THE WAR DISPATCHES
OF STEPHEN CRANE

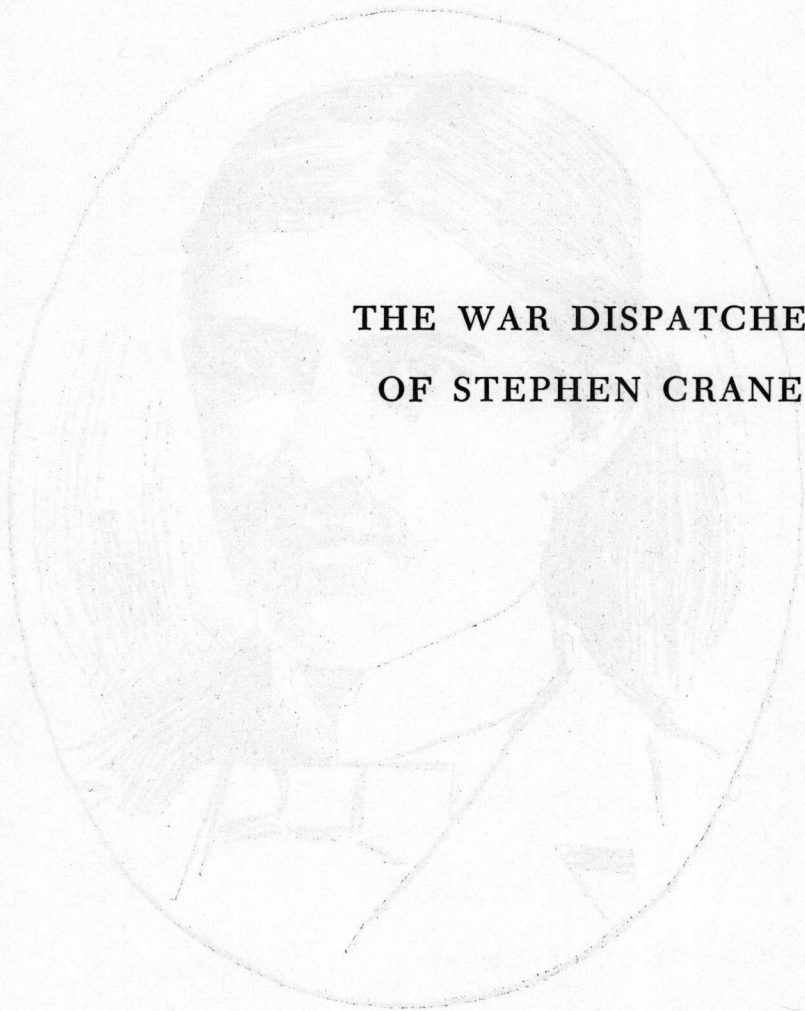

STEPHEN CRANE.

THE WAR DISPATCHES OF STEPHEN CRANE

Edited by

R. W. STALLMAN AND E. R. HAGEMANN

NEW YORK UNIVERSITY PRESS

1964

© 1964 New York University
Library of Congress Catalog Card Number: 64–12559
Manufactured in the United States of America

To

WILLIAM WOOSTER STALLMAN

and

ROBERT WOOSTER STALLMAN, JR.

To

JESSICA and MATTHEW HAGEMANN

PREFACE

He who would do good to another
Must do it in minute particulars.

BLAKE

In the first place, our thanks go to Roland Baughman, Head of Special Collections at Columbia University Libraries, for permission to reproduce the following pieces: The Spirit of the Greek People, The Eastern Question, Americans and Beggars in Cuba, and Drama in Cuba. For permission to publish these manuscripts, acknowledgment is also made to Alfred A. Knopf, Inc., copyright owner of all unpublished Crane manuscripts and letters. We also thank Kenneth A. Lohf, Assistant Librarian at Butler Library of Columbia University, for his constant aid; and for the same reason Harold Merklen, Research Librarian at the New York Public Library, and Miss Roberta Smith, Reference Librarian at the University of Connecticut.

Also B. Joseph O'Neil and Michael J. Venezia of the Research Services of the Boston Public Library; Rudolph C. Ellsworth, Assistant Reference Librarian at the Newberry Library, Chicago; Robert E. Scudder of the Free Library of Philadelphia; Donald C. Holmes, Chief of Photoduplication Service at the Library of Congress; Lester G. Wells, Rare Book Librarian at Syracuse University Library; Dr. David Erdman, Editor of the Bulletin of the New York Public Library; and Professor Jack W. Higgins of the University of Arizona. Also James B. Rhoads, Acting Chief of the Diplomatic, Legal and Fiscal Branch, The National Archives, Washington, D. C.

For aid in photocopying of materials: Mrs. Ruth Raines, Mrs. Carolyn King, and Mrs. Virginia Thorkelson at the University of Connecticut Library; also Robert Stallman, Jr., of Groton School. For typing of manuscript: Thomas Blank and Mrs. Virginia Stallman. For suggested leads in Crane research: Charles Honce of New York City, Charles Feinberg of Detroit, and Professors Scott Osborn, Arnold Schwab, and James B. Stronks. For data about Ravensbrook: Nicholas A. Pease, Esquire, of Limpsfield, Surrey, England.

For grants in aid of Crane research Stallman thanks the American Philosophical Society, the American Council of Learned Societies, and the University of Connecticut Research Foundation.

For their constant aid and courtesies Hagemann thanks the staff of the University of California Library at Los Angeles and makes grateful acknowledgments to Edward J. Hickey, Deputy Director for Administration, Passport Office, Department of State, Washington, D. C.; Elbert L. Huber, Archivist-in-Charge, Navy Branch, War Records Division, The National Archives; and Carl L. Lokke, Archivist-in-Charge, Foreign Affairs Branch, The National Archives. Also S. G. Pryor, Chief Librarian, *News-Chronicle* (London), for his invaluable aid in locating certain dispatches in the London *Westminster Gazette.* Also to the staff of the Bibliothèque Municipale at Marseilles, France, for aid in locating certain issues of *Le Sémaphore* (Marseilles).

Meanwhile we have prospered by the constant encouragement of Clifton Waller Barrett during the seven years we have been preparing *The War Dispatches of Stephen Crane.*

Editorially, we have tried to combine the conscientious duplication of original texts and holographs that scholars desire and Crane deserves with the easy accessibility that Crane himself would surely have wanted for the ordinary modern reader. Our only emendations have been in those instances where the newspaper or magazine we used as our source contained an obvious misprint, one that would seriously impede the reader's enjoyment of Crane's prose, and one where the correct version is beyond question (e.g., a comma instead of a period at the end of a sentence). These few emendations have been made tacitly. Present texts have been meticulously proofread against originals, and the reader can rest assured that whatever misspellings, solecisms, and inconsistencies he finds are what he would have found if he had picked up the newpaper or magazine in the 1890's. Certain misspellings were characteristic of Crane (for instance, he was partial to the word *portentious,* which is not to be found in any dictionary). Except where the bibliographical footnote indicates otherwise, the title of each item exactly reprints the original headline. The various heads that a modern journalist calls "decks," spreadeagled immediately under the headline, have been omitted except where they are of unusual interest, in which case they appear in the bibliographical footnote. Subheads that occur at intervals throughout individual articles, since they are with one or

two possible exceptions the work of a desk editor and not of Stephen
Crane, are enclosed in square brackets.

The following articles have never before appeared in book form:
Stephen Crane's Pen Picture of the Powers' Fleet Off Crete, Stephen
Crane Says Greeks Cannot Be Curbed, Imogene Carter's Pen Picture
of the Fighting at Velestino, War Seen Through a Woman's Eyes,
Crane at Velestino, The Blue Badge of Cowardice, Yale Man Arrested,
War's Horrors and Turkey's Bold Plan — I, War's Horrors and Turkey's
Bold Plan — II, How Novelist Crane Acts on the Battlefield, The Dogs
of War, Greeks Waiting at Thermopylae, A Fragment of Velestino, The
Little Stilettos of the Modern Navy Which Stab in the Dark, Sampson
Inspects Harbor at Mariel, With the Blockade on Cuban Coast, Hayti
and San Domingo Favor the United States, Narrow Escape of the
Three Friends, First American Newspaper to Open Headquarters on
Cuban Soil Is The World, Crane Tells the Story of the Disembarkment,
The Red Badge of Courage Was His Wig-Wag Flag, Stephen Crane
at the Front for the World, Roosevelt's Rough Riders' Loss Due to a
Gallant Blunder, Hunger Has Made the Cubans Fatalists, Artillery
Duel Was Fiercely Fought on Both Sides, Chased by a Big "Spanish
Man-o'-War," Night Attacks on the Marines and a Brave Rescue,
Spanish Deserters Among the Refugees at El Caney, Captured Mausers
for Volunteers, Regulars Get No Glory, A Soldier's Burial That Made a
Native Holiday, The Porto Rican "Straddle," Havana's Hate Dying,
Says Stephen Crane, Stephen Crane Sees Free Cuba, Stephen Crane
Fears No Blanco, Stephen Crane's Views of Havana, Stephen Crane
Makes Observations in Cuba's Capital, The Grocer Blockade, Memoirs
of a Private, The Private's Story, Stephen Crane in Havana, How They
Leave Cuba, How They Court in Cuba, Stephen Crane on Havana,
"You Must! — "We Can't!," Mr. Crane, of Havana, Spaniards Two, Our
Sad Need of Diplomats, In Havana As It Is To-Day, Mr. Stephen Crane
on the New America, Some Curious Lessons from the Transvaal, The
Great Boer Trek. The following pieces, as far as we know, have never
previously appeared in print: The Spirit of the Greek People, The
Eastern Question, and Americans and Beggars in Cuba.

Several articles not by Stephen Crane have also been included, and
they are set in Scotch type to distinguish them (see, for instance, p. 23).

As we will share whatever praise and blame are forthcoming, so
did we share the labor without any clear demarcation of responsibilities. In general, Stallman concentrated on finding and establishing the
texts, while Hagemann occupied himself with deviling for notes and
background information.

R.W.S.
E.R.H.

TABLE OF CONTENTS

* * *

* * *

* * *

1 THE GRECO-TURKISH WAR

Salonika

Gulf of
Salonika

Iannina

E P I R U S

T H E S S A L Y

Mati

Larissa

Arta

Domokos

Velestino

Volo

Gulf of
Volo

Halmyrós

Lamia

Levkes

Thermopylae

E U B O E A

Athens

Piraeus

PELOPONNESUS

Sparta

C R E T E

Introduction

DETERMINED to get to Cuba, Crane applied for a passport and declared his destinations were "Cuba, Mexico and the West Indies." His passport, which he received in mid-January 1897, describes him: gray eyes, aquiline nose, oval face, tawny mustache, and light hair. But to get to Cuba meant encountering the blockading patrol ships of the United States Navy and Revenue Cutter Service out to enforce the neutrality laws, and Crane's enthusiasm waned noticeably. "I have been for over a month among the swamps further South [of Jacksonville, Florida], wading miserably to and fro in an attempt to avoid our derned U.S. Navy. It can't be done. I am through trying. I have changed all my plans and am going to Crete." So he wrote his brother Edmund on March 11, and later to someone else he wrote: "I am going to Greece for the *Journal* and if the Red Badge is not all right I shall sell out my claim on literature and take up orange growing." [1]

In New York City by mid-March Crane and his artist-friend Corwin Knapp Linson met at a restaurant at Fourth Avenue and Twenty-third Street for a farewell dinner. "With a reserve characteristic of him when speaking of women," Crane told him of his intentions to marry Cora Taylor. "She could sail on the same steamer and be married in England. But there were tongues. 'The weasels would draw blood anyhow.' He hated to leave her alone, but his job was to go on to Greece and come back when the stew was over. 'What would you do, CK?' " [2] Well, Crane took Cora with him to Greece, but not on

1. From *Stephen Crane: Letters*, edited by R. W. Stallman and Lillian Gilkes (1960), p. 139.

2. In *My Stephen Crane*, by Corwin Knapp Linson, edited by Edwin H. Cady (1958), p. 101.

the same steamer.[3] He sailed on the Cunard's *Etruria* on March 20. And before Cora joined him in London he'd been entertained by the novelist Harold Frederic, whose *New York Times* tribute to Crane and *The Red Badge of Courage* (26 January 1896) prepared for their mutual friendship; by the Editor of Heinemann, Sydney Pauling, who arranged for Crane to cover the war in Greece for the *Westminster Gazette* (Heinemann published the English edition of *The Red Badge*, 1895); and by Richard Harding Davis, the popular fiction writer and correspondent whom the London *Times* employed to report the impending war between Greece and Turkey. At Davis' luncheon at the Savoy on March 31 Crane was presented to the famous dramatist James M. Barrie and other literary notables, including Anthony Hope. By then Cora was in London, and the next day they crossed the channel with Davis aboard and snubbing Cora. Writing home to mother, Davis described Cora as "a bi-roxide blonde who seemed to be attending to his [Crane's] luggage for him and whom I did not meet." He snubbed her because he knew who Cora was — the operator of a nightclub in Jacksonville, Florida, where Crane first met her in November 1896 at her Hotel de Dream.

Harold Frederic saw them off at Dover, and Davis parted with them in Paris to visit his brother Charles Belmont Davis in Florence before going on to Greece. Stephen parted with Cora and her traveling companion Mrs. Ruedy at Munich (the western terminal of the Orient Express), Cora and Mrs. Ruedy going overland to Turkey into Greece. Crane got to Marseilles, and "On Board French Steamer *Guardiana*" he filed his dispatch — "Pen Picture of the Powers' Fleet Off Crete" — on April 26. Cora in the role of woman correspondent at the front sent to some unidentified newspaper "War Seen Through a Woman's Eyes" with the dateline April 26. So she was in Greece, while Crane was in Crete.

On April 17 Turkey declared war on Greece, and Crane in Athens wrote that day his unpublished article: "Spirit of the Greek People." Spirit was all the Greeks could muster against the numerically superior and better-trained Turks. The war lasted barely one month.

Comically short in duration, the war had been long in coming. The demand of Greece for Crete's independence from Turkish rule had

3. Only two ships departed New York City for England during the period March 19–23. The *Etruria* sailed on the 20th and made Liverpool on the 27th. Crane was in London on the 29th and called first of all on Heinemann, his London publisher of *The Red Badge* (1895), *Maggie* (1896), *Black Riders* (1896), and *The Little Regiment* (1897). Forthcoming was Heinemann's issue of Crane's novel *The Third Violet* (1897). Heinemann was also Richard Harding Davis' publisher. Davis sailed on the *Germanic* on March 17.

gone unheeded at the Congress of Berlin in 1878, and for the next twenty years unrest and revolt and bloodshed rent the island. In 1889 a serious outbreak occurred, but the Sultan was able to crush it. The years that followed saw a reign of "stupid and cruel mismanagement." [4] The revolt of the Christian Cretans in 1895 spread throughout the island, and arms and men were sent there by the Greek nationalistic society *Ethneke Hetairia*. Public opinion called for war against Turkey, but the concert of Europe stepped in and restored an uneasy peace. By January 1897, however, Crete was once more in turmoil.

The Greek government sent a torpedo-boat flotilla under Prince George to Crete on February 10, and on the 13th Colonel Vassos landed with 2,000 men and proclaimed "the annexation of Crete to Greece." The concert of powers was incapable of action, giving the lie to their purpose; but they did proclaim Cretan autonomy, and a blockade was inaugurated by the concert of powers on March 21. Five days later Cretan insurgents flushed out Turkish defenders of the Akrotisi blockhouses and occupied them; but when the fleet of the powers opened fire on them, the Cretans fled. Crown Prince Constantine left Athens on March 27, amid much cheering, for the Thessalian frontier.

The act needed for hostilities to commence was committed by Greece when its irregulars crossed into Turkish territory in Thessaly and Macedonia. When Turkey declared war, the powers refused to intervene.

The war was fought mainly in northeastern Greece. And there was fighting in Epirus, where Crane first saw action. Greece was totally unprepared. In Thessaly some 60,000 Turks under Edhem Pasha moved against some 45,000 Greeks under Crown Prince Constantine, Duke of Sparta. The Crown Prince had no military experience, and he and his captains — except for brief stands and checks — never once succeeded in the field.[5]

Crane began with the Greek army in Epirus, the southwestern province of Turkey, and hearing of the hard fighting in Thessaly he went there by way of Athens, where he filed on April 29 his dispatch

4. From Mason Whiting Tyler, "The European Powers and the Near East, 1875–1908," *Research Publications of the University of Minnesota,* No. 17 (1925), 160. The editors have used Tyler's monograph for many details about Crete and Greece, also George Mylonas' *The Balkan States* (1947). A contemporary account of the Cretan situation may be found in *The Annual Cyclopedia and Register of Important Events of the Year 1897* (1900), pp. 241–253. A good brief account of the Greco-Turkish War appears in the *Encyclopædia Britannica*.

5. From "The Greek War as I Saw It," by Bennet Burleigh, *The Fortnightly Review*, LXVIII (15 July 1897), 140.

headed by the New York *Journal* as "Stephen Crane Says Greeks Cannot be Curbed" (*infra, page* 21).

A *Journal* correspondent in Crawfordsville, Indiana, filed that same day his interview with General Lew Wallace, author of *Ben Hur* and former Minister to Turkey, and this report, together with dispatches by Crane, by Cora Taylor under the pen name "Imogene Carter," by John Bass (head of the *Journal* field staff), and by Julian Ralph, appeared on April 30 on the same front page of the New York *Journal*. (See *infra*, pages 21–26.)

The temporary stand of Constantine at Mati ended in a stampede, and the popular feeling in Athens (as John Bass reports it) was that the people had been betrayed by their leaders. The withdrawal from Mati which Constantine ordered on April 23 quickly turned into a rout to Larissa. Scarcely pausing here, the Greeks fled to Pharsala. Here the Crown Prince reestablished some semblance of military order. His tactics, however, betrayed his military ignorance. With an amateurish flourish, he split his forces by sending a brigade to Velestino, forty miles from Pharsala. When the Turks reconnoitered Velestino on April 30 they were repulsed with heavy loss, and the Greeks claimed, with some justification, a brief victory. But they were premature in their enthusiasm, for on May 5 they were driven from their entrenchments at Pharsala by three divisions; the next evening they withdrew in fair order to Domokos. A concomitant withdrawal by the Greek general Smolenski occurred at Velestino. (General Smolenski, a Macedonian, achieved some fame early in the war by his defense of Ravenni.)

The commander in chief of the Turkish army in Thessaly, Edhem Pasha, did not hurry to attack and thereby he gave the Greeks time to take up positions at Domokos. Then on May 17 the two armies fought it out for the last time.

Surprisingly, the Turks were roughly handled. Attacking in three columns, their right was stopped; their center was blocked from overrunning the Greek trenches and suffered severe losses. Their left succeeded in menacing the Greek line of retreat, but once more the coming of night provided cover for the Greeks to withdraw.

Determined to hold Thermopylae, General Smolenski arrived from Velestino. But the Greek troops were demoralized. Czar Nicholas II at this point intervened to save the situation and spare further bloodshed. He sent a personal appeal to the Sultan, who responded by ordering that hostilities cease. An armistice was signed on May 20.

By modern standards of mass destruction incredibly light losses were inflicted on the battlefields of Epirus and Thessaly. Outnumbered two to one, the Greeks in Epirus under Colonel Manos held a line from Arta to Peta. The Turks bombarded Arta from April 18 to 21 but failed to carry it. Retiring to Philippiada, they fought a Greek force but gave way on April 23. In Epirus the Greeks thus managed a minor victory or two. Colonel Manos moved towards the Turkish capital of Epirus, Iannina, and at nearby Homopulos he held off strong attacks (April 28–29); but, reinforcements failing him, his withdrawal became a rout to the Arakhthos River and across it.

With reinforcements from Athens, Colonel Manos directed a three-prong attack into Turkish territory to cut off the Turkish garrison at Prevesa, at the entrance to the Gulf of Arta. The center column attacked the Turks at Strevina on May 13, but it was forced to retreat. The war was over in Epirus.

Epirus was a mere skirmish, and Crane didn't wait to see the end of it because he wanted to witness the Thessaly war sector, the real thing. He was back in Athens on the 27th, at the Grand Hotel D'Angleterre, with Cora. From Epirus Crane sent no dispatches, probably because there were no cable facilities thereabouts (the nearest station was on the island of Levkes). In Athens on the 28th Richard Harding Davis, arriving there from Florence via Brindisi, met Crane and reported to his mother:

> Stephen Crane came in last night having been searching for me all over Albania and to my satisfaction told me he had been in Crete all this time that I have been in Florence. So that he is not a day ahead of me as we start from here. . . . He has not seen as much as I have for several reasons but then when a man can describe battles as well as he can without seeing them why should he care.[6]

True, Crane had failed to cover his "beat"; and in this narrow sense of a reporter's duty he missed giving full value to his employer, William Randolph Hearst. But then Crane never was a mere "reporter." He was too much addicted to the exploitation of language to restrict himself to the routine "beat" reporter's factual account of a given scene or situation. What distinguishes any Crane sketch is the signature of the man in the way he uses words to recreate not so much the facts of the situation but rather an impression of it, what it felt like to him or to others then and there. Crane missed out on this skirmish or that, but then so did John Bass and Richard Harding Davis. They were absent from Mati, Meluna Pass, and Larissa: and in Athens the political confusion interested them not at all. On the day Crane returned from Epirus to Athens (April 27) a near revolution was touched off throughout the city by the news of the Greek reverses in Thessaly. Gunsmith

6. Quoted in "The 'Rivalry-Chivalry' of Davis and Crane," by Scott C. Osborn, *American Literature*, XXVIII (March 1956), 53–54.

shops were plundered, and wild demonstrations were made against the royal family. Foreign warships at Piraeus were alerted to stand by to protect the royal palace.[7] Crane glanced at this situation with cryptic sentences.

Off to Velestino on April 29 went Richard Harding Davis, John Bass, and Crane "accompanied by a Lady Stuart [Cora Taylor] who has run away from her husband to follow Crane. She is a commonplace dull woman old enough to have been his mother and with dyed yellow hair." So much for Cora. As for Crane, Davis adds in this same letter: "He seems a genius with no responsibilities of any sort to anyone, and I and Bass got shut of them at Velestino [on May 3] after having had to travel with them for four days."[8] Under the pen name "Imogene Carter" Cora's dispatch filed in Athens on April 29 reads: "I start today for the front of the Greek army to see how the men fight." And on May 6 she sent a dispatch by courier from the front: "I returned to Volo tonight [Thursday] from Velestino after witnessing a hard fight there." Crane and Cora chose to go on to Volo, a small town twelve miles east of Velestino and at the head of the Gulf of Volo, and so Davis and Bass were the only correspondents at Velestino when the battle there began. That was on May 4, but the next day:

> Crane came up for fifteen minutes and wrote a 1300 word story on that. He was never near the front but don't say I said so. He would have come but he had a toothache which kept him in bed. It was hard luck but on the other hand if he had not had that woman with him he would have been with us and not at Volo and could have seen the show toothache or no toothache.[9]

When Bass suggested an article about Davis' conduct under fire, Davis refused him permission to do so; so Bass wrote "How Novelist Crane Acts on the Battlefield" (*infra*, page 42). Davis wrote home: "why should he describe how the [London] *Times* correspondent acted

7. *Annual Register*, 1897 (London, 1898), pp. 22–23. Perhaps the Athens uprising is what Crane depicts in "The Man in the White Hat" (*infra*, p. 83). What street gathering Crane refers to here is not ascertainable since the situation is blurred into artful narrative. It's an effortless vignette.

8. Osborn quoting from Davis letter to family 16 May 1897. In his comedy "The Galloper," *Farces* (1906), based on the Greco-Turkish War, "Davis possibly modeled one of the characters upon Cora Taylor; in it an actress, 'an attractive, dashing-looking woman of the adventuress type,' who is pursuing her divorced war correspondent husband in an attempt to collect alimony, resembles Davis's conception of Cora."

9. Osborn introduces this passage thus: "Later in the day [May 4], however." But Crane wasn't there until May 5.

and say nothing about Crane who was there for the *Journal*. But there was nothing to be said about what Crane did except that he ought to be ashamed of himself . . . ." [10] Spiteful, Davis was much pleased that he'd beaten Crane. But Crane is in the clear by his admission that "Of the first two days' combat some other correspondents saw more than I did" — namely Davis and Bass. "I was rather laid up. . . . I arrived at noon on the second day [Wednesday, May 5]. I had been in skirmishes and small fights, but this was the first big battle." He remained with the Greek forces that night, and then "in the gray early morning the musketry fire was resumed." That refutes Davis' claim that Crane was on the scene for only "fifteen minutes," and so do the Bass sketch of Crane and the latter's impressionistic rendering of the battle of Velestino: "Crane at Velestino" (*infra*, page 28).

What happens in the sketch of Crane by John Bass spans far more than fifteen minutes: (1) Crane seats himself "on an ammunition box amid a shower of shells" and casually lights a cigarette. (2) He meditates on the quick work of the artillerymen, and Bass asks him:

"Crane, what impresses you most in this affair?"
The author of *The Red Badge of Courage* lighted another cigarette, pushed back his long hair out of his eyes with his hat, and answered quietly:
"Between two great armies battling against each other the interesting thing is the mental attitude of the men."

(3) By now the Greek army is in full retreat, and as the last mountain gun gets loaded onto mules Crane "quietly walked down the hill." Furthermore, "amid the singing bullets and smashing shells the novelist stopped, picked up a fat waddling puppy and immediately christened it Velestino, the Journal dog." Star correspondent of his day, the fabulous Davis resented any competitor — Crane or anyone else. Although Davis frequently championed Crane, Davis' remarks about him during the Greco-Turkish War and later during the Spanish-American War were (to quote Scott Osborn) "almost uniformly depreciatory." In an 1898 letter Davis wrote of Crane: "I don't like him myself." Unlike Davis, Crane never gave a damn whether you liked him or not.

The Greek army retreated to Domokos, and Crane and Cora retreated with the wounded and the refugees to Volo, where the helpless milled about. The Turks were near, and just as "the advance guard of the Turks reached the hilltops surrounding the town," Crane and Cora managed to get aboard a ship for Athens. It was a miserable voyage, and Crane was bitter that the Greek refugees had been refused help by foreign ships. He went ashore at the small fishing village

10. Osborn, *op. cit.*, p. 54.

of Oreos (Areos, as Crane spells it) "with a great crowd. This town consists of six houses already crowded." Seven hundred refugees, according to his reckoning, went ashore and squatted about the six houses.[11] Rounding the northwestern peninsula of Euboea, the ship sailed on for Chalkis, and here he found the pup "Velestino" — he'd been lost in crowded Volo. From Chalkis Crane dispatched by courier to Athens what the *Journal* headed as "The Blue Badge of Cowardice," as from Volo he had sent by courier his dispatch: "Crane at Velestino."

What Crane later wrote of Velestino, at a distance and with his full talents at his command (done in Athens after the war was over), is "A Fragment of Velestino" published in the London *Westminster Gazette* in early June. It is perhaps the finest sketch he ever wrote as war correspondent. It is not journalism, it is not fiction, but it employs some of his techniques in *The Red Badge of Courage*.

By drawbridge he crossed in a carriage the narrow Strait of Euripos, and lunched at Thebes. Finally he pulled into the capital and put the pup up "at the best hotel." [12] It was the Grand Hotel D'Angleterre. The date was about May 9. On the 18th he was aboard the *St. Marina* pulling out of Chalkis for Athens with a cargo of wounded from Domokos. A battle had been fought there on May 17; it was another defeat for the Crown Prince. In "War's Horrors and Turkey's Bold Plan" he reports on the retreat of the Greek army toward historic Thermopylae. He had gone from Athens north to Stylis (Stylida) on May 18, and he had seen the dust raised by Smolenski's retreating army. Thermopylae lay south across the Gulf of Lamia; Stylis is on its northern shore.

By steamer and schooner Stylis was evacuated of women and children and household goods — off to St. Marina, a few miles to the west. But bread had been left behind, and so Crane returned to Stylis, but he never found the stock of bread. He returned to St. Marina and sailed once more the Gulf of Euboea, and from Chalkis he returned to Athens.[13] He was back in Lamia on May 22, sending then his report "Greeks Waiting at Thermopylae." He mentions the truce signed on May 20. Crane refused to regard it as permanent: "I hope the armistice will be made to last long enough to give the Greek infantry some rest. They need it." Their rest was a long one — the war was over.

After sight-seeing in Greece, Crane in early June left by ship for Marseilles to meet Cora and her companion Mrs. Ruedy, who arrived by the overland route via Venice, in Paris. In Marseilles Crane was

11. Crane in "The Blue Badge of Cowardice" (*infra,* p. 33).

12. Crane in "The Dogs of War," in New York *Journal:* 30 May 1897.

13. An interesting account of what seems to be the same voyage occurs in "A Glimpse of the Late War," by Major C. E. Callwell, R.A., *Blackwood's Edinburgh Magazine,* CLXII (August 1897), 178–179.

arrested because he'd brought into France a pair of Greek twins, refugees named Ptolemy, without visas for them. They all got to England later in June,[14] including the dog "Velestino." He died on August 1 and was buried the next day with the dog collar given him by Sylvester Scovel, a close friend and fellow journalist. The novelist Harold Frederic had found quarters for the Cranes at Oxted, Surrey (in a house called Ravensbrook), and here Stephen lived with Cora as his common-law wife from July or August 1898 to January 1899. By then Crane was off to cover the Spanish-American War.

Several Crane sketches and stories about Greece appeared subsequent to the war's termination, including his best war sketches, which were published in seven parts in the *Westminster Gazette,* beginning on 3 May 1897, under the general title "With Greek and Turk." Instead of scattering these to follow chronological sequence, we have kept them together as a group. The most absorbing of the *Gazette* series is the seventh: "The Man in the White Hat," which is a parable constituting a fascinating piece of symbolism.

Certain of these sketches also appeared in identical or variant texts in the New York *Journal.* None of these has, however, been included here since that paper saw fit to tamper with Crane's dispatches, adding to or truncating them, and botching them with the egotistical "I" not found in the impersonal and more artistic *Gazette* versions.

The short story "Death and the Child" (*infra*, pages 87–103) also deals with the Greco-Turkish War, as does also Crane's novel *Active Service* (1899), of which he wrote the first draft in Havana, Cuba, late in 1898. Especially relevant is chapter XI, but as only certain portions are interesting we've decided to exclude the book altogether.

❋   ❋   ❋

STEPHEN CRANE'S PEN PICTURE
OF THE POWERS' FLEET OFF CRETE.

On Board French Steamer Guardiana, April 26. — Leaving Marseilles, the passengers of this ship had no intention of anything more than a tedious voyage to Athens without pause, but circumstances

14. In "London Letter," *The Critic*, XXVII (26 June 1897) Arthur Waugh reported having seen Crane in the Strand on June 10. Richard Harding Davis was also in the neighborhood.

Reprinted here for the first time from Louisville Courier-Journal: *9 May 1897.*

furnished us with a mild digression. In the early morning of the fourth day a ponderous headland[1] appeared to the north and we knew it to be the expected glimpse of Greece. Nevertheless some hours later another ponderous headland appeared to the southward,[2] and we could not arrange our geographical prejudices to suit this phenomenon until a man excitedly told every one that we had changed our course, that we were not bound for the Piree, but for the Bay of Suda in Crete.[3] He told us of mail bags for the fleet of the Powers and pointed to the headland and called it Crete. All this increased our importance vastly.

This headland was rough and gaunt, a promontory that one would expect in Iceland. It was of a warm color, resembling rusted iron. It towered grandly until one found in the sky above it some faint crystalline markings which later turned into a range of exalted snow-draped mountains. The blue sea glimmered to the foot of the rusty cape and the sun shone full on the silver peaks. The English commercial traveler who was cock-sure by education decided that with these mountains for their final stand the Cretans could never be conquered.

A scouting torpedo-boat as small as a gnat crawling on an enormous decorated wall came from the obscurity of the shore. Apparently it looked us over and was satisfied, for in a few moments it was returned to the obscurity. Crete spread high and wide precisely like a painting from that absurd period when the painters each tried to reproduce the universe on one canvas. It merely lacked the boat with

---

The importance of this dispatch is in its filing data: "On Board French Steamer Guardiana. *April 26. — Leaving Marseilles . . . ." What that proves is that Crane got to Greece by ship from Marseilles. The ship was the* Guadiana (*misspelled in the dispatch*); *it arrived from London March 30 and sailed April 3 for Greece, Turkey, and the Black Sea via Piraeus, Smyrna, the Dardanelles, Constantinople, and finally Batum. As Crane's dispatch tells us, the* Guadiana *was off Crete in the Bay of Suda on the fourth day* (*April 8*).

Ames Williams and Vincent Starrett in their Stephen Crane: A Bibliography (1948) *list "An Impression of the 'Concert'" (in* Westminster Gazette: 3 May 1897). "Stephen Crane's Pen Picture of the Powers' Fleet off Crete," *is identical with the former except in title and forms Part I of the* Westminster Gazette *series "With Greek and Turk." See infra, p. 60.*

1. Probably the island of Kithira.
2. Either Cape Spátha or the Akrotiri Peninsula on Crete.
3. Pirée is the French spelling of Piraeus, the port of Athens, five miles southwest of the capital, at the time a city with about 40,000 population. The Bay of Suda is on the northern coast of Crete in the northwest corner of the island. It bounds the Akrotiri Peninsula on the south.

a triangular sail and a pie-faced crew occupying the attention in the foreground. It was lonely and desolate like a land of Despair if it were not for the glory of the hills above all. Nothing lived there save the venomous torpedo-boat, which, after all, had been little more than a shadow on the water.

The Guardiana turned toward a faint indentation among the hills, a little cleft. The passengers had become excited and were for the most part grouped forward. Some Greeks from the steerage were crooning, incomprehensibly, but in a way that we hoped supported war and glory and general uproar for the sake of one's own country. Their small, black and rather shifty eyes shone like buttons.

But this strange island presented nothing to their gaze. It still gave no hint of house, man nor cattle. It was like one of those half-named countries of the remote north. If this was the island upon which the attention of Europe was fixed, it was certainly preserving an ulterior tranquility at any rate. Surely a little decent excitement could be expected. Surely a few men in white kilts could have turned out and chased a few men in red fez up and down the hillsides. One wondered where the chanting Greeks in the bow got their impetus. This great, high, sun-burned island was simply as thrilling as a bit of good pasturage for goats.

Meanwhile the steamer churned through the shimmering sea and at times from the cabin arose the thin wail of a baby that had objected without pause from Marseilles to the roll and heave of the ship.

A man with a glass discovered a tan-colored crease on one of the steep hillsides, and afterward it could be seen to be an earthwork. Below it the hills had parted and exhibited a steel-colored water-way.[4] The scene was always wide and fine, with its great stretches of blue bay and the towering heights, silent in the sunshine. At last a genius found that the flag over the redoubt was the Turkish flag, and the passengers stared at the tiny blood-red banner.

Gradually the hills slide aside, and impressively, like the scenes in a melodrama before the final tableau the water-way widened to an inner bay.[5] Then finally there were some faint etchings on the distances. They might have been like masts, but they were more like twigs. And before the steady ploughing advance of the steamer these twigs grew into the top-gear of war ships, stacks of tan, of white, of black, and fighting masts and the blaze of signal flags.

It was the fleet of the Powers; the Concert — the Concert — mind you, this most terrible creature which the world has known, con-

4. The entrance of Suda Bay, actually two promontories, north and south. There are redoubts, Turkish and Greek, in the hills above the bay.

5. Suda Bay.

structed out of the air and perhaps in a night. This fleet was the living arm and the mailed hand of the Concert.[6] It was a limb of Europe displayed, actual, animate. The babe who disliked the motion of the steamer continued to cry in the cabin.

At first the vessels in the distance were blended into a sort of prickly hedge. It was very unlike the pictures in the illustrated papers which appear always to have been sketched from balloons. As the Guadiana steamed forward, ship after ship became detached from the hedge and powerful ram-bows were drawn in formidable outline upon the water. When the Guadiana had come into the middle of the company she paused and her anchor chain roared.

Here they were — English, Russians, Germans, French, Italians, Turks and Austrians, all living peacefully in the same cage.[7]

The attention of the Guadiana was immediately divided in twelve ways. The seamen found the great flag-ship of France, the Admiral Charner,[8] and loved it with their eyes, while the English commercial traveler had a short, bitter quarrel with a fellow-countryman as to the identity of a certain ship — whether she was the Barfleur or the Camperdown.

These great steel animals sat in a little bay, menacing with their terrible glances a village of three rows of houses and a dock and vast stretches of hillsides, whereon there was not even a tree to shoot at for fun. A group of vicious little torpedoboats also waited impatiently. To one who did not care to feel that there was something in this affair which weighed as much as a planet it would be a joke of a kind. But it was the concert of Europe. Colossi never smile.

It was hard to decide which of these national exhibits was the most interesting. The French flag-ship was imposing in the weird and solemn complexion of her appearance. Her deck and sides were a wilderness of dull grey appliances. She looked like a factory, this monster, whereas the Camperdown, and more particularly the great Revenge, were so well-proportioned and trim that one had to refer

6. The combined fleet of the concert of powers, composed of naval units from England, Italy, Germany, Austria, France, and Russia, had been in Cretan waters for some weeks with the prime purpose of maintaining order in the area (in which the fleet was not too successful). The combined fleet was commanded by Rear Admiral Robert Hastings Harris, R.N., flagship HMS *Revenge*, second in command of the Mediterranean Squadron; K.C.M.G., 1898; K.C.B., 1900.

7. Turkish naval units were not a part of the combined fleet.

8. Flagship of Rear Admiral Pottiers, the *Admiral Charner* (1893) was an armored cruiser; tonnage (displacement): 4,716; length: 374 feet; speed: 15.5 knots; principal armament: two 5-inch and six 8-inch guns. (From Jane's *Fighting Ships*.)

to a memory of their tonnage before they became as impressive.[9]
Italy's squadron, to the novice, looked as well as any of them. Her
two battle-ships were large and powerful, and the Etna was obviously
the best cruiser in the harbor.[10] The Russian flag-ship[11] lay near the
French ships, while the Italians were rather close to the English. The
Kaiserine Augusta was aloof and alone.[12] On the other hand, the
Austrian hesitated in the middle of the situation.

Launches and gigs innumerable played around the Guadiana, and
officers of all kinds came up the side. The play of the launches and
gigs absorbed the attention of the passengers because a strong wind
was blowing down the harbor and it made the management of the
small craft enough of a trick. The French made the most uproar and
they were the authors of whatever bungling was done. They were at
the same time by far the proudest and most conscious. The eyes of the
world were upon them, surely, and they wanted to do everything with
such heaven born accuracy that they lost their minds at times.

Once, a launch from the Russian flag ship lay on the water waiting
for her officer who was on board the Guadiana to signal to come for
him. Her crew lounged under the weather bulwark and she swung
slowly and peacefully over the little waves. It was great then to see a
French launch come flying down the harbor, turn to pass on the lee
of the Russian launch and finally bat into her and scrape three yards
of paint from her side. The Russian seamen looked at the Frenchmen
and the Frenchmen laughed and nodded and chattered and apparently

9. HMS *Camperdown* (1885) was a modern ironclad; tonnage (displacement): 10,600; length: 325 feet; speed: 15 knots; principal armament:
four 17-inch and six 8-inch guns. HMS *Revenge* (1892) was another ironclad; tonnage (displacement): 14,150; length: 380 feet; speed: 15 knots;
principal armament: four 17-inch and ten 8-inch guns, plus two torpedo
tubes (submerged).

10. The "battle-ships" were probably the modern ironclads, *Re Um-
berto* (1888; 13,893 tons) and the *Sicilia* (1891; 13,298 tons); they were
regarded as among the most powerful ships in the world. The *Etna* (1885)
was a protected cruiser; length: 285 feet; speed: 16.5 knots; principal
armament: two 12-inch guns.

11. The *Nicholas I* (1889), flagship of Rear Admiral Andrief, and a
battleship; tonnage (displacement): 8,400; speed: 16 knots; principal armament: two 12-inch and four 9-inch guns. Its protective armor was up to
fourteen inches.

12. Apparently the *Kaiserin Augusta* (1892) was the only German
ship in the combined fleet. She was a heavily armed protective cruiser;
tonnage (displacement): 6,956 tons; length: 388 feet; principal armament;
twelve 8-inch guns. She was one of only two first-class cruisers in the
Imperial German Navy.

pointed out the incident as a bit of friendly wit. Whereupon the Russians smiled, faintly smiled.

Indeed at any time when a Russian boat was near a French one, the Frenchmen smiled with bright friendliness. And the echoing amiability of these men of the Czar was faint, certainly, merely like a shadow passing softly across the face of a stone figure, and to the onlooker there was something grim and strange in it.

Whenever officers came aboard of the mail steamer, the passengers crowded about them and to the Frenchmen this was food and wine, apparently. They flourished and expanded and waxed taller under this nourishment. They were sublime. As for the Russians, they didn't care. The Lieutenant who came for the British squadron's mail cared somewhat because seventy-five people crowded to hear him stagger through the French language, and it bored him. Down in the launch, however, there was a middy who was a joy. He was smaller than a sparrow, but — my soul — how bright and Napoleanic and forcible he was! He was as busy as a hive of bees. He had no time for poses and genuflections and other amusements. Once indeed he looked up from his business to the deck of the ship and this infant had a stern, quick glance, a man's eye. It was like hearing a canary bird swear to watch this tot put a speaking tube to his mouth. He was so small that a life-sized portrait of him could be painted on a sovereign, this warrior.

She would be a fool of a mother who would trust him in a pantry where there were tarts and his big sister can box his ears for some years to come, but, of course, there is no more fiery-hearted scoundrel in the fleet of the Powers than this babe. Of course he would drop to his knees and pray his admiral a hundred prayers if by this he could be at his station on the Camperdown and have her move into action immediately. Against what? Against anything. This is of the traditions that perforce are in the breast of the child. They could not be cut out of it under these circumstances. If another child of the Camperdown should steal this child's knife he might go to a corner and, and perhaps, almost shed tears, but no hoary admiral can dream of the wild slaughter and Hades on the bosom of the sea that agitate this babe's breast. He is a little villain. And yet may the god of all battle that sits above the smoke watch over this little villain and all bright little villains like him.

The stout boats from the war ships made ill-navigation for the native craft that for various purposes thronged about the steamer. Some unconcerned gigs' bow was forever bunting into a Cretan boat and causing the wildest panic, but pushing it aside and going ahead with gorgeous indifference. The native's nearest approach to redress was a jab in the eye with a boat-hook. It developed naturally that

these natives had voices like fifes and those who have never heard a
sacred concert in an insane asylum can not appreciate the objections
these men make to even the distant approach of a boat from a war
ship. They began to celebrate the terrors of a collision before there
was a probability of it and if by chance there should happen to be a
small crash, their cries were heart-rending. The twirling of their fingers
as they waved their hands tragically over their heads at these times
made a sight not to be seen in the west. This action seemed to stand
out in their minds as being more likely to carry them safely through
the crisis than a sudden and skillful application of the oars. But these
oars, after all, looked to the westerner to be as useful on the water as
scythes. However, when the natives unfurled their sails and tacked
for the shore, they were masters of their craft. All the boats then stood
on their lee gunwales and the water behind them boiled. The men
wore skirts and it was supposed to be exiomatic that none who wears
skirts could sail a boat.

All the afternoon the passengers remained on deck and watched
the fleet grouped on the bright bay. The launches were always speeding to and fro and from time to time a gig wherein the many oarsmen
caused it to resemble a water bug, walked over the water. The officers
on the Italian cruiser Etna had pistol practice from the stern and the
band on the Russian flag-ship played an uncanny melody. Late in the
afternoon the English torpedo destroyer Boxer, a long gray wasp of a
creature, came in from the sea.[13] She did not join the collection of
bottle-green scorpions on the Suda side of the harbor, but slid slowly
over to an anchorage near the Revenge. Then an Austrian torpedo-boat
— she was a bottle-green scorpion with a red and gold flag stuck in its
back — moved listlessly about among the ships. French sailors from
the flag-ship got a barge and their launch towed it down to the Guadiana after some freight which had been brought to them from Marseilles. The bringing of this barge alongside the Guadiana caused
scenes of the wildest disorder. The language used was material for
three riots in Dublin. All the same it was vastly exciting. These men
were in earnest about it. They were going to bring that barge alongside the steamer and one may be forgiven if one's temper gains an
advantage during the stress of unusual excitement. Twice the peevish
god of circumstance balked them and they were obliged to circle
widely down the wind and return for other tries. At last a line was
flung aboard and a sailor sprinted and caught it just as it was slipping
over-side. Then the blue sailor bonnets with their red pom-poms jostled
most surprisingly. There is one thing — a Frenchman can make a

13. HMS *Boxer* (1894) was a destroyer (also called a torpedo-boat
destroyer); tonnage (displacement): 4,300; length: 200 feet; speed: about
25 knots; principal armament: one 4-inch and five small quick-fire guns.

festival even of pulling on a rope. These tars had a perfectly delicious time at it. Perhaps the presence of an audience had something to do with the matter. Finally, when the barge was lined alongside, the French officer came aboard the steamer, his face beaming with a smile of victory.

In the meantime, against the darkening hills, strings of signal flags would suddenly burn out in splendid flashes and often the little voices of bugles called over the water. Smoke was drifting from the enormous funnels of some of the battle ships.

Down the bay a fat tub of a thing appeared, puffing like an old woman and making trouble enough on the water for a Cunarder moving sideways. It took an infinite time for her to come up, but when at last she steamed laboriously past everybody went to the rail and grinned. It was the Turkish dispatch boat arrived from her anchorage opposite the fort.[14] She had come three miles. It was wonderful. How she could come three miles puzzled the ablest mariners. She was flimsy enough to have an effect like a pane of glass; one felt that one could see through her. There is nothing in the United States Revenue Marine to compare with her. There was a collection of red flags on the bridge and over her trailed the red banner.

The decks of the Guadiana had been glad all day with the blue and gilt of the naval officers, and now into our experience and into this assemblage behold the Turks! Around the ship lay the power of Christian Europe and now here was the other thing, here was the Turk. Here was the creature that had pulled Europe's nose, boxed its ears, kicked it down stairs and told it to go to the devil, all the time asking it to be quite patient, that the creature was really governed by the most amiable impulse and all would be right in time, making it finally furious enough for deadly assault and then ending by harnessing it and driving it off gaily. Surely the art of procrastination should be taught more if by it you can stab a man's children and then convince him that you are only feeding them with buns and that he owes you a sixpence for the buns.

Naturally, then, this Turk was interesting. He didn't care, however. He was rather tall and well made, and had the face of a man — a man who could think, a man who could fight. He was fit for problems and he was fit for war, this fellow. The collar of his uniform was heavily flowered with gold, and a saber dangled to his spurred heels. He wore glasses, and about his eyes was the calm, studious expression that one expects in professors at colleges. Unconsciously to us, perhaps, many of us have fashioned our idea of the Turk on this hang-dog photograph

14. Fort Paleocastro was on the southern promontory of the entrance to the bay.

of the Sultan, which has been produced everywhere.[15] Probably this Turk was no nearer the controlling type, but, then, it was good to find him where one expected at least to find something fat and greasy.

In the array of genius that had boarded the ship there was even a little French officer of cavalry, in a plum-colored coat and blue trousers, all heavily braided in black. He was rather acrobatic in his manner, and it seems that it was particularly necessary that he should do a great deal of flying about in the ensuing festivities. Then there were some consular officers, and they also flew. But in the midst of all this pallaver, the Turk had the calmness of sense, the unconcern of a man who did not find it necessary to feel intimidated by the adjacent intellects. Once when he was free his glance remained reflectively for a time on these battle ships: arrayed Europe.

The Guadiana at last hove anchor and departed from Suda Bay, and behind her the fleet again blended gradually into a hedge. For a long time the tall tan stacks of the Camperdown and the long, gray hull of the Kaiserin Augusta remained distinct, but eventually, in the twilight, the fleet was only a great black thing, and afterward it was nothing. The hand of Europe was hidden by the hills lying in evening peace.

THE SPIRIT OF THE GREEK PEOPLE

Athens, Greece; April 17. — In this time of change and surprise, it is[1] good to find something that does not move with either tide, possessing a stability that enables badgered correspondents to remark upon it without being confused when their articles appear in print to find[2] by that time that the situation has been reversed. This unchangeable element is the spirit of the Greek people.

There is a kind of government that can make every man a soldier but there is no[3] government that can make every man desire to be a

15. This portrait was reproduced with the story as printed in the Louisville *Courier-Journal*. The Sultan of Turkey was Abdul Hamid II, who reigned 1876–1909.

Title added by the Editors to the untitled two-page holograph in the Crane Collection at Columbia University Libraries. This addition to the Crane canon is published here for the first time.

1. *well* cancelled.
2. *that* cancelled.
3. *man which* cancelled.

soldier. The population of Greece is for this time practically a population of soldiers. The[4] arming of the nation has progressed steadily for weeks and it is now about complete. It may be that this consumation will be directly followed by a return to the farms and flocks and fishing-boats but the best informed here deem it[5] improbable. Greece has made a bludgeon to be used on somebody's head and it is not likely that she will stir porridge with it of her[6] accord. Some of these confounded spectators who are so busy will have to stop a pretty row. The intention of Greece is war.

In view of this fact, the Place de la Constitution in front of the royal palace[7] has been interesting.[8] At all hours of the day the victims who have come from everywhere to be robbed by the hotel-proprietors in the vicinity[9] have been aroused by the blare of bugles, the great roaring cheers of recruits mingled with the loud approbation of the populace. There is one thing about a Greek crowd, it never howls. From descriptions of the modern Greek made by the correspondents of London[10] Conservative journals one rather expects him to howl. But he dont howl; these crowds cheer in a deep-throated and meanful way that stirs the heart. They are serious; constantly the news comes[11] from the frontier that the Greek soldiers are kept[12] from fighting — pitching into the Turks — only by the superb control which the officers have over them. They are insane to get at their ancient foes. Their enthusiasm is of the kind that has[13] the dignity in it. Ask any Greek[14] on the street his opinion of the situation and he will say: "We must fight. There is nothing else to do."

"Well, but the Powers?" you say to[15] him.

"Ah, yes, the Powers! Well, we must fight anyhow. Does it seem right to you that the Powers should bully Greece in this way? Look at the poor Cretans. Those men put their flesh against walls and capture a Turkish fort. Then as they stand panting after their victory, the fleet of the Powers shells them. Afterwards, perhaps, some Turkish troops assail a Cretan outpost and the[16] ships sit idly on the water

4. *army* cancelled.
5. *highly* cancelled.
6. *own* cancelled.
7. *is* cancelled.
8. *at these times* cancelled.
9. *are* cancelled.
10. Originally *c* in manuscript.
11. Originally *comess;* first *s* cancelled.
12. Originally *keep; ep* cancelled and *pt* added above the line.
13. *a w* cancelled.
14. *here* cancelled.
15. *them* cancelled.
16. *rigging* cancelled.

and watch it. They say they are there in the interests of peace but they do not stop the fighting, do they? No, they simply stop Cretan victories, it seems? I do not know what you may term it but to me it is infamous. Nevertheless you will see. The Cretans will not submit. It may be a spectacle of these islanders opposed to the force of Europe." [17]

"And Greece?"

"We must fight. How can we do anything but fight? Can we submit to this series of impositions? The Powers have settled our affairs for us before, have they not? And always allowed Turkey to cheat us in the end. This time we shall fight. And it is better to be defeated than shamed."

This talk sounds like[18] four glasses of cognac on the shady sidewalk before a cafe but it is not that kind strictly. It may be said truly to represent the attitude of the Grecian people.

STEPHEN CRANE SAYS
GREEKS CANNOT BE CURBED.
By Stephen Crane.

ATHENS, April 29. — I was with the Greek army in the campaign toward Yanina, the principal town of Epirus, the southwestern province of Turkey, when I heard the first rumors of the hard fighting in Thessaly.[1]

The journey from Arta overland to Thessaly requires a longer time than it does to go by the way of Athens, and so I have been

17. *and Greece* cancelled.
18. *the* cancelled.

***

Reprinted here for the first time from New York Journal: *30 April 1897. Under the headline "War in the East as Seen by the Journal's Correspondents," five articles were published side by side on the front page: (1) Crane's article; (2) "Woman Correspondent at the Front" by "Imogene Carter" (see infra, p. 25); (3) "Gallant Greeks Would Continue War" (which in some editions of the Journal for April 30th was headed: "Greeks Not Alarmed") by John Bass, who was the head of the Journal's contingent of correspondents in the field; (4) Julian Ralph's "Salonica Expecting a Bombardment"; (5) "Lew Wallace Tells How Greece May Win" by Julius Chambers.*

1. That is, the northeastern section of Greece, composed of the provinces (nomarchies) of Arta, Trikalla, and Larissa.

fortunate enough to arrive in the capital in time to witness another popular outburst of the Athenians.

Crowds are in the streets, in the square before the King's[2] palace, and in every place of public congregation.

Practically every man in Athens is arming to go and fight the Turks. Every train into the city is loaded with other troops. Yesterday crowds broke into the gun shops and took the practicable weapons. It was unanimous throughout all classes. To-day Greece is armed to fight for her life.

Today I went to a shop and found no one there but a boy seated on a box.

"Where is the proprietor?" said I.

"He has gone to the war," said the boy.

This man had taken no time to arrange his affairs in careful detail. He might have been gone out to buy a cigar in another shop. The shelves were stripped and the counters were bare.

"The proprietor has nailed fast the lid of a great box in which are the things. I cannot sell you anything," the boy said hastily. "I am going to the front."

In my hotel here, which is usually very English and impressive, they are shy on waiters, porters and call boys. These men have gone to the war. There is a battalion now preparing that uses as uniforms the stable clothes of a squadron of cavalry already gone. In fact, this is not a king's war, not a parliament's war, but a people's war.

It is absurd to say that the Greeks undertook this contest because they believed they would take Constantinople in a fortnight. No nation ever had a truer sense of the odds. The concert of Europe had calmly informed them of possible consequences; there had been a general movement to impress Greece with her danger, but the Greeks said: "Well, we must fight, anyhow."

There will a great deal happen before these people of the mountains care to pause.

❉   ❉   ❉

2. George I (1845–1913) ruled Greece, 1863–1913. He was the second son of Christian IX of Denmark (1818–1906). His civil list was approximately $260,000 a year, including $20,000 a year each from England, France, and Russia.

Despite his rather lowly place among the royalty of Europe, George I possessed powerful relatives. His wife was the Grand Duchess Olga, niece of Alexander II, the Czar-Liberator of Russia. Nicholas II, present Czar of Russia, was his nephew, son of his sister Dagmar, wife of Alexander III. Another sister, Alexandra, was the Princess of Wales, wife of the future Edward VII of England. George I was also related by the marriage of his eldest son to the Emperor of Germany.

GALLANT GREEKS WOULD CONTINUE WAR.

By John Bass.

ATHENS, April 29. — The popular feeling that the people have been betrayed by their leaders in the now famous stampede from Mati is, for the time, quieted. An incident showing the temper of the Greek people happened during the demonstration gotten up by Gennadius, who made a speech in which he called the King a traitor, and demanded that the royal family be driven from the country.

Then at the head of numerous rabble, he marched to the palace, which was entirely unguarded. Alone he entered on violence bent, and demanded to see the King.

"His Majesty does not receive today," said the doorkeeper.

"I am sorry," replied Gennadius. Coming out he informed the rabble that His Majesty did not receive him. He then entered a carriage and drove away in triumph, followed by a crowd. The situation has many opera comique elements. The safety of the King lay in the shrewd removal of the palace guards through the advice of one of the Ministers.

Greeks burst into tears when the Thessalian rout is mentioned. The Crown Prince's successor, General Smolenski, was elected in the following way at Pharsala: He had one competitor, General Mavromichalis, his personal enemy, who, pistol in hand, kept his division from stampeding, shooting down five of his men.

Mavromichalis was about to be elected when he arose and said:

"Gentlemen, my comrade General Smolenski, is better versed in military science than I, and I retire in his favor."

The people are anxious to try issues again under these two patriotic leaders, and another great battle is probable.

Ex-Premier Delyannis recently said in an interview making an attack on the King:

"I was never in favor of war. I permitted it to save the King's crown."

LEW WALLACE TELLS HOW GREECE MAY WIN.

By Julius Chambers.

CRAWFORDSVILLE, Ind., April 29. — "The situation for Greece is indeed critical, but all is not lost if she be the nation of heroes that I think and believe her to be. She can end the war in her favor in a week, badly as she is pressed at this very hour," said General Lew Wallace, former Minister to Turkey and immortalized as the author of "Ben-Hur" and "The Prince of India."

"How can Greece yet save herself?" I asked.

[GREECE'S NAVY CAN SAVE HER.]

"Her fleet can perpetuate her destiny," exclaimed General Wallace. "Turkey hasn't a man-of-war worthy of the name. Greece has some modern ships. Her sailors are as good as any in the world. Why, then, does she hesitate? A single man-of-war off Zeraglio Point, with her decks cleared for action, could dictate peace in an hour. Why do they threaten Salonica? Why waste good powder in the gulf of Arta? Are they made, or do they still trust in the god of Mount Olympia?"

SALONICA EXPECTING A BOMBARDMENT.
By Julian Ralph.

SALONICA, April 29. — From Vienna to Nish, in Servia, and to the Turkish frontier all the news was of Greek defeats, and everywhere there was great rejoicing, because the Greek is detested in all of Southeastern Europe.

In Austria-Hungary and Servia it is said that the Greek individual is equal to three Oriental Jews, therefore Austria-Hungary and Servia all presented a broad grin at the constant news of Greek reverses.

In Servia they told me:

"We are delighted. We are happy and at peace for the first time in our history."

[THE TURKS DISPLEASED.]

But when I reached Salonica all this was changed. There were two sides to the story. While it is true the Turks gained a great victory at Melouna and at Larissa, yet the Greeks had been vanquishing the Turks at other points and destroying towns along the coast near this place. So great was Turkish discontent with the way the war is carried on that they actually started Osman Pasha, Turkey's sole Marshal, to infuse new courage into the army.

The hero of Plevna is very old. It is like asking Bismark to take the field or sending Victoria around England stump speaking at a general election, but he is idolized by every Turk. His mere name is a tower of strength.

I find Salonica quiet and at peace amid its own foul smells, but all say: "The quiet is only today. God knows what will be tomorrow."

[GREEK FLEET IS CLOSE.]

The Greek fleet of ten war vessels is only twenty miles distant, and has already bombarded two towns. It is likely any moment to give sixteen hours' notice to the people to quit the town before bombardment.

Austrian and Italian war ships lie in the harbor ready to take care of their fellow countrymen and all strangers needing protection. In all houses of the better class men have their wives and children in readiness for flight, curios boxed up and valuables of all sorts put in portable packages, and yet nothing of a panic meets the eye.

Jews swarm the streets selling goods and counting money; Albanian doormen in quilted white petticoats bask in chairs in the sunshine, and in the concert halls music and beer flow together, and men and women flirt, drink and smoke together as if the fate of Babylon will never be repeated.

WOMAN CORRESPONDENT AT THE FRONT.
By Imogene Carter.

ATHENS, April 29. — I start to-day for the front of the Greek army to see how the men fight. I learn that even the English nurses have returned from the hospitals of the army because the Turks fire on the Red Cross flag with the same enthusiasm with which they fire on the lines of battle.

Reprinted here from New York Journal: *30 April 1897. This was one of the five articles published simultaneously under the heading "War in the East as Seen by the Journal's Correspondents," and was the first of three articles by Cora published in that newspaper over the pen name "Imogene Carter." On this occasion, the headlines were: "Woman Correspondent at the Front. / Goes for the* Journal */ Imogene Carter Braves Perils of the Field of War. / Only Woman on the Scene / Not Daunted by the Stories of Turks Firing on Nurses. / By Imogene Carter." She was not, however, the "only woman on the scene." Harriet Boyd was in Greece writing for the* Journal, *which described her on May 5 as the "Only Woman War Correspondent at Front."*

The first piece written by Cora was "War Seen Through a Woman's Eyes," which contains some striking, Crane-like writing but was apparently not considered suitable for her debut in the Journal, *for it was not published until May 14.*

From this and other rumors I am quite sure that the Journal will have the only woman correspondent within even the sound of the guns.

Acquaintances among the foreign residents here all strongly advise me not to go. At first I was flatly refused letters of introduction to people at the front in an effort to make my going impossible, but, as a matter of fact, I do not believe altogether in the point of view of the women of Athens, and, at any rate, I am going.

IMOGENE CARTER'S PEN PICTURE OF THE FIGHTING AT VELESTINO.
By Imogene Carter.

ATHENS, May 9. — By Courier from the Front. — I returned to Volo to-night (Thursday)[1] from Velestino after witnessing a hard fight there. I spent most of the time with the Second Battery of mountain howitzers.

The reinforced Turks, under Osman Pasha,[2] made a heavy attack upon the Greek right and left wings.

I was among the last of the correspondents to leave the field. Shells screamed about me as I went toward the station, and I had one narrow escape.

The soldiers were amazed at the presence of a woman during the fighting.

Our train was shelled on the way to Volo. We expected a panic here last night, despite the presence of English, French and Italian men-of-war.

The arrival of Turks is looked for at any moment.

WAR SEEN THROUGH A WOMAN'S EYES.

ATHENS, April 26. — To a woman, war is a thing that hits at the heart and at the places around the table. It does not always exist to her mind as a stirring panorama, or at least when it does she is

Reprinted here for the first time from New York Journal: *10 May 1897.*

1. Thursday was May 6, although the article is datelined May 9.
2. Gazi Osman Pasha had been dispatched recently from Constantinople to assume command in this sector.

Reprinted here in full for the first time from New York Journal: *14 May 1897.*

not thinking of battles save in our past tense historic way, which
eliminates the sufferings. One cannot, however, be in any part of
Greece at this time without coming close to the meaning of war,
war in the present tense, war in complete definition. I have seen the
volunteers start amid flowers and tears and seen afterward the tears
when the flowers were forgotten. I have seen the crowds rave before
the palace of the King, appealing to him for permission to sacrifice,
as if death was a wine. I have seen the wounded come in hastily and
clumsily bandaged, unwashed and wan, with rolling eyes that expressed that vague desire of the human mind in pain for an impossible
meadow wherein rest and sleep and peace come suddenly when one
lies in the grass. In Athens this is war — the tears of mothers, the
cheers of the throng and later the rolling eyes of the wounded. In
Athens one can get an idea of war which satisfies, it is true, the correspondents of many London newspapers, but surely this is not the
whole of war. War here is tears and flowers and blood and oratory.
Surely there must be other things. I am going to try and find out
at the front.

It is an encouraging prospect. People point to the hospital
corps and say: "Look! Do you see the cartridge belts around the
waists of these men who wear the Red Cross, the emblem of mercy?
Do you see that they carry rifles? Do you know what it means? No?
It means that a Turk fires on a hospital as quickly as he fires on
charging infantry. Do you know what they do to prisoners? Do you
know what they do to an enemy's wounded on the field? Do you
know what becomes of the women they capture? No? Well, no
license of words can describe the horrors of this last thing. The most
common Turkish outrages are the ones that don't get into print. We
assure you this on the word of every one who knows. The facts
simply can't be printed. This American journalism is very strange to
our minds. Why don't they send a man?"

"They have sent many men," I reply, "but now they want to
know what a woman thinks of a battle." The Greeks then solemnly
shake their heads. All this is very enfeebling. Nevertheless one cannot remain in this atmosphere long without gaining something from
the resolution and fortitude of this Greek people.

Imogene Carter

❋   ❋   ❋

CRANE AT VELESTINO.

ATHENS, May 10. — (By Courier from Volo.) — When this war is done Velestino will be famed as its greatest battle.

The Greeks began with a reverse at Larissa, and the world expected the swiftest possible conclusion, but Velestino has proved that Greek soldiers when well led can cope successfully with Turks, even though outnumbered.

This battle has proved them good fighters, long fighters, stayers. It must have surprised the world after Larissa. I know all Greece rejoiced, and this battle's effect upon the Greek soldiers is like champagne.

It made them perfectly happy. To be sure, the army retreated from Velestino, but it was no fault of this army. The commander bit his fingers and cursed when the order came to retreat. He knew that his army had victory within its grasp. For three days he had been holding the Turks beautifully in check, killing them as fast as they fell upon him. In the middle of intoxication of victory came the orders to fall back. Why? Reverses or something of the sort in other places may have been the reason, if there was a reason.

Smolenski knew, of course, that his retreat sacrificed Volo, and he raged like a soldier and a general.[1] But, like a soldier and a general, he obeyed orders and the Turks occupied Velestino. And this after a three days' successful fight. The troops were jubilant, the commander

---

Reprinted here for the first time from New York Journal: *11 May 1897. In another edition this same day the* Journal *published a variant account entitled:* "Stephen Crane at Velestino/Journal's Special Correspondent Describes the Battle." *Internal evidence indicates that Crane wrote both of these dispatches.*

Crane's dispatch was sent to Athens by courier from Volo probably on May 7, while Cora Taylor's "Imogene Carter's Pen Picture of the Fighting at Velestino," *in* Journal *May 10, was sent from Volo on May 6.*

1. Constantine Smolenski is a general only by courtesy of this dispatch. He was one of ten senior colonels in the Greek army and "the ablest Greek artillery officer." Cf. Frederick Palmer, *Going to War in Greece* (1897), p. 64. "Colonel Smolenski," said the *Illustrated London News* (5 June 1897), "comes of an old Slav family. He has a strong face, black piercing eyes, and an abrupt manner. In his dress he is very particular, always wearing white gloves, and he emphasises any orders he gives with his small riding-cane." Smolenski served as Minister of War prior to the outbreak of hostilities.

confident — and then the Crown Prince ordered a retreat.[2] My notion is that the Turks must have turned the far left of the Greeks. Probably by now New York knows more than Volo on this point.

[TROOPS WERE CONFIDENT.]

Anyhow, the Turks could never have turned the Greeks' right, and we who saw the worst of it feel doubts concerning the violence of the combat on the left.

The orders of retreat have crushed every man of this command. How the soldiers talked! Nobody wanted to fall back, save the few who would have fallen back anyhow. The Greeks understood the vastly superior number of the Turks, but they had whipped the vastly superior number of Turks three days and wanted to do it again.

Some other correspondents saw more of the battle than I did. I was rather laid up and had hurried on from Pharsala when I learned of the strong attack on Velestino. I knew that the taking of Velestino practically uncovered the base of the army at Volo, and so did not spare myself. But I only arrived at noon of the second day [Wednesday, May 5]. I had seen skirmishes and small fights, but this was my first big battle.

The roll of musketry was tremendous. From a distance it was like tearing a cloth; nearer, it sounded like rain on a tin roof and close up it was just a long crash after crash. It was a beautiful sound — beautiful as I had never dreamed. It was more impressive than the roar of Niagara and finer than thunder or avalanche — because it had the wonder of human tragedy in it. It was the most beautiful sound of my experience, barring no symphony. The crash of it was ideal.

This is one point of view. Another might be taken from the men who died there.

[MANY TURKS SLAIN.]

The slaughter of the Turks was enormous. The fire of the Greeks was so fierce that the Turkish soldiers while charging shielded their eyes with their hands. Eight charges the Turks made on this day, and they were repulsed every time. The desperate Turkish cavalry even attacked their enemy on a steep, rocky hill. The insane, wicked squad-

2. The Crown Prince (Duke of Sparta) was Constantine (1888–1923), later Constantine I, King of Greece, 1913–1917, 1920–1922, and brother-in-law of the then German Emperor. What follows shortly in the dispatch is one of Crane's frequent gibes at the Prince, once glowingly described as "quite six feet high, with a splendid athletic figure . . . a veritable picture of health and manly beauty," and a nobleman who spoke English very well. See *Illustrated London News*, CX (24 April 1897), 549; there is a pencil sketch of him on p. 547.

rons were practically annihilated. Scattered fragments slid slowly back, leaving the plain black with wounded and dead men and horses. From a distance it was like a game. There was no blood, no expression, no horror to be seen.[3]

All the assaults of the Turks this day resulted disastrously to them. The Greek troops fought with the steadiness of salaried bookkeepers, never tired, never complaining. It was a magnificent exhibition. The Greeks fought all the time with the artillery fire on them, even in a musketry lull, but nobody minded anything. The Turks were in great numbers, and fought according to the precepts of their religion. But the Greeks were never daunted and whipped them well. Sometimes it was fighting among gaunt hills, sometimes fighting on green plains; but always the Greeks held their position.

When night came shells burst infrequently, lighting the darkness. By the red flashes I saw the wounded taken to Volo. There was very little outcry among them. They were mostly silent.

In the gray early morning the musketry fire began again. It rattled from hill to hill, batteries awoke, and soon the whole play was resumed.

The Turkish guns were superior to those of the Greeks, who had mostly mountain howitzers. The Turkish artillery consisted principally of regulation field pieces, and I learned to curse the German officers who directed their fire. I think these officers are the normal results of German civilization, which teaches that a man should first of all be a soldier; ultimately he becomes simply a soldier, not a man at all. I consider these German officers hired assassins. One has strong feelings under such circumstances as these.[4]

[WAR IS NOT SWIFT.]

I watched for a long time the blue-clad Greek infantry march into position across a small plain. War takes a long time. The swiftness of chronological order of battle is not correct. A man has time to get shaved, or to lunch or to take a bath often in battles the description of which read like a whirlwind.

While I watched the Turks changed their attack from the Greek right on the plain to the Greek left on the rocky hill. Then the fighting became obscured from view. The Greeks lay in trenches, snugly flat-

3. The variant reading has it: "No blood, no expressions of horror were to be seen; there were simply the movements of tiny doll tragedy."

4. Crane seems to be following the popular belief of the time. G. W. Steevens was with the Turkish army throughout the brief war. He asserts that he never once saw a German officer officially attached to the Turks. "The Turkish army beat the Greeks in its own wonderful way." See *With the Conquering Turk: Confessions of a Bashi-Bazouk* (1901), p. 296.

tened against the dirt, firing carefully, while the Turks loomed close before them. Every ridge was fringed with smoke.

I saw soldiers in the trench ease off and take a drink from their canteens, twist their cartridge belts to put the empty links behind them, or turn around to say something to a comrade. Then they went at it again.

I noticed one lieutenant standing up in the rear of a trench rolling a cigarette, his lips wide apart. In this careless attitude a shot went through his neck. His servant came from the trench and knelt weeping over the body, regardless of the battle. The men had to drag him in by the legs.

The reserves coming up passed a wayside shrine. The men paused to cross themselves and pray. A shell struck the shrine and demolished it. The men in the rear of the column were obliged to pray to the spot where the shrine had been.

An officer of a battery sent a man to the rear after another pair of field glasses, the first pair having been smashed by a musket ball. The man brought a bottle of wine, having misunderstood. Meanwhile the Turks were forming on a little green hill 1,200 yards off. The officer was furious over the man's mistake, but he never let go of that bottle of wine.

A member of the Foreign Legion came from the left, wounded in the head. He was bandaged with magnificent clumsiness with about nine yards of linen. I noticed a little silk English flag embroidered on his sleeve.[5] He was very sad and said the battle was over. Most wounded men conclude that the battle is over.

[FUTILE ATTEMPT TO TURN FLANK.]

News came from the left that the Turks had tried to turn the flank and failed. I saw no correspondents and supposed them all to be in the thick of the fray.

The Turks formed on the right and moved slowly across the plain and the battery of howitzers opened on them.

I saw troops moving to the rear to prevent a possible flank attack in the direction of Volo.

The fight on the plain to the right began. Masses of Turkish troops like shadows slowly moved toward the Greek trenches indicated by gray lines of smoke. Shots began to rake the trenches on the hill and to also rake the battery to the rear. I hoped the Greeks on the plain would hurry and drive the Turks from their position. They did it

5. Most likely the Philhellenic Legion, made up of foreign volunteers, including some fourteen Englishmen (five of whom were wounded in this battle) and a number of Italians — the so-called "Garibaldians."

gallantly in a short, ferocious infantry fight. The bit of woods where the fight occurred seemed on fire. There was a great rattling and banging and then the Turks went out defeated. There was general rejoicing all along the Greek line, the officers walked proudly; the men in the trenches grinned. Then, mind you, just at this time late in the afternoon, after another successful day, came the order to retreat.

Smolenski had apparently received the brunt of the fighting. Yet the centre and left near Karadjah and at Pharsala had again retired. No one could explain it. We were not aware of the situation they faced, but it seemed an extraordinary order.

They say Smolenski wept.[6]

I went down to see the retreat. A curious thing was that the Turks seemed to understand the order as quickly as we did. They moved up batteries with startling rapidity for the Turks. Your correspondent got well shelled on his way.

[MADE AN ORDERLY RETREAT.]

The retreat was not disorderly, but wrathful and sullen. A regiment of Ephzones, the kilted men,[7] 2,000 strong, came down to cover the retreat and in the twilight, brightened by Turkish shells, the Greeks slowly withdrew.

An order to advance and get whipped scares no soldiers, but an order to retreat scares a good many. No retreat can be as orderly as an advance. But this was distinctly a decent retreat. The troops moved at the usual time and kept well together.

A train came, the last Greek train to run on this road for a long time. It received a heavy fire. I wanted to see the engineer, but could not. There are few better men than this engineer even in the Greek army. A complication of a railroad accident and bombardment is a bad disease. All the way down on the train a man covered with bloody bandages talked to me in wild Greek.

6. There seems to be some disagreement as to the time when the order was received. One account puts it at 4 A.M. In any case, the order was simple and to the point: "I withdraw this evening with the army to Domokos; rejoin there immediately." Smolenski was furious and is reported to have said: "The Prince's men are the same as mine. They can win battles against the Turks if some one will lead them." From "The Greek War as I Saw It," by Bennet Burleigh, *Fortnightly Review*, LXVIII (15 July 1897).

7. The Evzones were light infantrymen or riflemen, a select corps, usually recruited from the mountains of Greece. Their uniform was, and still is, the colorful skirt and tufted shoes.

I send this from Volo and before you print it the Turks will be here.[8]

THE BLUE BADGE OF COWARDICE.

ATHENS, May 11 — (By Courier from Chalkis). — Back fell the Greek army, wrathful, sullen, fierce as any victorious army would be when commanded to retreat before the enemy it had defeated.

There was no "God save the King" in the few cries that went up from Smolenski's men. They knew the grief and indignation of their brave general, and they knew he had to obey the order of the Crown Prince Constantine. The men cursed the faint-heartedness of the Prince who will rule them, and the officers turned away because in their hearts was the same bitterness that doubled the weight of the soldier's equipments.[1]

So the army withdrew, and the Turks came on. The Greeks knew how disastrous this retreat must be. They knew Volo must be occupied by the enemy, and they guessed more might fall because of the incomprehensible order of the King's son.

The Turks are slow by God's requirement, so vast numbers of

8. The account here is at odds with the variant reading: "I wanted to see the engineer, but was in somewhat of a hurry myself. Still I saw him. He was a daisy.

"The complication of a railroad accident and a bombardment at the same time is a bad disease, and the engineer in bloody bandages talked to me in wild Greek. I cannot quote him. I send this from Volo and before you print it the Turks will be here."

Reprinted here for the first time from New York Journal: *12 May 1897.*

1. The Crown Prince had both his defenders and his detractors, and Crane is probably partly correct in his scorn for Constantine on the battlefield. One contemporary of Crane defended the Prince to some extent and quoted the royal young man as saying that "the cadre of officers was deplorably weak," that the Greeks had "no idea of the meaning of the word discipline," and that Smolenski was a "mutinous swashbuckler" who deserved a court martial for his conduct at Domokos. See "Greece and Its Rulers," *The Saturday Review*, LXXXIV (25 September 1897), 334. However, the editors, in a subsequent story, "The King of Greece and Ourselves," disagreed and attacked the Prince, among others, for the fiasco.

women and children got safely aboard ships in the harbor of Volo. There was no particular panic, because of the strong Greek fleet in the harbor and the foreign war ships.

The foreign consuls all had their flags up and the consulates were crowded in anticipation of the coming of the Turk.

Volo is a beautiful town, a Summer resort in time of peace for wealthy Greeks. The houses are gay with awnings and the situation high on the mountain side overlooking the harbor is charming.

[SHIPS THRONGED WITH FUGITIVES.]

Every available ship in the harbor was employed to transport fugitives — except one, the one which above all others should have been employed in the work. This was the English Red Cross ship, and its non-employment was due to a particular and splendid ass, the surgeon in charge. He had some rules — God knows what they were — and he was the kind of fool to whom a rule is a holy thing. This ship came away light when thousands of war victims suffered for the lack of just the aid she could have given. The blame is not on the English Red Cross, but on the accursed idiot, who, by the devil's luck, was in charge. I promise myself the pleasure of writing about him later on.[2]

Every Greek battle ship was loaded with refugees. Fifteen hundred were on the Hydra alone.[3] The condition of these people was pitiable in the extreme. Many of them were original refugees from Larissa and other Northern points, who, flying before the march of the Turks, came to Volo as a place of certain harbor. Now they are obliged to flee even from there.

The foreign war ships naturally refused to assist the people to safety, but it seems to me that had a United States vessel been there Americans would have regarded such a course as the reverse of natural. The pleasant hypothesis by which the foreigners squared their consciences was that there was no need of flight.

2. Apparently Crane soon forgot the man. The Editors have not located such an article nor have they been able to identify either the "surgeon in charge" or the Red Cross ship.

3. *Hydra*, steel-built, along with her sister ships, the *Spetsai* and *Psara*, was constructed in France, 1889–1890; tonnage (displacement): 4,885; principal armament: three 10.6-inch and four 5.9-inch Canet guns and seven 6-pound quick-fire guns.

The Greek Navy was small and ineffectual. In addition to the above-named ships, there were two other armor-clads, the *Basileus Georgios* (1,770 tons; 1867) and the *Basilissa Olga* (2,060 tons; 1869); seventeen torpedo boats, two Nordenfelt submarine torpedo boats, two corvettes, twelve gunboats, and two very small cruisers. During the war the navy was mostly inactive, except for rather useless bombardments.

[THE TURK NOT LAMBLIKE.]

The London Times says the Turks are mild, woolly lambs. I saw at Epirus a Greek officer who had fallen wounded into Turkish hands. His body was headless when I saw it, and I do not consider the Turks as woolly lambs. I think the haste of the people rather natural.

Your correspondent left Volo when the advance guard of the Turks reached the hill tops surrounding the town. The decks of every ship in the harbor except the English Red Cross ship was simply packed with women and children. Most of the men of these families were away fighting. Even the little sail boats and fishing smacks carried a heavy quota.

It was the great sudden evacuation of Volo which I had the luck to prophesy to you two weeks ago.

The Greek naval officers said they would not fire on the Turks because the town is Grecian, though it is expected the Turks will burn it. There will be a curious situation here when the Turks are in possession and the Greek war ships lie four hundred yards away. I noticed the Greeks had their torpedo nets ready for lowering.

While the Turks came over the hills the right wing of the Greek army was falling back to Salmyros.[4] Smolenski, I think, is sure to make such a stand there as he did at Velestino. But will it do any good? There is a feeling that should the main army retire from Domoko — and the Greek army is more afraid of such an order from the Crown Prince than it is of the Turks — Smolenski will get that same old order to retreat, regardless of a success at Salmyros.

While I write the glad news has come that the Crown Prince will not retreat further while the army lives. Everybody believes it. If it is true, the big ridge back of Domokos will be drenched with blood. There is where the hard fighting will be done — not at Domokos as the report goes.[5] Domokos can be flanked, but the ridge is ideal for a defending army. It will be a sight worth seeing when the Turkish waves roll up against it.

[SWARMING ON THE SHIPS.]

But that fight is still in the future, and here at hand the scenes on the transports and merchant ships make one tired of war. Women and children are positively in heaps on the decks. They have no food, and they will be landed where they can.

I asked one of the officers how they expected to feed the people.

4. Halmyros is misspelled in Crane's dispatch as *Salmyros*.
5. The fighting at Domokos turned out to be decisive. Crane missed it, and so did Richard Harding Davis.

He answered that they did not expect to feed them — that they could not feed them.

I went with a great crowd to Areos. This town consists of six houses already crowded. The refugees came ashore carrying their household goods. They camped on the fields by great bonfires. These peasant women are patient, suffering in curious silence, while the babies wail on all sides.

This is war — but it is another picture from that we got at the front.

The Greek naval officers, with their eyes full of tears, swore to me the Turks would pay for all this misery. But the Turks probably will not; nobody pays for these things in war.

Eight thousand people at least fled from Volo. Their plight makes a man hate himself for being well fed and having some place to go. For instance, 700 fugitives landed at the village of six houses.

Who will feed them? There is no food. The mind of an American naturally turns to the wealth and charity of his own people. But such charity would be too late. Anyhow, organized American charity would likely proceed like the English Red Cross idiot. It is a case for the opening of skies, but no skies open. I wish I knew what is to become of these poor people. Warships are made to kill men, not to save men; otherwise the foreign warships at Volo would have assisted the stricken people. The Greek officers say the refugees landed at Areos, Helmyros, and Chalkis will have to wait for provisions to be dispensed by the Government at Athens. My calculation, and I know the elements with which to figure, is that this relief will be six days in coming.

[THE ARMY OUT OF PROVISIONS.]

Rumor has it that the army at Domokos is very short of provisions. I do not see many chances for the people outside the war programme getting food.

I cannot guess what the immediate future holds in store for Greece. The Crown Prince's message that he will not fall back again has re-inspired the troops. They are tired of falling back. The main body of troops would gladly give the Turks another battle. They accept their reverses with fine impassivity, and will fight well if provisions hold out and ammunition lasts.

The Turks move so sluggishly that no one can tell when they will get anywhere. They took almost three days to make the twenty miles from Velestino to Volo. Such marching gives the Greeks their opportunity.

I told some Greek officers to-day that in our country the Northern army fought for two years without winning a victory. They shrugged their shoulders and mildly said that fighting under such circumstances must be hard work.

Rumors are thick here. Every day a new one appears, generally referring to an intervention by the powers.

To-day we learn that the story has been told of a great panic at Volo. There was no panic; simply a most pitiable emigration.

YALE MAN ARRESTED.

ATHENS, May 13. — George Montgomery, an American graduate of Yale, '92,[1] was arrested several days ago at the Greek outpost near Pharsala. He was in the company of Baron Bindter, an Austrian, and was arrested for prowling where he had no business.

Bindter is the correspondent of an Austrian newspaper, who was arrested once by officials of the insurgents in Crete for calmly breaking the rules of war.

At the time of their arrest the two men were wandering between the lines with no particular care where they were. Montgomery wore a Turkish fez and had a Turkish servant.

When they were brought to Athens the populace was inflamed at the sight of the two men, who appeared like Turkish spies. The people spat upon them.

The men have been released. Montgomery is correspondent of the London Standard.

❂   ❂   ❂

Reprinted here for the first time from New York Journal: 14 May 1897.

1. George Redington Montgomery, B.A. 1892, Ll.B. 1894, B.D. 1900, and Ph.D. 1901; Alumni Lecturer in the Divinity School 1911–1912 and Assistant Professor of French 1919–1920. See *Historical Register of Yale University* (New Haven, 1939), p. 396.

Montgomery, along with a reporter named Maud, both representing the London *Graphic*, and John Bass, had investigated the Turkish massacres in Armenia in 1896.

WAR'S HORRORS AND TURKEY'S BOLD PLAN — I
By Julian Ralph.

Nisch, Servia, May 19. — What most interests foreigners at the seat of war in Thessaly is the question what Turkey is doing. Not merely fighting Greece. On the contrary, that is the least thing she is doing. The faster the Greeks run, the more earnestly Turkey prepares for war; the nearer the end of the Greek war approaches, the faster Turkey masses new troops, heaps up ammunition on Greek soil, builds great camps and buys more horses.

I was at Larissa for four days seeing a huge blue procession pour in its thousands, and when I turned homeward I found the situation still unaltered, the great blue serpent was winding new folds along to meet me and join the army. Beside the road at Larissa, Elassona, Melouna, Serbije, Cozeni and Sorovitch were military caps. At Cozeni, Haffizi Pasha, the Vall, called me to the window of the residence and showed me a large body of newly arrived troops, all armed with new Mauser rifles, who halted and gave a ringing cheer for the Padishah, as all Turks call the Sultan.

"Four thousand reinforcements there," said he, "and yesterday four thousand others came."

[SWARMING TO THE FRONT.]

Finally, when I returned to Salonica, I learned that an average number of sixteen hundred soldiers had been passing daily to the front, and that eighty thousand men were massed at the seat of war on April 25, and the force already on the field was close to one hundred and fifty thousand. The minimum number arranged for is three hundred thousand, with two hundred thousand more of reserves within easy call. Every day I asked what it meant.

Little by little what seems to be the truth leaked out — what I am going to tell I believe to be the whole truth and nothing but the truth. If I am right it is the most important news I have written for many years. Bulgaria and Albania both take warning by the fate of Greece, and both see as plainly as the rest of the world the wonderful evidence of Turkey's vitality, earnestness and pugnacity. Moreover, Bulgaria has got what it asked for and Turkey is now taking care of

Reprinted here for the first time from New York Journal: 23 May 1897. This and Crane's dispatch dated May 22 appeared side by side under the common headline: "Stephen Crane and Julian Ralph Tell of War's Horrors and Turkey's Bold Plan." At the bottom of the same page the Sunday Journal ran John Bass's "How Novelist Crane Acts on the Battlefield." (See infra, p. 42.)

Albania by accepting thousands of Albanian volunteers for the campaign to Thessaly, at the same time massing Anatolian troops in Albania and along the Albanian frontier. No, the truth is a thousand times more important.

When Greece began to defy the European concert and harass the Turkish outposts the Sultan was anxious for peace and very much averse to war, but he was overpowered by two members of the Government, who assured him if he did not declare war he would anger the people and lose the throne.

[THE COWARDLY SULTAN.]

He is the biggest coward on earth, so great a coward that finding Ghazi Osman idolized by the people he not only made the hero of Plevna practically a prisoner in the Yildiz Klosk, but ever since has put him in the royal carriage every day because he believes his enemies would not shoot nor dynamite the monarch if the hero sat by his side. Yielding to unwelcome advice the Sultan sent Ghazi Osman to supersede Edhem Pasha, but when Osman arrived at Salonica, while I was there, the Sultan was terrified by the popular welcome accorded the hero and hurried him back to the palace and removed the military governor of Salonica, whom he fancied was responsible for the behaviour of the people toward Osman.

Terrified by threats of his Ministers the Sultan declared war; as soon as war was declared the same palace influences that now have the upper hand in Turkey began a new line of insidious arguments in favor of impressing Europe with the great strength of the manifold resources and complete independence of the Ottoman Empire. The Sultan's counsellors said to him: "Do you not see that Greece successfully defies all Europe, and yet is not a thousandth part as strong as Turkey." Continuing, his advisers said: "You have been deceived too long. Turkey has been the cat's-paw of its own foolish fears of Europe. We now know the helplessness of the Christian nations and their inability to combine. Let us mobilize a grand army on the soil we have captured in Greece. Let us heavily garrison each Greek town we have taken, and when the war ends let us make our own terms and declare our huge army shall not be removed until our demands are satisfied."

[READY TO DEFY EUROPE.]

This I gather from officers who are members of a progressive young Turkish party and from foreign consul attaches in Turkey and from others who have the right to believe they know the subterranean forces at work within the Government of Constantinople. Between three hundred thousand and half a million soldiers are now being massed in Thessaly, Macedonia and Epirus, and I believe they will remain as silent backing of Turkey's demands when Europe intervenes to arrange terms of peace.

Greece has set her a great example and taught her a lesson; she feels all her strength and it gives her newborn confidence; she is ashamed of her past subjection and aspires to rank as one of the great powers hereafter. A dozen times I said to the Turkish officers:

"Are you going to give up the territory you captured?"

"Never."

"But the Sultan pledged his word not to make this a war of conquest."

"Yes, but a higher than the Sultan's, the power of the entire ruling class of Turks forced this war, and that power feels that Turkey has only taken what belongs to us by former ownership and we have paid a high price for it with our blood."

WAR'S HORRORS AND TURKEY'S BOLD PLAN – II
By Stephen Crane.

Athens, May 22 (On Board the St. Marina, Which Left Chalkis, Greece, May 18.) We are carrying the wounded away from Domokos. There are eight hundred bullet-torn men aboard, some of them dead. This steamer was formerly used for transporting sheep, but it was taken by the Government for ambulance purposes. It is not a nice place for a well man, but war takes the finical quality out of its victims, and the soldiers do not complain. The ship is not large enough for its dreadful freight. But the men must be moved, and so 800 bleeding soldiers are jammed together in an insufferably hot hole, the light in which is so faint that we cannot distinguish the living from the dead.

Near the hatch where I can see them is a man shot through the mouth. The bullet passed through both cheeks. He is asleep with his head pillowed on the bosom of a dead comrade. He had been awake for days, doubtless, marching on bread and water, to be finally wounded at Domokos and taken aboard this steamer. He is too weary to mind either his wound or his awful pillow. There is a breeze on the gulf and the ship is rolling, heaving one wounded man against the other.

[WOUNDED TAKEN TO ATHENS.]

Some of the wounded were taken off at Chalkis; the others will be taken to Athens, because there is not room for them in the Chalkis

Reprinted here for the first time from New York Journal: 23 May 1897.

hospitals. Already we have travelled a night and a day under these cheerful circumstances that war brings to some of those who engage in it.

When we with our suffering freight arrived at Piraeus they were selling the newspaper extra, and the people were shouting, "Hurrah! Hurrah for war!" And while they shouted a seemingly endless procession of stretchers proceeded from the ship, the still figures upon them.

There is just enough moaning and wailing to make a distinct chorus above the creaking of the deck timbers over that low hole where the lamps are smoking.

[RETREAT TOWARD THERMOPYLAE.]

This is Wednesday, I think.[1] We are at Stylidia. All day there have been clouds of dust upon the highroad over which Smolenki's division is retreating toward Thermopylae. The movement completely uncovers this place, and the Turks are advancing from Halmyros.

One long line of dust marked the road across the green plain where Smolenski marched away. And the people stared at this and then at the great mountains in back of the town, whence the Turks were coming. All the household goods of the city were piled on the pier. The town was completely empty, except for two battalions of Smolenski's rear guard, who slept in the streets, worn out, after a twenty hours' march. We loaded the steamer and schooner with women and children, and household goods. The anchor was raised by two man-of-war's men, three fugitives, and one Greek Red Cross nurse.

[SUFFERING OF WOMEN AND CHILDREN.]

The refugees generally seemed dazed. The old women particularly, uprooted from the spot they had lived so long, kept their red eyes turned toward the shore as they sat on their rough bundles of clothes and blankets.[2]

Our deck looked like an emigrant quarter of an Atlantic liner, except for the sick soldiers. The Journal steamer then went to St. Marina and landed the hospital stores.

Lieutenant-Colonel Caracolas came aboard there, much disturbed because some bread had been left at Stylidia. He was at the head of

1. Actually, it was Tuesday, May 18.
2. Some twenty-five years later, Ernest Hemingway, as correspondent for the Toronto *Daily Star*, covered the retreat of the Greek army — under the general command of this same Constantine — from Eastern Thrace; and he was as shaken by the misery of it and the suffering of it as was Crane. See Charles A. Fenton's *The Apprenticeship of Ernest Hemingway: The Early Years* (1958), pp. 180–186.

the commissary department of Smolenski's division. He asked us if we would try to get the bread. We agreed and found another schooner. We told the captain we were going to take him to Stylidia and he flatly refused to go. There was no time for argument; our extra bluejackets, seven in number, promptly stormed the schooner and took it by assault. I guess the captain of the schooner is talking of the outrage yet. The bluejackets got us a hawser, raised the anchor, and we towed the protesting schooner back to Stylidia, with the captain on the bow, gesticulating violently throughout the voyage. Incidentally we never found the bread.

We steamed back to St. Marina and found Dr. Belline, chief surgeon of the Greek army. He was worried about the safety of the hospital at St. Marina, but no orders had been issued for its removal. The obvious thing to do was to get orders from Thermopylae headquarters, and we carried the doctor across the gulf. He got the orders promptly and we took him back to St. Marina and took aboard the wounded men and Red Cross nurses of the hospital. The last boat had left the shore when a soldier came and said something to the interpreter, who shook his head negatively. The soldier turned quietly away.

On board the steamer your correspondent idly asked the interpreter what the soldier had said, and he answered that the soldier had asked for transportation to Chalkis on the ground that he was sick. The interpreter thought the man too well to go on a boat containing wounded men.

We sent ashore and after some trouble found the soldier. He was ill with fever, was shot through the calf of the leg and his knees were raw from kneeling in the trenches.

There is more of this sort of thing in war than glory and heroic death, flags, banners, shouting and victory.

❊　❊　❊

HOW NOVELIST CRANE ACTS ON THE BATTLEFIELD.
By John Bass.

ATHENS, May 21. — At Velestino I was greatly interested to see how the Journal correspondent, the well-known novelist Stephen Crane, would act in a real battle. Your correspondent followed him

Reprinted here for the first time from New York Journal: *23 May 1897.*

up the steep hill to where the Greek mountain battery, enveloped in smoke, was dropping shells among the black lines of Turkish infantry in the plain below. Your correspondent sought shelter in a trench and cautiously watched the pale, thin face of the novelist as the latter seated himself on an ammunition box amid a shower of shells and casually lighted a cigarette.[1]

Stephen Crane did not appear surprised, but watched with a quiet expression the quick work of the artillerymen as they loaded, fired and jumped to replace the small cannon overturned by the recoil.

I was curious to know what was passing in his mind, and said: "Crane, what impresses you most in this affair?"

The author of *The Red Badge of Courage* lighted another cigarette, pushed back his long hair out of his eyes with his hat and answered quickly:

"Between two great armies battling against each other the interesting thing is the mental attitude of the men. The Greeks I can see and understand, but the Turks seem unreal. They are shadows on the plain — vague figures in black, indications of a mysterious force."

By this time the Greek army was in full retreat.

As the last mountain gun was loaded on the mules Stephen Crane quietly walked down the hill. The Turkish artillery had drawn nearer, and amid the singing bullets and smashing shells the novelist stopped, picked up a fat waddling puppy and immediately christened it Velestino, the Journal dog.[2]

1. This incident had already been reported in Chicago *Post*: 13 May 1897. "The information is cabled to us that Stephen Crane sat on an ammunition box and lit a cigarette while under fire. While it has been impressed upon us before that he ranked high, we had not supposed that he actually aspired to the championship of inspired idiocy."

2. See *supra*, pp. 9–11. Velestino also figures in the next dispatch from Crane. But in *Cora Crane: A Biography of Mrs. Stephen Crane*, by Lillian Gilkes (1960), there is a photograph of this dog with the inscription in Cora's hand: " 'Velestino.' Picked up by Mrs. Stephen Crane in the midst of the battle of Velestino Greece." This contradicts Bass's claim that Stephen rescued it.

THE DOGS OF WAR

ON the left of the pup, lines of Greek infantry lay on the high, bare hills, firing without intermission. Gray smoke went up and backward from all these lines. Sometimes wounded men came from there and passed the pup as he sat reflecting in the roadway. Directly in his front a mountain battery of the Greeks was roaring, and the horses and mules of the command were browsing the grass in a sheltered place not far from the pup. Some soldiers in blue overcoats lay in an up-turned furrow of brown trenches.

If the pup had studied the vast green plain on his right he would have seen black lines and lines still fainter than black, and these lines were all Turks. Frequently a crescendo of hoots and hurtling noises was in the air above him and the shells crashed as they struck. More-over, there was sometimes a curious singing of great insects. But for all these things the pup did not care.

He was a little pup, not larger than a kitten, but he was fat and fairly smothered in long white wool, marked here and there with black, and he had every indifference of a fat pup. Two soldiers came that way on their return to the front, and, seeing him, paused. One stooped and offered him gently a bit of hard biscuit, but he had been used to other food, and, with the insolence of babyhood, he scorned the generosity of these men who had stopped under fire to give him assistance. They laughed then, and stroked his long hair and went away to their business.

The pup's interest was always the thing directly under his nose. He was really in the battle of Velestino, but what he wanted to do was to waddle in his curious way among the stones of the roadway and

---

Reprinted here for the first time from New York Journal: *30 May 1897.*

Other Crane dog stories include "Dark Brown Dog," in Cos-mopolitan: March 1901, and "Black Dog: A Night of Spectral Terror," in New York Tribune: 24 July 1892. "Jack," a dog story extant in three unfinished drafts, is in the Clifton Waller Barrett Crane Collection at the University of Virginia. It is described in "Stephen Crane: Some New Stories (Part III)," edited by R. W. Stallman, Bulletin of The New York Public Library: January 1957. Still another dog story, or rather a start at one, exists in a single page of holograph in the Crane Collection at Columbia Libraries. It was reproduced as the cover-design for the University of Con-necticut Fine Arts Magazine in 1961 for the first time. "Yellow Undersized Dog," a Bowery sketch, appeared in the Denver Re-publican: 16 August 1896.

smell at them and fall over them whenever he forgot that he was top
heavy. Although he was not larger than a cake of soap, he had
something elephantine in his movement. His little legs were still very
weak, and he sprawled and spraddled over the road in a way that one
would expect of a baby elephant. Once a cavalryman with orders
galloped past him, and a hoof of the gray charger missed him by little,
but he didn't care for that, either. He was busy with his geological
survey.

The Journal correspondent came along from the firing line at that
time and stopped when he saw the dog. The dog had been trying to
scratch his near ear with his off hind leg, but he stopped when he saw
the Journal correspondent. They looked at each other in reflective
silence. The pup had a crafty eye, and he put his head on one side and
surveyed the correspondent with much attention to detail. Another
shell came closer then, and your correspondent said: "Come on, pup."
He took the pup in his arms.

The dog was naturally named Velestino at once. There was a
thought in the correspondent's mind of calling him Loot. But then
he was not really loot. He was simply a Greek pup deserted by his
relatives and friends in a most trying hour, who had accepted the assistance of a correspondent of the New York Journal. His home had
probably been in one of the stone huts that stood here and there along
the road, now all lonely. His owners had probably scuttled out at word
of the coming of the Turks. But he didn't care about this, either. He
simply lolled on the correspondent's arm and blinked fatly at the
passing landscape.

When the correspondent arrived at where his horses awaited him,
he gave the pup Velestino into the hands of his Greek boy and stood
and admonished him sternly for five minutes about the inadvisability
of losing that pup. The boy grinned, and took Velestino in his arms.

Later the pup got under a particularly heavy artillery fire. While
the correspondent's party were crossing a bit of plain, the Turks opened
fire on a near-by house. One would have thought they had opened
on the pup, because they came nearer to the pup than they did to the
house. There was some excitement. The stragglers in the road scurried
everywhere. The correspondent had a bit of trouble with his horse,
which had been hurt in the back by some kind of fragment, and when
it was all over, he looked around for the pup, the two servants and
the other horses, and there was none.

Late that night[1] in Volo a knock came to the correspondent's
door, and, as he called out, it opened and the Greek boy appeared,
with a bow and a grin.

"Where is the pup?" said the correspondent, instantly.

1. May 6.

The Greek boy had brought a great piece of shell, which he said had almost killed him, and he exhibited it proudly.

"Where is the pup?"

The boy said he was sure he was going to be killed when he heard the shell, and he now considered his escape to be a miracle. The correspondent arose impressively to his feet. "Where is the pup?"

Well — poor Velestino — poor correspondent — they were united only to be immediately parted. The boy said that he had brought the pup to Volo and had given it to a man to hold while he unsaddled his horse. The man ran away with Velestino.

There were dispatches to be sent, and the wires were muddled in a way that was simply scandalous. The correspondent left for Athens, reflecting from time to time upon the virtues of his lost pup.

Volo is, ordinarily, 300,000 miles from Athens. In time of war, it is the square of 300,000. Every route is impossible. All the steamers are on war business. All the carriages have vanished. There are no horses. It requires more energy to travel now in Greece than it does to do a three months' campaign. The correspondent struggled as far as Chalkis,[2] with phenomenal good fortune. He was taking his breakfast in the restaurant there when he observed a peasant come in and walk toward the rear of the place. This man had a pup inside his shirt, and the little woolly head projected. The correspondent said to his dragoman:[3] "That is my dog." The dragoman laughed. "There are a million dogs like that in Greece, sir."

"No, there ain't. I tell you that is my dog."

As the peasant with the pup disappeared through a door in the rear, the correspondent and the dragoman rushed after him. In a courtyard they found the peasant delivering the pup to another dragoman, the servant of an English correspondent. But the correspondent took his pup. "It is my dog."

"No. It isn't," said the dragoman of the English correspondent. "I got him at Volo."

"You got him at Volo, did you? Well, I got him at Velestino. He belongs to the New York Journal and it doesn't matter what you say, you can't have him."

"Well" —

"Shut up."

"Well, he has cost me two drachms[4] for his food and care. Pay me that and it is all right."

Velestino thus rejoined the correspondent. His hotel bills were

2. Chalkis is the capital of Euboea (or Negroponte), largest island of the Greek archipelago.

3. An interpreter or professional guide in Near Eastern countries.

4. The monetary unit of Greece, usually spelled *drachmas*.

paid and he was invited to some bread and milk. The rounds he fought with this bread and milk were simply too exciting for words. He was not satisfied with putting all of his features in the plate. He waded up to his knees, and his subsequent cargo was, altogether, out of proportion to his displacement. His shape became suddenly like that of a toy balloon. But it filled him with a sort of glad satisfaction which was noticeable in his rollicking tipsy-sailor walk.

On his way to Athens the pup received constant ovations. The Greek boy was on the box, and he elaborated his own experiences, and incidentally the experiences of the pup. People gazed at Velestino with awe. He was such a wee thing that the correspondent was not sure whether he was going to grow to be a cow or a caterpillar, but the kilted mountaineers that studied him said that he was of the famous shepherd dog breed of the Greeks and was destined to be a big dog.

"Wait until he grows," they said, "and then, if even a hundred bad men approach your house, you need not fear." Looking at Velestino, asleep in a fluffy ball in the carriage, the correspondent rather thought that the number of bad men was over the limit.

At Thebes, while the correspondent lunched, Velestino waddled, or, rather, fell around the floor of the cafe. The boys of the village congregated about him, and the Greek child, who thought he had been almost killed, dilated on the experiences of himself and the dog. All these popular honors the pup accepted with his usual sublime indifference. He interested himself in certain surprising physical eccentricities. For instance, every time he tried to run he fell on his nose. When he tried to catch his tail he fell on his shoulder. In fact, he was so much of a pup that he could fall in almost any direction with equal abandon. These manoeuvres were also conducted without regard to the interest and admiration of the populace.

People do not usually talk about dogs, and so, before he reached Athens, he was easily the most famous dog in Greece. In Athens itself he was put up at the best hotel, and the honors he received befitted his social position.

At present he is with your correspondent. He has a personal attendant engaged at a fabulous salary. He is well-known here already, and his appearance on the street causes popular demonstration. But he don't care.

GREEKS WAITING AT THERMOPYLAE

Lamia, May 22, via Athens, May 23. — Still backward fall the Greek soldiers. First it was Velestino, then Domokos, next it will be Thermopylae.

They have had a hard time of it. Their fiercest fighting has been rewarded, not with victory, but with orders to retreat. They have had a fierce, outnumbering enemy before them and a rear fire from the vacillating Crown Prince. They have had a campaign that has made officers cry like hysterical women with weariness and disappointment; they have been marched uselessly day and night, have starved and suffered and lost, and yet they are stout hearted and anxious for another fight.

[ONLY EVZONES LEFT BEHIND.]

The main body of the army has already marched away for the new position. Only the Thermopylae division, 15,000 strong, remains at Lamia.

I have grown to know this division. They are mainly Evzones. They are always last when the Greek army retreats and first when it advances.

Here they are in their old position, the rest of the Greek army miles away, and the Turks so near that their advance is plainly visible from the top of the old Acropolis, about four miles away. As they come closer I recognize them as Circassian cavalry.[1] There are the elements of a first-class scrap right here in the range of my field glass.

There is a rumor all through the town and the army of an armistice, but the Greeks have no thought that the war is over. They all believe they will fight again soon and are glad of it.

[PREPARATION FOR RESISTANCE.]

There is no let up of preparations for a stout resistance to the Turks at the historic pass. Nine fresh battalions arrived here late this evening from Athens, and they are eager for a chance.

I hope the armistice will be made to last long enough to give the Greek infantry some rest. They need it.

Plans for truces are nice things, but I really don't know that they are always possible of fulfilment. There is a strong probability

Reprinted here for the first time from New York Journal: 24 May 1897.

1. A warlike people from Circassia in the northwest section of the Caucasus, between the mountains and the Black Sea.

that the next fight will be begun by Turkish irregulars. These are men from the wild mountains of Albania, who are in the war business exclusively. They don't know an armistice from a pie or a truce from a trilobite, and the shooting will surely go on with them in the game.

[TALES OF CRUELTIES PLENTIFUL.]

I hear the most dreadful tales of their cruelty, but have not been able to substantiate one. If the stories are true, the cruelties probably occur miles out on the flanks, where the Turkish irregulars raid villages.

I have been asking Greek soldiers if they were not tired of it; if they did not want the war stopped.

"No! we want to fight more," has been the invariable reply.

The officers, or many of them, on the other hand, seem to have had enough. Ask them the same question and they shrug their shoulders and say:

"What can we do? It is better to cease."

Maybe they appreciate the situation better than the men in the ranks; maybe the hasty orders to retreat that are always coming are more significant to them. Whatever the reason, they are willing to stop.

[NEW THERMOPYLAE STRONG.]

None of the soldiers admits the possibility of losing Thermopylae. Really, the new position is very strong. Although the pass has been widened and much changed since Leonidas's fight, it is still an ideal place to hold an enemy in check and here, if the war goes on according to the rules of the game and the supreme authority lets the Greek army do what is in it to do the advance of the Turks may be dammed. I would like to write a dispatch telling of a full blown Greek victory for a change.

*　*　*

Four Parodies of Crane as War Correspondent

ST-PH-N CR-N-[1]

BRINDISI, April 24. — Able students of the art of war who read my "Red Badge of Courage" said that beyond a doubt I must have borne arms in our Civil War but as a matter of fact, I wasn't even borne in arms until a year or so after it was finished. Now, if I could write so graphic and convincing an account of a conflict, the varying colors of which had faded and gone before I came upon the scene, it follows that I ought to be able to write an account of the present Graeco-Turkish war that shall be at least as highly colored as any other man's and that too from a point where I am able to give my whole attention to writing and mixing my colors and am in no danger from stray bullets. From what the critics say, I know all about war without ever having been near one. What have I to expect by being on the scene except an incapacitating wound? It is more fair to those who sent me out as war correspondent that I stay here in Italy. So I will give my imagination free play and sling in lots of color, and there's not one man in a million can tell where I'm wrong if I am.

I have just received the following despatch: — "Athens, April 24. It is learned here that a desperate battle was fought at Mati yesterday."

The fight must have been between the Greeks and the Turks and so it was full of my favorite color, red — Turkey red. The Turkish and Greek troops lay encamped before Mati. A huge and laborious fog wallowed and pirouetted by turns, shutting out the operations of the armies from the knowledge of my contemporaries, Richard Harding Kipling and Rudyard Davis. Now and again a Greek youth filled with patriotic fire of an exceedingly effective shade of scarlet would swear volubly in Greek, but as I am not a linguist I am unable

1. Reprinted from *The Critic:* 1 May 1897; appears also in J. B. Gilder's *The Month:* June 1897.

It is the last of three parodies, the other two being of "R-dy-rd K-pl-ng" and "R-ch-rd H-rd-ng D-v-s." The trio appears over the name "Charles Battell Loomis," the poet and humorist (1861–1911). In all three word *despatch* is so spelled.

to spell his conversation either phonetically or after my own system. The effect of the Greek fire which is of course in constant use in the army was to color the fog beautifully and make Richard Harding think he was at a pyrotechnic display at Coney Island. Shortly after four o'clock the Turks were ordered to win the battle and they pressed forward with religious frenzy, waving their bundles of shoestrings, just as they do on Broadway. A giant Turk stubbed his toe and fell to sobbing piteously, but unmoved at the sight the rest swept on uttering huge yellow oaths that it would tax even my ingenuity to spell. One Turk who had been in business in New York and had returned to fight for his country ran along crying irrelevantly, "This is a heluva note. Wanta shoestring? This is a heluva note. Wanta shoestring? Five cent."

At half-past four the Greeks heard a pale green rumble and they knew that the Turks were upon them. The Greek youth remembered that other youth who fired the Ephesian dome, and he spoke of it to a tall Greek who stood next him, but he received no response. A squirrel sat upon a cannon and cracked cannon balls with saucy gibberings, unspellable. Red and brown and green ants hurried this way and that as if scenting the coming danger. The Greek youth remembered his mother. She would be making doughnuts full of grease about this time and he cried silently. A short Greek by his side looked blue for a minute, and then at a remark from the youth he changed color. The fog as if rejoiced at balking the efforts of Davis and Kipling wallowed at intervals of five minutes.

Then there was a Turkish crash, cream color with a selvedge of red and the ants and the youth and the squirrel were gone and the Turks had won the battle of Mati.

                                                   Charles Battell Loomis.

I HAVE SEEN A BATTLE[2]

I have seen a battle.
I find it is very like what
I wrote up before.
I congratulate myself that
I ever saw a battle.
I am pleased with the sound of war.
I think it is beautiful.
I thought it would be.

2. Reprinted from New York *Tribune:* 18 May 1897.

I am sure of my nose for battle.
I did not see any war correspondents while
I was watching the battle except
I.

THE GREEN STONE OF UNREST[3]

By S———n Cr———e

A Mere Boy stood on a pile of blue stones. His attitude was regardant. The day was seal brown. There was a vermillion valley containing a church. The church's steeple aspired strenuously in a direction tangent to the earth's center. A pale wind mentioned tremendous facts under its breath with certain effort at concealment to seven not-dwarfed poplars on an un-distant mauve hilltop.

The Mere Boy was a brilliant blue color. The effect of the scene was not un-kaleidoscopic.

After a certain appreciable duration of time the Mere Boy abandoned his regardant demeanor. The strenuously aspiring church steeple no longer projected itself upon his consciousness. He found means to remove himself from the pile of blue stones. He set his face valleyward. He proceeded.

The road was raw umber. There were in it wagon ruts. There were in it pebbles, Naples yellow in color. One was green. The Mere Boy allowed the idea of the green pebble to nick itself into the sharp edge of the disc of his Perception.

"Ah," he said, "a green pebble."

The rather pallid wind communicated another Incomprehensible Fact to the paranthine trees. It would appear that the poplars understood.

"Ah," repeated the Mere Boy, "a Green Pebble."

"Sho-o," remarked the wind.

The Mere Boy moved appreciably forward. If there were a thousand men in a procession and nine hundred and ninety-nine should suddenly expire, the one man who was remnant would assume the responsibility of the procession.

The Mere Boy was an abbreviated procession.

The blue Mere Boy transported himself diagonally athwart the larger landscape, printed in four colors, like a poster.

3. A parody by Frank Norris first published in the San Francisco *Wave:* 24 December 1897. Reprinted in *Frank Norris of "The Wave,"* edited by Oscar Lewis (1931).

On the uplands were chequered squares made by fields, tilled and otherwise. Cloud-shadows moved from square to square. It was as if the Sky and Earth were playing a tremendous game of chess.

By and by the Mere Boy observed an Army of a Million Men. Certain cannon, like voluble but non-committal toads with hunched backs, fulminated vast hiccoughs at unimpassioned intervals. Their own invulnerableness was offensive.

An officer of blue serge waved a sword, like a picture in a school history. The non-committal toads pullulated with brief red pimples and swiftly relapsed to impassivity.

The line of the Army of a Million Men obnubilated itself in whiteness as a line of writing is blotted with a new blotter.

"Go teh blazes b'Jimminey," remarked the Mere Boy. "What yeh's shooting fur? They might be people in that field."

He was terrific in his denunciation of such negligence. He debated the question of his ir-removability.

"If I'm goin' teh be shot," he observed; "If I'm goin teh be shot, b'Jimminey —— "

                    *   *   *

A Thing lay in the little hollow.

The little hollow was green.

The Thing was pulpy white. Its eyes were white. It had blackish-yellow lips. It was beautifully spotted with red, like tomato stains on a rolled napkin.

The yellow sun was dropping on the green plain of the earth, like a twenty-dollar gold piece falling on the baize cloth of a gaming table.

The blue serge officer abruptly discovered the punctured Thing in the Hollow. He was struck with the ir-remediableness of the business.

"Gee," he murmured with interest. "Gee, it's a Mere Boy."

The Mere Boy had been struck with seventy-seven rifle bullets. Seventy had struck him in the chest, seven in the head. He bore close resemblance to the top of a pepper castor.

He was dead.

He was obsolete.

As the blue serge officer bent over him he became aware of a something in the Thing's hand.

It was a green pebble.

"Gee," exclaimed the blue serge officer. "A green pebble, gee."

The large Wind evolved a threnody with reference to the seven un-distant poplars.

BY STEPHEN CRANE[4]

The American fleet came redly on like a bunch of waving bandana handkerchiefs. The air was full of prunes as a plum pudding. The whitish-green rattle of the rapid-fire guns was exacerbatingly shrill.

The Spanish met the onslaught with a mauve determination. Ecruly they stood at the posts shepherds doggedly.

The two fleets hurtled in a magenta hurtle. They feinted and thrust with a deep canary-yellow vigor. The battle looked like two overturned garbage-cans on a hot night. The shells whistled sealbrownly. The death screams of the Spaniards were full of purplish pink despair. One Spaniard with a cerise voice like the aftermath of an aurora borealis screamed paintily his desire to kill the Americanos.

Then with a blackish white tremor, strong battleships sank greenly chromely black into the water. A gauntly greenish smell tore the air. The whole thing looked like a German pouring dark wine into a dingy funnel.

Admiral Dewey had won.

✿   ✿   ✿

THE EASTERN QUESTION

If there is one[1] man in Europe who is now more apparent than another it is the man who understands the Eastern question. He outnumbers the tinkers and the bakers and the butchers already on the

4. This parody of Crane by James Huneker appeared in *The Musical Courier* (3 August 1898) with a note: "The Buffalo *Enquirer* prints the following war correspondence from the front. It neglects to state whether the dispatches were received by wire or by freight."

Reproduced here for the first time from the holograph in the Crane Collection at Columbia University Libraries. There are six holograph sheets of which the first and most of the second are in Cora Taylor's hand, Crane taking over at the sentence: "And yet it puts to flight the brains of Europe." At the top of the first sheet the figure 2000 (representing wordage) is encircled and underlined is the phrase "not used." It is signed on the final sheet

1. *a* cancelled.

continent of Europe and in Great Britain alone his census dwarfs that of the people who like ale and roast beef. It is thought that someday he may go on strike in which case existence must necessarily cease. Half of the business of Europe would at once be paused.

The great advantage of understanding the Eastern question is that you can lecture other people about it and for obvious reasons make them wish that they understood it too. But it is essentially an accomplishment that benifits only the vocal organs and vanity. It is now a matter of record that when a man thinks he comprehends this puzzle well enough to risk his goods, his home, or his life on it he learns perhaps to his astonishment that it is still the most subtle and evasive creation that the Turk has yet achieved in long years of successful political[2] legerdemain. In fact the Turk is nothing if not the Eastern question. He is the Eastern question. It is his proffession. It has been his business for a long time to mystyfy and seduce and trick his neighbors and he does it with the skill that comes from perfect devotion to the game.

I have said that the limits of advantageous comprehension of the Eastern question lies in the vocal organs and that if a man risks his goods, his home, or his life on this knowledge he comes suddenly upon a great disaster. Greece understood the Eastern question and she has lost a vast amount even if she has not altogether lost her goods, her home and her life. But then the great powers[3] understood the Eastern question and if they have not lost their self respect it is because it must have been fastened to them with a great many more tacks than is common. There has always been a calamity in store for the philosophy of statesmanship which believed itself to be compitent to deal with the Turk at his own particular stunt. Any body who has studied the negotiations between Turkey and the Powers over what the Sultan shall be paid in money, land and national advantages for the victories of his soldiers[4] should see plainly that the christian statesman of Europe is perfectly incompetent to play the game of diplomacy for one moment with the masters of the art at Constantinople.

"Stephen Crane." There is neither title (the above having been added by the Editors) nor date. It was written some time after the Greco-Turkish War, probably in England, and is an addition to the Crane canon. The manuscript contains many misspellings and deletions. All of the former are reproduced in our transcript, but only as many of the latter as seem interesting.

2. *economical* cancelled.
3. *thought* cancelled.
4. *can* cancelled.

The Turk invariably makes a monkey and a fool of any white man who deals with him in these matters. History does not show a purely diplomatic victory over the Turk. This is almost proof that diplomacy is composed too much of lies and procrastination to be the high art which Europeans love to name it.

Anyone who has been in the Orient[5] can percive in the manoe-vurings of the Sultans ministers during this great international crisis the very methods displayed which dumbfounded the traveler when he argued the price of a rug in the bazaar. And yet it puts to flight the brains of Europe. With every apparent advantage of force on their side, not to mention the great and important one of general harmony of purpose, the embassadors of the Powers fail to bring the Turk to the point in less time than it would require to build a railroad from Pittsburgh to Philadelphia.

Long ago the Powers told the Turks to evacuate Thessaly. In reply, the Turk appoints civil officials to administer the government of the province as if it were a suburb of Constantinople. At the time of sweeping indignation he will reply that it is a shame to make him evacuate Thessaly when he has taken so much trouble to establish a good civil regime.

The embassadors inform Tewfik Pasha that[6] his government will be paid £4.000000 as indemnity.

Tewfik thinks that he will compromise on £4500000. In the bazaar you name your final price and the merchant thinks you are a liar. He promptly refuses to sell for that price. He must have a little, just a little, more. He squirms and squeaks and squeals over it until he is satisfied that you are serious — then he accepts with thrilling alacrity. Afterward you wonder if you can learn[7] from the book of judgment how much you have over-paid this rascal.

So if the Porte says that four million pounds will not re-pay Turkey the cost of this war, the chances are fifty to one that the Porte lies. The other five hundred thousand pounds is simply the regular raise of the oriental vendor of fruits. In American poker terms it may be called a hike.

But it is in Crete particularly that Turkey has made a complete exhibition of Europe until the whole affair might perhaps be noted as resembling a Sunday inspection at an idiot asylum. It has not yet been disputed that if while Turkey was engaged with Greece, the Powers had keep their hands from Crete, that towering island in the Mediter-ranean would not now be free. The inhabitants are Christians in the

5. *Constantinople* cancelled.
6. *he shall* cancelled.
7. *see* cancelled.

proportion of five to one Mussulman and they are islanders as well as mountaineers, the two kinds of people who are most famous for fighting. Despite the talk of easy victories Turkey's hands were quite busy during the war with Greece and she would not have sent too many battalions to Crete. The Cretans would have conquered their own island. But by a number of roundabout and solemn manuvres, Europe herself steps in between the Cretans and their liberty under the impression that a fight on this little island will, if the Cretans are supported by the Greeks, result in a general up-heaval of Europe. The contrary is proved to them by a war on the continent itself which involves only Turkey and Greece and certain German sympathies and ends apparently at that point. But the Powers having grabbed this bear by the tail, find no precedent in diplomacy for relinquishing this grip and hang on heroically until Crete's opportunity is completely lost and hang on still more under the impression that having once hung on, it would be improper to let go.

Europe that has always pretended to find the Turk the one odious ingredient in the continental punch proceeds to defend the Turk at every point. She cleans his knives and washes his dishes for him. She shoots at the Christian in an outburst of indignation. She performs all other feats that are expected of a good Turk. The guns of the Camperdown, larger than any guns that have been in action in the past history of the world, make their initial appearance in an enthusiastic bombardment of the Christian as he attempts his freedom. The Turk is attacked and at once they devote a great deal of energy and practically all the naval forces in the Mediterranean to his protection.

Devious excuses occur. Since[8] the war between Greece and Turkey took away any vestige of cause[9] why the Powers should occupy[10] Crete, the Powers advanced as their reason that if they withdrew their forces the Mohammeddans would be massacred by their over-whelming Cretan foes.[11] Is it massacres then that the Powers seek to prevent? If Crete is not to be vacated because there is a prospect of massacre, why was not Armenia occupied on the proof of massacre? Of course[12] to occupy Armenia is a difficult military proposition but then we are

8. *When* cancelled.

9. *reason* cancelled.

10. *blockade* cancelled.

11. *This remains a proposition yet to be proven because the Cretans have never had that particular and supreme reputation for massacre which is the heritage of the Turk. If they have never yet have massacred anybody it is legal to exempt them, partially at least, from this charge. Furthermore* cancelled.

12. The bottom of the page is torn off for the length of about three words.

speaking of the Powers who can do anything even to the adoption of a collective title which does not evidently belong to them. In fact it is further plain that the Powers have even no right to use the word massacre. With the prevention of massacres they have nothing to do. During the massacres in Armenia they called upon each other to recognize a sacred duty and then they contented themselves with this empty expression. As far as their sacred duty was concerned they let it be eaten by the dogs. It is proved that the Concert of Europe formed for the purpose of preventing bloodshed is an idle collation which continues to allow admirals to [*lacuna*] with unfailing regularity. When this farce is termed Peace, or, Humanity, it is a crime. With these things it has nothing[13] in common. It is a private establishment of sailors and ships combined under the influence of a mistake to enforce a certain expedient. And when[14] the necessity for the expedient no longer exists, they raise semblances of it on the fighting-tops of the war-ships of the squadrons and proceed bravely in the same way. They refuse to define themselves because they cannot define themselves. They do not know. Questions as to their identity throw them into spasms of indignation. The whole affair dies down into a wearisome confusion of explanations on the part of governmental mouth-pieces in nearly every legislative chamber of Europe.

In the meantime the perplexed British citizen mumbles something about the work of the unseen hand of Russia while France cries out against German duplicity. Russia laments the strength of English influence at Constantinople and Germany blames the ambition of France.

But we who have never understood the Eastern question are at last able to see one thing clearly and that is the Turk seated coolly upon a pinnacle of success regarding with a singular smile the nations that have patronized him so long. This victory does not lie merely in the defeat of Greece; there is a far[15] greater victory in the effect of this sudden disclosure, this coming from behind the glass, and appearing to astonished Europe as a gentleman in very fair health indeed. And from this vantage, he gaily waves the scalps of all the diplomats[16] that have come against him.

They had called him the sick man of Europe but when he chose he showed them that at any rate he could knock together the heads of the nations. As far as the Concert was concerned, if it's back was turned and if he felt in the humor, he quite often kicked it sharply and emphatically although perhaps not always in accordance with the law of pugilism.

13. *to do* cancelled.
14. *this expedient* cancelled.
15. *larger aspect* cancelled.
16. *of Europe* cancelled.

One could hardly have the temerity to[17] observe the emotions of this gigantic creature, the Concert, at this particular hour. It would be an intrusion too grievous. Nor would one dare to scan the colossal countenance, broken with surprise and pain. It no doubt feels itself to[18] be an immense and hideous bit of nonsense. It went into a thing with a great deal of solemnity and with all sorts of kow towing and salamming on all sides and with a loud declaration to do it's own will in a certain matter and there rose up from the dark East a little man in a red fez who took it by the hair and mopped the world with it.

❈   ❈   ❈

17. *think* cancelled.
18. *have made an* cancelled.

From *"With Greek and Turk"*,

II. A FRAGMENT OF VELESTINO.[1]

The sky was of a fair and quiet blue. In the radiantly bright
atmosphere of the morning the distances among the hills were puzzling
in the extreme. The Westerner could reflect that after all his eye was
accustomed to using a tree as a standard of measure, but here there
were no trees. The great bold hills were naked. The landscape was in-

---

*The following sketches — instead of being scattered chronolog-
ically in the text of Crane's Greco-Turkish War sketches — are presented here as a unit. They are reprinted here for the first time
from the London* Westminster Gazette: *"With Greek and Turk."*

*Part I, captioned "An Impression of the 'Concert,'" is identical
with the Louisville* Courier-Journal *sketch entitled "Stephen
Crane's Pen Picture of the Powers' Fleet Off Crete" (9 May 1897),
which text we have used on pp. 11–19, supra, as the opening
sketch of Crane's Greco-Turkish War series.*

Part II consists of "A Fragment of Velestino," in Westminster Gazette *for June 3, 4, and 8 (1897). Part I appeared there
on May 3, whereas Part II did not begin until a month later, and
for this gap the* Gazette *Editor issued an apology. In much short-
ened form "A Fragment of Velestino" first appeared in the New York*
Journal *(13 June 1897) captioned: "That Was the Romance,/This
Is the Reality,/A Battle To-day in Greece/ — a Fact./by/Stephen
Crane."*

The portions omitted from the New York Journal *are indicated in our reproduction of the text of the* Westminster Gazette
by brackets.

*Parts V and VI — captioned "Some Interviews" — appeared in
the* Gazette *on June 14 and 15, and Part VII, "The Man in the
White Hat," concluded the series on June 18. "Some Interviews"
represents what the* Journal *published on June 20 under the heading: "My Talk With 'Soldiers Six.' By Stephen Crane./The*
Journal's *Special War Correspondent at the Front in the Turko-
Greek War."*

1. Spelled *Velestimo* throughout this series.

deed one which we would understand as being Biblical. A tall lean
shepherd was necessary to it. Furthermore, the rocks were grey, save
when a reddish tinge of lurking ores appeared on their rough surfaces.

There was a wide highway curving sinuously because of the
grades. A trail for pack animals took less account of these grades, and
cut a way over the ridge far straighter than the road. In the distance
lay the town of Volo. It is in two parts. The port, with the business
district, lies flat on the water's edge, while another portion is separated
sufficiently to have another name, and is fastened to the side of an
enormous mountain. Tiny house appears above tiny house, and streets
can be seen from end to end. In fact, the mountain side is so steep that
the entire town there is displayed as if one looked at a lithograph.
One can only dream of the view of the blue gulf there to be obtained,
and of the soft splendour of the fall of evening. Lights in the houses
at night seem like stars to the people on the plain, and to those far
out in ships. Many wealthy Athenians once preferred to spend there
the summer months. The highroad was a broad, glaring, yellow band
in the Oriental sunshine, but no dust arose from it on this morning
because there were no carts, no old crazy carriages. The trail was even
bereft of donkeys. The road led to Velestino, and since the blue of
early morning there had been curious sounds from there — the rolling
boom of the guns, and the hot, dry crackle of the infantry fire, which
grew more hot and more dry as the sunshine became stronger. On
the quay at Volo, five miles away, one could see a vast concourse of
people, fugitives mainly, but the harbour contained one little steamer.

On the lonely road from Velestino there appeared the figure of
a man. He came slowly and with a certain patient steadiness. A great
piece of white linen was wound under his jaw, and finally tied at the
top of his head in a great knot like the one grandma ties when she
remedies her boy's toothache. The man had a staff in his hand, and
he used it during his slow walk. He was in the uniform of the Greek
infantry, and his clothes were very dusty — so dusty that the little
regimental number on his shoulder could hardly be seen. Under other
circumstances one could have sworn that the man had great smears of
red paint on his face. It was blood. It had to be blood; but then it was
weirdly not like blood. It was dry, but it had dried crimson and
brilliant. In fact, this hue upon his face was so unexpected in its
luridness that one first had to gaze at this poor fellow in astonishment.
He had been shot in the head, and bandaged evidently according to
the ability of the nearest comrade. Now, as he went slowly along two
things smote the sense of the observer: first, the terrible red of the
man's face, which was of the quality of flame as it appears in old
pictures; and second, this same old ridiculous knot in the linen at the
top of the head, which simply emphasized one's recollection of New

England and the mumps. As he reached the top of the ridge Volo was under his vision. His calm, patient glance swept over it. To the things about him he paid no evident regard. He was hurt, and he had known enough of the hospital at Volo to have the thing become almost an instinct with him now. He was hurt, and he was going to Volo. Even as he plodded across the ridge a train loaded with other wounded rolled down the valley. It had started a long time after he had started, and it would be at Volo much sooner, but one can, perhaps, under-stand why he did not wait for it at Velestino. A rabbit when it is hurt does not wait for a train — it crawls away immediately into the bushes; and so this man had started for Volo.

Behind him was the noise of the battle, the roar and rumble of an enormous factory. This was the product, not so well finished as some, but sufficient to express the plan of the machine. This wounded soldier explained the distant roar. He defined it. This — this and worse — was what was going on. This explained the meaning of all that racket. Gazing at this soldier with his awful face, one felt a new respect for the din.

Withal, one could muse upon the inexpressible and vast crime of by some chance addressing a flippant remark to this man. There was a dignity in his condition, a great and reaching dignity. It was of a kind that would have made marshals step aside for him at a king's levy. Five miles of lonely road was still between him and Volo. He plodded steadily on, and became a dim and dimming figure.

The right flank of this wing of the Greek army was on a plain. In fact, this plain cut through the right flank and extended to the rear of the centre. Afterward it narrowed to a valley and passed on behind the left flank. The railroad came out from Volo towards Larissa across the plain, and a junction was formed at Velestino with the railroad that went to Pharsala, where lay the Crown Prince with the larger part of the Greek army. The Velestino portion of the army was primarily covering the railroad, because the railroad, besides being a railroad, and useful therefore in many military ways, was the connexion be-tween Volo, the base of supplies, and the troops at Pharsala. [The part of the army at Velestino had its position on hills, when that was pos-sible, but the railroad made a wide curve on the plain to turn toward Pharsala, and this wretched plain extended quite to Larissa, from which direction the Turks were pouring. So the Greek commander had not alone the task of battle with an enemy superior in force, but his great duty was to protect this important communication. Strate-gically, then, Velestino was the centre of the Greek position, although nominally it was the right flank, and strategically the railroad was an infernal nuisance.]

Dust arose from the road on the plain where a cavalryman, his dark green uniform grey from the dust, his slanted carbine bobbing on his back, was galloping somewhere with orders. Long thick lines of troops were to be seen. They faced various ways, but mainly towards that part of the plain which extended in the direction of Larissa. There were trenches along the railroad track turned up in rich new earth. Many men in the blue of Greece lay in them. Some were asleep, sprawled out on their backs; some were eating hard-tack, cutting with their knives with great difficulty, holding the bread and paring away as a cobbler does with a shoe. One strolled off with a great number of canteens. A large group was listening to someone's news from the fighting front. Most of the infantry officers had gone to chat with the officers of a mountain battery which was in the rear of the other line. The guns sat each in its own tiara-shaped entrenchment. They were tilted, with an air of having been knocked under the chin and told to hold their heads up. The officer said something rather good perhaps, and the others all laughed appreciatively but carelessly, their legs wide apart, their caps set rakishly, like a lot of peacefully garrisoned hussars after evening parade. And yet from the hills on the left of their line the guns were roaring and the infantry fire was rattling and rattling, in spasms, light, heavy, heavy, light, describing all the moods of the battle that was raging there. People imagine battle to be one long muscular contortion with a mental condition corresponding to it. But just as it is impossible for a man to have convulsions eternally and without rest, so it is essential that when the other fellows are against the enemy the soldier should be superior to worrying too much about it. His turn will come; he will get all the worry that is due to him. In the meantime let him gossip, with his legs wide apart, and pass around the cigarettes. One would not have thought these officers to be vitally interested in the outcome of this fight. Later, an order to move struck a lazy and indifferent battalion of infantry. Then the change was obvious. The officers' faces became instantly hard, stern, military. The commands were so sharp as to sound almost impassioned. They had got their cause to worry. Meanwhile the officers of the battery continued to laugh and talk.

Apparently the Greek lines here lay in the form of two sides of a triangle, with the apex rather sharp. It was the result of the outreaching curve of the railroad, and the necessity for its defence, and this necessity adjusted to the topography of the country, as well as the gods would allow. The town of Velestino was in this apex. Velestino, before a friendly army sat down upon it, had been a most beautiful town. Even friendly armies can but destroy the more subtle effects of nature, although they substitute a wilder beauty of their own creation. Velestino has about it a great number of fine trees, which in Greece is very unusual. Many of the houses were quite buried in foliage, and it was impossible to see the Turks towards Larissa owing to the many strips of forest on the plain. All the houses of any importance were tightly closed and barred, every door, every window. The huts of the peasants, made from stone-like cobbles were not closed and barred, because they seemed never to have had doors, but the interiors were mere dark vacancies. It was a deserted village. One walked the streets wondering of the life that had been, and if it would ever return. It is a human thing to think of a community that has been, and here was one with all its important loves, hates, friendships; all its games, spites, its wonderful complexity of relation and intercourse, suddenly smitten by the sledge of chance and rendered nothing — nothing but a few vacant staring houses. The spectator notes then that some villager had carefully repaired his front gate, and the chance-comer's sense of the futility of repairing that front gate causes him to know more of life for a moment than he had known before.

[There was a mosque and minaret — evidence of a former Turkish occupation — near the foot of the hill. A little square faced the mosque, and there was a pool, a still and lovely pool. On its mirror-like surface it reflected part of the old dome of the mosque, and reproduced completely the round and pointed little minaret. Some cattle, deserted probably by their owner, came quietly down to the pool to drink. The sky was blue. A gentle wind rustled the foliage over a garden wall. To be sure, there was a soldier nursing a sore foot under the porch of the mosque, but even with him this scene in the angle formed by two lines of battle was eminently peace. And yet there was a curious sound in the square — spit — spit — spit; and with this sound a long tenor humming. Little clouds of dust flew from the roadway. Spit — spit. The little square, by baleful chance, had fallen under fire. Some Turks were firing at another thing, and consequently they were hitting this square. Spit — spit — spit. The cattle drank, gratefully rolling their fine and melancholy eyes. They were up to their knees in the cool water, and the pool reflected their stout dun-coloured bodies. By strange chance they walked into the pool at a place which caused the mosque to be between them and the line of fire. They lazily swished their long tails, and as for this spitting and kicking of dust within ten yards of them, it was as if it were not happening.

A certain part of the Greek nature, or rather the nature of certain Greeks, can in action make it clear to the Anglo-Saxon that he has another way of doing things. There was a battery of howitzers on a hill above the mosque and the bullet-swept square. The captain of this battery walked out to his position at middle-rear. He addressed his men. His chest was well out, and his manner was gorgeous. If one could have judged by the tone, it was one of the finest speeches of the age. It was Demosthenes returned and in command of a battery of howitzers. There was in it a quality of the best kind of sentiment. One waited for the answering cheers of the men. The poor devils of men are always obliged to give answering cheers to the patriotic orations on the field. But what was the captain saying? He was merely order-ing the gunners to elevate their pieces for a range of sixteen hundred metres.

From this hill one was enabled to see Turks. Down in the square the bullets might have been dropping from the clouds. Down in the square one ran a danger of being killed by some Turk who would not know that he did it, and who had never really intended, nor could he intend, to do that particular thing. It is a dreadful idea. But on this hill the Turks could be seen and the Turks could see the battery, and if a man was killed he could consider that there had been a certain election on the part of some Turk. It was very different down in the square.

The gunners having raised their pieces according to the captain's appeal, the guns were fired one by one. These little howitzers remind one somehow of children. When one exploded it threw itself back-wards in a wild paroxysm as does some angry and outraged child. And then the men ran to it and set it on its pins again, and straightened it out and soothed it. The men were very attentive and anxious. One of these howitzers would remain quiet then for a time, and all the trouble would be over. Then suddenly it would have another fit, and neces-sitate the scampering of a whole squad to set it right again. They were foolish little guns, peevish, intolerable as to their dispositions. It was a wonder the men would take so much trouble with them.

Out on the green plain there was a dark line, heavier than a shadow, and lighter than a hedge. Most of the plain was hidden from this hill by a higher hill forward and to the left, but this dark line afforded the essential interest. It was the Turks.]

III. A FRAGMENT OF VELESTINO (CONTINUED).

[It is a great thing to survey the army of the enemy. Just where and how it takes hold upon the heart is difficult of description. Of course there is all the usual reflection concerning the chances of being killed, but there is another element, important and strong, and at the same time elusive to a degree. It has perhaps something to do with the enemy's persistent and palpable determination to kill you if pos-sible. Here are a vast number of men convened evidently for this sole purpose. You can repeat to yourself, if you like, the various stated causes of the war, and mouth them over and try to apply them to the situation, but they will fail to answer your vague interrogation. The mind returns to the wonder of why so many people will put themselves to the most incredible labour and inconvenience and danger for the sake of this — this ending of a few lives like yours, or a little better or a little worse.] This army on the plain was a majestic thing. It expressed power — power — power. The force one felt to be in those long dark lines was terrible. It could let two seas meet, this thing. A soldier in the trenches suddenly screamed and clasped his hands to his eyes as if he had been struck blind. He rolled to the bottom of the trench, his body turning twice. A comrade, dazed, whistling through his teeth, reached in his pocket and drew out a hunch of bread and a handkerchief. It appeared that he was going to feed this corpse. But he took the handkerchief and pressed it on the wound and then looked about him helplessly. He still held the bread in his other hand, because he could not lay it down in the dirt of the trench. As for most of the men, they accepted this visitation in silence, merely turning their eyes to look at the body, and then perhaps shaking their heads mournfully while a strange wonder and wistful questioning of the future were in some glances. [The crest of the hill had been a field of meagre but ripe grain. It had been trampled now until little of it appeared, although a yellow wisp or two might be trying to struggle out from under one of the ammunition boxes of the battery, all painted a light blue and scattered thickly over the field. To the rear lay a dead horse, and a number of blood-red poppies, miraculously preserved from the countless feet, bloomed near it.] Continually there was in the air a noise as if someone had thrown an empty beer-bottle with marvellous speed at you. Shells just whined and sang in a sort of arc of sound — an arc both in volume and in key. It was great to hear others go like immense birds flashing across the vision on their swift journey. The rapid flapping of their wings was perfectly obvious. Sometimes the blinding explosions of these shells dug holes on the hill among the trampled grain and the few poppies.

There was great trouble on the other hill in front and extending far to the left. Its summit was a long fringe of grey smoke floating backwards. The volleys were rattling and crackling from one end of the hill to the other. Sometimes the pattering of individual firing swelled suddenly to one long beautiful crash that had something in it of the fall of a giant pine amid his brethren of the mountain side. It was the thunder of a monstrous breaker against the hard rocks. At times it was these things, and at times it was just the crack-crack-crackety crack-crackle of burning timbers. Altogether the troops on the ridge were heavily engaged, and, as if by concert, the plain on the right became dotted with litle puffs of smoke. The captain of the battery was furnished with a new and large number of marks. It was during the attendant excitement of this situation that he sent a man to the rear for another pair of field-glasses. His first pair had suffered a rifle-ball wound. The man misunderstood the order, and he came with a bottle of wine. He stood until the captain should finish talking with a subaltern. There was a look of pious satisfaction on his face at having concluded his errand with wisdom and celerity. Suddenly the captain reached for his field-glasses and got instead a bottle of wine. Astonishment and incredulity mingled on his face. He looked sternly at the soldier and harangued him on the necessity of not being an idiot during battle. His gestures were wild and rapid. Nevertheless, he did not relinquish his fast grip on the bottle of wine. Presently he went along the lines giving an order, and sometimes he absent-mindedly waved the bottle towards the Turks. He looked down at last and saw that he still grasped the bottle. He went then and gave it into the care of the trusty corporal who commanded the horse and mule squad below the hill. When the actors are under fire, small dramas of this kind may be interesting to the spectator.

It was about this time, too, that a column of infantry marching to support the troops on the hill had its prayers interrupted. There was a small stone shrine at the side of the trail. It contained a little holy picture of a saint, a little chromo in red and green, with a frame of gilt paper. Under this picture was a little lamp, wherein oil was sometimes burned. It was the common wayside shrine of the Greek Church. The soldiers had been marched a long way. Their faces were warm with sweat. Their blanket-rolls lay heavily upon their shoulders. Their haversacks knocked awkwardly upon their tired hips. Their rifles and double rows of long Gras cartridges[2] must have each appeared weighty enough to sink a yacht. Moreover, many of the men still wore their thick winter overcoats, as is rather a custom among Greek soldiers, no matter how warm may be the Oriental sunshine.

This weary column reached the little shrine, which was less than

2. The Gras Rifle, Model 1874, caliber .433, single-shot, bolt action, and not the Model 1874F, converted to caliber .317. The Model 1874 weighed, with bayonet, 10½ pounds and had an overall length, including bayonet, of seventy-two inches. The rifle had been condemned by the French Government and sold to the Greeks at eight francs each. The cartridges were sixteen years old, weighed 471 grains, and were useless at even intermediate ranges, although the weapon was sighted to 1,968 yards. See "Greece and Its Rulers," *The Saturday Review*, LXXXIV (25 September 1897), 333–335, and *The World Almanac* (1897), p. 349.

The Turks were armed with the superior Mauser, caliber .301, which held five cartridges (235 grains) in the magazine, weighed 9.9 pounds, and had a muzzle velocity of 2,067 feet per second, as compared to 1,411 for the Gras.

three hundred yards from the advanced firing line. The men at the front crossed themselves and prayed. Suddenly a great hooting shell struck the base of the shrine and lifted the structure in the air. It fell with a ringing smash, demolished. There was a spectacle of the nearest men scurrying in every direction to escape the flying stones, and as they ran the fingers of many of them were still at their chests as they had been when making the sign of the cross before the coming of the shell. The men in the rear of the column, finding no shrine, prayed quietly facing its ruins.

[Naturally one wants now to be informed of the complexion of the battle. Who was winning? Was victory with the blue field and white cross of the Greeks? Or was it with the crimson banner of the Moslems? If a reader of a casual article of this kind wishes to know who was winning this battle, depend upon it there were men present upon the field who considered the question to be one of surpassing importance. But none knew. How could he know? The battlefield was spread over miles of ground. It had a multitude of phases. No one could judge whether it was to be well or ill for Turk or Greek in the final measure of the day. People would like to stand in front of the mercury of war and see it rise or fall, and they think they ought to demand it, more or less, in descriptions of battle; but it is an absurd thing for a writer to do if he wishes to reflect in any way the mental condition of the men in the ranks, and the knowledge of a captain is very little better. Perhaps the general ignorance extends to colonels, who in this army command from two to five thousand men. A subordinate commander knows this — he knows he was attacked and that he repulsed the enemy or didn't repulse the enemy. He knows that he attacked, and won or lost; whether or not this was vitally important to the fortunes of the day he cares to learn, but probably he can't find out. In the meantime, the men know this or less.

On this day in particular there was a rumour through the army that the Turks were attacking in force. This is what was known. The Turks were attacking in force.

Stragglers moving towards Volo told many tales. The Greeks were on the edge of a great victory. The Greeks were on the verge of a great defeat. The right flank had been driven back; the right flank had advanced. The centre was crushed; the centre was holding its own. The left flank was turned; the left flank had taken a height in its front.

The column of infantry that had witnessed the destruction of the shrine was composed of new troops. The men had never been in battle. Indeed, three days previously they had marched down the streets of Athens with flowers in their gun-barrels and smiles on their faces, certain that war was but a fête. Later they had learned that it was mainly hard work, and now they were evidently going to be taught that it contained certain elements of fighting. The summit of the ridge was still a long grey fringe of smoke, and a tremendous banging came from there. As the battalion reached the foot of the steep, stragglers were coming down. Some were in a great hurry. The new men looked at them uneasily. "Well, how is it going?" they asked. Some of the stragglers said "good," in assured tones, but others shook their heads sadly and made little reply. As the column slowly climbed the steep the men's countenances became very thoughtful. There was a reason for this, too, outside of any perturbations of new men. The Greek army had been taught the horrors of panic. As for the Larissa panic, the tale of it was probably vastly exaggerated, but the tradition of the thing now has its influence in the army. The Greek soldier fighting on the defensive will probably stick to his trench as long as any man, but it will not do to shake a soldier's confidence from the rear. Even a war correspondent could find it in him to turn a wary eye occasionally in that direction, lest a retreat be suddenly ordered and tumultuously begun, and a journey with an army that has succeeded in routing itself is more instructive than pleasant. As has been said, the terrors of a rapid retreat were now a tradition in this army, and it was not good. Really, if orders to fall back are in the air, a man wants to be the first to note them afar, and he is apt to glance often over his shoulder to make sure he is not missing their arrival. It seems absolutely certain that this was all that was the matter with these new troops. To go in and help whip the Turks — that was a fair proposition. That was why they had come. But what about a retreat, some kind of a weird and incomprehensible order to retreat that would get them cut up outrageously, practically have them destroyed? It is true that troops should not trouble themselves with a commander's business, but it is also true that a commander should remember that his men's brains are obliged to work, and he is careful, if he is a good soldier, of the kind of mental food with which he provides them. There had been, however, a conspiracy of general incompetency and stupidity to engrave the word retreat in the middle of the brain of the Greek soldier, and in his natural mental processes it occurs.]

When the battalion came to the top of the ridge it found a great green plain spread out before it, and the plain was ruddy, almost brazen, in the light of the late afternoon sun. The distances here were magnificent. One could see even the long snowy summit of Mount Olympus in the far north, and as for the central plain of Thessaly, it was simply a great map. But these natural splendours did not occupy any serious part of the battalion's attention. The men had been projected into the middle of a good fight. Obliged to wait for a time, they peered cautiously over the crest of the ridges. Below and in front some yards there was a trench, and in this trench there were perhaps forty

Greek soldiers. These soldiers had hollowed little places on the top of the trench, and had added the protection of stones. When a soldier had loaded his rifle, he rested it in this groove, and, taking aim at some tiny black figures on a knoll that arose from the plain half a mile away, he fired. The shiny Gras jumped a trifle with the explosion, and then the soldier rolled half on his back and drew his piece in to be again loaded. They were quite leisurely at this time. [To the rear lay the body of a youth who had been killed by a ball through the chest. This youth had not been a regular soldier, evidently; he had been a volunteer. The only things military were the double cartridge belt, the haversack, and the rifle. As for the clothes, they were of black cloth with a subtle stripe or check in it, and they were cut after a common London style. Beside the body lay a black hat. It was what one would have to call a Derby, although from the short crown there was an inclination to apply the old name of dicer. There was a rather high straight collar and a little four-in-hand scarf of flowered green and a pin with a little pink stone in it.

This dead young Greek had nothing particularly noble in his face. There was expressed in this thing none of the higher thrills to incite, for instance, a company of romantic poets. The lad was of a common enough type. The whole episode was almost obvious. He was of people in comfortable circumstances; he bought his own equipment, of course. Then one morning news sped to the town that the Turks were beating. And then he came to the war on the smoke, so to speak, of the new fires of patriotism which had been immediately kindled in the village place, around the tables in front of the café. He had been perhaps a little inclined to misgiving, but withal anxious to see everything anyhow, and usually convinced of his ability to kill any number of Turks. He had come to this height, and fought with these swarthy, hard-muscled men in the trench, and, soon or late, got his ball through the chest. Then they had lifted the body and laid it to the rear in order to get it out of the way.]

IV. A FRAGMENT OF VELESTINO (CONCLUDED).

The fire from the ridge had been undergoing one of the merely crackling periods. Now, however, it blazed up again. These wonderful little figures amid the green and brown fields of the plain had increased vastly in numbers. Little trickling streams of them began to flow slowly along the lines of the old hedges and ditches. In one place there was a great long heavy streak of them. It was more than human to see even the colour of a fez from the height. As for a gesture, any expression at all, it could not be seen. And this quality provided the picture with its extraordinary mysticism. These little black things streaming from here and there on the plain, what were they? What moved them to this? The power and majesty of this approach was all in its mystery, its inexplicable mystery. What was this thing? and why was it? Of course Turks, Turks, Turks; but then that is a mere name used to describe these creatures who were really hobgoblins and endowed with hobgoblin motives. In the olden times one could have had a certain advantage of seeing an enemy's eyes. If one was anxious about the battle, one could have perhaps witnessed the anxiety of the enemy. Anything is better than a fight with an enemy that wears the black velvet mask of distance.

The trenches on the left part of the height became tumultuous with smoke and long thin rifle flashes. As the dark streams, rivulets, of the enemy poured along the plain, a large number of batteries open,[3] and great black shells, whirling and screaming, fled over the heads of the men in the trenches. There was going to be a good tight little fight.

The heads of the loose skirmishing columns of the enemy became hidden in rolling masses of smoke. The Turks were shooting low. Few bullets went over the trench. Many fell below it, and a certain number with great regularity went pum — pum — pump into the earthwork. The lieutenant in command of this trench walked slowly to and fro in the rear of his men. He was a fine-looking young chap with a bronzed skin and a clear eye, showing below the banded and peaked cap with its crown and arms. His dark coat fitted him bravely. There were two silver stars on the vivid scarlet facing at his throat. His light blue trousers were hidden below the knee by black walking boots. In fact, he looked like a soldier, and he wore his clothes as a soldier wears his clothes. He was trim, lithe, muscular — a man to whom campaigning has begun to be easy work. As he walked to and fro under this strong fire he did not evince any fear, nor did he evince any strutting contempt. From time to time as he glanced up or to one side towards the particularly close path of some missile there was in his gaze more of a decent respect than of any other emotion — once he turned and rapidly called out to his men a new order concerning the range. The bullet that came there struck him in the throat — squarely in the throat. He fell like a flash — as if someone had knocked his heels from under him from behind. On the ground his arms made one long stiff and shivery gesture, and then he lay still. For a moment his men had a clear case of rattle, simply rattle. It was as when the captain is washed off the bridge at sea during a storm. There are two things lost — the captain, and what the captain knows about managing ships in

3. Obviously a misprint for *opened*.

storms. For a moment, these soldiers were wild-eyed. They screamed
at each other. But then another trench with the rest of the company in
it was very close. This trench was not a lone ship. The men settled down
again to fighting.

[All processes of battle are slower than accounts of them. There
is plenty of time for everything if your side is holding its own. A big
battle is not a whirlwind of many events, although many of the events
may be of themselves whirlwinds. There are many pauses, many waits
during a big battle, when apparently one would have time to lunch
in great comfort. This statement can be accepted provisionally. This
battle deals with the Turk. The Turk when he moves forward approaches with the celerity of a stone chariot going the other way. To be
sure, he can carry a height with a wild rush and a roar, but first he
has got to play around the question and fool with the enemy and
lose some men.]

The Turks were merely crawling across the plain towards the
height. There was a Greek battery of the inevitable mountain howitzers, and its captain was inhaling more pure joy than had been his
for many months. He had a raking fire on a dark slow column of
Turkish infantry, and in the late afternoon atmosphere he could see
the crimson outburst of shell after shell directly in the midst of it.
The broad purple double-stripe on the captain's trousers flashed everywhere amid the men and guns of the battery. He had gone suddenly
to his station at middle-rear, and paused there once, when there came
to him a tall, pale young man in civilian garb. He was obviously
English, and to this distinction was added a wild, wild eye. He carried
a large bottle, loudly labelled "Poison," and a blanket.

He addressed the captain in rascally French. "Monsieur," he said,
"I have come to take care of the wounded: can you tell me where they
are?" The captain went away and superintended the firing of the two
guns of the first section. When he returned to middle-rear, he said in
excellent English, "Sir, if you speak in English instead of French I
may be able to understand you better." He went away and superintended the firing of the second section. When he returned to middle-
rear the pale young man said to him, "Look here: you have insulted
me, and I demand satisfaction." The captain went away and superintended the firing of the third section. When he returned he said, "I
am sorry if I have offended you, and I can't give you satisfaction because I am very busy now, and so, if you will allow me, it gives me
pleasure to apologise at once." He went away to refire the first section.
The tall, pale youth wandered gloomily and vacantly down the hill,
and as straggling soldiers saw him coming with his great bottle of
poison clasped in his arms they sheered off.

And now began the infantry fight at the foot of the height. In this light of the concluding day both sides in the conflict were dim to the view. There was a vast amount of smoke, and bullets came and went from everywhere. The whole of this sharp, hard attack was incoherent, and the strength of the drama of it was in this incoherence. There was even no cheering to indicate the success of Turk or Greek. Only the roar of the guns and the terrific crashing of the musketry. It was the most ferocious attack the Turks had made that day, and perhaps the most formidable. The Turks did not come like a flood, nor did the Greeks stand like adamant. It was simply a shifting, changing, bitter, furious struggle, where one could not place odds nor know when to run.

[A lot of Turks charged across the field, not in a line or anything approaching it, but in a sort of a herd, and they ran very slowly, very slowly, and with bowed heads. In this charge one could see this formidable precept: "If it is the will of God that I will be killed, why, I will be killed, but if not —" And they ran slowly with the idea of finding out. If they ran rapidly, and took an earthwork and so on, they could do a whole lot before they learned anything of the will of God. But no. They ran slowly, sometimes holding shielding arms up to their faces, and reflectively wondering of God's decision. Now, this is only as it appeared.

One can imagine that a slow charge of this kind over open ground does not stand every chance of success. The side of the ridge from the top almost to the bottom was a snarling, flaming thing. Twenty moments of uproar elapsed, and then there were no Turks in front save a great number of dead ones, and none of these lay close enough for one to see that the fez was red. There was no indication of posture, no expression, no human character — just some small dark blots on a green field. It was the same suggestion always — a battle with the undefined, with phantoms.]

The din did not abate on many other parts of the field, but here, on this height, there was a general pause. There were dead in the trenches, but the living were rejoicing. The new battalion had been placed in trenches, where it had had a fair shot at the Turks. It had probably done a great deal of high shooting, but then it was a fact never to be known. Turks had been killed, and everyone who fired a careful shot was in the credit of the repulse. [Meanwhile the Turco-German artillery had not ceased its fire, and the quiet celebration in the Greek trenches was conducted with a certain amount of caution. When a shell fell among the rocks it flung dangerous fragments of stone in all directions.]

A little to the rear, the captain of a mountain battery had called to a trusty corporal who commanded the horse and mule squad, and the corporal brought a bottle of wine. The captain and his subalterns perched on blue ammunition boxes and finished this wine with some bread and cheese from goats' milk. It was a cheerful party.

A venerable colonel of infantry sat on a rock and chaffed his line officers. They stood around him smiling. In the twilight on the height there was, in fact, a general satisfaction. Meanwhile one of a party of four privates who were carrying away the dead body of a Greek major stumbled in the dark, and his three comrades rebuked him sharply and unreasonably.

There were some mountaineer volunteers in great woolly grey shepherds' cloaks. They were curious figures in the evening light, perfectly romantic if it were not for the modernity of the rifles and the shining lines of cartridges. With the plain a sea of shadow below, and the vague blue troops of Greece about them in the trenches, these men sang softly the wild minor ballads of their hills. As the evening deepened many men curled in their blankets and slept, but these grey-cloaked mountaineers continued to sing. Ultimately the rays of the moon outlined their figures in silver light, and it was not infrequently that shells from the persistent Turco-German batteries threw a sudden red colour on their curious garb and on the banner of their village which hung above them. They sang of war, and their songs were new to the sense, reflecting the centuries of their singing, and as the ultimate quiet of night came to the height this low chanting was the only sound. This ended one day at Velestino.

V. SOME INTERVIEWS.

Many newspapers, particularly in America, have celebrated in type their correspondents' interviews with the King of Greece and with the Crown Prince, and with others who have had only a little more to do with the war. Here are some interviews with the Grecian soldier.[4]

4. The New York *Journal* (20 June 1897) published what the London *Westminster Gazette* headed as "Some Interviews" under the title "My Talk With 'Soldiers Six'." and the opening variant paragraph is worth quoting for comparison with the above *Gazette* version: "ATHENS, June 1. — Since everybody has interviewed the King and the Crown Prince and Smolenski, it occurred to me that it might be well to interview the private soldier. There is more of him than there is of the King or of the Crown Prince or of Smolenski, and as he has had rather a hand in whatever has been done, it seemed fair to give him a chance to express his opinion." Some of the most celebrated interviews were those with the King and Crown Prince of Greece written by James Creelman for the New York *World*. He also interviewed certain of the Greek ministers.

They may be this, they may be that, they may be anything, but they are reported with care and some conscience, and perhaps they contain a suggestion from time to time of a view-point which has not been particularly heeded.

One soldier sat by the roadside nursing a sore foot. I gave him a cigarette, and he smiled. I said to him: "How many fights have you been in?"

"Three. One on the frontier, and then at Pharsala and at Domoko."

"How did you feel in your first fight?"

"Well, when the first bullets came — just one, two, three — I didn't care. Afterwards, when they made more noise, I grew afraid, but yet afterwards it was all right."

"How did you feel in your other battles?"

"I didn't think about it."

"Did you ever see a comrade that you knew intimately killed at your side?"

"No; that has not happened."

"Do you want to fight more?"

"Yes! Certainly!"

"Do all the other private soldiers want to fight more?"

"I think so."

"A great deal is said of the army wishing to stop the war. It does not, then?"

"The officers may want to stop."

"Are not the officers of your regiment good officers?"

"No."

"Why?"

"When an order comes to retreat, they go first."

"But in action they stand up back of the trenches. That is not easy. And then see how many officers are killed."

"Well, this may be in other regiments."

"What effect have these consecutive orders to retreat had upon the soldiers?"

"Oh, it has broken their hearts."

"Whose was the fault?"

"The Crown Prince's, I think."

"Is he not a good soldier?"

"No. He is for ever turning pale and ordering us to fall back."

"But you like the King?"

"No."

"Why not?"

"He is not a good Greek. To be sure, he was not born a Greek,[5]

5. As noted earlier, King George I was not in any way a Greek. His full name and title, before accession to the vacant Greek throne, was Prince

but he is King, and a King of the Greeks ought to be more Greek than the Greeks."

"Do your comrades feel as you?"

"Yes."

"If your regiment is ordered to Athens after the war, what will it do? Will there be trouble?"

"I don't know. For my part, I want to go quietly home."

"How do your comrades feel about it?"

"Who knows what may happen?"

In Lamia there was an euzone, one of the kilted mountaineers, with a small rakishly piratical scarlet fez. He sat alone because, in the first place, he was a man of the hills, and, in the second place, because the other soldiers in the place were town-bred, and knew him as we know a "hay-seed." And, in the third place, he sat alone because he considered that the euzone had done the best of the fighting. He was a swarthy, flash-eyed chap, holding himself like a chief, and paying no heed to the chatter about him.

I said to him: "Which is harder, marching or fighting?"

"Marching," he answered promptly.

"How many fights have you been in?"

"Oh, about ten."

"How did you feel in your first fight?"

"I am not sure. There were seventy of us holding in check a battalion of Turks. It was in a pass of the mountains. I think I was wondering how long we could hold them in check."

"How about the other fights?"

"Oh, perhaps they were the same. At Velestino I had fun. We killed many Turks. Only when we covered that accursed retreat of ours were we hurt any."

"Do you want to fight more?"

"Certainly."

"Do all your comrades want to fight more?"

"Of course."

"Are the officers of your regiment good officers?"

"Yes."

"What effect have these successive orders to retreat had upon the soldiers?"

"We hate them. Often and often we are ordered to retreat, I tell you, when it is absurd. The euzonoi are usually ordered to cover these

---

Christian William Ferdinand Adolphus George of Schleswig-Holstein-Sonderburg-Glücksburg. His elective title was "King of the Hellenes."

retreats, too. It is harder than any battle if the Turks come quickly."

"Whose was the fault?"

"Our leader's."

"Whom do you mean?"

"Well, our regiment is under Smolenski. I don't mean him. He is a great chieftain. I mean the head of the whole army."

"Who?"

"The head of the whole army."

"Why is it his fault?"

"He orders all these retreats. He has taught us to retreat. The men of the hills did not know how."

"Well?"

"Well?"

"Um! After the war will you go home directly?"

"No! How can I go home if the war ends this way? I am disgraced. I am the shamed son of my father. I cannot go home."

"What do you wish to do?"

"I wish to fight the Turk until Greece is saved from dishonour. We are not beaten. At Larissa, at Velestino, we were not beaten. Yet here we are at Lamia."

"But you must understand the importance of flank movements. Perhaps you were doing well on your part of the line, but how about the flanks? The Turks are many. We had in our army once a man named Sherman, who used the same way of winning that the Turks use against you now. He made finally a great victory."

"I know nothing of the man you name, but I know we were not flanked at Velestino. We were not flanked at Domoko."

My third victim was a young corporal in the infantry. He was of rather wealthy people in Athens. He had been educated in France, and was altogether a new type to find in any army save this Greek army. Here you are likely to find anybody in the ranks. On second thoughts it bears a resemblance in this way to our armies during the Civil War.

"Which is harder — marching or fighting?"

"Marching."

"What impressed you in your first battle?"

"I was much afraid of the shells."

"And in later battles?"

"I was still afraid of the shells."

"Did not the whistling of the bullets affect you more?"

"No."

"You have been under very heavy artillery fire?"

"Yes."

"Where?"

"At Domoko."

"Did you see anybody hurt by a shell?"

"Yes. A splinter laid open an officer's cheek."

"Was the infantry fire heavy in your front?"

"Not very heavy."

"What was the loss in your battalion from the Turkish infantry fire?"

"We lost twenty-eight men in killed and wounded."

"All from infantry fire?"

"All but the officer who was struck by the splinter."

"It strikes me that you would be about twenty-seven times more afraid of the bullets than of the shells?"

"Yes, but then the shells are very loud."

"Do you want to fight any more?"

"Yes."

"Why?"

"Because Greece has not had a fair chance. She has been betrayed."

"By whom?"

"I cannot say. We think it was somebody high in command."

"How high in command?"

"Well — very high."

"Do your comrades also wish to fight more?"

"Yes."

"Do they also think Greece has been betrayed?"

"Yes."

"By whom?"

"They think as I think."

VI. SOME INTERVIEWS (CONTINUED).

In front of the doors of a house that was being used as a field hospital many stretchers were crowded awaiting their turns, as carriages in front of a New York theatre around eight o'clock crowd and await their turns. The hospital was simply packed already, and these stretchers remained a long time waiting. The prostrate figures of the wounded men were for the most part very still, quietly still, already like the dead. Their faces were yellow from suffering — seldom pallid, almost always yellow. Blankets usually covered them, but sometimes a blue trouser leg with dark bloodstains upon it projected from beneath the covering. The men were flat on their backs, and looked at nothing. Through the door of the hospital could be seen a white-clothed surgeon, erect, serene, but swift-fingered. He was calm enough to be sinister and terrible in this scene of blood. He had every necessary casual mannerism of a surgeon facing his patients, but it was ghoulish anyhow. This thing was a banquet for him.

Sometimes a man came out with his arm in a sling, or his head bandaged, or his jaw tightly bound. They went off somewhere and sat down. Carriers would come out and get a stretcher and take it in to the surgeon. The business of the hospital went on in this way, smoothly, for hours and hours, fed regularly as a mill by water, by the stream of wounded from the scene of the late battle. A hundred yards away there was some long grass and daisies, and a peasant asleep in the shade of olive trees, while his donkey browsed near him.

Four men had brought an euzone on a stretcher and laid him on the outskirts of the crowd of stretchers thronging about the hospital door. This euzone had been shot through the leg just above the knee. He did not lie flat on his back like the others. He had turned his body and was reclining on one elbow. One side of him was a man shot vitally, and the laboured movement of his breathing caused the blanket over his chest to rise and fall. On the other side of the euzone was an officer shot through the head — worse than a corpse, because his eyes looked here, there, everywhere in slow sweeps.

The euzone was smoking a cigarette. He had drawn the blanket up to shield the fact evidently as an ordinary precaution lest some surgeon detect it and upbraid him for a thing so utterly in opposition to the etiquette of his condition. But he was having a bully time with that cigarette. He was having more fun than a barrel of monkeys. Every puff was long and profound and comforting. Perhaps he had been far out in the front — these euzonoi are always in front — where there was no tobacco, and then he has been wounded and brought here — here he could crib a cigarette. The wound in his leg be blowed.

When the correspondent saw this euzone smoking a cigarette at this time and in this place it was a beautiful thing and he hoped the surgeon wouldn't catch him. He wanted to give the euzone another cigarette, or some tobacco and papers, or a match — indeed anything to help on this crime — but he did not dare. The correspondent simply grinned at the euzone and the euzone grinned at the correspondent.

"Does your wound hurt you?"

"No."

"Is it a bad wound?"

"I think so."

"Well, then, perhaps it hurts you?"

"Perhaps it does."

"Are you satisfied? Are you going home?"

"No. I think I will be well soon. Then I will come back."

"Which is harder — marching or fighting?"

"Well, I have seen hard fighting, but I think long marches are worse than fights."

"What do you think of the Turkish artillery?"

"I don't understand why they don't kill everybody. But they do not. The cannon always affect me a little, but I have never seen anyone hurt by them, only a horse."

"Are all these orders to retreat good, do you think?"

"One of them."

"Which?"

"The order to retreat from Domoko. We were lost if we tried to hold Domoko, I know. My regiment was out on the left flank."

"Whom do you blame for the other retreats?"

"The Royal Family. They are cowards. They are not Greeks. They are foreigners."

"Did you ever kill a Turk?"

"Oh, many."

"Are you sure?"

"Oh, certainly."

"How do you know?"

"Well, I think I have killed many, but I am not sure. Anyhow, I know that I killed one, because it was in the mountains, and my shot was the only shot fired from our side then, and I saw him tumble down the rocks."

"What is your business in time of peace?"

"I take care of a flock in the hills."

They came for the euzone, then. It was his turn. They carried him towards this dreadful portal. It was the gates of Hades. As the bearers drew near it the euzone took one more puff at his cigarette and then threw it away.

In Thurka Pass[6] a member of the Foreign Legion was filling his canteen from a spring. He really held rank on one of the standing armies of Europe, and had enlisted in this Foreign Legion in order to get some experience. The Foreign Legion in this war has provided its members with rather a deal of experience.

"Well, how do you like it?"

"The deuce! It is a great bore — all these retreats."

"Whom do you blame?"

"I am inclined to think it is the Crown Prince."

"Is he not a good soldier?"

"He is a duffer."

6. Thurka Pass is in the Othris mountains, northwest of Lamia and southeast of Domokos, roughly halfway between the two towns.

"Do the Greek troops fight well?"

"When they are well led they fight as well as any troops."

"To your mind, the difficulty is where, then?"

"General funk at headquarters. The retreat from Larissa was conducted in the most absurd fashion. Do you know, the staff was in such a hurry that they forgot the foreign legion entirely — forgot to give us any orders whatever. We saw the whole army going back, and there we were without an order. Our captain said, 'Well, we will stay here until we see the Turks coming, anyhow.' We waited a decent time and no Turks came, and then we plodded off to Velestino."

"Do you want to fight any more?"

"Yes, under certain circumstances. I haven't got enough fighting, but I have got enough of this kind of management."

"You are certain that it is the bad management of the Greek army, and not altogether the good management of the Turkish army, causes these situations?"

"Yes."

Ten soldiers in Lamia were pounding on the closed and barred doors of a café. It was after the battle of Domoko, and Lamia was even then almost a deserted city.

The doors remained obdurate, and the soldiers waxed enthusiastic in assault. One man brought a great stone and banged it against a door. The door broke and fell aside, disclosing, inside, other doors of glass. Another soldier fetched a small wooden table from the plaza and hurled it through the glass doors. Then they reached in, unlocked the doors, and entered the café.

The proprietor went wild and woolly mad. The soldiers said they wanted coffee. The proprietor swore by his gods that they could have no coffee in his shop. The soldiers said they wanted coffee. The proprietor called upon Heaven to curse him and nine generations if he gave these men coffee. The soldiers said that they wanted coffee. The proprietor said that he had no coffee. The soldiers said that they wanted coffee.

Now, there is a trick known to the Oriental. This is it. Suddenly the proprietor went to the charcoal furnaces and began to prepare the coffee, meanwhile chatting with the soldiers as amiably as a village priest. His rage was all forgotten — forgotten, mind you; not hidden, but forgotten. Nor did the soldiers for their part reproach him for his previous obstinacy. The incident was closed. It was now as if they had entered the coffee-house in the ordinary way and ordered coffee from the ordinary polite proprietor. This is the trick known to the Oriental. The correspondent entered the breach made by the ten soldiers and ordered coffee. There was a soldier there among the ten of a type I know. In the photograph galleries in Athens there are many portraits of bearded gentlemen in kilts festooned with 500 yards of cartridge belt, and gripping their Gras rifles ferociously. By the Athenians they are supposed to be away killing battalion after battalion of Turks. I know that type too, and I have never seen them do anything. Generally speaking, they are a pack of humpty-dumphties. But this brown-faced quiet lad, with his lamb-like eyes and gentle, considerate ways, I know him too, and he will stick to a trench, and stick and stick, and go without water and food, and fight long and still stick, until the usual orders come to fall back. Barring the genuine euzone, this gentle lad is the best man in Greece, even if he does wear the regulation uniform. When he gets up on his legs and retires, he may get shot in the back by the close Turks, and if he be taken to a hospital some philanthropic doctor from London may, when observing his wound, think that he is a coward. But this is just in passing and wholly exceptional. The main point is that this lad is a soldier, and he has fought as a proportion of the French fought from Alsace back to Paris.

"Which is harder — marching or fighting?"

"Marching — as we have been marched."

"Are you tired of fighting?"

"Oh, no."

"How about these retreats? Who is to blame?"

"I cannot say exactly, but we all believe it is the fault of the Crown Prince."

"Do you remember the cries of 'À Berlin!' and that afterwards the French people blamed the whole affair on the heads of the State, when as a matter of truth it was everybody's fault that they were well thrashed?"

"Yes, I remember. But even if it was everybody's fault in that case it is not consequently proven that it is everybody's fault in this case. We think not."

"It may be something of a general opinion throughout the world that your case in Greece parallels the previous case in France?"

"If by the world you mean Europe, we have learnt to expect injustice and stupidity from the Powers of Europe, and if that is their opinion, as you say, I am perfectly willing to recognise it as an exhibition of intellect."

"What do you think of the successive retreats?"

"The Crown Prince always thinks his army beaten long before it is really beaten. Some men learn war in a day. These are the men who immediately plunge right in it up to their necks. There are others who never learn it, because they always remain on the edge of battle merely. The Crown Prince is one of these last. He has never been farther than the edge, and his immediate staff are known to be so careful of the person of his Highness that they seldom leave him to go closer themselves."

"You are severe."

"I am a soldier. I have been fortunate enough to have been wounded for Greece. I have lived on nothing practically for months, and marched many miles, and fought a few battles. I have a right to name any man who I am sure has not done his duty by Greece, and I name the Crown Prince."

"Did not he say, or at least was he not reported to have said, at Domoko that there he would stand or fall with his men?"

"Yes, such was the report. But where is Domoko now? It is in the hands of the Turks. As before, the Crown Prince thought that he was beaten. These quotable sentiments are sometimes unfortunate. I know from experience."

"Why?"

"Well, when I left Athens there was a considerable celebration by my family and friends — tears and flowers, added to a Spartan injunction from my mother. I believe I replied with a Spartan sentence, too. It is very difficult."

"When all these disappointed troops return to Athens what will they do?"

"I do not know."

"Will they wreak vengeance?"

"Perhaps."

"Upon whom?"

"Upon the King."

VII. THE MAN IN THE WHITE HAT.

A great crowd had gathered in the Place de la Constitution[7] in front of the Royal Palace because it was understood that the editor of one of the Athenian journals was to come and address the populace

7. The Place de la Constitution was to the north and east of the Acropolis and was the center of "traffic" for Greeks and strangers alike in Athens. The principal street of the city was the Rue du Stade which connected the Place de la Constitution with the Place de la Concorde. Other important thoroughfares were the Rue de Hermès and the Boulevard de l'Université.

On the east side of the Place was the Palace in front of which were laid out oranges, oleanders, and other southern trees. The Palace garden bounded the Palace on the east and south. The Palace itself was erected in

from a position in front of a well-known café.[8] Over the tops of some trees and above a stone terrace reared the quiet dwelling of the King, its windows all heavily curtained as if it had closed its eyes purposely to this scene in the square below it. The old building was sallow in the glare of the sun. A string of tramcars was for ever tooling one way or the other way on the avenue which crossed on the terrace at the middle of the square, and dust from the travel blew white across the face of the Palace.[9] The crowd when they looked up the slant of the plaza could see a little sentry-box, and in it an euzone of the Royal Guard, framed as a mummy is framed in its case.

The editor was late. He was also a deputy and, as the Chamber was then in session, he was supposed to be engaged there. The crowd did not display much impatience while awaiting him. For one thing, a swarm of newsboys suddenly came racing around the corner, hoarsely shouting as charging savages might shout. They plunged headlong into this concentration of their prey, dispensing papers and making change with rapidity, meanwhile yelling. This onslaught incited the crowd to bestow their interest elsewhere for a certain time, and it came to pass that when the hero of the minute finally appeared it took rather long for the news to reach the Athenians, who were standing calmly in their places and reading.

He had white hair. He was almost venerable. He had the mobile mouth of a poet and the glance of surpassing vanity. He wore a tall hat, grey in scheme, moulded in a curious form. We usually lay the burden of responsibility for this shape upon the men of 1840, or of any date which lies far enough behind us. But it was an impressively-shaped hat. It was the hat of violence. It was the hat of insurrection. It proclaimed terror. In New York this hat would foreshadow the cessation of the cable-car, the disappearance of the postman, the subterranean concealment of the cook, the supreme elevation of the price of beer — all the horrors of municipal war. No one could wear this terrible and revolutionary hat unless he was a deputy of the Two-Miles-beyond-the-Extreme-Edge of the Radicals. Where this hat of anarchy and inhumanity appears, there comes change. If you study the history of the famous revolutions you will be taught to tremble at

---

1834–1838. It was a large building, adorned in front with a Doric colonnade and built of Pentellic marble and limestone.

8. Most of the large hotels and better cafés were on the Place. It is possible here that Crane is referring to the Café Zacharatos (at the corner of the Rue du Stade, on both sides), or possibly to the Café des Étrangers or the Café d'Orient.

9. At the time two tramway lines skirted the Palace on the east and west.

this headgear. In the black sea of men this floating hat glowed — glowed with threats.

There was at first a great deal of cheering by some twenty men who seemed to be the immediate escort of the white hat. Their enthusiasm was imparted gradually. After a time the welcome was general. A great cry rolled up from the square. It brought people swiftly to the windows of the hotels that fronted on the square.

The man in the white hat mounted a small iron café-table. It was like a pedestal; suddenly the white hat shone high above the crowd. The journalist and deputy was about to begin his speech when there was a sudden new onslaught of newsboys whose yells precluded any chance of his being heard. He was obliged to remain quietly on his little table until these wolves had sated themselves upon the money of the crowd. In the sentry-box near the Palace steps was still the immovable and indifferent figure of the euzone of the Royal Guard. In the clear air one could see plainly the fissures in the mountain afar off behind the Palace, and this mountain, rearing above the sallow dwelling of the King, was beginning to turn faintly purple — a prophecy of evening.

Finally the man in the white hat was enabled to begin his oration. He was interrupted by cheers from time to time. His incendiary hat bobbed from the ferocity of his gestures. Why was Greece shamed? Whose fault was it? He would go to the King — he would speak to the King — now — this instant — and ask him why was Greece shamed? What treacherous serpent had coiled in the path of Greece? And let the King answer!

A mighty roar came from the crowd or from a part of the crowd. Really, one could never tell how many people were seriously in the thing, and how many were there only to see it. And amid these loud acclamations the hero of the minute was helped down from his table, and, escorted by hundreds of his countrymen, began a formidable march upon the Palace of the King.

As the throng swarmed out upon the trodden place directly in front of the Palace, the euzone on guard came out of his sentry-box and began to pace deliberately up and down in front of the steps. He did not look at the advancing crowd or heed it in any way.

The deputy left his myriad followers and went to the Palace door. The euzone, a step above, walked thoughtfully to and fro before them.

A murmur arose at the back of the crowd. It was the audible machinery, the temper of the people, revolving and revolving toward turbulence. This throng was spread out like a wind-shaken lake to this one sentry who paced slowly before it.

Once the humming of voices in its crescendo almost reached the point of action. Then this kilted soldier, this simple child of the hills, darted a look at the crowd, and this look was so full of scorn, deep and moving scorn, that it must have been felt to the pits of their stomachs.

He stooped and picked from the ground a handful of pebbles. He raised his arm and, still profoundly deliberate and with supreme disdain, this solitary figure on the Palace steps flung the handful of pebbles straight into the upturned faces of the Athenians.

Meanwhile the hero of the minute was met at the door by an old servitor. In a voice full of dignity and quiet strength, the hero of the minute said: "I wish to see the King."

The old servitor replied to him tranquilly with this objection: "The King does not receive to-day."

There was a moment of silence while the peaceful old servitor stood with his hand on the door.

There are few statesmen that have been met on the threshold of an ambitious success by the cool words: "The King does not receive to-day." The hero of the minute stood irresolute. The servitor stood waiting. "Oh-um!" said the statesman at last. "Well!" — he went away.

When the white hat reappeared to the crowd they cheered clamourously. With the same quiet dignity which had marked his bearing throughout the more trying part of the incident, the man of the white hat took his seat in a landau which his admirers had brought for him. As he passed through the streets his trooping followers cheered and cheered the victor, and from time to time he modestly lifted in recognition his tall, white hat.[10]

10. Such café "revolutions" were common apparently. Frederick Palmer, in his *Going to War in Greece,* made much fun over one he saw activated in the Place and sarcastically remarked that it was in "the foremost café whence the King receives his orders, evolved from the chatter and gesticulations of the idle, who form a conspicuous majority in Athens."

❖ ❖ ❖

DEATH AND THE CHILD

i

THE PEASANTS who were streaming down the mountain trail had, in their sharp terror, evidently lost their ability to count. The cattle and the huge round bundles seemed to suffice to the minds of the crowd if there were now two in each case where there had been three. This brown stream poured on with a constant wastage of goods and beasts. A goat fell behind to scout the dried grass, and its owner, howling, flogging his donkeys, passed far ahead. A colt, suddenly frightened, made a stumbling charge up the hillside. The expenditure was always profligate, and always unnamed, unnoted. It was as if fear was a river, and this horde had simply been caught in the torrent, man tumbling over beast, beast over man, as helpless in it as the logs that fall and shoulder grindingly through the gorges of a lumber country. It was a freshet that might sear the face of the tall, quiet mountain; it might draw a livid line across the land, this downpour of fear with a thousand homes adrift in the current — men, women, babes, animals. From it there arose a constant babble of tongues, shrill, broken, and sometimes choking, as from men drowning. Many made gestures, painting their agonies on the air with fingers that twirled swiftly.

The blue bay, with its pointed ships, and the white town[1] lay below them, distant, flat, serene. There was upon this vista a peace that a bird knows when, high in air, it surveys the world, a great, calm thing rolling noiselessly toward the end of the mystery. Here on the height one felt the existence of the universe scornfully defining the pain in ten thousand minds. The sky was an arch of stolid sapphire. Even to the mountains, raising their mighty shapes from the valley, this headlong rush of the fugitives was too minute. The sea, the sky, and the hills combined in their grandeur to term this misery inconsequent. Then, too, it sometimes happened that a face seen as it passed on the flood reflected curiously the spirit of them all, and still more.

Published in Harper's Weekly: *19 and 26 March 1898; reprinted in* The Open Boat and Other Stories, *1898; also in* Work of Stephen Crane, *XII* (*1927*).

Crane's story takes place at the battle of Velestino, as the terrain here described is the same as in his Westminster Gazette *sketch: "A Fragment of Velestino" (supra, p. 60). Velestino was, after all, the one battle of the Greco-Turkish War that Crane knew.*

1. The little "white town" is the pretty summer resort Volo on the Gulf of Volo.

One saw then a woman of the opinion of the vaults above the clouds. When a child cried, it cried always because of some adjacent misfortune — some discomfort of a pack-saddle or rudeness of an encircling arm. In the dismal melody of this flight there were often sounding chords of apathy. Into these preoccupied countenances one felt that needles could be thrust without purchasing a scream. The trail wound here and there, as the sheep had willed in the making of it.

Although this throng seemed to prove that the whole of humanity was fleeing in one direction — with every tie severed that binds us to the soil — a young man was walking rapidly up the mountain, hastening to a side of the path from time to time to avoid some particularly wide rush of people and cattle. He looked at everything in agitation and pity. Frequently he called admonitions to maniacal fugitives, and at other times he exchanged strange stares with the imperturbable ones. They seemed to him to wear merely the expressions of so many boulders rolling down the hill. He exhibited wonder and awe with his pitying glances.

Turning once toward the rear, he saw a man in the uniform of a lieutenant of infantry marching the same way. He waited then, subconsciously elate at a prospect of being able to make into words the emotion which heretofore had been expressed only in the flash of eyes and sensitive movements of his flexible mouth. He spoke to the officer in rapid French, waving his arms wildly, and often pointing with a dramatic finger. "Ah, this is too cruel, too cruel, too cruel! is it not? I did not think it would be as bad as this. I did not think — God's mercy! — I did not think at all. And yet, I am a Greek; or, at least, my father was a Greek. I did not come here to fight; I am really a correspondent; you see? I was to write for an Italian paper. I have been educated in Italy; I have spent nearly all my life in Italy — at the schools and universities. I knew nothing of war! I was a student — a student. I came here merely because my father was a Greek, and for his sake I thought of Greece. I loved Greece; but I did not dream — "

He paused, breathing heavily. His eyes glistened from that soft overflow which comes on occasion to the glance of a young woman. Eager, passionate, profoundly moved, his first words while facing the procession of fugitives had been an active definition of his own dimension, his personal relation to men, geography, life. Throughout he had preserved the fiery dignity of a tragedian.

The officer's manner at once deferred to this outburst. "Yes," he said, polite, but mournful; "these poor people — these poor people! I do not know what is to become of these poor people."

The young man declaimed again: "I had no dream — I had no dream that it would be like this! This is too cruel — too cruel! Now I want to be a soldier. Now I want to fight. Now I want to do battle for the land of my father." He made a sweeping gesture into the north-west.

The officer was also a young man, but he was bronzed and steady. Above his high military collar of crimson cloth with one silver star upon it appeared a profile stern, quiet, and confident, respecting fate, fearing only opinion. His clothes were covered with dust; the only bright spot was the flame of the crimson collar. At the violent cries of his companion he smiled as if to himself, meanwhile keeping his eyes fixed in a glance ahead.

From a land toward which their faces were bent came a continuous boom of artillery fire. It was sounding in regular measures, like the beating of a colossal clock — a clock that was counting the seconds in the lives of the stars, and men had time to die between the ticks. Solemn, oracular, inexorable, the great seconds tolled over the hills as if God fronted this dial rimmed by the horizon. The soldier and the correspondent found themselves silent. The latter in particular was sunk in a great mournfulness, as if he had resolved willy-nilly to swing to the bottom of the abyss where dwelt secrets of this kind, and had learned beforehand that all to be met there was cruelty and hopelessness. A strap of his bright new leather leggings came unfastened, and he bowed over it slowly, impressively, as one bending over the grave of a child.

Then, suddenly, the reverberations mingled until one could not separate one explosion from another, and into the hubbub came the drawling sound of a leisurely musketry fire. Instantly, for some reason of cadence, the noise was irritating, silly, infantile. This uproar was childish. It forced the nerves to object, to protest against this racket, which was as idle as the din of a lad with a drum.

The lieutenant lifted his finger and pointed. He spoke in vexed tones, as if he held the other man personally responsible for the noise. "Well, there!" he said. "If you wish for war, you now have an opportunity magnificent."

The correspondent raised himself upon his toes. He tapped his chest with gloomy pride. "Yes! There is war! There is the war I wish to enter. I fling myself in. I am a Greek — a Greek, you understand. I wish to fight for my country. You know the way. Lead me! I offer myself." Struck with a sudden thought, he brought a case from his pocket, and, extracting a card, handed it to the officer with a bow. "My name is Peza," he said simply.

A strange smile passed over the soldier's face. There was pity and pride — the vanity of experience — and contempt in it. "Very well," he said, returning the bow. "If my company is in the middle of the fight, I shall be glad for the honour of your companionship. If my company is not in the middle of the fight, I will make other arrangements for you."

Peza bowed once more, very stiffly, and correctly spoke his thanks. On the edge of what he took to be a great venture toward death, he discovered that he was annoyed at something in the lieutenant's tone. Things immediately assumed new and extraordinary proportions. The battle, the great carnival of woe, was sunk at once to an equation with a vexation by a stranger. He wanted to ask the lieutenant what was his meaning. He bowed again majestically. The lieutenant bowed. They flung a shadow of manners, of capering tinsel ceremony, across a land that groaned, and it satisfied something within themselves completely.

In the meantime the river of fleeing villagers was changed to simply a last dropping of belated creatures who fled past stammering and flinging their hands high. The two men had come to the top of the great hill. Before them was a green plain as level as an inland sea. It swept northward, and merged finally into a length of silvery mist. Upon the near part of this plain, and upon two grey, treeless mountains at the sides of it, were little black lines from which floated slanting sheets of smoke. It was not a battle, to the nerves; one could survey it with equanimity, as if it were a tea-table. But upon Peza's mind it struck a loud, clanging blow. It was war. Edified, aghast, triumphant, he paused suddenly, his lips apart. He remembered the pageants of carnage that had marched through the dreams of his childhood. Love he knew; that he had confronted alone, isolated, wondering, an individual, an atom taking the hand of a titanic principle. Like the faintest breeze on his forehead, he felt here the vibration from the hearts of forty thousand men.

The lieutenant's nostrils were moving. "I must go at once," he said. "I must go at once."

"I will go with you, wherever you go," shouted Peza, loudly.

A primitive track wound down the side of the mountain, and in their rush they bounded from here to there, choosing risks which in the ordinary caution of man would surely have seemed of remarkable danger. The ardour of the correspondent surpassed the full energy of the soldier. Several times he turned and shouted: "Come on! Come on!"

At the foot of the path they came to a wide road which extended toward the battle in a yellow and straight line. Some men were trudging wearily to the rear. They were without rifles; their clumsy uniforms were dirty and all awry. They turned eyes dully aglow with fever upon the pair striding toward the battle. Others were bandaged with the triangular kerchief, upon which one could still see, through bloodstains, the little explanatory pictures illustrating the ways to bind various wounds — "Fig. 1," "Fig. 2," "Fig. 7." Mingled with the pacing soldiers were peasants, indifferent, capable of smiling, gibbering about the battle, which was to them an ulterior drama. A man was leading a string of three donkeys to the rear, and at intervals he was accosted by wounded or fevered soldiers, from whom he defended his animals with ape-like cries and mad gesticulations. After much chattering they usually subsided gloomily, and allowed him to go with his sleek little beasts unburdened. Finally he encountered a soldier who walked slowly, with the assistance of a staff. His head was bound with a wide bandage, grimy from blood and mud. He made application to the peasant, and immediately they were involved in a hideous Levantine discussion. The peasant whined and clamoured, sometimes spitting like a kitten. The wounded soldier jawed on thunderously, his great hands stretched in claw-like graspings over the peasant's head. Once he raised his staff and made threat with it. Then suddenly the row was at an end. The other sick men saw their comrade mount the leading donkey, and at once begin to drum with his heels. None attempted to gain the backs of the remaining animals. They gazed after him dully. Finally they saw the caravan outlined for a moment against the sky. The soldier was still waving his arms passionately, having it out with the peasant.

Peza was alive with despair for these men who looked at him with such doleful, quiet eyes. "Ah, my God!" he cried to the lieutenant, "these poor souls! — these poor souls!"

The officer faced about angrily. "If you are coming with me, there is no time for this." Peza obeyed instantly and with a sudden meekness. In the moment some portion of egotism left him, and he modestly wondered if the universe took cognizance of him to an important degree. This theatre for slaughter, built by the inscrutable needs of the earth, was an enormous affair, and he reflected that the accidental destruction of an individual, Peza by name, would perhaps be nothing at all.

With the lieutenant, he was soon walking along behind a series of little crescent-shaped trenches, in which were soldiers tranquilly interested, gossiping with the hum of a tea-party. Although these men were not at this time under fire, he concluded that they were fabulously brave, else they would not be so comfortable, so at home, in their sticky brown trenches. They were certain to be heavily attacked before the day was old. The universities had not taught him to understand this attitude. At the passing of the young man in very nice tweed, with his new leggings, his new white helmet, his new field-glass case, his new revolver holster, the soiled soldiers turned with the same curiosity which a being in strange garb meets at the corners of streets. He might as well have been promenading a populous avenue. The soldiers volubly discussed his identity.

To Peza there was something awful in the absolute familiarity of each tone, expression, gesture. These men, menaced with battle, displayed the curiosity of the café. Then, on the verge of his great encounter toward death, he found himself extremely embarrassed, composing his face with difficulty, wondering what to do with his hands, like a gawk at a levee.

He felt ridiculous, and also he felt awed, aghast at these men who could turn their faces from the ominous front and debate his clothes, his business. There was an element which was new-born into his theory of war.

He was not averse to the brisk pace at which the lieutenant moved along the line. The roar of fighting was always in Peza's ears. It came from some short hills ahead and to the left. The road curved suddenly and entered a wood. The trees stretched their luxuriant and graceful branches over grassy slopes. A breeze made all this verdure gently rustle and speak in long silken sighs. Absorbed in listening to the hurricane racket from the front, he still remembered that these trees were growing, the grass-blades were extending, according to their process. He inhaled a deep breath of moisture and fragrance from the grove, a wet odour which expressed the opulent fecundity of unmoved nature, marching on with her million plans for multiple life, multiple death.

Farther on, they came to a place where the Turkish shells were landing. There was a long, hurtling sound in the air, and then one had sight of a shell. To Peza it was of the conical missiles which friendly officers had displayed to him on board warships. Curiously enough, too, this first shell smacked of the foundry — of men with smudged faces, of the blare of furnace fires. It brought machinery immediately into his mind. He thought that if he was killed there at that time, it would be as romantic to the old standards as death by a bit of falling iron in a factory.

ii

A child was playing on a mountain, and disregarding a battle that was waging on the plain. Behind him was the little cobbled hut of his fled parents. It was now occupied by a pearl-coloured cow, that stared out from the darkness, thoughtful and tender-eyed. The child ran to and fro, fumbling with sticks, and making great machinations with pebbles. By a striking exercise of artistic licence, the sticks were ponies, cows, and dogs, and the pebbles were sheep. He was managing large agricultural and herding affairs. He was too intent on them to pay much heed to the fight four miles away, which at that distance resembled in sound the beating of surf upon rocks. However, there were occasions when some louder outbreak of that thunder stirred him from his serious occupation, and he turned then a questioning eye upon the battle, a small stick poised in his hand, interrupted in the act of sending his dog after his sheep. His tranquillity in regard to the death on the plain was as invincible as that of the mountain on which he stood.

It was evident that fear had swept the parents away from their home in a manner that could make them forget this child, the first-born. Nevertheless, the hut was cleaned bare. The cow had committed no impropriety in billeting herself at the domicile of her masters. This smoke-coloured and odorous interior contained nothing as large as a humming-bird. Terror had operated on these runaway people in its sinister fashion — elevating details to enormous heights, causing a man to remember a button while he forgot a coat, overpowering every one with recollections of a broken coffee-cup, deluging them with fears for the safety of an old pipe, and causing them to forget their first-born. Meanwhile the child played soberly with his trinkets.

He was solitary. Engrossed in his own pursuits, it was seldom that he lifted his head to inquire of the world why it made so much noise. The stick in his hand was much larger to him than was an army corps of the distance. It was too childish for the mind of the child. He was dealing with sticks.

The battle-lines writhed at times in the agony of a sea-creature on the sands. These tentacles flung and waved in a supreme excitement of pain, and the struggles of the great outlined body brought it near and nearer to the child. Once he looked at the plain, and saw some men running wildly across a field. He had seen people chasing obdu-rate beasts in such fashion, and it struck him immediately that it was a manly thing, which he would incorporate in his game. Consequently he raced furiously at his stone sheep, flourishing a cudgel, crying the shepherd calls. He paused frequently to get a cue of manner from the soldiers fighting on the plain. He reproduced, to a degree, any move-ments which he accounted rational to his theory of sheep-herding, the business of men, the traditional and exalted living of his father.

iii

It was as if Peza was a corpse walking on the bottom of the sea, and finding there fields of grain, groves, weeds, the faces of men, voices. War, a strange employment of the race, presented to him a scene crowded with familiar objects which wore the livery of their commonness placidly, undauntedly. He was smitten with keen aston-ishment; a spread of green grass, lit with the flames of poppies, was too old for the company of this new ogre. If he had been devoting the full lens of his mind to this phase, he would have known that he was amazed that the trees, the flowers, the grass, all tender and peaceful nature, had not taken to heels at once upon the outbreak of battle. He venerated the immovable poppies.

The road seemed to lead into the apex of an angle formed by the two defensive lines of the Greeks. There was a struggle of wounded men, and of gunless and jaded men. These latter did not seem to be frightened. They remained very cool, walking with unhurried steps, and busy in gossip. Peza tried to define them. Perhaps during the fight they had reached the limit of their mental storage, their capacity for excitement, for tragedy, and had then simply come away. Peza remembered his visit to a certain place of pictures, where he had found himself amid heavenly skies and diabolic midnights — the sunshine beating red upon desert sands, nude bodies flung to the shore in the green moonglow, ghastly and starving men clawing at a wall in darkness, a girl at her bath, with screened rays falling upon her pearly shoulders, a dance, a funeral, a review, an execution — all the strength of argus-eyed art; and he had whirled and whirled amid this universe, with cries of woe and joy, sin and beauty, piercing his ears until he had been obliged to simply come away. He remembered that as he had emerged he had lit a cigarette with unction, and advanced promptly to a café. A great hollow quiet seemed to be upon the earth.

This was a different case, but in his thoughts he conceded the same causes to many of these gunless wanderers. They, too, may have dreamed at lightning speed, until the capacity for it was overwhelmed. As he watched them, he again saw himself walking toward the café, puffing upon his cigarette. As if to reinforce his theory, a soldier stopped him with an eager but polite inquiry for a match. He watched the man light his little roll of tobacco and paper and begin to smoke ravenously.

Peza no longer was torn with sorrow at the sight of wounded men. Evidently he found that pity had a numerical limit, and when this was passed the emotion became another thing. Now, as he viewed them, he merely felt himself very lucky, and beseeched the continuance of his superior fortune. At the passing of these slouched and stained figures he now heard a reiteration of warning. A part of himself was appealing through the medium of these grim shapes. It was plucking at his sleeve and pointing, telling him to beware of these soldiers only as he would have cared for the harms of broken dolls. His whole vision was focused upon his own chance.

The lieutenant suddenly halted. "Look," he said; "I find that my duty is in another direction; I must go another way. But if you wish to fight, you have only to go forward, and any officer of the fighting line will give you opportunity." He raised his cap ceremoniously. Peza raised his new white helmet. The stranger to battles uttered thanks to his chaperon, the one who had presented him. They bowed punctiliously, staring at each other with civil eyes.

The lieutenant moved quietly away through a field. In an instant it flashed upon Peza's mind that this desertion was perfidious. He had been subjected to a criminal discourtesy. The officer had fetched him into the middle of the thing, and then left him to wander helplessly toward death. At one time he was upon the point of shouting at the officer.

In the vale there was an effect as if one was then beneath the battle. It was going on above, somewhere. Alone, unguided, Peza felt like a man groping in a cellar. He reflected, too, that one should always see the beginning of a fight. It was too difficult to thus approach it when the affair was in full swing. The trees hid all the movements of troops from him, and he thought he might be walking out to the very spot which chance had provided for the reception of a fool. He asked eager questions of passing soldiers. Some paid no heed to him; others shook their heads mournfully. They knew nothing, save that war was hard work. If they talked at all, it was in testimony of having fought well, savagely. They did not know if the army was going to advance, hold its ground, or retreat. They were weary.

A long, pointed shell flashed through the air, and struck near the base of a tree with a fierce upheaval, compounded of earth and flames. Looking back, Peza could see the shattered tree quivering from head to foot. Its whole being underwent a convulsive tremor which was an exhibition of pain and, furthermore, deep amazement. As he advanced through the vale, the shells continued to hiss and hurtle in long, low flights, and the bullets purred in the air. The missiles were flying into the breast of an astounded nature. The landscape, bewildered, agonized, was suffering a rain of infamous shots, and Peza imagined a million eyes gazing at him with the gaze of startled antelopes.

There was a resolute crashing of musketry from the tall hill on the left, and from directly in front there was a mingled din of artillery and musketry firing. Peza felt that his pride was playing a great trick in forcing him forward in this manner under conditions of strangeness, isolation, and ignorance; but he recalled the manner of the lieutenant, the smile on the hilltop among the flying peasants. Peza blushed, and pulled the peak of his helmet down on his forehead. He strode on firmly. Nevertheless, he hated the lieutenant, and he resolved that on some future occasion he would take much trouble to arrange a stinging social revenge upon that grinning jackanapes. It did not occur to him, until later, that he was now going to battle mainly because at a previous time a certain man had smiled.

iv

The road moved around the base of a little hill, and on this hill a battery of mountain guns was leisurely shelling something unseen. In the lee of the height, the mules, contented under their heavy saddles, were quietly browsing the long grass. Peza ascended the hill by a slanting path. He felt his heart beat swiftly. Once at the top of the hill, he would be obliged to look this phenomenon in the face. He hurried with a mysterious idea of preventing by this strategy the battle from making his appearance a signal for some tremendous renewal. This vague thought seemed logical at the time. Certainly this living thing had knowledge of his coming. He endowed it with the intelligence of a barbaric deity. And so he hurried. He wished to surprise war, this terrible emperor, when it was only growling on its throne. The ferocious and horrible sovereign was not to be allowed to make the arrival a pretext for some fit of smoky rage and blood. In this half-lull, Peza had distinctly the sense of stealing upon the battle unawares.

The soldiers watching the mules did not seem to be impressed by anything august. Two of them sat side by side and talked comfortably; another lay flat upon his back, staring dreamily at the sky; another cursed a mule for certain refractions. Despite their uniforms, their bandoleers and rifles, they were dwelling in the peace of hostlers. However, the long shells were whooping from time to time over the brow of the hill, and swirling in almost straight lines toward the vale of trees, flowers, and grass. Peza, hearing and seeing the shells, and seeing the pensive guardians of the mules, felt reassured. They were accepting the conditions of war as easily as an old sailor accepts the chair behind the counter of a tobacco-shop. Or it was merely that the farm boy had gone to sea, and he had adjusted himself to the circumstances immediately, and with only the usual first misadventures in conduct. Peza was proud and ashamed that he was not of them — these stupid peasants who, throughout the world, hold potentates on their thrones, make statesmen illustrious, provide generals with lasting victories, all with ignorance, indifference, or half-witted hatred, moving the world with the strength of their arms, and getting their heads knocked together, in the name of God, the king, or the stock exchange — immortal, dreaming, hopeless asses who surrender their reason to the care of a shining puppet, and persuade some toy to carry their lives in his purse. Peza mentally abased himself before them, and wished to stir them with furious kicks.

As his eyes ranged above the rim of the plateau, he saw a group of artillery officers talking busily. They turned at once, and regarded his ascent. A moment later a row of infantry soldiers, in a trench beyond the little guns, all faced him. Peza bowed to the officers. He understood at the time that he had made a good and cool bow, and he wondered at it; for his breath was coming in gasps — he was stifling from sheer excitement. He felt like a tipsy man trying to conceal his muscular uncertainty from the people in the street. But the officers did not display any knowledge. They bowed. Behind them Peza saw the plain, glittering green, with three lines of black marked upon it heavily. The front of the first of these lines was frothy with smoke. To the left of this hill was a craggy mountain, from which came a continual dull rattle of musketry. Its summit was ringed with the white smoke. The black lines on the plain slowly moved. The shells that came from there passed overhead, with the sound of great birds frantically flapping their wings. Peza thought of the first sight of the sea during a storm. He seemed to feel against his face the wind that races over the tops of cold and tumultuous billows.

He heard a voice afar off: "Sir, what would you?" He turned, and saw the dapper captain of the battery standing beside him. Only a moment had elapsed.

"Pardon me, sir," said Peza, bowing again.

The officer was evidently reserving his bows. He scanned the newcomer attentively. "Are you a correspondent?" he asked.

Peza produced a card. "Yes; I came as a correspondent," he replied. "But now, sir, I have other thoughts. I wish to help. You see? I wish to help."

"What do you mean?" said the captain. "Are you a Greek? Do you wish to fight?"

"Yes; I am a Greek; I wish to fight." Peza's voice surprised him by coming from his lips in even and deliberate tones. He thought with gratification that he was behaving rather well. Another shell, travelling from some unknown point on the plain, whirled close and furiously in the air, pursuing an apparently horizontal course, as if it were never going to touch the earth. The dark shape swished across the sky.

"Ah," cried the captain, now smiling, "I am not sure that we will be able to accommodate you with a fierce affair here just at this time, but — " He walked gaily to and fro behind the guns with Peza, pointing out to him the lines of the Greeks, and describing his opinion of the general plan of defence. He wore the air of an amiable host. Other officers questioned Peza in regard to the politics of the war. The king, the ministry, Germany, England, Russia — all these huge words were continually upon their tongues. "And the people in Athens, were they — ?" Amid this vivacious babble, Peza, seated upon an ammunition-box, kept his glance high, watching the appearance of shell after shell. These officers were like men who had been lost for days in the forest. They were thirsty for any scrap of news. Nevertheless, one of them would occasionally dispute their informant courteously. What would Servia have to say to that? No, no; France and Russia could never allow it. Peza was elated. The shells killed no one. War was not so bad! He was simply having coffee in the smoking-room of some embassy where reverberate the names of nations.

A rumour had passed along the motley line of privates in the trench. The new arrival with the clean white helmet was a famous English cavalry officer, come to assist the army with his counsel. They stared at the figure of him, surrounded by officers. Peza, gaining sense of the glances and whispers, felt that his coming was an event.

Later, he resolved that he could, with temerity, do something finer. He contemplated the mountain where the Greek infantry was engaged, and announced leisurely to the captain of the battery that he thought presently of going in that direction and getting into the fight. He reaffirmed the sentiments of a patriot. The captain seemed surprised. "Oh, there will be fighting here at this knoll in a few minutes," he said orientally. "That will be sufficient. You had better stay with us. Besides, I have been ordered to resume fire." The officers all tried to dissuade him from departing. It was really not worth the trouble. The battery would begin again directly; then it would be amusing for him.

Peza felt that he was wandering, with his protestations of high patriotism, through a desert of sensible men. These officers gave no heed to his exalted declarations. They seemed too jaded. They were fighting the men who were fighting them. Palaver of the particular kind had subsided before their intense preoccupation in war as a craft. Moreover, many men had talked in that manner, and only talked.

Peza believed at first that they were treating him delicately; they were considerate of his inexperience. War had turned out to be such a gentle business that Peza concluded that he could scorn this idea. He bade them an heroic farewell, despite their objections.

However, when he reflected upon their ways afterward, he saw dimly that they were actuated principally by some universal childish desire for a spectator of their fine things. They were going into action, and they wished to be seen at war, precise and fearless.

v

Climbing slowly to the high infantry position, Peza was amazed to meet a soldier whose jaw had been half shot away, and who was being helped down the steep track by two tearful comrades. The man's breast was drenched with blood, and from a cloth which he held to the wound drops were splashing wildly upon the stones of the path. He gazed at Peza for a moment. It was a mystic gaze, which Peza withstood with difficulty. He was exchanging looks with a spectre; all aspect of the man was somehow gone from this victim. As Peza went on, one of the unwounded soldiers loudly shouted to him to return and assist in this tragic march. But even Peza's fingers revolted. He was afraid of the spectre; he would not have dared to touch it. He was surely craven in the movement of refusal he made to them. He scrambled hastily on up the path. He was running away!

At the top of the hill he came immediately upon a part of the line that was in action. Another battery of mountain guns was here, firing at the streaks of black on the plain. There were trenches filled with men lining parts of the crest, and near the base were other trenches, all crashing away mightily. The plain stretched as far as the eye could see, and from where silver mist ended this emerald ocean of grass, a great ridge of snow-topped mountains poised against a fleckless blue sky. Two knolls, green and yellow with grain, sat on the prairie, confronting the dark hills of the Greek position. Between them were the lines of the enemy. A row of trees, a village, a stretch of road showed faintly on this great canvas, this tremendous picture; but men, the Turkish battalions, were emphasized startlingly upon it. The ranks of troops between the knolls and the Greek position were as black as ink. The first line, of course, was muffled in smoke; but at the rear of it, battalions crawled up, and to and fro, plainer than beetles on a plate. Peza had never understood that masses of men were so declarative, so unmistakable, as if nature makes every arrangement to give information of the coming and the presence of destruction, the end, oblivion. The firing was full, complete, a roar of cataracts, and this pealing of concerted volleys was adjusted to the grandeur of the far-off range of snowy mountains. Peza, breathless, pale, felt that he had been set upon a pillar, and was surveying mankind, the world. In the meantime dust had got in his eye. He took his handkerchief and mechanically administered to it.

An officer with a double stripe of purple on his trousers paced in the rear of the battery of howitzers. He waved a little cane. Sometimes he paused in his promenade to study the field through his glasses. "A fine scene, sir," he cried airily, upon the approach of Peza. It was like a blow in the chest to the wide-eyed volunteer. It revealed to him a point of view.

"Yes, sir; it is a fine scene," he answered.

They spoke in French. "I am happy to be able to entertain monsieur with a little fine practice," continued the officer. "I am firing upon that mass of troops you see there, a little to the right. They are probably forming for another attack."

Peza smiled. Here again appeared manners — manners erect by the side of death.

The right-flank gun of the battery thundered; there was a belch of fire and smoke; the shell, flung swiftly and afar, was known only to the ear, in which rang a broadening, hooting wake of sound. The howitzer had thrown itself backward convulsively, and lay with its wheels moving in the air as a squad of men rushed toward it; and later, it seemed as if each little gun had made the supreme effort of its being in each particular shot. They roared with voices far too loud, and the thunderous effort caused a gun to bound as in a dying convulsion. And then occasionally one was hurled with wheels in air. These shuddering howitzers presented an appearance of so many cowards, always longing to bolt to the rear, but being implacably held up to their business by this throng of soldiers who ran in squads to drag them up again to their obligation. The guns were herded and cajoled and bullied interminably. One by one, in relentless program, they were dragged forward to contribute a profound vibration of steel and wood, a flash and a roar, to the important happiness of men.

The adjacent infantry celebrated a good shot with smiles and an outburst of gleeful talk.

"Look, sir," cried an officer once to Peza. Thin smoke was drifting lazily before Peza, and, dodging impatiently, he brought his eyes to bear upon that part of the plain indicated by the officer's finger. The enemy's infantry was advancing to attack. From the black lines had come forth an inky mass which was shaped much like a human tongue. It advanced slowly, casually, without apparent spirit, but with an insolent confidence that was like a proclamation of the inevitable.

The impetuous part was all played by the defensive side.

Officers called; men plucked each other by the sleeve. There were shouts — motion. All eyes were turned upon the inky mass which was flowing toward the base of the hills, heavily, languorously, as oily and thick as one of the streams that ooze through a swamp.

Peza was chattering a question at every one. In the way, pushed aside, or in the way again, he continued to repeat it: "Can they take the position? Can they take the position? Can they take the position?" He was apparently addressing an assemblage of deaf men. Every eye was busy watching every hand. The soldiers did not even seem to see the interesting stranger in the white helmet, who was crying out so feverishly.

Finally, however, the hurried captain of the battery espied him, and heeded his question. "No, sir! No, sir! It is impossible!" he shouted angrily. His manner seemed to denote that if he had had sufficient time he would have completely insulted Peza. The latter swallowed the crumb of news without regard to the coating of scorn, and, waving his hand in adieu, he began to run along the crest of the hill toward the part of the Greek line against which the attack was directed.

vi

Peza, as he ran along the crest of the mountain, believed that his action was receiving the wrathful attention of the hosts of the foe. To him, then, it was incredible foolhardiness thus to call to himself the stares of thousands of hateful eyes. He was like a lad induced by playmates to commit some indiscretion in a cathedral. He was abashed; perhaps he even blushed as he ran. It seemed to him that the whole solemn ceremony of war had paused during this commission. So he scrambled wildly over the rocks in his haste to end the embarrassing ordeal. When he came among the crowning rifle-pits, filled with eager soldiers, he wanted to yell with joy. None noticed him, save a young officer of infantry, who said: "Sir, what do you want?" It was obvious that people had devoted some attention to their own affairs.

Peza asserted, in Greek, that he wished above everything to battle for the fatherland. The officer nodded. With a smile he pointed to some dead men, covered with blankets, from which were thrust upturned dusty shoes.

"Yes; I know, I know," cried Peza. He thought the officer was poetically alluding to the danger.

"No," said the officer, at once. "I mean cartridges — a bandoleer. Take a bandoleer from one of them."

Peza went cautiously toward a body. He moved a hand toward a corner of a blanket. There he hesitated, stuck, as if his arm had turned to plaster. Hearing a rustle behind him, he spun quickly. Three soldiers of the close rank in the trench were regarding him. The officer came again, and tapped him on the shoulder. "Have you any tobacco?" Peza looked at him in bewilderment. His hand was still extended toward the blanket which covered the dead soldier.

"Yes," he said; "I have some tobacco." He gave the officer his pouch. As if in compensation, the other directed a soldier to strip the bandoleer from the corpse. Peza, having crossed the long cartridge-belt on his breast, felt that the dead man had flung his two arms around him.

A soldier, with a polite nod and smile, gave Peza a rifle — a relic of another dead man. Thus he felt, besides the clutch of a corpse about his neck, that the rifle was as unhumanly horrible as a snake that lives in a tomb. He heard at his ear something that was in effect like the voices of those two dead men, their low voices speaking to him of bloody death, mutilation. The bandoleer gripped him tighter; he wished to raise his hands to his throat, like a man who is choking. The rifle was clumsy; upon his palms he felt the movement of the sluggish currents of a serpent's life; it was crawling and frightful.

All about him were these peasants, with their interested countenances, gibbering of the fight. From time to time a soldier cried out
in semi-humorous lamentations descriptive of his thirst. One bearded
man sat munching a great bit of hard bread. Fat, greasy, squat, he
was like an idol made of tallow. Peza felt dimly that there was a distinction between this man and a young student who could write
sonnets and play the piano quite well. This old blockhead was coolly
gnawing at the bread, while he — Peza — was being throttled by a
dead man's arms.

He looked behind him, and saw that a head, by some chance,
had been uncovered from its blanket. Two liquid-like eyes were staring
into his face. The head was turned a little sideways, as if to get better
opportunity for the scrutiny. Peza could feel himself blanch. He was
being drawn and drawn by these dead men, slowly, firmly down, as to
some mystic chamber under the earth, where they could walk, dreadful figures, swollen and blood-marked. He was bidden; they had commanded him; he was going, going, going.

When the man in the new white helmet bolted for the rear, many
of the soldiers in the trench thought that he had been struck. But those
who had been nearest to him knew better. Otherwise they would have
heard the silken, sliding, tender noise of the bullet, and the thud of
its impact. They bawled after him curses, and also outbursts of self-
congratulation and vanity. Despite the prominence of the cowardly
part, they were enabled to see in this exhibition a fine comment upon
their own fortitude. The other soldiers thought that Peza had been
wounded somewhere in the neck, because, as he ran, he was tearing
madly at the bandoleer — the dead man's arms. The soldier with the
bread paused in his eating, and cynically remarked upon the speed of
the runaway.

An officer's voice was suddenly heard calling out the calculation
of the distance to the enemy, the readjustment of the sights. There
was a stirring rattle along the line. The men turned their eyes to the
front. Other trenches, beneath them, to the right, were already heavily
in action. The smoke was lifting toward the blue sky. The soldier with
the bread placed it carefully on a bit of paper beside him as he turned
to kneel in the trench.

vii

In the late afternoon the child ceased his play on the mountain
with his flocks and his dogs. Part of the battle had whirled very near
to the base of his hill, and the noise was great. Sometimes he could
see fantastic, smoky shapes, which resembled the curious figures in
foam which one sees on the slant of a rough sea. The plain, indeed,
was etched in white circles and whirligigs, like the slope of a colossal

wave. The child took seat on a stone, and contemplated the fight. He was beginning to be astonished. He had never before seen cattle herded with such uproar. Lines of flame flashed out here and there. It was mystery.

Finally, without any preliminary indication, he began to weep. If the men struggling on the plain had had time, and greater vision, they could have seen this strange, tiny figure seated on a boulder, surveying them while the tears streamed. It was as simple as some powerful symbol.

As the magic clear light of day amid the mountains dimmed the distances, and the plain shone as a pallid blue cloth marked by the red threads of the firing, the child arose and moved off to the unwelcoming door of his home. He called softly for his mother, and complained of his hunger in the familiar formulae. The pearl-coloured cow, grinding her jaws thoughtfully, stared at him with her large eyes. The peaceful gloom of evening was slowly draping the hills.

The child heard a rattle of loose stones on the hillside, and, facing the sound, saw, a moment later, a man drag himself up to the crest of the hill and fall panting. Forgetting his mother and his hunger, filled with calm interest, the child walked forward, and stood over the heaving form. His eyes, too, were now large and inscrutably wise and sad, like those of the animal in the house.

After a silence, he spoke inquiringly: "Are you a man?"

Peza rolled over quickly, and gazed up into the fearless and cherubic countenance. He did not attempt to reply. He breathed as if life was about to leave his body. He was covered with dust; his face had been cut in some way, and his cheek was ribboned with blood. All the spick of his former appearance had vanished in a general dishevelment, in which he resembled a creature that had been flung to and fro, up and down, by cliffs and prairies during an earthquake. He rolled his eye glassily at the child.

They remained thus until the child repeated his words: "Are you a man?"

Peza gasped in the manner of a fish. Palsied, windless, and abject, he confronted the primitive courage, the sovereign child, the brother of the mountains, the sky, and the sea, and he knew that the definition of his misery could be written on a wee grass-blade.

Stephen Crane in Greece, May 1897. Permission of Mr. Ames Williams.

Stephen Crane on the Three Friends *off Cuba, 1898.*
Photograph by Frances Cabané Scovel Saportas.

2   THE SPANISH-AMERICAN WAR

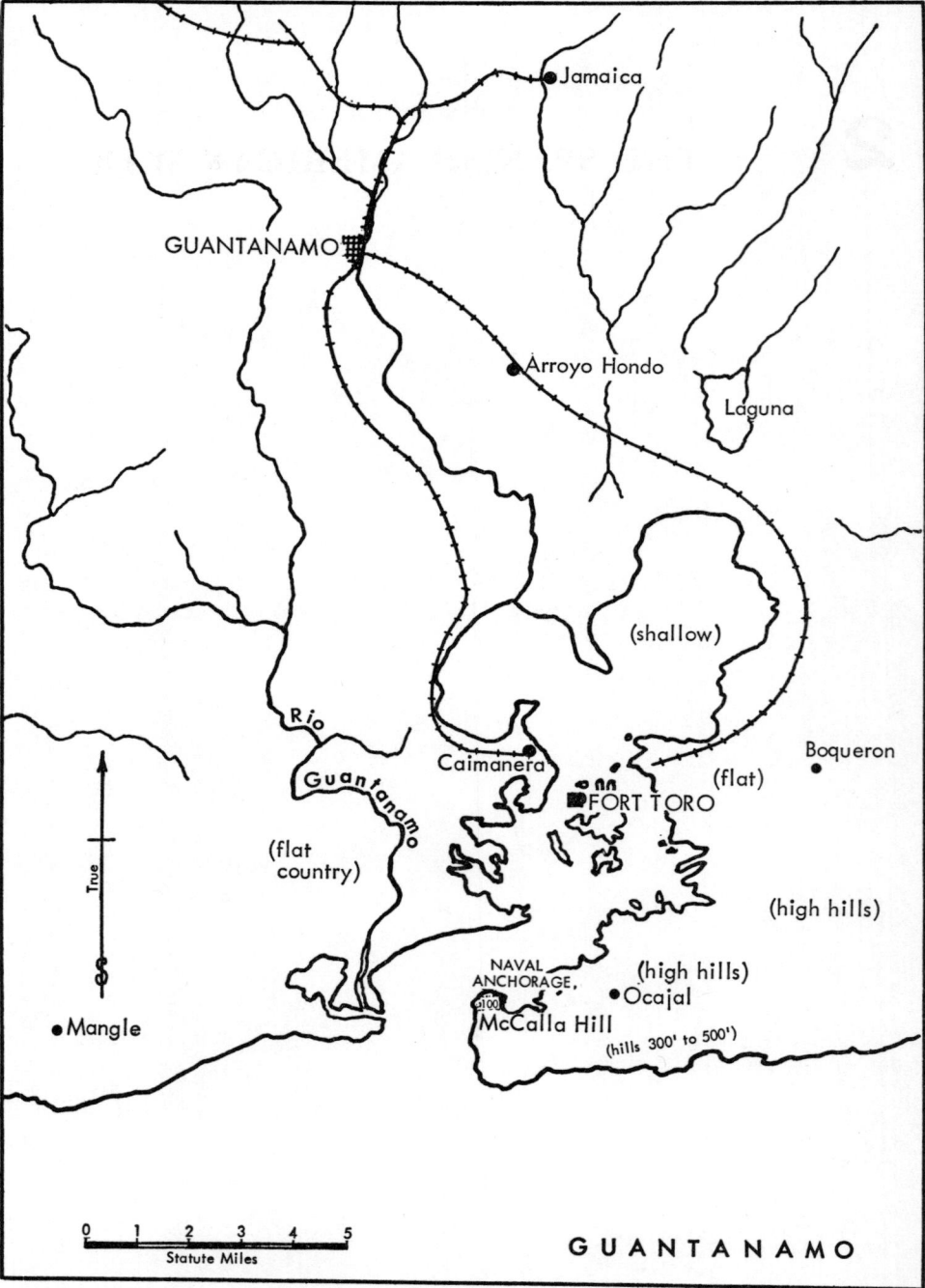

GUANTANAMO

Introduction

Crane had no talent for news of the type demanded by his editors and that explains why Crane remains today interesting — he wrote only what he felt interested him. He was, however, a star reporter, and the editors for whom he worked made a point of putting his name in their front page headlines again and again.

His fellow reporters — Ralph Paine and Ernest McCready, for instance — treated Crane affectionately as the genius of *The Red Badge of Courage* who as war correspondent, however, was the irresponsible artist lagging in his assignments. Crane's dispatches were out of place in the yellow journalism of Pulitzer's *World*; "if they had appeared in a more literary medium they would have carried more weight," said the *Literary Digest* (15 October 1898). Crane was a Special Correspondent, a *literary* correspondent as distinguished from the general run of newspaper historians reporting what their editors demanded: mere facts. His primary interest was in what the soldiers felt. Crane would agree with George W. Steevens' credo as reporter: "I only say what I saw." Said Crane to a school chum who wanted to write but could not get down the real thing: "You've got to feel the things you write if you want to make an impact on the world." Crane's credo as reporter and as fiction-writer is the same as Joseph Conrad declared in his 1897 Preface to his *Nigger of the "Narcissus"*: ". . . by the power of the written word to make you hear, to make you feel — it is, before all, to make you *see*. That — and no more, and it is everything."

Crane's journalistic output in Spanish-American War dispatches, sketches, and stories is fantastic. Some of it reads today as rather dull copy: "The Terrible Captain of the Captured Panama" (New York

World: 28 April 1898), "Inaction Deteriorates the Key West Fleet" (*World:* 6 May 1898), and "Sayings of Turret Jacks in Our Blockading Fleets" (*World:* 15 May 1898). Such items are not included here unless they provide background information that seems worth having.

As our volume aims to present mainly newspaper sketches and war dispatches not reprinted since their original appearance in Crane's day, we do not represent Crane as short-story author except on a few occasions. Is "The Price of the Harness" a short story or a sketch? A short story (to define it) is shorter than a novella and still shorter than a novel; but *what* distinguishes the short story from the sketch is the ingredient of a conflict between two opposing forces or ideas or conditions (in "The Price of the Harness" it is a condition of no choice). A sketch reports a conflict, whereas a short story recreates it. "Marines Signalling Under Fire at Guantanamo" is obviously a sketch. It is short, but it is not for that reason a short story. It is simply an account of what happened. It is the same with "The Sergeant's Private Madhouse." These sketches lack the ingredient of thematic import, by which such a short story as "The Price of the Harness" transcends mere sketch reporting. Perhaps "The Sergeant's Private Madhouse" borders between sketch and short story, but there is no doubt about such Spanish-American War sketches as "God Rest Ye, Merry Gentlemen," "The Revenge of *The Adolphus*," and "The Lone Charge of William B. Perkins" — not included in this collection. They are sketches, not short stories. (Perkins is Ralph D. Paine, who retells the same thing, the source situation of Crane's sketch, in his own *Roads of Adventure.*)

Edward Garnett's description of Crane as "an interpreter of the significant surface of things" applies to his journalism as well as his novels, for in his dispatches and sketches Crane reveals in a few strokes the inner life by its outer surface. No other reporter wrote in Crane's paint-brush style. He chose suggestive incidents and rendered them visually and metaphorically — in contrast to today's newspapermen who use metaphors "as sparingly as a Montclair housewife employs garlic," as A. J. Liebling put it.

Chivalrous Richard Harding Davis judged Crane's "Marines Signalling Under Fire" to be one of the finest examples of descriptive writing in the Cuban campaign, and he singled out "The Red Badge of Courage was His Wig-Wag Flag" and "Stephen Crane's Vivid Story of the Battle of San Juan" as among the best eye-witness accounts the war produced. In an article on "Our War Correspondents in Cuba and Puerto Rico" published in *Harper's Magazine* in May 1899, "Richard Lion Harding" — as he was nicknamed — admitted that "Mr. Crane easily led all the rest. Of his power to make the public see what he sees it would be impertinent to speak."

In Crane the personal element predominates, and that is why he was the butt of ridicule in parodies and snarling remarks in newspapers throughout the United States during both years of his war reporting. But he was not the failure as a journalist that almost every critic has labelled him. These war dispatches ask for and reward our reappraisal of Crane as journalist.

In mid-July 1898 Crane was fired by the business manager of the New York *World,* Don Carlos Seitz, who had known Crane in the days when they belonged to the Lanthorne Club in New York City. Seitz knew that Crane had submitted some twenty dispatches to the *World,* but he said in his 1924 biography of Joseph Pulitzer that Crane submitted only one dispatch of any merit and that this dispatch imperiled the *World* because it accused the Seventy-first New York Regiment of cowardice at San Juan. Crane was at San Juan, but he didn't write that dispatch — his friend Sylvester Scovel wrote it. The *World's* "CONDUCT OF 71ST NEW YORK" appeared there on 16 July 1898, dispatched from Jamaica the previous day, and Crane was back in the United States by then; he was at Old Point Comfort, Virginia, on the 13th. (Also, all Crane's Cuban War dispatches in the acknowledged canon were signed by Crane, whereas this *World* article was unsigned.)

The charge of cowardice by the 71st was seized upon by William Randolph Hearst's *Journal* as a slander on heroes, and Pulitzer, embarrassed, began raising a fund for a memorial to be erected on the battlefield in memory of the New York men in the 71st and in the Rough Riders. It is said that Teddy Roosevelt on learning of the Pulitzer Memorial declared that no Rough Rider could sleep in the same grave with the cowardly dead of the 71st.

For writing an article he never wrote Crane has been damned for forty years, Seitz's slander being repeated by Walter Millis in his *Martial Spirit* (1931), by Seitz once more in his 1933 *Bookman* sketch, by Gregory Mason in his *Remember the Maine* (1939), and by W. A. Swanberg in his *Citizen Hearst* (1961). The record was first set straight by war correspondent Edward Marshall in his *Story of the Rough Riders* (1899): the *World* discharged Sylvester Scovel "for telling the truth about the Seventy-First N.Y. Volunteers and for returning a blow." (The Cuban campaign ended with the surrender ceremonies in the plaza of Santiago de Cuba, at which Sylvester Scovel swung his fist at General Shafter!)

The *World* fired Crane when he came back from Cuba in July by refusing to reimburse him $23 for new clothing he had purchased to replace his old outfit, and so he said goodbye and signed up with Hearst's *Journal* for the Puerto Rican campaign. Their grudge against him was that he had filed for a rival newspaper the dispatch Edward

Marshall wrote, Crane walking five or six miles to the coast to file his friend's dispatch. Marshall wrote it some hours after being shot near the spine (at Las Guásimas on June 23). Crane had to walk it because he could get no horse or mule. At Siboney he arranged for a stretcher to get Marshall back to the coast, and then Crane trudged in the heat to the field hospital where Marshall was lying and saw to it that he was properly conveyed to the coast.

Our war with Spain, which — like the Greco-Turkish War — was long in coming but short in duration, had its beginnings in the revolt of the Cubans on 25 February 1895 against Spanish rule of the island. After General Valeriano Weyler's appointment as Captain General of the Spanish forces in Cuba in 1896, American newspapers whipped up the war-passion. Nicknamed the "Butcher" by Hearst's *Journal*, Weyler became the butt of atrocity stories about Cubans suffering in concentration camps, imprisoned in "filthy and fever-charged stockades," and about mothers and children mutilated, etc. Many correspondents approached no nearer to Cuba than Key West and yet they reported "eye-witness" accounts of incidents they never saw, relying on the exaggerated stories of the Cuban insurgents. They created war propaganda, and thereby the circulation of their newspapers increased. It was the era of "Jingo Journalism," and the New York *Journal*, *World*, *Herald*, and *Sun* exploited the Cuban situation. The leading propaganda organs were the *World* and the *Journal*; Joseph Pulitzer's *World* was engaged in a death-struggle against the intruding William Randolph Hearst's *Journal*.

War with Spain finally became a fact, instead of a probability or a wish, when the battleship *Maine* exploded in Havana harbor on 15 February 1898 (what caused the explosion has never been indisputably determined), and President McKinley, who had resisted the popular fervor for war, asked Congress for a declaration of war on Monday, April 25. Two days before he had issued his first call for 125,000 volunteers. That day Crane, having been rejected by the Navy, signed with the *World*. He had left Cora at Ravensbrook in the village of Oxted, Surrey, where they had settled in England after their returning from Greece in June 1897, and he sailed on the steamer *Germanic*, probably from Queenstown, Ireland, on April 14 at 12:25 p.m. The White Star Line's *Germanic* was off Fire Island on April 21 (9:51 p.m.) and arrived at the Bar that night (11:53 p.m.), docking at Pier 45. Crane had been absent from New York City thirteen months to the day. In Madrid that day diplomatic relations between Spain and the United States were broken, and in New York City that day the *World* whipped up a flag parade to arouse the patriotism of the city to "fighting pitch" by flinging "the starry banner of freedom to the winds." It was all over by the time Crane got off the *Germanic*.

Crane joined the *World* as second choice; he couldn't pass the Navy's surprisingly rigid physical requirements; so, then, he reported the war instead of fighting it. By hook or crook he was determined to experience war once more and thereby challenge the possibility of death that haunted him.

The second phase of the war, the Puerto Rican campaign, Crane covered for Hearst's *Journal.* He boarded a tug at Pensacola and shoved off to see war again. Charles Michelson was with him and later wrote that "Crane revealed the wreck of an athlete's frame — once square shoulders crowded forward by the concavity of a collapsed chest; great hollows where the once smooth pitching muscles had wasted; legs like pipestems — he looked like a frayed white ribbon, seen through the veil of green as the seas washed over him." As the tug pitched and rolled in the Gulf Stream and the men vomiting from seasickness jerked convulsively, Crane remarked that men died with "just such a spasm."

By August 25 Crane was in Havana, having illegally slipped into the city by posing as a tobacco buyer. Such a disguise would have been easy to carry off. He probably simply sailed into the harbor and debarked after August 13 when the blockade was lifted. The harbor was deserted. Food was scarce, and prices were inflated; scavengers flourished. Havana was sad, filthy, deadened; and his dispatches from that city betray a world-weariness, a general lassitude, and an occasional bitterness. He was a man trying to regain his balance; himself and no one else was his egocentric concern. He ignored Cora and her pressing problems of existing in England without him — and without money. He was in isolation so as to put himself back together again in his own peculiar way and in his own pace of time.

Crane left Havana and got to New York City about the middle of November. On December 20 he cabled Cora, and in the first week of January 1899 he sailed on the *Manitou* from New York City. The *Manitou* sailed on New Year's Eve 1898. Earlier that day Theodore Roosevelt had taken the oath of office as Governor of the State of New York, and at noon the next day Spanish rule ceased in Cuba.

Crane had been absent from Cora two days short of nine months when the *Manitou* tied up in the Royal Albert Dock on January 11.

✿   ✿   ✿

THE LITTLE STILETTOS OF THE MODERN NAVY WHICH STAB IN THE DARK

IN the past century the gallant aristocracy of London liked to travel down the south bank of the Thames to Greenwich Hospital, where venerable pensioners of the crown were ready to hire telescopes at a penny each, and with these telescopes the lords and ladies were able to view at a better advantage the dried and enchained corpses of pirates hanging from the gibbets on the Isle of Dogs.[1] In those times the dismal marsh was inhabited solely by the clanking figures whose feet moved in the wind like rather poorly constructed weather cocks.

But even the Isle of Dogs could not escape the appetite of an expanding London. Thousands of souls now live on it and it has changed its character from that of a place of execution, with mists, wet with fever, coiling forever from the mire and wandering among the black gibbets, to that of an ordinary, squalid, nauseating slum of London, whose streets bear a faint resemblance to that part of Avenue A which lies directly above Sixtieth street in New York.[2]

Down near the water front one finds a long brick building, three storied and signless, which shuts off all view of the river. The windows, as well as the bricks, are very dirty, and you see no sign of life, unless some smudged workman dodges in or out through a little door. The place might be a factory for the making of lamps or stair rods or any ordinary commercial thing. As a matter of fact the building fronts the ship yard of Yarrow, the builder of torpedo boats, the maker of knives for the nations, the man who provides everybody with a certain kind of efficient weapon. One then remembers that if Russia fights England, Yarrow meets Yarrow; if Germany fights France, Yarrow meets Yarrow; if Chili fights Argentina, Yarrow meets Yarrow.

Besides the above-mentioned countries, Yarrow has built torpedo boats for Italy, Austria, Holland, Japan, China, Chili, Ecuador, Brazil Costa Rica and Spain. There is a keeper of a great shop in London who is known as the Universal Provider; if a general conflagration of war should break out in the world, Yarrow would be known as one of the Universal Warriors, for it would practically be a battle between Yarrow, Armstrong, Krupp and a few other firms. This is what makes interesting the dinginess of the cantonment of the Isle of Dogs.

Reprinted here for the first time from New York Journal: *24 April 1898.*

1. The Isle of Dogs is south of the West India Docks and an area within a sudden bend of the Thames River.
2. Crane lived at 1064 Avenue A in 1893.

The great Yarrow forte is to build speedy steamers of a tonnage of not more than 240 tons. This practically includes only yachts, launches, tugs, torpedo boat destroyers, torpedo boats, and of late shallow-draught gunboats for service on the Nile, Congo and Niger. Some of the gunboats that are now shelling dervishes from the banks of the Nile below Khartoum[3] were built by Yarrow. Yarrow is always in action somewhere. Even if the firm's boats do not appear in every coming sea-combat, the ideas of the firm will, for many nations, notably France and Germany, have bought specimens of the best models of Yarrow construction in order to reduplicate and reduplicate them in their own yards.

When the great fever to possess torpedo boats came upon the powers of Europe England was at first left far in the rear. Either Germany or France to-day has in her fleet more torpedo boats than has England.[4] The British tar is a hard man to oust out of a habit. He had a habit of thinking that his battle ships and cruisers were the final thing in naval construction. He scoffed at the advent of the torpedo boat. He did not scoff intelligently, but because, mainly, he hated to be forced to change his ways.

You will usually find an Englishman balking and kicking at an innovation up to the last moment. It takes him some years to get an idea into his head, and when finally it is inserted he not only respects it, he reveres it. The Londoners have a fire brigade which would interest the ghost of a Babylonian as an example of how much the method of extinguishing fires could degenerate in two thousand years. And in 1897, when a terrible fire devastated a large part of the city, some voices were raised challenging the efficiency of the brigade.[5] But that part of the London County Council which corresponds to our fire commissioners laid their hands upon their hearts and solemnly assured the public that they had investigated the matter and had found the London fire brigade to be as good as any in the world. There were some isolated cases of dissent, but the great English public as a

3. On April 8, 1898, in the Sudan, Anglo-Egyptian forces defeated the dervishes under Mahmud near the Atbara River.

4. Here — and later in the article — Crane has his facts wrong. France possessed a total of 245 torpedo boats of all classes, England 192, and Germany 134.

5. Apparently Crane had in mind the fire of 5 February 1897, in London, when a large block of warehouses used for storing furniture in Camden Town was completely destroyed; and just the day before, February 4, the shipbuilding yard of the Fairfield Engineering Company on the Clyde was almost totally destroyed with damage estimated at nearly £100,000.

whole placidly accepted these assurances concerning the activity of the honored corps.

For a long time England blundered in the same way over the matter of torpedo boats. They were authoritatively informed that there was nothing in all the talk about torpedo boats. Then came a great popular uproar, in which people tumbled over each other to get to the doors of the Admiralty and howl about torpedo boats. It was an awakening as unreasonable as had been the previous indifference and contempt. Then England began to build. She has never overtaken France or Germany in the number of torpedo boats, but she now heads the world with her collection of that marvel of marine architecture — the torpedo boat destroyer. She has about sixty-five of these vessels now in commission, and has about as many more in process of building.[6]

People ordinarily have a false idea of the appearance of a destroyer. The common type is longer than an ordinary gunboat — a long, low, graceful thing, flying through the water at fabulous speed, with a great curve of water some yards back of the bow and smoke flying horizontally from the three or four stacks.

Rushing this way and that way, circling, dodging, turning, they are like demons.

The best kind of modern destroyer has a length of 220 feet, with a beam of 26½ feet. The horse power is about 6,500, driving the boat at a speed of thirty-one knots or more. The engines are triple expansion, with water tube boilers. They carry from seventy to a hundred tons of coal, and at a speed of eight or nine knots can keep the sea for a week; so they are independent of coaling in a voyage of between 1,300 and 1,500 miles. They carry a crew of three or four officers and about forty men.[7]

They are armed, usually, with one twelve-pounder gun and from three to five six-pounder guns, besides their equipment of torpedoes. Their hulls and top hamper are painted olive, buff, or, preferably, slate, in order to make them hard to find with the eye at sea.

Their principal functions, theoretically, are to discover and kill

6. *The World Almanac* for 1899 listed the strength of torpedo-boat destroyers as follows: England, 103; France, 18; United States, 16; and Germany, 10.

7. The torpedo-boat destroyers were even more powerful and remarkable than Crane describes them. One, HMS *Albatross,* had a guaranteed speed of 32 knots, or about 36¾ m.p.h. Faster than this, yet, was HMS *Express* with a speed of 33 knots. They were the fastest vessels in the world at the time. The building program of the Royal Navy for 1896–1897 provided for twenty-eight such destroyers. (Our data about ships derive from Jane's *Fighting Ships;* Whittaker's *Almanack;* etc.)

the enemy's torpedo boats, guard and scout for the main squadron, and perform messenger service. However, they are also torpedo boats of a most formidable kind, and in action will be found carrying out the torpedo boat idea in an expanded form. The four destroyers of this type now building at the Yarrow yards are for Japan.

The modern European ideal of a torpedo boat is a craft 152 feet long with a beam of 15¼ feet. When the boat is fully loaded a speed of 24 knots is derived from her 2,000-horse-power engines. The destroyers are all twin screw, whereas the torpedo boats are commonly propelled by a single screw. The speed of 24 knots is for a run of three hours. These boats are not designed to keep at sea for any great length of time, and cannot raid toward a distant coast without the constant attendance of a cruiser to keep them in coal and provisions. Primarily they are for defence. Even with destroyers, England, in lately reinforcing her foreign stations, has seen fit to send cruisers in order to provide help for them in stormy weather.

Some years ago it was thought the proper thing to equip torpedo craft with rudders, which would enable them to turn in their own length while running at full speed. Yarrow found this to result in too much broken steering gear, and the firm's boats now have smaller rudders, which enable them to turn in a larger circle.

At one time a torpedo boat steaming at her best gait always carried a great bone in her teeth. During manoeuvres the watch on the deck of a battle ship often discovered the approach of the little enemy by the great white wave which the boat rolled up at her bows during her headlong rush. This was mainly because the old-fashioned boats carried two torpedo tubes set in the bows, and the bows were consequently bluff.

The modern boat carries the greater part of her armament amidships and astern on swivels and her bow is like a dagger. With no more bow-waves and with these phantom colors of buff, olive, bottle-green or slate, the principal foe to a safe attack at night is bad firing in the stoke-room, which might cause flames to leap out of the stacks.

A captain of an English battle ship recently remarked: "See those five destroyers lying there? Well, if they should attack me I would sink four of them, but the fifth one would sink me."

This was repeated to Yarrow's manager, who said: "He wouldn't sink four of them if the attack were at night and the boats were shrewdly and courageously handled." Anyhow, the captain's remark goes to show the wholesome respect which the great battle ship has for these little fliers.

The Yarrow people say there is no sense in a torpedo flotilla attack on anything save vessels. A modern fortification is never built near enough to the water for a torpedo explosion to injure it, and, although some old stone flush-with-the-water castle might be badly crumpled, it would harm nobody in particular even if the assault were wholly successful.

Of course, if a torpedo boat could get a chance at piers and dock gates they would make a disturbance, but the chance is extremely remote if the defenders have ordinary vigilance and some rapid fire guns. In harbor defence the searchlight would naturally play a most important part, whereas at sea experts are beginning to doubt its use as an auxiliary to the rapid fire guns against torpedo boats. About half the time it does little more than betray the position of the ship. On the other hand, a port cannot conceal its position anyhow, and searchlights would be invaluable for sweeping the narrow channels.

There could be only one direction from which the assault could come, and all the odds would be in favor of the guns on shore. A torpedo boat commander knows this perfectly. What he wants is a ship off at sea with a nervous crew staring into the encircling darkness from any point in which the terror might be coming.

Hi, then for a grand, bold, silent rush and the assassin-like stab!

In stormy weather life on board a torpedo boat is not amusing. They tumble about like bucking bronchos, especially if they are going at anything like speed. Everything is battered down as if it were soldered, and the watch below feel that they are living in a football, which is being kicked every way at once.

And finally, while Yarrow and other great builders can make torpedo craft which are wonders of speed and manoeuvring power, they cannot make that high spirit of daring and hardihood which is essential to a success.

That must exist in the mind of some young lieutenant who, knowing well that if he is detected, a shot or so from a rapid fire gun will cripple him if it does not sink him absolutely, nevertheless goes creeping off to sea to find a huge antagonist and performs stealthily in the darkness an act which is more peculiarly murderous than most things in war.

If a torpedo is caught within range in daylight, the fighting is all over before it begins. Any common little gunboat can dispose of it in a moment if the gunnery is not too Chinese.

SAMPSON[1] INSPECTS HARBOR AT MARIEL

On Board United States Flagship, New York. Havana, April 29, via Key West, April 30.

The flagship New York at daybreak this morning was at her station to the northeast of Havana. In her company were the Newport and the Ericsson. The flagship shaped a course to the westward, meeting and speaking, off Havana, the Wilmington, Algonquin, Indiana, Iowa, Detroit, and Mangrove.[2]

Reprinted here for the first time from New York World: 1 May 1898. Crane had switched from the Journal to the World, but by mid-August he returned to the New York Journal.

1. "Just plain, pure, unsauced accomplishment" — that is Crane's tribute to William T. Sampson, whom he thought the most interesting personality of the war (see *infra*, p. 277).

The Dewey of the Atlantic, Sampson and his fleet aimed to intercept the enemy fleet under Admiral Pascual Cervera y Topete, who had sailed from the Cape Verde Islands on April 29. But he had to detach part of his command to defend the Eastern seaboard, and Cervera at Martinique read the newspapers revealing Sampson's maneuvers — Sampson had been betrayed by the American yellow press announcing that his destination was Puerto Rico! So, then, Cervera changed course away from Puerto Rico to head for Santiago de Cuba, where he arrived on May 19 to seek the protection of its channel.

While Sampson was off on the *New York* to meet General Shafter, Cervera's ships broke away, and the American fleet under Commodore W. S. Schley gave chase and destroyed the enemy vessels on July 3. While the Navy fought the decisive battle of the war, Sampson was preparing to land for his conference with Shafter — he was wearing leggings and spurs! As for Schley — "a blustering clown whose chief contribution to victory was to turn his own ship away from the battle and bellow, 'Give them hell, bullies!'" — all that remained was for Schley and Sampson to dispute the laurels, and Sampson did so for the rest of his life. See "The Spanish-American War," by William Manchester, *Holiday*, 30 (September 1961).

2. USS *New York* (1893) was an armored cruiser; tonnage (displacement): 8,200; length: 380 feet; speed: 21 knots; principal armament: six 8-inch and twelve 4-inch guns. USS *Indiana* (1895) was a first-class "battleship;" tonnage (displacement): 10,288; length: 358 feet; speed: 15:6 knots; principal armament: four 13-inch and eight 8-inch guns. USS *Iowa* (1897) was another first-class "battleship"; tonnage (displacement): 11,-410; length: 360 feet; speed: 16.5 knots; principal armament: four 12-inch and eight 8-inch guns. USS *Detroit* (1896) was an unprotected cruiser; tonnage (displacement): 2,089; length: 257 feet; speed: 16.4 knots; principal armament: nine 5-inch guns.

It was rumored on board that we were bound for Mariel [3] to see if the Spaniards were erecting new batteries there.

The Newport left us and the Porter came in from the horizon. Thereafter the torpedo-boats Ericsson and Porter remained, one on each quarter. As Havana was passed the squadron presented rather an imposing appearance with five newspaper despatch boats pounding along in the rear.

We were within long range, but the fortifications did not open fire. The enemy apparently has been perfecting his batteries to the eastward of Morro Castle.

The bay of Mariel, thirty-five miles to the west of Havana, was reached in the middle of the afternoon. An old Martello tower[4] stands on the point to the left of the entrance, and on a higher point to the right, stand a blockhouse of the kind that sentinel the trocha.[5]

There is a big old-fashioned smooth-bore battery near the blockhouse. These seemed to constitute the sole defenses.

The entrance to the bay is very narrow and faces due north. There is only fourteen feet of water on the bar. The flagship steamed up within easy rifle range of the shore, but a more lifeless and desolate place could hardly be imagined. At the great tobacco warehouses on the edge of the bay there was no movement. The town beyond seemed like a cemetery around the large church.

However, on the green palm-covered mountains to the left smoke raised in slanting lines. Two little gunboats and four schooners lay in the bay. The flagship could not get in very close, but was satisfied, perhaps, that the five smooth-bores, the Martello tower and the blockhouse were not very worthy of attention by the flagship. The New York continued her way down the coast toward Cabanas, thirteen miles away.

USS *Newport* (1896) was a composite gunboat; tonnage (displacement): 1,000; length: 168 feet; speed: 12.2 knots; principal armament: six 4-inch guns. USS *Ericsson* (1894) was a steel torpedo boat; tonnage (displacement): 120; length: 149 feet; speed: 24 knots. It was the first ship ever launched on inland waters (Dubuque, Iowa). USS *Wilmington* (1895) was a light-draft (9 feet) gunboat; tonnage (displacement): 1,397; length: 250 feet; speed: 15.8 knots; principal armament: eight 4-inch guns.

USS *Algonquin* was a revenue cutter, transferred to the auxiliary Navy, and the USS *Mangrove* was a lighthouse tender.

3. Mariel, an important city and harbor, was about twenty miles west from Havana on the northern coast of the island.

4. A fort of circular shape and constructed of masonry.

5. A fortified line of trenches, blockhouses, wire entanglements, etc., that spread across the island at various points. These cordons were used by the Spanish as defense against the Cuban insurgents.

On the route the little Castine[6] swooped out of the northwest with a motionless white-clad lookout high on the head of her single mast. She was sent back toward Mariel.

The junior officers of the flagship were at supper in the steerage, when about 8 o'clock the foggy voice of the boatswain could be heard roaring on the gun deck:

"Man the port battery!"

The boatswain of the New York has a voice like the watery snuffle of a swimming horse. It is delightfully terrible, and no ballad singer could hope for such an ovation as he will have whenever he shouts "Man the port battery!"

Below decks was empty in a moment. The cruiser was off Cabanas[7] and almost opposite the ruined hacienda of a tobacco plantation, from a point near which a troop of Spanish cavalry had dismounted and opened a musketry fire upon her.

The afterport 4-inch gun of the New York, taking a range of 3,700 yards immediately sent a shell into that vicinity, and this shot was followed by six others from the afterport guns.

When the flagship came about, Capt. Chadwick[8] himself aimed the after-starboard 4-inch gun. By this time the cavalry had decided that the engagement was over and were proceeding up a hill. The captain's shell dropped into the middle of their formation and they wildly scattered.

The flagship then placidly continued her way back toward Mariel. The venture ended, leaving only one thoroughly dissatisfied man on board. Gunner's Mate Lentile, whose station is in the after turret, grumbled bitterly because those two eight-inch guns, "General Lee" and "Stonewall Jackson," were not called upon to disperse the Spanish soldiers.

Meanwhile, the Spaniards are now probably gathered around some cognac bottles: "Ah, we fifty Spanish soldiers, we fought to-day a great battleship. Yes, we fifty men — a little band of fifty men — we fought a great ship. More cognac! Just think how easily we can thrash these Americans when fifty men can fight the flagship!"

The signal officer on the after bridge states as the silent fleet passed Mariel in the earlier afternoon a man in a small boat was fishing in the harbor. He had his back to the squadron and did not turn his head.

6. USS Castine (1892) was a gunboat; tonnage (displacement): 1,177; length: 204 feet; speed: 16 knots; principal armament: eight 4-inch guns.

7. To the west of Mariel; a minor harbor.

8. Captain French E. Chadwick, U.S.N., commanding the New York, who, despite thirty-seven years' Naval service, was one of the junior captains in the fleet.

However, one of the gunboats had better eyesight, and upon seeing the New York bolted so abruptly that she dragged half the mud in the bay loose with her anchor. Her men could be seen moving excitedly to and fro on her decks. She was within an easy range of three miles, but in direct line with the town.

The coast from Havana to Cabanas is high and beautifully wooded, with lofty mountains in the background. This part of the island must be at all times more healthy than low-lying Florida and more suitable for military movements.

The flagship has returned to her station. The torpedo-boats are evidently keeping Havana rather nervous to-night, for the searchlights have been frantically flashing on the horizon.

WITH THE BLOCKADE ON CUBAN COAST

(On Board World Tug Three Friends,[1] Off the Coast of Cuba, May 6, via Tampa, May 8.)

A day on the Cuban blockade.

The coast of Cuba, a high, wooded bank, with ranges of hills in the background, lay ten miles to the south. The flagship New York lifted her huge slate-colored body moodily over the quiet waves, disclosing from time to time a bit of blood-red hull below the water-line. Some officers in various degrees of white duck were grouped on the quarterdeck and on the after bridge. The signal men were sending aloft

Reprinted here for the first time from New York World: *9 May 1898.*

1. Crane wrote this dispatch off the coast of Cuba aboard the *Three Friends* on May 6. Sometime that summer (in July ?) he wrote while aboard the *Three Friends* a Whilomville story, "His New Mittens."

In "Hunger Has made Cubans Fatalists" (*infra*, p. 161), Crane describes his disappointment on being too late to catch the *Three Friends*, and his association with this tug figures in many Crane dispatches collected in this volume. The *Three Friends* figured in the story of the *Commodore* disaster. Because of governmental red tape, it was not sent to the rescue of the men on the rafts until it was too late.

Photographs of the *Three Friends* and her crew are reproduced in Ralph Paine's *Roads of Adventure* (1922); she is also reproduced in Lillian Gilkes' *Cora Crane* (1960). The photograph of Crane aboard the *Three Friends* reproduced in John Berryman's *Stephen Crane* (1950) shows him "ten or fifteen years older than the handsome youth posing in a Greek studio [in Greece] a year before."

a line of flags, holding talk with a faint gray thing far away, the only other ship on the sweeping expanse of sea.

To those who imagine the blockade of Cuba to be a close assembling of ships about the mouth of Havana Harbor this would be confusing. It does not represent the popular idea of the blockade; but, nevertheless, on six days out of eight and twenty-two hours out of twenty-four this is the appearance of the Cuban blockade.

To the eastward another steamer lifted a vague shadow over the horizon, and an officer instantly remarked that it was the torpedo-boat Porter, although how he could identify this vacillating, uncertain form is known only to seamen.

In a short time the Porter, rolling and tumbling in a sea that scarcely moved the New York, glided into the lee of the flagship. As she reeled from side to side her deck twirled as if it was spinning on an axle from bow to stern. Her crew, a sooty collection of men in the nondescript clothing of real torpedo-boat service, turned their faces toward the flagship.

The commander, standing just behind the conning tower, lifted a megaphone to his lips. His voice rang clear to everybody aboard the flagship.

"I have to report, sir, that two of the enemy's torpedo gunboats tried to escape yesterday from Havana and were chased back by the Iowa and the Wilmington. One has since gotten out and gone to the eastward."

These sentences, spoken very deliberately, with a pause after every word, made everybody prick up his ears.

"Oh, ho!" said the junior officers; "this is not so bad, after all."

Below, officers just off the early morning watches were having a belated breakfast — two slices of toast, bacon and coffee. Other officers in bath robes departed toward the tubes.

Somebody was rattling away on the piano, the tones of which on this huge steel-bulwarked and compartmented mass penetrate only to the gun-deck through the medium of an open hatch. On the gun-deck the jack tars were asleep, writing or working, or in some cases grouped to discuss in angry despair the improbability of an immediate fight. One was sewing, scowling and with pursed lips, as attentive and serious over the task as a seamstress. Two paced nervously to and fro, explaining to each other their idea of a headlong assault on Havana. Others were thoughtfully polishing the guns.

The New York strolled westward on a line parallel with the coast. The Wilmington appeared close in shore to the east. The Porter loafed listlessly astern of the flagship, her keen bow and three slanted stacks lifting and falling with infinite grace over the choppy sea. See that yellow band on her forward funnel? Well, that is the easiest way to distinguish her from the Dupont.[2]

The extremes of the coast line were misty, but an officer defined a certain depression in the hills as indicating the position of Havana.

The flagship steamed slowly in shore. Newspaper despatch boats, as if able to scent excitement or interest, loomed up to the north, a bunch of them, with every funnel streaming thick smoke, coming on furiously.

The details of Havana grew slowly out of the mist. Morro Castle,[3] low to the water, bared an outline which, strangely enough, was exactly like a preconception of it conceived from pictures. On the sides of the hills to its right were two long, straight yellow scars, modern batteries.

With immense dignity the New York steamed at a distance of six miles past the Havana fortifications. The deck forward was crowded with observant jacks, and the quarter-deck was crowded with officers. The canvas surrounding the forward bridge allowed only the busts of officers to be seen, motionless heads in profile, crooked elbows with hands up holding glasses, which were all turned toward the grim capital. Far at sea were two faint, castellated, moving islands — the Iowa and the Indiana. Everybody thought the Spanish batteries would open on the flagship. Everybody on board the flagship hoped so. The newspaper boats pounded eagerly along in the rear. But Havana remained silent, enigmatical. The only fun was allowing the imagination to dwell upon the emotions, gestures, orations which were hidden behind the six miles which separated the ships from Havana.

Meanwhile the Wilmington had turned and headed off to sea. It was reported that she, at any rate, had been fired upon by the batteries, but no action was visible to the eye, other than the movement of innumerable waves and slow forging of the warships.

Presently the Iowa and Indiana disappeared. The Wilmington turned and resumed her beat to the eastward. The Porter sped away on some mission or to return to her station. And again the New York was alone, save for the two dim points on the horizon.

Over a brilliant sea she swung again to the northeast. The bugle for the regular call to quarters pealed through the ship, even when the houses of Havana could be counted, and, as usual, the marines and a division of blue jackets formed on the quarter deck. After inspection

2. USS *Dupont* (1897) was a torpedo boat; tonnage (displacement): 165; length: 175 feet; speed: 28.5 knots.

3. Morro Castle was a fortification on the east side of the entrance to Havana harbor; it was constructed by the Spanish in 1589–1597. Another fortification with the same name was at Santiago, Cuba.

they took their trot about the deck in perfect rhythm to the music of the band, which played a rollicking, fascinating melody.

It was a peaceful scene. In fact it was more peaceful than peace, since one's sights were adjusted for war.

✻   ✻   ✻

FRANK NORRIS' PEN PORTRAIT
OF STEPHEN CRANE
ABOARD *THE THREE FRIENDS*

While we screwed and floundered our way back to Key West the correspondents wrote out their stories. It will be long before I forget the picture which the Young Personage made while at work upon his "stuff." Table there was none and the plunging of the boat made it out of the question to write while sitting in a chair. The correspondents took themselves off to the cabin and wrote while sitting in their bunks. The Young Personage was wearing a pair of duck trousers grimed and fouled with all manner of pitch and grease and oil. His shirt was guiltless of color or scarf and was unbuttoned at the throat. His hair hung in ragged fringes over his eyes. His dress-suit case was across his lap and answered him for a desk. Between his heels he held a bottle of beer against the rolling of the boat, and when he drank was royally independent of a glass. While he was composing his descriptive dispatches which some ten thousand people would read in the morning from the bulletins in New York I wondered what the fifty thousand who have read his war novel and have held him, no doubt rightly, to be a great genius, would have said and thought could they have seen him at the moment.

✻   ✻   ✻

Reprinted from *"News Gathering at Key West,"* The Letters of Frank Norris, *edited by Franklin Walker* (1956), *pp. 10–18.*

THRILLING ADVENTURES OF WORLD SCOUT IN CUBA.

KEY WEST, May 7. — After being in Havana, in the service of The World and of the United States Government, since April 13, I am again in my own country, and free from the constant danger that beset me in Cuba. There is a reward of $2,000 for my capture, and if I had been discovered in Cuba I was certain of summary execution.

My legs are covered with festering sores from poison that crept into abrasions resulting from running and crawling through the jungle. My tongue is slightly swollen from lack of water. Thanks to the alertness and kindness of Capt. C. C. Todd, U.S.N., and of the naval officers and men of the gunboat Wilmington, I am again on the soil of my own land. My last experience in getting out of Havana is freshest in my mind and I will tell that first.

After making two trips to the appointed place where I expected to meet The World's despatch boat and failing each time to be picked up, I found on returning to Havana that I was incessantly watched. So I determined to get away from the place which could no longer furnish me a bit of information, and I made up my mind to get to the coast. Filling a bottle of water I started.

I had been told that every day boats from the American fleet had been seen to approach the shore. The Spaniards expected that either an attempt was to be made to land an expedition or that somebody was to be taken off shore. If I once reached the beach, I had made up my mind that if I could not signal a ship, I would get a log or any wreckage I might find and trust to the tide or current to take me away from the shore. Perhaps I might be picked up, perhaps not, but at any rate I was better off on a floating log in the Gulf stream than on dry land surrounded by Spaniards.

I left Havana at 4.45 o'clock in the morning on May 3. Passing through Regla, I got off the train at the Guanabacoa station. Walking through the town I met a farmer driving a herd of cows. Scrap-

By Charles H. Thrall, reprinted here from New York World: 8 May 1898.

The subheads read: "How Charles H. Thrall, Yale Graduate and Prominent Business Man, Three Times in One Week Entered and Left Havana./Rescued a Wreck by U.S.S. Wilmington./Twice Failing to Find a Vessel Awaiting Him on the Coast, He Returned to City and Calmly Made Notes of the Fortifications." On the same page (p. 19) appeared "Stephen Crane's Pen Portrait of C. H. Thrall" (infra, p. 129).

ing up an acquaintance with him and pretending I was going out to look at some land, I walked along, helping him herd the cattle.

I was soiled and unkempt, with a week's growth of beard on my face. I looked like a cow-herder. We passed the line of forts without difficulty, and we found an encampment of about 2,000 cavalry stretched along the hills for about a mile. I left the farmer after we got by the last soldier and struck into the bush.

Through the tangle of undergrowth I followed the general direction of my two former trips, keeping away from the points where I had found soldiers before. About sixty soldiers saw me at a distance of half a mile and began rifle practice, making me their target. The Mauser bullet makes a sound like the scream of an angry cat, and it appeared to me that I was surrounded by a colony of felines that was holding a primary election. But my luck did not desert me. Not touched by a single missile, I promptly changed my course and made off into the bush, where I could not be seen. Soon after that I struck the shore.

[CLOSE TO DEATH ON THE CUBAN COAST.]

I knew that across that stretch of beautiful, opalescent water lay my country and freedom. Would I escape this time? The question was of importance to me, and I was anxious for a quick response. In my haste to get away from the soldiers who were firing at me I had lost my bottle of water. Nearly dead with thirst, I staggered out on the sandy beach and sank to the ground. I soon gained strength to get to my feet, and then I saw one of my own ships offshore with the glorious Stars and Stripes waving over her stern.

Frantic with desire to attract attention, I signalled with my handkerchief. I waved it wildly, but could not see that I had attracted attention. Despair almost seized me. Then I thought that my signal might be too small to be seen, so I tore off my shirt, tied the sleeves to a stick and waved it. The ship was headed to the west when I first saw her. My signals were again unheeded. On she went without noticing me. Despair filled my mind. Then I began to look about for material for a raft. Up and down the beach I ran like a wild man.

I attempted to lift logs that fifty men could not have carried into the water. Again exhausted, I stopped, staggered and fell. I must have fainted from hunger, thirst and exhaustion. When my senses returned, after a few moments, I sought the shade, and soon felt more myself. My heart leaped when I saw that the United States ship had turned in its patrol duty and was now coming back toward me. Running to where I had dropped my shirt, I again hoisted my signal of distress.

Once more she passed about two miles offshore. This time I did not waste energy in a wild endeavor to throw the forest into the sea. I rested a few minutes and went back into the country about a mile for water. Much refreshed by the few swallows I secured, I went again to the coast.

There was my ship, and I signalled again. This time my signals were seen. She stopped and, thank God, was lowering a boat. The boat came in with a flag of truce flying, and when near enough Lieut. A. C. Almy, who said he was from the U.S.S. Wilmington, asked me who I was and what I wanted.

I told him that I was a correspondent for the New York World, who had been in Havana since April 13, and that I was trying to get back where I could communicate with my paper.

Lieut. Almy ordered his men to pull in close to the breakers and I waded to my waist. The jackies grabbed me and hauled me into the boat. Her bow was already pointed to sea, and in ten minutes I was on board the Wilmington. I was hardly able to stand. Capt. Todd and his men could not do too much for me. I shall ever remember their many kindnesses.

[ADMIRAL SAMPSON SENDS FOR MR. THRALL.]

I remained on board the Wilmington the night of May 3. The next morning the flagship signalled the Wilmington to put on board the Leyden, which was to transfer me to the flagship New York, as Rear-Admiral Sampson wanted to see me. The World's tug Triton was coming alongside to take me off and carry me to Key West, but the Wilmington obeyed orders, ran to the Leyden and put me on board that vessel.

At this moment the New York signalled the Wilmington to protect the landing of the Leyden's cargo on the Cuban coast. We started for the point where the cargo was to be put ashore. While there I again heard the scream of the Spanish bullets. After the skirmish, and when the Spaniards were in retreat, I went on shore and found a lot of my friends among the Cuban forces. When we went offshore the Leyden, in pursuance of her orders, put me on the flagship. After the capture of the Lafayette we ran to this port.

Sylvester Scovel has already sent to The World a story of our meeting on the coast of Cuba on April 22. After bidding him farewell I went with my insurgent guard back to the camp at Mosquito, three miles in the country. That afternoon Col. Delgado gave me a guard to accompany me to Evstions, in the suburbs of Havana.

I reached Havana proper that night. On the train from Marinao I first heard that the American fleet was off Havana. When I reached the city crowds were running about the streets in a state of frenzy. Women were wringing their hands and calling upon the saints to save them. Children clung to their skirts, wild with fright and terror of incomprehensible dangers that beset them.

Jumping into a coach, I went to the vicinity of the short batteries in the neighborhood of the Reina Battery. Everything was in confusion — not a single thing in readiness. Havana could have been taken at that moment without a struggle.

[WILD FLIGHT OF PEOPLE FROM HAVANA.]

After that quiet was restored, and next day every man inhabitant in the city who could be impressed was set at work in batteries and defenses. All theatres and places of amusement closed their doors. Everybody that had ready money took passage on foreign ships that were in the harbor.

Gelats, the banker, paid $9,000 for passage for himself and family to Bermuda. After I had been about the city and had got what I considered sufficient information I started out for the rendezvous appointed by The World's correspondent. I discovered that a reward of $2,000 had been offered for my capture. The authorities had searched Regla for me, understanding that I had returned with an expedition. This added somewhat to the difficulty of getting out of the city.

But it was necessary that I should cross the bay to Regla, there secure my guide, and start for the appointed place on the coast east of Morro. I was well known in Havana, and naturally had to disguise myself.

Dressed as a farmer and with a clean-shaven face I walked down the sloping streets of Havana to the boat landing at Paula. Picking up one of the harbor boats I sailed across the bay to the Regla shore. I had a friend with me. We met our guide and tramped through Regla on the way to Guanabacoa.

About one mile out of Regla we questioned our guide as to how we should break through military lines. He said the only way he knew of was to march boldly by the guards' house. We let him go back and went straight through Guanabacoa. On the outskirts the guard stopped us. We told him that we did not want to go through the lines, but that we were merely waiting for some people coming in from the country.

We waited until the sergeant of the guard went into the house, when we began talking to the soldiers. Watching our chance, in about half an hour we made a run for it, expecting every minute to hear the firing begin and the whistle of the rifle balls.

From there we made our way through the brush about eight

miles to a point on the coast, arriving there about 9 o'clock at night. On reaching the coast we saw a boat three miles further east making signals to us. We answered, but were not seen. So we stayed there until 4 o'clock in the morning.

Our sufferings were horrible. We had walked fifteen miles without a drop of water. We tried to make ourselves seen. No answer came, and just before daylight we decided that we must make our way back. Some of the intrenchments at Cojima could be seen outlined against the western sky. We crept up under the banks of the fortifications and lay there until daylight. We found a line of intrenchments all around Cojima and about 5,000 regular troops in the town.

[TAKES NOTES OF THE FORTIFICATIONS.]

When I got back into Havana I found they were taking the guns out of the Alfonso XII. They could not get her boilers repaired, so they took her heavy battery of 6-inch guns and mounted them on shore.

I hung about the fortifications from La Punta to Vedado all that day. They mounting a new battery on La Punta of two 6-inch breech-loading rifles.

On all the other batteries large forces of men were at work piling up sand in front of the emplacement. In constant danger of discovery, I knew that my life was not worth much if once the military authorities picked me up. They suspected I was in Havana, as was evidenced by the reward offered.

A second rendezvous had been appointed for me April 29. I started again to the eastward. This time I avoided the towns. I went across the bay again in a small boat and started for the open country, at a point where there were no houses. I went right up to the Cojima road, crossing the road at a point midway between Cojima and Guanabacoa. Beyond the road I had to break through the line of forts which are located more than 2,000 feet apart with a sentry box between. There I made a run for it. The soldiers saw me and opened fire, but did not pursue me.

Running at the top of my speed, I seemed to feel a stimulus each time a bullet whistled by or started up a little cloud of dust as it struck the ground. Out of breath and distressed with the violence of my exertions, I finally reached the brush. I glanced back from this concealment at the Spanish soldiers who did not know how close they came to getting $2,000 reward for my capture.

After about a mile and a half in the jungle, I found a barricade blocking the trail. Thinking there must be some soldiers behind it, I crawled forward a hundred yards on my hands and knees, and, getting up on my feet, I came face to face with a sentry, who was not fifty yards away.

[ASTONISHED THE SPANISH GUARD.]

His astonishment was evidently as great as mine. I thought the game was up, but had no thought of surrendering. Without arms I could not attack him and I had to take to my heels. Three times that Spaniard fired at me. He must have been nervous, for I got away without a scratch. I started for the coast through the brush in a northeasterly direction and struck the coast about 4 o'clock.

I waited in hiding all night, hoping for The World's despatch boat. No boats appeared near shore. Straining my eyes all night out over the heaving waters I could see nothing. I knew that I had not been deserted and knew that efforts were being made to find me. Surely they must succeed.

But luck or fate was against me. My signals were unseen. I knew that as daylight approached I must again get back to Havana. I made a long detour and went back again through Guanabacoa and Regla, reaching Havana about 3 o'clock on the afternoon of 1st Saturday. There was nothing for me to do but to carry out the mission which took me into the enemy's fortified city.

Until May 3 I walked about the city, noting every point about which information may be of benefit to my country when her forces are called upon to make an attack on the town. The story of my third trip to the coast and rescue had already been told.

The distress in Havana is already severe. Food and clothing sent there by the Americans for the relief of the reconcentrados have been appropriated by the Spaniards, and not a particle of them will ever reach those for whom they were intended.

Charles H. Thrall.

❖   ❖   ❖

STEPHEN CRANE'S PEN PICTURE
OF C. H. THRALL.

KEY WEST, May 7. — Charles H. Thrall is a graduate of Yale and has for years represented extensive American manufacturing interests in Cuba. We had been hearing a good deal about Thrall for a

Reprinted here from New York World: 8 May 1898.

long time. Everybody was aware of his immensely precarious situation, and everybody heaved a sigh of relief when he at last was known to be safe on board one of the American warships.

Dressed in the universal linen or duck and with a straw hat on the back of his head, Thrall differs little from a certain good type of young American manhood. The striking thing about him now is his eyes. The expression of them will doubtless change as he breathes more of the peace of the American side, but at present they are peculiarly wide open as if strained with watching. They stare at you and do not seem to think, and at the corners the lids are wrinkled as if from long pain. This is the impress of his hazardous situation still upon him. As for his own deeds, he talks as little and wants to talk as little as most intrepid men.

Ask him of the situation in Havana, however, and he is eager at once. He says that the first day of the blockade brought tremendous confusion to Havana. Even in the batteries everything was pell-mell. In the city white-faced people thronged the streets.

"Oh! they are going to open fire! they are going to open fire!"

On the second day the populace was calmed mainly because they were sleepy. They had been up all the previous night. On the third day almost everybody who went upon the streets was rounded up and put to work upon the fortifications. They were paid $2 a day. As the days passed on and no bombardment ensued the spirit of the populace changed.

They decided that the fleet was afraid. When Thrall left, they were feeling very gay and content. It was also reported in Havana that the Spanish fleet had whaled the life of Admiral Dewey's squadron in the East. Blanco is daily issuing proclamations about this thing and that thing. He issued one calling upon the insurgents to enlist in the Spanish army under the command of the traitor chieftan, Juan Parra. Thrall says that as far as he knows, no aspirants for this distinction have appeared.

The 2d of May being a great patriotic fete day among all Spaniards, the people in Havana were certain that the American fleet would attack on that day, and they were looking for it. They had a gambler's confidence in winning any game if it was played on their lucky day. Thrall's story of the American Major, W. D. Smith, who was arrested as a spy in Havana recently, will doubtless remain all that can be told of one of the melancholy and mysterious chapters of the war.

The man must be dead by this time.

HAYTI AND SAN DOMINGO FAVOR
THE UNITED STATES.

PORTO PLATA. San Domingo.[1] May 15. — Opinion and the direction of sympathy in the island of Hayti might at this time be of particular interest, since Hayti's proximity to Cuba and Porto Rico has rendered a singular experience of the Spanish and his ways.

The World's despatch boat, the Three Friends, was in Cape Haytien yesterday. Cape Haytien[2] is the northern port of the republic of Hayti. It is situated at the side of a wide and deep roadstead, while splendid green mountains rise directly from its suburbs. It has the miscellaneous quality of all seaport towns. Among its population are negroes from every part of the West Indies.[3] It is, in fact, a kind of eddy which has caught driftwood from every imaginable quarter of this vast collection of islands. Most of the people speak English, French and Spanish.

Everybody was found to be talking of nothing else but the war between America and Spain. The French cable company was issuing daily bulletins, very absurd, usually in detail and quite pro-Spanish, which were eagerly consumed by the people.

When inquiries were made as to their sympathies they were not backward in declaring their position. It was found that in the little but decidedly influential colony of foreign merchants the French and the Germans were all openly rooting for Spain. They liked Spain, they said; they did not like the United States and, anyhow, they were certain that the Spanish squadrons would surely down Admiral Sampson's ships.

There was one venerable Frenchman, perhaps the doyen[4] of the corps of foreign merchants, who positively refused to believe even then that Dewey had been victorious at Manila. We gently offered him such familiar information as we possessed, but he shook his old gray head in derision and scorn.

Reprinted here for the first time from New York World: *24 May 1898.*

1. At this time Porto Plata (Puerto Plata) was a town of about 5,000. Haiti and Santo Domingo make up the island of Hispaniola. Santo Domingo is now known as the Dominican Republic.
2. Or Cap Haitien, population about 29,000.
3. In 1905, an ecclesiastical census established the population of Haiti at about 1,400,000, nearly all Negroes or mulattoes. In fact, scarcely more than 200 Europeans lived in the country.
4. That is, the senior or oldest member; the dean.

"All lies!" he said. "All lies by this — what you call? — damn tele-graph."

[ENGLISHMEN OUR FRIENDS.]

It was another matter with the handful of Englishmen. They were completely American in feeling. One could not distinguish between them and the born Americans. As an addition, there was the captain of a Nova Scotian bark, who had nothing on his ship from a foretop-sail to a drink that was not the property of any American that chose to ask for it.

The natives, drooping about the dirty, sun-smitten streets, would have no basis of information upon which to form an opinion if it were not for the comings, goings, all the changes which take place amid a semi-maritime population. Thus have they been brought into direct relations with the Spaniard. They hate him. A negro merchant said to me:

"The history of Spain is the history of cruelty."

This same merchant has many friends in Havana, and recently when a rumor was current there that the American fleet was off Cape Haytien, bound eastward, his friends cabled him for information. He answered deceptively. He explained yesterday that really it was not any of his business, but he could not bring himself to do anything which might even indirectly be of service to any part of the Spanish cause.

[SOME WHO FEAR US.]

This is largely representative of the feeling of the people, but there is also a party who will look without satisfaction upon a com-plete success of the American arms. They say: "If Cuba and Porto Rico go it will probably be our turn after a while, eh?" They feel that the signal for the expansion of the giant republic is also a signal of certain danger to their integrity as an independent nation. This senti-ment seemingly inspires the Haytien army, as much as that weirdly absurd institution can be inspired by anything. The negro soldiers think chiefly of bread, bananas and rum, but they have somehow had it gimleted into their skulls that the Americans menace their country. Yesterday one of The World correspondents casually was examining the gun-rack in the town's guard-room. The weapons were old Reming-tons of 1865, and the correspondent was interested in them mainly as antiques. He did not notice the glowering soldiers, and turned pres-ently to ask how many men formed the garrison of Cape Haytien. The soldier to whom this question was addressed stared angrily at the correspondent, spat on the ground and, throwing his arm out in a defiant gesture, said: "Plenty! plenty!" The correspondent was then able to perceive that he had been taken for an American committee of investigation.

[WORLD BOAT CHEERED AT PORTO PLATA.]

Here at Porto Plata, in the sister republic of San Domingo, one finds the same condition of feeling, with a higher exponent of intelligence. San Domingo is always mental superior of Hayti. Porto Plata has been largely under Spanish influence, but little of it now remains beyond the language. As the Three Friends steamed in to her anchorage this morning a crowd of people gathered on the green headland that shields the little cove and cheered the famous tug as if she were really the Campania. Flags and handkerchiefs fluttered from every fist. There is a considerable Cuban colony here, and only the requirements of journalism prevent us from being feted to-night by an enthusiastic populace, with a band and a dinner and all other modern excitements.

As in Cape Haytien, the group of French and German merchants is pro-Spanish. Moreover, the British Consul[5] has a Spanish wife, and this fact seems to prevent him from getting facts into any kind of perspective. But the natives are for us. They see in the destiny of the United States a destiny for themselves. They want to be let alone, but they want to follow the great republic in the making of a western world which will one day outshine the old civilization of the East. The citizen of San Domingo is a good deal of a man. He has not too much of the jealousy and suspicion that corrodes and perverts the Haytien; he is able to grasp modernity and apply it. He has distinctive ideas about sewage. There is not a town in a Spanish colony so clean, bright, cheering in every way, as this Porto Plata. And, mark you, as soon as a tropical town becomes clean its intelligence can be rated as of superior excellence.

In short, then, we find the French and Germans invariably against us; the English and the natives almost invariably with us, and the more clean and modern the people the more they favor us.

5. The English Vice-Consul in Porto Plata was one Charles McGrigor.

NARROW ESCAPE OF THE THREE FRIENDS.

Key West, May 20.

Exceeding industry on the part of the naval commanders of the Cuban blockading fleet causes life in the service of newspapers to be full of interest.

More than one despatch boat flying the pennant of a newspaper has been held up at midnight by shells that had every serious intention, but it remained for The World's tug Three Friends to hold an interview last night with the United States gunboat Machias[1] which probably climaxes the situation.

We were all greatly entertained over an immediate prospect of being either killed by rapid-fire guns, cut in half by the ram or merely drowned, but we do not now anticipate that a longing for diversion will cause us to seek the vicinity of the Machias on a dark night for some months.

We had sailed from Key West on a mission that had nothing to do with the coast of Cuba, and that night, steaming due east and some thirty-five miles from the coast, we did not think we were liable to an affair with any of the fierce American cruisers.

Suddenly a familiar signal of red and white lights flashed like a brooch of jewels on the pall that covered the sea. It was far away and tiny. Answering lanterns sprang at once to the masthead of the Three Friends. The warship's signals vanished and the sea presented nothing but a smoky black stretch, lit with the hissing white tops of the flying waves. A thin line of flame swept from a gun. Thereafter followed one of those silences which have become so peculiarly instructive to the blockade-runner. Somewhere in the darkness we knew that a slate-colored cruiser, red below the water-line and with a gold scroll on her bows, was flying over the waves toward us, and a time was approaching when our identity had to be bawled across the wind and made clear to the warship in a blamed sight less than seventeen parts of a second if we didn't care to be smashed instantly into smithereens.

The pause was long. Then a voice spoke from the sea through a megaphone. It was faint, but clear. "What ship is that?"

"The World tug Three Friends," thundered the first mate. No one

---

Reprinted here for the first time from New York World: *29 May 1898. Subhead reads: "A Story of the Week by Stephen Crane."*

1. Tonnage (displacement): 1,177; length: 204 feet; speed: 15.4 knots; principal armament: eight 4-inch guns. It had a shallow draft of only twelve feet. The ship was named for the city of Machias, Maine.

hesitates over his answer in cases of this kind. Everybody was desirous of imparting the fullest information in the shortest possible time. We wished for one of the flaming electric signs of upper Broadway.

There was another pause. Then out of the darkness flew an American cruiser, silent as death, handled as ferociously as if the devil commanded her. Again the little voice hailed from the bridge: "What ship is that?" Evidently the reply to the first hail had been misunderstood or not heard. This time the voice rang with menace — menace of destruction — and the last word was intoned savagely and strangely, as one would explain that the cruiser was after either fools or the common enemy.

The yells in return did not stop her; she was hurling herself forward to ram us amidships, and the people on the little Three Friends looked at a tall, swooping bow, and it was keener than any knife that has ever been made. As the cruiser lunged every man imagined the gallant and famous Three Friends cut into two parts as neatly as if she had been cheese.

But of course there was a sheer, and a hard sheer, to starboard, and toward our quarter swung a monstrous thing, larger than any ship in the world — the U.S.S. Machias. She had a freeboard of about three hundred feet, and the top of her funnel was out of sight in the clouds. No living man has ever seen so big a ship as was the Machias last night. No living man has seen anything so sharp as her ram. And at a range of twenty paces every gun on her port side swept deliberately into perfect aim.

We all had an opportunity of looking several miles down the muzzles of this festive artillery before came the inevitable collision.

Then the Machias reeled her steel shoulder against the wooden side of the Three Friends, and up went a roar as if a vast shingle roof had fallen. The tug staggered, dipped as if she meant to pass under the warship, and finally righted, trembling from head to foot. The cries of the splintered timbers ceased. Men on the tug found time to say: "Well, I'll be —— ——." The Machias backed away into the darkness even as the Three Friends drew slowly ahead.

Later, from some hidden part of the sea, the bullish eye of a searchlight looked at us and the widened white rays bathed us in light.

Then there was another hail.

"Hello, Three Friends!"

"Aye, aye."

"Are you injured?"

"No, sir."

The incident was closed, but it had impressed us. The worst or the best of it was that when the Three Friends had met the Machias last before this terrific, bloodthirsty charge — it was late one afternoon off Cardenas — we had received this plaintive hail:

"Have you any onions, potatoes or eggs?" The gunboat had been on station for three weeks. Forthwith we had patriotically given up our last spud to the country's defenders. These, then, were the ungrateful people who came at us with such dangerous fury. We wanted to demand the return of our potatoes.

But, after all, this one thing is certain. If we had been a Spanish gunboat there would not have been enough left of us to patch a tooth. This is the satisfaction we gain from our short interview with that fiery, blood-curdling crowd on the United States gunboat Machias.

✿　✿　✿

FIRST AMERICAN NEWSPAPER TO OPEN HEADQUARTERS ON CUBAN SOIL IS THE WORLD.

MOLE ST. NICHOLAS, Hayti, June 19. — The New York World is the first newspaper to establish permanent headquarters on Cuban soil. This has been done almost under the guns of Santiago's forts. It was accomplished last Friday,[1] when Sylvester Scovel,[2] Stephen Crane, and Alex. Kenealy, of the World staff of correspondents, landed at Cuero, thirteen miles west of Santiago.

The correspondents, with attendants, signalling apparatus and two horses, were taken to Cuero on the despatch boat Triton. After landing a third horse was purchased from a native. A camp has been set up, over which float the Cuban flag, with The World's banner. From this point constant communication will be kept up by couriers with the Cuban army that guards the mountain passes and

---

Reprinted here for the first time from New York World: *20 June 1898. The* World's *correspondent for this article — unidentified — is not Crane. It was most likely Alexander Kenealy.*

1. June 17.

2. Sylvester Scovel of the New York *World*. "He had won his laurels in the field with Máximo Gómez and the Cuban insurgent forces as a correspondent of the most remarkable bravery, dash, and resourcefulness, taking his life in his hands and succeeding where others had failed. He had been imprisoned by order of the Spanish Captain-General [Blanco] and sentenced to be shot. The protests of the American Government saved him and he had rejoined the insurgents. His nerve and audacity were proof against dismay." Ralph D. Paine in *Roads of Adventure* (1922).

approaches to Santiago, and by despatch boats to the fleet and the nearest cable stations.

The country about is nearly all in the hands of the Cubans, but there are daily incursions by foraging parties of Spanish soldiers, and skirmishes are very frequent. Before the correspondents landed from the Triton a Cuban boat was seen putting out from the shore. Suddenly a horseman galloped down the beach and made signals to the boat, which returned and brought him off to the Triton. He proved to be Col. Hernandez, of the Cuban army, who had landed at Banes and had been pursued by Spaniards. He was made welcome and gave much valuable information, which was forwarded to Admiral Sampson.

After the World camp had been gotten in shape Messrs. Scovel and Crane started up into the mountains, with an escort of Cuban soldiers, to get a view of the harbor of Santiago, where Cervera's warships are anchored. They obtained information which Admiral Sampson particularly wanted. They will be taken on the despatch boat Three Friends to-morrow[3] to the flagship and report. The Three Friends will call at the camp at stated intervals for news, which will be hurried to the nearest cable office. The advantage of this enterprise in news gathering, both to World readers and the naval and military authorities, cannot be over-estimated.

❋   ❋   ❋

CRANE TELLS THE STORY
OF THE DISEMBARKMENT.

DAIQUIRI, June 22, 5:10 P. M. — Ten minutes ago the great crowd of soldiers working at the landing — the troops filing off through the scrub, the white duck jack tars in the speeding launches and cutters,

3. June 20.

Reprinted here for the first time from New York World: 7 July 1898.

This dispatch was not published until July 7, and on the same page the World (infra, p. 154) also published "Stephen Crane at the Front for the World," which was filed at Siboney on June 24.

Our sequence for Crane dispatches adheres — with some exceptions — to the filed dispatch dates rather than to the sequence of publication dates.

the ragged Cuban infantry — all burst into a great cheer that swelled and rolled against the green hills until your heart beat loudly with the thrill of it. The sea, thronged with transports and cruisers, was suddenly ringing with the noise of steam whistles from the deep sea-lion roar of the great steamers to the wild screams of the launches. For on a high plateau overlooking this hamlet was silhouetted a band of men and a flagstaff. One man was hauling upon some halyards, slowly raising to the eager eyes of thousands of men the Stars and Stripes, symbol that our foot is firmly and formidably planted.

[DIFFICULT WORK.]

Since this morning troops have been landing, boat after boat. About a hundred yards back from the beach the companies are formed and then marched off to the westward, disappearing amid the trees. A ceaseless groundswell makes the handling of the boats at the dock a difficult matter, but the blue-jackets from the warships work hard and patiently, to and fro, to and fro. The job seems endless. Sometimes boats get in the breakers and fill, then there is more labor for the jackies. But they say nothing. In fact, it is a day of universal back-breaking work, but on the plateau floats the flag. That is enough.

The Cubans — those who are not out on far out-post duty — stand looking, looking, looking. They stand in their tatters, brown bodies sticking out of a collection of rags, and survey what is to them an endless string of men. The Second Massachusetts[1] is all ashore and moved out. The regulars come fast. To some unoccupied squads an insurgent points out many sacks of cocoanuts left by the Spaniards. Whoop! The way in which the regulars fall upon this loot is a marvel. Instantly every man in sight is eating pieces of white cocoanut. The insurgents chop the fruit with their machetes for their friends. An ambitious private desires two cocoanuts. He hauls out a handful of silver and begins to pantomime at a Cuban. The man shakes his head. He signifies that the American can have two cocoanuts — yes. But buy them — no.

[ANXIOUS CUBANS.]

In one of the cottages on the slope Gen. Castillo[2] has his head-quarters, where men gallop every five minutes with reports from here, there and everywhere where the vigilant Cubans are scouting. It is reported that the Spaniards have already retreated some miles. Not

1. The Second Massachusetts Volunteers, Colonel E. P. Clark commanding, 1st Brigade, 2d Division; they were one of two volunteer infantry units landed at Siboney, the other being the 71st New York.

2. General Demetrio Castillo, serving under General Calixto Garcia, commanding the Cuban forces.

a shot has yet been fired. The men act as if they were still at Tampa; there is no excitement, no nerves. The regulars are businesslike and extremely placid. Gen. Norton,[3] tall and gray, has gone forward to arrange his lines. Meanwhile the flames from a burning blockhouse sends gusts of intense heat down the slope. In the shops which the Spaniards had fired stands a Baldwin locomotive so gray with ashes that it seems like a ghost. Out into the cove sweeps a long, high iron dock for loading iron ore.[4] It is American property and is untouched by American shells. The Spaniards were evidently in too much of a hurry to harm it. In the yard of one of the houses of the village lies an overturned bathtub. A Cuban officer has hastily explained that it must have belonged to one of the Americans when the company was operating. The Spaniards, he remarked, really have no use for bath tubs. They use powder, one layer over another.

The men from the ships are hungry for news from New York and Washington. They demand it of the correspondents, not knowing that most of us have been far longer without news from New York and Washington than any soldier of them all. Then they ask innumerable questions about the Spaniards. Are they hard fighters, do we think? Can they shoot straight? How long can Santiago hold out? Are the Spanish ships really in the harbor? Where is the Vizcaya?[5] How about the marines at Guantanamo?

[AN EXCITING NIGHT.]

Bugles sound the assembly. Men hurry off to join their companies. Sergeants come looking for stragglers. And still the boatloads continue

3. Brigadier General Henry W. Lawton, commanding 2d Division, V Corps. The dispatch incorrectly reads "Norton" for "Lawton."

4. Prior to the invasion, Daiquiri, a minor landing point on the coast east of Santiago, was connected by a narrow-gauge railroad with Vinente and outlying mines in the area.

5. The *Vizcaya* was captained by Don Antonio Eulate, who was subsequently blown overboard in battle. "Watterlogged, wounded, and menaced by sharks, he was hauled aboard the *Iowa*. The *Iowa*'s guard presented arms, and the ham in Don Antonio sprang to life. Straightening slowly, he unbuckled his sword-belt, kissed the hilt, and offered it to Capt. Robley Evans with a charming bow. Naturally it was refused. The don then turned seaward and extended a hand toward his sinking ship. 'Adios, Vizcaya!' he cried brokenly. At that moment the *Vizcaya*, with a superb sense of timing, vanished in a blossom of flame." From William Manchester's "The Spanish American War," *Holiday*, 30 (September 1961).

The *Vizcaya*, after hauling down her colors and going aground burning, exploded, and as she exploded the USS *Texas* raced past her with her crew giving a victorious shout. But Captain Jack Philip quickly silenced it: "Don't cheer, men; those poor devils are dying."

to come. A barge loaded with bags of something is being warped into the dock. The formidable craft is in command of a man with a rasping voice, who jaws away loudly and incessantly.

At last it has happened. A boat has been overturned. Men of the Tenth Cavalry,[6] tied in blanket rolls and weighty cartridge belts, are in the water. It is horrible to think of them clasped in the arms of their heavy accoutrements. Wild excitement reigns on the pierhead; lines are flung; men try to reach down to the water; overboard from launches and cutters go blue-jackets, gallant blue-jackets, while over all the hubbub tears the sound of that same rasping voice, screaming senselessly to do this and do that. * * * Well, two of them are gone — killed on the doorstep of Cuba, drowned a moment before they could set foot on that island which had been the subject of their soldierly dreams.

Dusk calls out the crimson glare of the burning shops in the ruins of which stands the ghostly locomotive. The Cuban soldiers have occupied the houses of the village, and as they gather around their camp-fires some of them sing native melodies — weird, half-savage airs — accompanied by the booming of improvised drums. Night has come; a search-light flashes pallidly over the foliage, throwing into gleaming relief the myriad leaves.

THE RED BADGE OF COURAGE WAS HIS WIG-WAG FLAG

GUANTANAMO CAMP, June 22. — It has become known that Captain Elliott's[1] expedition against the guerillas was more successful

6. A regular U.S. Army unit, the Tenth Cavalry, a Negro regiment, was commanded by Major Stevens T. Norvell and was a part of the 2d Brigade, Cavalry Division, commanded by Major General Joseph Wheeler, ex-Confederate cavalry general.

Reprinted here for the first time from New York World: 1 July 1898.

1. George Frank Elliott (1846–1931); at the time of this foray he was fifty-two years old. Already his participation in the skirmish on June 11 was to advance him three numbers in grade for "eminent and conspicuous conduct." His subsequent career was just as brilliant and meteoric in rapid promotion. He served in the Philippines 1899–1900 and commanded the Marines at Novaleta (8 October 1899). His last field action was as commanding officer of the expeditionary brigade of Marines in Panama (1903–1904). During these four years he rose from major (1899) to brigadier

than any one could imagine at the time. The enemy was badly routed, but we expected him to recover in a few days, perhaps, and come back to renew his night attacks. But the firing of a shot near the camp has been a wonderfully rare thing since our advance and attack.

Inasmuch as this affair was the first serious engagement of our troops on Cuban soil, a few details of it may be of interest.

It was known that this large guerilla band had its headquarters some five miles back from our camp, at a point near the seacoast, where was located the only well, according to the Cubans, within four or five leagues of our position.[2] Capt. Elliott asked permission to take 200 marines and some Cubans to drive the enemy from the well and destroy it. Col. Huntington[3] granted this request, and it was my good fortune to get leave to accompany it.

After breakfast one morning the companies of Capt. Elliott and Capt. Spicer[4] were formed on the sandy path below the fortified camp, while the Cubans, fifty in number, were bustling noisily into some kind of shape. Most of the latter were dressed in the white duck clothes of the American jack-tar, which had been dealt out to them from the stores of the fleet. Some had shoes on their feet and some had shoes slung around their necks with a string, all according to taste. They were a hard-bitten, undersized lot, most of them negroes, and with the stoop and curious gait of men who had at one time labored at the soil. They were, in short, peasants — hardy, tireless, uncomplaining peasants — and they viewed in utter calm these early morning preparations for battle.

---

general (1903), when he was named commandant. He gained promotion to major general in 1908.

At Guantanamo Captain Elliott commanded Company "C." He figures in Crane's dispatch "Marines Signalling Under Fire at Guantanamo" (*infra*, p. 148), and so do Lt. Lucas and Col. Huntington.

2. The Spanish well was almost directly south, roughly two miles distance across country, from the Marines' position. It was situated on a trail that skirted the coast and at the bottom of a small valley surrounded on three sides by the steep Cuzco Hills, ranging up to some 350 feet in height.

A league is approximately three miles; thus the nearest water supply, excepting the well, was twelve to fifteen miles distance.

3. Lieutenant Colonel Robert W. Huntington commanded the First Battalion of Marines at Guantanamo. His career was nearing the end. He entered service on 5 June 1861. Less than two months after the Guantanamo affair, he was promoted colonel, his highest rank. He retired in 1900 and died 3 November 1917.

4. William F. Spicer was a veteran of sixteen years' service with the Corps; he had been a captain for six of them.

And also they viewed with the same calm the attempts of their ambitious officers to make them bear some resemblance to soldiers at "order arms." The officers had an idea that their men must drill the same as marines, and they howled over it a good deal. The men had to be adjusted one by one at the expense of considerable physical effort, but when once in place they viewed their new position with unalterable stolidty. Order arms? Oh, very well. What does it matter?

Further on the two companies of marines were going through a short, sharp inspection. Their linen suits and black corded accoutrements made their strong figures very business-like and soldierly. Contrary to the Cubans, the bronze faces of the Americans were not stolid at all. One could note the prevalence of a curious expression — something dreamy, the symbol of minds striving to tear aside the screen of the future and perhaps expose the ambush of death. It was not fear in the least. It was simply a moment in the lives of men who have staked themselves and have come to wonder which wins — red or black?

And glancing along that fine, silent rank at faces grown intimate through the association of four days and nights of almost constant fighting, it was impossible not to fall into deepest sympathy with this mood and wonder as to the dash and death there would presently be on the other side of those hills — those mysterious hills not far away, placidly in the sunlight veiling the scene of somebody's last gasp. And then the time. It was now 7 o'clock. What about 8 o'clock? Nine o'clock? Little absurd indications of time, redolent of coffee, steak, porridge, or what you like, emblems of the departure of trains for Yonkers, Newark, N. J., or anywhere — these indications of time now were sinister, sombre with the shadows of certain tragedy, not the tragedy of a street accident, but foreseen, inexorable, invincible tragedy.

Meanwhile the officers were thinking of business; their voices rang out.

The sailor-clad Cubans moved slowly off on a narrow path through the bushes, and presently the long brown line of marines followed them.

After the ascent of a chalky cliff, the camp on the hill, the ships in the harbor were all hidden by the bush we entered, a thick, tangled mass, penetrated by a winding path hardly wide enough for one man.

No word was spoken; one could only hear the dull trample of the men, mingling with the near and far drooning of insects raising their tiny voices under the blazing sky. From time to time in an hour's march we passed pickets of Cubans, poised with their rifles, scanning the woods with unchanging stares. They did not turn their heads as we passed them. They seemed like stone men.

The country at last grew clearer. We passed a stone house knocked to flinders by a Yankee gunboat some days previously, when it had been evacuated helter skelter by its little Spanish garrison. Tall, gaunt ridges covered with chaparral[5] and cactus shouldered down to the sea, and on the spaces of bottom-land were palms and dry yellow grass. A halt was made to give the Cuban scouts more time; the Cuban colonel,[6] revolver in one hand, machete in the other, waited their report before advancing.

Finally the word was given. The men arose from the grass and moved on around the foot of the ridges. Out at sea the Dolphin[7] was steaming along slowly. Presently the word was passed that the enemy were over the next ridge. Lieut. Lucas[8] had meantime been sent with the first platoon of Company C to keep the hills as the main body moved around them and we could now see his force and some Cubans crawling slowly up the last ridge.

The main body was moving over a lower part of this ridge when the firing broke out. It needs little practice to tell the difference in sound between the Lee[9] and the Mauser. The Lee says "Prut!" It is a fine note, not very metallic. The Mauser says "Pop!" — plainly and frankly pop, like a soda-water bottle being opened close to the ear. We could hear both sounds now in great plenty. Prut — prut — pr-r-r-rut — pr-rut! Pop — pop — poppetty — pop!

It was very evident that our men had come upon the enemy and were slugging away for all they were worth, while the Spaniards were

5. Thick shrubbery and thorny bush.

6. Lieutenant Colonel Enrique Tomás.

7. While the *Dolphin* shelled the shore, Crane with the Marines was on the coast. USS *Dolphin* (1884) was a steel Navy dispatch boat, with a three-masted schooner rig; tonnage (displacement): 1,486; length: 240 feet; speed: 15.5 knots; principal armament: three 4-inch guns.

8. First Lieutenant Lewis Clarke Lucas was platoon leader of Company "C," 1st Battalion. A graduate of the U.S. Naval Academy in 1889, he was appointed second lieutenant in 1891 and promoted first lieutenant in 1892.

9. The Winchester-Lee rifle, adopted by the Navy in the mid-1890's, was regarded as one of the best small arms in existence, especially after its performance at Guantanamo, its first trial in actual combat. It was a bolt-action, straight-pull rifle, caliber .236; its magazine held five lightweight (168 grains) cartridges, each man carrying 180 rounds. Particular advantages of the weapon were its high muzzle velocity (2,400 feet per second) and its penetrating power; for example, in a test it was found that the bullet penetrated sixty-two inches into hard pine from a distance of five feet.

Except for minor differences, the Spanish Mauser was the same as that carried by the Turks in the Greco-Turkish War.

pegging away to the limit. To the tune of this furious shooting Capt. Elliott with Lieut. Bannon's[10] platoon of C Company scrambled madly up the hill, tearing themselves on the cactus and fighting their way through the mesquite. To the left we could see that Capt. Spicer's men had rapidly closed up and were racing us.

As we swung up the crest we did not come upon Lucas and his men as we expected. He was on the next ridge, or rather this ridge was double-backed, being connected by a short transverse. But we came upon Mauser bullets in considerable numbers. They sang in the air until one thought that a good hand with a lacrosse stick could have bagged many.

Now the sound made by a bullet is a favorite subject for afternoon discussion, and it has been settled in many ways by many and eminent authorities. Some say bullets whistle. Bullets do not whistle, or rather the modern bullet does not whistle. The old-fashioned lead missile certainly did toot, and does toot, like a boy coming home from school; but the modern steel affair has nothing in common with it.

These Mauser projectiles sounded as if one string of a most delicate musical instrument had been touched by the wind into a long faint note, or that overhead some one had swiftly swung a long, thin-lashed whip. The men stooped as they ran to join Lucas.

Our fighting line was in plain view about one hundred yards away. The brown-clad marines and the white-clad Cubans were mingled in line on the crest. Some were flat, some were kneeling, some were erect. The marines were silent; the Cubans were cursing shrilly. There was no smoke; everything could be seen but the enemy, who was presumably below the hill in force.

It took only three minutes to reach the scene of activity, and, incidentally, the activity was considerable and fierce.

The sky was speckless; the sun blazed out of it as if it would melt the earth. Far away on one side were the white waters of Guantanamo Bay; on the other a vast expanse of blue sea was rippling in millions of wee waves. The surrounding country was nothing but miles upon miles of gaunt, brown ridges. It would have been a fine view if one had had time.

Then along the top of our particular hill, mingled with the cactus and chaparral, was a long, irregular line of men fighting the first part of the first action of the Spanish war. Toiling, sweating marines; shrill, jumping Cubans; officers shouting out the ranges, 200 Lee rifles crashing — these were the essentials. The razor-backed hill seemed to reel with it all.

10. Second Lieutenant Philip M. Bannon, platoon leader of the second platoon, Company "C," under Elliott.

And — mark you — a spruce young sergeant of marines,[11] erect, his back to the showering bullets, solemnly and intently wigwagging to the distant Dolphin!

It was necessary that this man should stand at the very top of the ridge in order that his flag might appear in relief against the sky, and the Spaniards must have concentrated a fire of at least twenty rifles upon him. His society was at that moment sought by none. We gave him a wide berth. Presently into the din came the boom of the Dolphin's guns.

The whole thing was an infernal din. One wanted to clap one's hands to one's ears and cry out in God's name for the noise to cease; it was past bearing. And — look — there fell a Cuban, a great hulking negro, shot just beneath the heart, the blood staining his soiled shirt. He seemed in no pain; it seemed as if he were senseless before he fell. He made no outcry; he simply toppled over, while a comrade made a semi-futile grab at him. Instantly one Cuban loaded the body upon the back of another and then took up the dying man's feet. The procession that moved off resembled a grotesque wheelbarrow. No one heeded it much. A marine remarked: "Well, there goes one of the Cubans."

Under a bush lay a D Company private shot through the ankle. Two comrades were ministering to him. He too did not seem then in pain. His expression was of a man weary, weary, weary.

Marines, drunk from the heat and the fumes of the powder, swung heavily with blazing faces out of the firing line and dropped panting two or three paces to the rear.

And still crashed the Lees and the Mausers, punctuated by the roar of the Dolphin's guns. Along our line the rifle locks were clicking incessantly, as if some giant loom was running wildly, and on the ground among the stones and weeds came dropping, dropping a rain of rolling brass shells. And what was two hundred yards down the hill? No grim array, no serried ranks. Two hundred yards down the hill there was a — a thicket, a thicket whose predominant bush wore large, oily, green leaves. It was about an acre in extent and on level ground, so that its whole expanse was plain from the hills. This thicket was alive with the loud popping of the Mausers. From end to end and from side to side it was alive. What mysterious underbrush! But — there — that was a bit of dirty, white jacket! That was a dodging head! P-r-r-rut!

This terrible exchange of fire lasted a year, or probably it was twenty minutes. Then a strange thing happened. Lieut. Magill [12] had

11. This is Sergeant John H. Quick, U.S.M.C. See, infra, p. 153.

12. Second Lieutenant Louis J. Magill, graduate of the Academy and platoon leader, second platoon, Company "A."

been sent out with forty men from camp to reinforce us. He had come up on our left flank and taken a position there, covering us. The Dolphin swung a little further on and then suddenly turned loose with a fire that went clean over the Spaniards and straight as a die for Magill's position. Magill was immensely anxious to move out and intercept a possible Spanish retreat, but the Dolphin's guns not only held him in check, but made his men hunt cover with great celerity. It was no extraordinary blunder on the part of the Dolphin. It was improbable that the ship's commander[13] should know of the presence of Magill's force, and he did not know from our line of fire that the enemy was in the valley. But at any rate, in the heat and rage of this tight little fight there was a good deal of strong language used on the hill.

Suddenly some one shouted: "There they go! See 'em! See 'em!" Forty rifles rang out. A number of figures had been seen to break from the other side of the thicket. The Spaniards were running.

Now began one of the most extraordinary games ever played in war. The skirmish suddenly turned into something that was like a grim and frightful field sport. It did not appear so then — for many reasons — but when one reflects, it was trap-shooting. The thicket was the trap; the Dolphin marked the line for the marines to toe. Coveys of guerillas got up in bunches of five or six and flew frantically up the opposite hillside.

There were two open spaces which in their terror they did not attempt to avoid. One was 400 yards away, the other was 800. You could see the little figures, like pieces of white paper. At first the whole line of marines and Cubans let go at sight. Soon it was arranged on a system. The Cubans, who cannot hit even the wide, wide world, lapsed into temporary peace, and a line of a score of marines was formed into a firing squad. Sometimes we could see a whole covey vanish miraculously after the volley. It was impossible to tell whether they were all hit, or whether all or part had plunged headlong for cover. Everybody on our side stood up. It was vastly exciting. "There they go! See 'em! See 'em!"

Dr. Gibbs,[14] Sergt.-Major Goode, shot at night by a hidden enemy;

13. Commander Henry W. Lyon, U.S.N., with thirty-six years' service.

14. Acting Assistant Surgeon John Blair Gibbs, U.S.N.R., and Sergeant Charles H. Smith, U.S.M.C., were killed on the night of June 11–12. On Gibbs see, *infra*, p. 000. On the first day of combat, June 11, Crane had chills, and Gibbs gave him some quinine. Some three weeks later Crane had yellow fever and hallucinations. Crane recorded his plight in his "War Memories" — see, *infra*, p. 291.

Dunphy and McColgan,[15] the two lads ambushed and riddled with bullets at ten yards; Sergt. Smith, whose body had to be left temporarily with the enemy — all these men were being terrifically avenged. The marines — raw men who had been harassed and harassed day and night since the first foot struck Cuba — the marines had come out in broad day, met a superior force and in twenty minutes had them panic-stricken and on the gallop. The Spanish commander had had plenty of time to take any position that pleased him, for as we marched out we had heard his scouts heralding our approach with their wood-dove-cooing from hilltop to hilltop. He had chosen the thicket; in twenty minutes the thicket was too hot for his men.

The firing-drill of the marines was splendid. The men reloaded and got up their guns like lightning, but afterward there was always a rock-like beautiful poise as the aim was taken. One noticed it the more on account of the Cubans, who used the Lee as if it were a squirt-gun. The entire function of the lieutenant who commanded them in action was to stand back of the line, frenziedly beat his machete through the air, and with incredible rapidity howl: "Fuego! fuego! fuego! fuego! fuego!" He could not possibly have taken time to breathe during the action. His men were meanwhile screaming the most horrible language in a babble.

As for daring, that is another matter. They paid no heed whatever to the Spaniards' volleys, but simply lashed themselves into a delirium that disdained everything. Looking at them one could hardly imagine that they were the silent, stealthy woodsmen, the splendid scouts of the previous hours.

At last it was over. The dripping marines looked with despair at their empty canteens.[16] The wounded were carried down to the beach on the rifles of their comrades. The heaven-born Dolphin sent many casks of water ashore. A squad[17] destroyed the Spanish well and burned the commander's house; the heavy tiles rang down from the caving roof like the sound of a new volley. The Cubans to the number of twenty chased on for a mile after the Spaniards.

A party went out to count the Spanish dead; the daylight began to soften. Save for the low murmur of the men a peace fell upon all the brown wilderness of hills.

15. Acting Sergeant Major Henry Good was killed on the night of June 12–13. Private William Dunphy and James McColgan were killed the first day ashore, June 10. Crane spent that night watching trenches being dug.

16. Captain Spicer was prostrated by the heat and had to be taken aboard the *Dolphin*.

17. The detachment was commanded by Lt. Lucas.

In the meantime a blue-jacket from the Dolphin appeared among the marines; he had a rifle and belt; he had escaped from a landing party in order to join in the fray. He grinned joyously.

Possible stragglers were called in. As the dusk deepened the men closed for the homeward march. The Cubans appeared with prisoners and a cheer went up. Then the brown lines began to wind slowly homeward. The tired men grew silent; not a sound was heard except where, ahead, to the rear, on the flank, could be heard the low trample of many careful feet.

As to execution done, none was certain. Some said sixty; some said one hundred and sixty; some laughingly said six. It turns out to be a certain fifty-eight — dead. Which is many.

As we neared camp we saw somebody in the darkness — a watchful figure, eager and anxious, perhaps uncertain of the serpent-like thing swishing softly through the bushes.

"Hello!" said a marine. "Who are you?"

A low voice came in reply: "Sergeant of the guard."

Sergeant of the guard! Saintly man! Protector of the weary! Coffee! Hardtack! Beans! Rest! Sleep! Peace!

MARINES SIGNALLING UNDER FIRE AT GUANTANAMO

They were four Guantanamo marines, officially known for the time as signalmen, and it was their duty to lie in the trenches of Camp McCalla, that faced the water, and, by day, signal the *Marblehead*[1]

First published in McClure's Magazine: *February 1899; also appeared in* Wounds in the Rain, *1900. The present text is taken from* The Work of Stephen Crane, *IX (1926).*

Richard Harding Davis considered Crane's dispatch (to quote Ames Williams) "one of the finest examples of descriptive writing of the war. Incidentally, Crane was no idle spectator during this engagement, but lent a hand to the Marines for which he was officially commended to the Secretary of the Navy by the commanding officer of the Marine detachment, Captain G. F. Elliott." From New Colophon: *April 1948.*

1. Ralph D. Paine, on whom Crane drew for his sketch "The Lone Charge of William B. Perkins," retells this incident in his *Roads of Adventure* (1922), pp. 244–245. USS *Marblehead* (1892) was an unprotected cruiser; tonnage (displacement): 2,089; length: 257 feet; speed: 18.7 knots; principal armament: ten 5-inch guns.

with a flag and, by night, signal the *Marblehead* with lanterns. It was my good fortune — at that time I considered it my bad fortune, indeed — to be with them on two of the nights when a wild storm of fighting was pealing about the hill; and, of all the actions of the war, none were so hard on the nerves, none strained courage so near the panic point, as those swift nights in Camp McCalla. With a thousand rifles rattling; with the field-guns booming in your ears; with the diabolic Colt automatics clacking; with the roar of the *Marblehead* coming from the bay, and, last, with Mauser bullets sneering always in the air a few inches over one's head, and with this enduring from dusk to dawn, it is extremely doubtful if any one who was there will be able to forget it easily. The noise; the impenetrable darkness; the knowledge from the sound of the bullets that the enemy was on three sides of the camp; the infrequent bloody stumbling and death of some man with whom, perhaps, one had messed two hours previous; the weariness of the body, and the more terrible weariness of the mind, at the endlessness of the thing, made it wonderful that at least some of the men did not come out of it with their nerves hopelessly in shreds.

But, as this interesting ceremony proceeded in the darkness, it was necessary for the signal squad to coolly take and send messages. Captain McCalla always participated in the defence of the camp by raking the woods on two of its sides with the guns of the *Marblehead*. Moreover, he was the senior officer present, and he wanted to know what was happening. All night long the crews of the ships in the bay would stare sleeplessly into the blackness toward the roaring hill.

The signal squad had an old cracker-box placed on top of the trench. When not signalling they hid the lanterns in this box; but as soon as an order to send a message was received, it became necessary for one of the men to stand up and expose the lights. And then — oh, my eye, how the guerillas hidden in the gulf of night would turn loose at those yellow gleams!

Signalling in this way is done by letting one lantern remain stationary — on top of the cracker-box, in this case — and moving the other over to the left and right and so on in the regular gestures of the wig-wagging code. It is a very simple system of night communication, but one can see that it presents rare possibilities when used in front of an enemy who, a few hundred yards away, is overjoyed at sighting so definite a mark.

How, in the name of wonders, those four men at Camp McCalla were not riddled from head to foot and sent home more as repositories of Spanish ammunition than as marines is beyond all comprehension. To make a confession — when one of these men stood up to wave his lantern, I, lying in the trench, invariably rolled a little to the right or left, in order that, when he was shot, he might not fall on me. But the squad came off scatheless, despite the best efforts of the most formidable corps in the Spanish army — the Escuadra de Guantanamo. That it was the most formidable corps in the Spanish army of occupation has been told me by many Spanish officers and also by General Menocal and other insurgent officers. General Menocal was Garcia's chief of staff when the latter was operating busily in Santiago province. The regiment was composed solely of practicos, or guides, who knew every shrub and tree on the ground over which they moved.

Whenever the adjutant, Lieutenant Draper,[2] came plunging along through the darkness with an order — such as: "Ask the *Marblehead* to please shell the woods to the left" — my heart would come into my mouth, for I knew then that one of my pals was going to stand up behind the lanterns and have all Spain shoot at him.

The answer was always upon the instant: "Yes, sir."

Then the bullets began to snap, snap, snap, at his head, while all the woods began to crackle like burning straw. I could lie near and watch the face of the signalman, illumed as it was by the yellow shine of lantern-light, and the absence of excitement, fright, or any emotion at all on his countenance was something to astonish all theories out of one's mind. The face was in every instance merely that of a man intent upon his business, the business of wigwagging into the gulf of night where a light on the *Marblehead* was seen to move slowly.

These times on the hill resembled, in some ways, those terrible scenes on the stage — scenes of intense gloom, blinding lightning, with a cloaked devil or assassin or other appropriate character muttering deeply amid the awful roll of the thunder-drums. It was theatric beyond words: one felt like a leaf in this booming chaos, this prolonged tragedy of the night. Amid it all one could see from time to time the yellow light on the face of a preoccupied signalman.

Possibly no man who was there ever before understood the true eloquence of the breaking of the day. We would lie staring into the east, fairly ravenous for the dawn. Utterly worn to rags, with our nerves standing on end like so many bristles, we lay and watched the east — the unspeakably obdurate and slow east. It was a wonder that the eyes of some of us did not turn to glass balls from the fixity of our gaze.

Then there would come into the sky a patch of faint blue light. It was like a piece of moonshine. Some would say it was the beginning of daybreak; others would declare it was nothing of the kind. Men would get very disgusted with each other in these low-toned arguments held in the trenches. For my part, this development in the

2. Herbert L. Draper was promoted to captain in March 1899. He was a graduate of the United States Naval Academy (1887). He died on duty at Hong Kong (19 September 1901).

eastern sky destroyed many of my ideas and theories concerning the dawning of the day; but then, I had never before had occasion to give it such solemn attention.

This patch widened and whitened in about the speed of a man's accomplishment if he should be in the way of painting Madison Square Garden with a camel's-hair brush. The guerillas always set out to whoop it up about this time, because they knew the occasion was approaching when it would be expedient for them to elope. I, at least, always grew furious with this wretched sunrise. I thought I could have walked around the world in the time required for the old thing to get up above the horizon.

One midnight, when an important message was to be sent to the *Marblehead*, Colonel Huntington came himself to the signal-place with Adjutant Draper and Captain McCauley, the quartermaster. When the man stood up to signal, the colonel stood beside him. At sight of the lights, the Spaniards performed as usual. They drove enough bullets into that immediate vicinity to kill all the marines in the corps.

Lieutenant Draper was agitated for his chief. "Colonel, won't you step down, sir?"

"Why, I guess not," said the grey old veteran in his slow, sad, always gentle way. "I am in no more danger than the man."

"But, sir — " began the adjutant.

"Oh, it's all right, Draper."

So the colonel and the private stood side to side and took the heavy fire without either moving a muscle.

Day was always obliged to come at last, punctuated by a final exchange of scattering shots. And the light shone on the marines, the dumb guns, the flag. Grimy yellow face looked into grimy yellow face, and grinned with weary satisfaction. Coffee!

Usually it was impossible for many of the men to sleep at once. It always took me, for instance, some hours to get my nerves combed down. But then it was great joy to lie in the trench with the four signalmen, and understand thoroughly that that night was fully over at last, and that, although the future might have in store other bad nights, that one could never escape from the prison-house which we call the past.

ii

At the wild little fight at Cusco there were some splendid exhibitions of wigwagging under fire. Action began when an advanced detachment of marines under Lieutenant Lucas, with the Cuban guides, had reached the summit of a ridge overlooking a small valley where there was a house, a well, and a thicket of some kind of shrub with great broad oily leaves. This thicket, which was perhaps an acre in extent, contained the guerillas. The valley was open to the sea. The distance from the top of the ridge to the thicket was barely two hundred yards.

The *Dolphin* had sailed up the coast in line with the marine advance, ready with her guns to assist in any action. Captain Elliott, who commanded the two hundred marines in this fight, suddenly called out for a signalman. He wanted a man to tell the *Dolphin* to open fire on the house and the thicket. It was a blazing, bitter hot day on top of the ridge with its shrivelled chaparral and its straight, tall cactus-plants. The sky was bare and blue, and hurt like brass. In two minutes the prostrate marines were red and sweating like so many hull-buried stokers in the tropics.

Captain Elliott called out: "Where's a signalman? Who's a signalman here?"

A red-headed mick — I think his name was Clancy; at any rate, it will do to call him Clancy — twisted his head from where he lay on his stomach pumping his Lee, and, saluting, said that he was a signalman.

There was no regulation flag with the expedition, so Clancy was obliged to tie his blue polka-dot neckerchief[3] on the end of his rifle. It did not make a very good flag. At first Clancy moved a way down the safe side of the ridge and wigwagged there very busily. But what with the flag being so poor for the purpose, and the background of ridge being so dark, those on the *Dolphin* did not see it. So Clancy had to return to the top of the ridge and outline himself and his flag against the sky.

The usual thing happened. As soon as the Spaniards caught sight of this silhouette, they let go like mad at it. To make things more comfortable for Clancy, the situation demanded that he face the sea and turn his back to the Spanish bullets. This was a hard game, mark you — to stand with the small of your back to volley firing. Clancy thought so. Everybody thought so. We all cleared out of his neighbourhood. If he wanted sole possession of any particular spot on that hill, he could have it for all we would interfere with him.

It cannot be denied that Clancy was in a hurry. I watched him. He was so occupied with the bullets that snarled close to his ears that he was obliged to repeat the letters of his message softly to himself. It seemed an intolerable time before the *Dolphin* answered the little signal. Meanwhile we gazed at him, marvelling every second that he had not yet pitched headlong. He swore at times.

Finally the *Dolphin* replied to his frantic gesticulation, and he

---

3. The badge of the Rough Riders was a blue polka-dot neckerchief tied to the rifle.

delivered his message. As his part of the transaction was quite finished — whoop! — he dropped like a brick into the firing line and began
to shoot; began to get "hunky" with all those people who had been
plugging at him. The blue polka-dot neckerchief still fluttered from
the barrel of his rifle. I am quite certain that he let it remain there
until the end of the fight.

The shells of the *Dolphin* began to plough up the thicket, kicking
the bushes, stones, and soil into the air as if somebody was blasting
there.

Meanwhile, this force of two hundred marines and fifty Cubans
and the force of — probably — six companies of Spanish guerillas were
making such an awful din that the distant Camp McCalla was all alive
with excitement. Colonel Huntington sent out strong parties to critical
points on the road to facilitate, if necessary, a safe retreat, and also
sent forty men under Lieutenant Magill to come up on the left flank
of the two companies in action under Captain Elliott. Lieutenant
Magill and his men had crowned a hill which covered entirely the
flank of the fighting companies, but when the *Dolphin* opened fire,
it happened that Magill was in the line of the shots. It became necessary to stop the *Dolphin* at once. Captain Elliott was not near Clancy
at this time, and he called hurriedly for another signalman.

Sergeant Quick[4] arose and announced that he was a signalman.
He produced from somewhere a blue polka-dot neckerchief as large
as a quilt. He tied it on a long, crooked stick. Then he went to the
top of the ridge and, turning his back to the Spanish fire, began to
signal to the *Dolphin*. Again we gave a man sole possession of a
particular part of the ridge. We didn't want it. He could have it and
welcome. If the young sergeant had had the smallpox, the cholera,
and the yellow fever, we could not have slid out with more celerity.

As men have said often, it seemed as if there was in this war a
God of Battles who held His mighty hand before the Americans.
As I looked at Sergeant Quick wigwagging there against the sky,
I would not have given a tin tobacco tag for his life. Escape for him
seemed impossible. It seemed absurd to hope that he would not be hit;
I only hoped that he would be hit just a little, little, in the arm, the
shoulder, or the leg.

4. Sergeant John H. Quick, who figures in Crane's "The Red Badge of
Courage Was His Wig-Wag Flag" (*supra,* p. 140) as "a spruce young
sergeant of marines, erect, his back to the showering bullets, solemnly and
intently wigwagging to the distant Dolphin."

Sergeant Quick was awarded the Congressional Medal of Honor for
gallantry at Cuzco (14 June 1898); and a certain Private John Fitzgerald,
U.S.M.C., who was probably one of the four signalmen, received the C.M.H.
for gallantry at Cuzco — but not until 1910.

I watched his face, and it was as grave and serene as that of a man writing in his own library. He was the very embodiment of tranquillity in occupation. He stood there amid the animal-like babble of the Cubans, the crack of rifles, and the whistling snarl of the bullets, and wigwagged whatever he had to wigwag without heeding anything but his business. There was not a single trace of nervousness or haste.

To say the least, a fight at close range is absorbing as a spectacle. No man wants to take his eyes from it until that time comes when he makes up his mind to run away. To deliberately stand up and turn your back to a battle is in itself hard work. To deliberately stand up and turn your back to a battle and hear immediate evidences of the boundless enthusiasm with which a large company of the enemy shoot at you from an adjacent thicket is, to my mind at least, a very great feat. One need not dwell upon the detail of keeping the mind carefully upon a slow spelling of an important code message.

I saw Quick betray only one sign of emotion. As he swung his clumsy flag to and fro, an end of it once caught on a cactus pillar, and he looked sharply over his shoulder to see what had it. He gave the flag an impatient jerk. He looked annoyed.

STEPHEN CRANE AT THE FRONT FOR THE WORLD.

SIBONEY, June 24. — And this is the end of the third day since the landing of the troops. Yesterday was a day of insurgent fighting and rumors of insurgent fighting. The Cubans were supposed to be fighting somewhere in the hills with the regiment of Santiago de Cuba, which had been quite cut off from its native city. No American soldiery were implicated in any way in the battle. But to-day is different. The mounted infantry — the First Volunteer Cavalry — Teddie's Terrors —

Reprinted here for the first time from New York World: *7 July 1898. Immediately following this article and on the same page (p. 8) the* World *published "Crane Tells the Story of the Disembarkment" (supra, p. 137). The subheads read as follows: "The Author of 'The Red Badge of Courage,' the Most Notable War Story of Recent Years, Written Before He Ever Saw an Actual Engagement, Was in the Thick of Battle with the Rough Riders./ He Tells the Real Story of Their Glorious Baptism of Fire./ Heedless of Danger That Surrounded Them, Noisily, Carelessly They Went to Death with Superb Courage — The Heroism of Marshall, the Correspondent, and Other Thrilling Episodes Brought Intimately Before the Reader."*

Wood's Weary Walkers — have had their first engagement.[1] It was a bitter hard first fight for new troops, but no man can ever question the gallantry of this regiment.

As we landed from a despatch boat we saw the last troop of the mounted infantry wending slowly over the top of a huge hill. Three of us promptly posted after them upon hearing the statement that they had gone out with the avowed intention of finding the Spaniards and mixing it up with them.

[THROUGH THE THICKETS.]

They were far ahead of us by the time we reached the top of the mountain, but we swung rapidly on the path through the dense Cuban thickets and in time met and passed the hospital corps, a vacant, unloaded hospital corps, going ahead on mules. Then there was another long lonely march through the dry woods, which seemed almost upon the point of crackling into a blaze under the rays of the furious Cuban sun. We met nothing but blankets, shelter-tents, coats and other impedimenta, which the panting Rough Riders had flung behind them on their swift march.

In time we came in touch with a few stragglers, men down with heat, prone and breathing heavily, and then we struck the rear of the column. We were now about four miles out, with no troops nearer than that by the road.

I know nothing about war, of course, and pretend nothing, but I have been enabled from time to time to see brush fighting, and I want to say here plainly that the behavior of these Rough Riders while marching through the woods shook me with terror as I have never before been shaken.

1. Crane is describing the battle at Las Guásimas, which occurred on 24 June 1898. Leonard Wood commanded the unit at Las Guásimas. Although a colonel of the volunteers, his permanent rank was assistant surgeon with the rank of captain. Wood (1860–1927) was one of the important military and political figures of his time. He took his M.D. at Harvard University (1884) and began his career as an infantry officer. He fought against Geronimo and was awarded the Congressional Medal of Honor. He met Roosevelt in 1897, and the two of them organized the First United States Volunteer Cavalry shortly after the outbreak of war. Wood was the colonel commanding and Roosevelt the lieutenant colonel. Wood's later career, although marked by quarrels and spectacular shifts of opinion, was a brilliant one, climaxed by his appointment (1910) as Chief of Staff of the Army. In 1920 he made an unsuccessful bid for the Republican nomination for the presidency.

Theodore Roosevelt (1858–1919) became the twenty-sixth President of the United States, 1901–1909. He had been assistant secretary of the Navy, 1896–1898, resigning to organize the "Rough Riders."

[SUPERB COURAGE.]

It must now be perfectly understood throughout the length and breadth of the United States that the Spaniards have learned a great deal from the Cubans, and they are going to use against us the tactics which the Cubans have used so successfully against them. The marines at Guantanamo have learned it. The Indian-fighting regulars know it anyhow, but this regiment of volunteers knew nothing but their own superb courage. They wound along this narrow winding path, babbling joyously, arguing, recounting, laughing; making more noise than a train going through a tunnel.

Any one could tell from the conformation of the country when we were liable to strike the enemy's outposts, but the clatter of tongues did not then cease. Also, those of us who knew heard going from hillock to hillock the beautiful coo of the Cuban wood-dove — ah, the wood-dove! the Spanish-guerilla wood-dove which had presaged the death of gallant marines.

For my part, I declare that I was frightened almost into convulsions. Incidentally I mentioned the cooing of the doves to some of the men, but they said decisively that the Spaniards did not use this signal. I don't know how they knew.

[SILENCE — ACTION!]

Well, after we had advanced well into the zone of the enemy's fire — mark that — well into the zone of Spanish fire — a loud order came along the line: "There's a Spanish outpost just ahead and the men must stop talking."

"Stop talkin', can't ye, —— it," bawled a sergeant.

"Ah, say, can't ye stop talkin'?" howled another.

I was frightened before a shot was fired; frightened because I thought this silly brave force was wandering placidly into a great deal of trouble. They did. The firing began. Four little volleys were fired by members of a troop deployed to the right. Then the Mauser began to pop — the familiar Mauser pop. A captain announced that this distinct Mauser sound was our own Krag-Jorgensen.[2] O misery!

2. The standard arm of the Army at the time, the rifle had been invented by Captain O. Krag and E. Jörgensen of Norway. Adopted in 1892, the rifle was caliber .308, had a length without bayonet of 49.10 inches and a weight with bayonet of 10.4 pounds. Its magazine held five cartridges, weighing 264 grains each. The weapon was sighted to 2,200 yards and had a muzzle velocity of 2,000 feet per second. Restricted to the regular Army only, it was never very popular in this country. There were three models, 1892, 1896, and 1898; the latter was the standard arm until the adoption of the Model 1903 (Springfield) rifle.

Then the woods became aglow with fighting. Our people advanced, deployed, reinforced, fought, fell — in the bushes, in the tall grass, under the lone palms — before a foe not even half seen. Mauser bullets came from three sides. Mauser bullets — not Krag-Jorgensen — although men began to cry that they were being fired into by their own people — whined in almost all directions. Three troops went forward in skirmish order and in five minutes they called for reinforcements. They were under a cruel fire; half of the men hardly knew whence it came; but their conduct, by any soldierly standard, was magnificent.

[GREEN HEROES.]

Most persons with a fancy for military things suspect the value of an announcedly picked regiment. Better gather a simple collection of clerks from anywhere. But in this case the usual view changes. This regiment is as fine a body of men as were ever accumulated for war.

There was nothing to be seen but men straggling through the underbrush and firing at some part of the landscape. This was the scenic effect. Of course men said that they saw five hundred, one thousand, three thousand, fifteen thousand Spaniards, but — poof — in bush country of this kind it is almost impossible for one to see more than fifty men at a time. According to my opinion there were never more than five hundred men in the Spanish firing line. There might have been aplenty in touch with their centre and flanks, but as to the firing there were never more than five hundred men engaged. This is certain.

The Rough Riders advanced steadily and confidently under the Mauser bullets. They spread across some open ground — tall grass and palms — and there they began to fall, smothering and threshing down in the grass, marking man-shaped places among those luxuriant blades. The action lasted about one-half hour. Then the Spaniards fled. They had never had men fight them in this manner and they fled. The business was too serious.

Then the heroic rumor arose, soared, screamed above the bush. Everybody was wounded. Everybody was dead. There was nobody. Gradually there was somebody. There was the wounded, the important wounded. And the dead.

[MARSHALL'S COURAGE.]

Meanwhile a soldier passing near me said: "There's a correspondent up there all shot to hell."

He guided me to where Edward Marshall[3] lay, shot through the body. The following conversation ensued:

"Hello, Crane!"

"Hello, Marshall! In hard luck old man?"

"Yes, I'm done for."

"Nonsense! You're all right, old boy. What can I do for you?"

"Well, you might file my despatches. I don't mean file 'em ahead of your own, old man — but just file 'em if you find it handy."

I immediately decided that he was doomed. No man could be so sublime in detail concerning the trade of journalism and not die. There was the solemnity of a funeral song in these absurd and fine sentences about despatches. Six soldiers gathered him up on a tent and moved slowly off.

3. Davis Edward Marshall (1869–1933), an active newspaperman and writer all his life. He commenced journalism as Sunday editor of the New York *Press* in 1888; then concentrated on slum tenement housing for a number of years. In 1896–1897, he did editorial work and foreign correspondence for the New York *Journal* and in 1897–1898 foreign correspondence and Sunday editorial work for the *World*. He was in Cuba for the *Journal*.

An old friend of Crane on Park Row, Marshall befriended him from the start. He tried but failed to get Crane's *Maggie* serialized in his own New York *Press*. He knew Crane also as a fellow member of the Lantern Club, a group of New York newspapermen meeting weekly there with guest speakers, and now here was Crane covering the Cuban War for a rival newspaper.

Marshall, hit by a bullet near the spine, dictated his dispatch to Crane. The day was hot, says Marshall in his "Stories of Stephen Crane," *Literary Life* (1900). "The thermometer — had there been such an instrument in that God-forsaken and man-invaded wilderness — would have shown a temperature of something like 100 degrees. Yet Stephen Crane — and mind you, he was there in the interest of a rival newspaper — took the dispatch which I managed to write five or six miles to the coast and cabled it for me. He had to walk, for he could get no horse or mule. Then he rushed about in the heat and arranged with a number of men to bring a stretcher up from the coast and carry me back on it. He was probably as tired then as a man could be and still walk. But he trudged back from the coast to the field hospital where I was lying and saw to it that I was properly conveyed to the coast."

Busy in getting Marshall's dispatch to Siboney, Crane lost out meanwhile on most of the fighting at Las Guasimas. Marshall, who subsequently wrote *The Story of the Rough Riders* (1899), reports that Pulitzer's *World* cut Crane short in retaliation for aiding his rival newspaper. In mid-August Crane switched to the *Journal,* where he had sent his first dispatches in April.

"Hello!" shouted a stern and menacing person, "who are you? And what are you doing here? Quick!"

"I am a correspondent, and we are merely carrying back another correspondent who we think is mortally wounded. Do you care?"

The Rough Rider, somewhat abashed, announced that he did not care.

[NEW YORK TO THE FORE!]

And now the wounded soldiers began to crawl, walk and be carried back to where, in the middle of the path, the surgeons had established a little field hospital.

"Say, doctor, this ain't much of a wound. I reckon I can go now back to my troop," said Arizona.

"Thanks, awfully, doctor. Awfully kind of you. I dare say I shall be all right in a moment," said New York.

This hospital was a spectacle of heroism. The doctors, gentle and calm, moved among the men without the common-senseless bullying of the ordinary ward. It was a sort of fraternal game. They were all in it, and of it, helping each other.

In the mean time three troops of the Ninth Cavalry were swinging through the woods, and a mile behind them the Seventy-first New York was moving forward eagerly to the rescue. But the day was done. The Rough Riders had bitten it off and chewed it up — chewed it up splendidly.

ROOSEVELT'S ROUGH RIDERS' LOSS DUE TO A GALLANT BLUNDER.

PLAYA DEL ESTE, June 25.— Lieut. Col. Roosevelt's Rough Riders,[1] who were ambushed yesterday, advanced at daylight without any particular plan of action as to how to strike the enemy.

Reprinted here for the first time from New York World: *26 June 1898. The same dispatch about the blunder of the Rough*

1. The First U.S. Volunteer Cavalry — the so-called Rough Riders — was organized by Theodore Roosevelt and Leonard Wood. It was composed of cowboys and bluebloods, frontier democracy and socialites of the American aristocracy. "Lean, slit-eyed plainsmen with names like Cherokee Bill and Rattlesnake Pete served beside men from Boston's Somerset Club and the Knickerbocker Club of New York, crack polo players, tennis champions, steeplechase riders, Princeton linemen, Yale's finest high-jumper, and a whole contingent from Teddy's Harvard, led by two ace quarterbacks. The

The men marched noisily through the narrow road in the woods, talking volubly, when suddenly they struck the Spanish lines.

Fierce fire was poured into their ranks and there began a great fight in the thickets.

Nothing of the enemy was visible to our men, who displayed much gallantry. In fact, their bearing was superb, and couldn't have been finer.

They suffered a heavy loss, however, due to the remarkably wrong idea of how the Spanish bushwhack.[2]

It was simply a gallant blunder.

Riders appeared in the Philadelphia Press on June 26, under the headline: "Stephen Crane Calls It a Blunder." Above it is Admiral Sampson's dispatch: "Sampson Withdraws Charge of Mutilation." It had been alleged that the bodies of four marines killed in the outpost of Guantanamo were mutilated, but the apparent mutilation "was probably due to the effect of small caliber bullets fired at short range, and I withdraw the charge of mutilation."

"Denies Mutilation of Bodies," in Philadelphia Press for June 26, is listed in the Williams-Starrett Crane Bibliography as by Crane, but this article was dispatched by Sylvester Scovel.

socialites were a minority, but they saw to it that the entire regiment was outfitted with equipment unavailable to the regulars. . . . They also gave the unit a distinct tone, which was demonstrated during the siege of Santiago: when regimental bands were ordered to join in the national anthem, the Rough Riders played *Fair Harvard*." (From "The Spanish-American War," by William Manchester, *Holiday*, 30 September 1961.)

2. The *World's* reporter George Rea reported on June 25: "Cubans Warned Col. Wood In Vain of an Ambush." (This article appeared the next day on the same page as Crane's dispatch: "Roosevelt's Rough Riders' Loss Due to a Gallant Blunder.") The advance of the American pickets, said Rea, "is so rapid that tomorrow they will be in sight of Santiago City. The cavalry all fought dismounted. It is reported that the Cubans warned Col. Wood that there was a Spanish ambuscade, but he refused to heed the warning." Their baptism of fire sobered his men, "teaching the necessary lesson to the entire army to use caution in fighting bushwhackers."

HUNGER HAS MADE CUBANS FATALISTS

SIBONEY, June 27. — The day is hot and lazy; endless Cuban infantry straggling past the door of our shack send the yellow dust in clouds. The Thirty-third Michigan is landing in dribbles upon the beach.[1]

Reprinted here for the first time from New York World: 12 July 1898. The headlines are as follows: "Hunger Has Made Cubans Fatalists/No Cheering When Shafter's Forces Landed at Daiquiri./They Are Good Scouts, But —/American Troops Do Not Look With Favor on Them and They Do Not Understand Us./Rough Riders Surprised Them/Steady Advance in Face of Deadly Fire Filled Them with Wonder and Admiration." Note that these headlines refer only to the first part of the article.

William Rufus Shafter (1835–1906) had had a long, but not distinguished, career in the Army, beginning with volunteer service in the Civil War. In 1897 he had been promoted brigadier general. Subsequent to the Spanish-American War he commanded the Departments of the East, California, and Columbia. He was promoted to major general in June 1898.

In Charge! The Story of the Battle of San Juan (1961), A. C. M. Azoy says, "A big man, nearly six feet tall, with big hands and a big head of tousled gray hair, Shafter unfortunately measured almost as much from front to back as he did up and down, and was therefore a source of never-ending inspiration for the gibing pens and pencils of newspaper reporters and cartoonists." He weighed 300 pounds, he had gout, and he could not function efficiently in the Cuban hills and heat. He belonged in Gilbert and Sullivan: " 'His immense abdomen hung down, yes, actually hung down between his legs,' one officer wrote home, and T. R. [Roosevelt] remarked bitingly that 'Not since the campaign of Crassus against the Parthians has there been so criminally incompetent a general as Shafter.' "

"Special platforms were built so he could mount his horse, but since the animal sagged pathetically, he rode around most of the time in a buckboard with his afflicted foot wrapped in burlap, or lay prostrate in his tent, his bullfrog jowls pulsing like bellows" (William Manchester, "The Spanish-American War," Holiday, 30 [September 1961]).

At the start of the campaign Shafter told off the press in his quarrel with Richard Harding Davis of the Herald, and at the end he had a row with Sylvester Scovel of the World — Scovel

---

1. The Thirty-third Michigan (44 officers and 878 men) and a battalion of the Thirty-fourth Michigan were attached to Brigadier General H. M. Duffield's brigade down from Camp Alger, Virginia.

Four Red Cross nurses[2] — the first American women to set foot on Cuban soil since the beginning of the war — came ashore from the State of Texas[3] a few minutes ago, and the soldiers, disheveled, dirty, bronzed, gazed at them with all their eyes. They were a revelation in their cool white dresses.

Life occasionally moves slowly at the seat of war. This makes two days of tranquillity. The Spaniards, when they fled from the conflict with Roosevelt's men and the First and Tenth Regular Cavalry, took occasion to flee a considerable distance; in fact, they went nearly into Santiago de Cuba.

No army can move ahead faster than its rations, and although here we picture the impatience of the bulletin-board crowds who fancy that war is not a complication composed of heat, dust, rain, thirst, hunger and blood, yet it is impossible for the army to move faster than it does at present.

The attitude of the American soldier toward the insurgent is interesting. So also is the attitude of the insurgent toward the American soldier. One must not suppose that there was any cheering enthusiasm at the landing of our army here. The American soldiers looked with silent curiosity upon the ragged brown insurgents and the insurgents looked stolidly, almost indifferently, at the Americans.

[CUBANS ARE FATALISTS.]

The Cuban soldier, indeed, has turned into an absolutely emotionless character save when he is maddened by battle. He starves and he makes no complaint. We feed him and he expresses no joy. When you come to think of it, one follows the other naturally. If he had retained the emotional ability to make a fuss over nearly starving to death he would also have retained the emotional ability to faint with joy at sight of the festive canned beef, hard-tack and coffee. But he exists with the impenetrable indifference or ignorance of the greater part of the people in an ordinary slum.

---

swung a haymaker at Shafter's jaw. Azoy has it that Shafter dodged; Manchester says that Scovel punched Shafter in the face. Says Paine: "It was a flurried blow, without much science behind it, and Scovel's fist glanced off the general's double chin, but it left a mark there, a red scratch visible for some days. Then, indeed, was the militant young journalist hustled away and locked up. It was an incident of war without precedent" (Roads of Adventure [1922], p. 266).

2. In charge of the Red Cross nurses was Clara Barton.

3. State of Texas was the Red Cross ship, which sailed from Key West on June 20. Aboard was George Kennan of The Outlook, a well-known correspondent and writer.

Everybody knows that the kind of sympathetic charity which loves to be thanked is often grievously disappointed and wounded in tenement districts, where people often accept gifts as if their own property had turned up after a short absence. The Cubans accept our stores in something of this way. If there are any thanks it is because of custom. Of course, I mean the rank and file. The officers are mannered both good and bad, true and dissembling, like ordinary people.

But there is no specious intercourse between the Cubans and the Americans. Each hold largely to their own people and go their own ways. The American does not regard his ally as a good man for the fighting line, and the Cuban is aware that his knowledge of the country makes his woodcraft superior to that of the American. He regards himself also as considerable of a veteran and there has not yet been enough fighting to let him know what immensely formidable persons are your Uncle Samuel's regulars.

When that fighting does come he will see, for marksmanship and steadiness, such a soldier as could never have come into his visions. The fighting of the Rough Riders, by the way, surprised him greatly. He is not educated in that kind of warfare. The way our troops kept going, going, never giving back a foot despite the losses, hanging on as if every battle was a life or death struggle — this seemed extraordinary to the Cuban.

The scene of the fight on the 24th is now far within our lines. The Spanish position was perfect. They must have been badly rattled to have so easily given it up at the attack of less than 2,000 men. Here now the vultures wheel slowly over the woods.

The gallantry of the First Regular Cavalry has not been particularly mentioned in connection with the first fight. There were five correspondents present under fire and we were all with the Rough Riders. We did not know until after the action that the First Regular Cavalry had been engaged over on the right flank.[4] But when a second sergeant takes out a troop because its captain, lieutenant, and first sergeant all go down in the first five minutes' firing there has been considerable trouble.

[REGULARS NOT APPRECIATED.]

In fact our admiration for our regulars is a peculiar bit of business. We appreciate them heartily but vaguely, without any other medium of expression than the term, "the regulars." Thus when it comes down to action no one out of five correspondents thought it important to be with the First Regular Cavalry.

And their performance was grand! Oh, but never mind — it was

4. Here at Las Guásimas on June 24 one squadron of the First Regiment of Cavalry, U.S.A., was engaged.

only the regulars. They fought gallantly of course. Why not? Have they ever been known to fail? That is the point. They have never been known to fail. Our confidence in them has come to be a habit. But, good heavens! it must be about time to change all that and heed them somewhat, even if we have to make some of the volunteers wait a little.

Scovel[5] and I swam two Jamaica horses ashore from the Triton,[6] found some insurgents and took a journey into the hills. Col. Cebreco's little force we found encamped under the palms in thatched huts with sapling uprights. The ragged semi-naked men lay about in dirty hammocks, but their rifles were Springfields, 1873[7] and their belts were full of cartridges. The tall guinea grass[8] had been trodden flat by their bare feet.

We asked for a guide and the colonel gave us an escort of five men for our ride over the mountains. The first ridge we rode up was a simple illumination as to why the insurgents if they had food and ammunition could hold out for years. There is no getting men out of such hills if they choose to stay in them. The path, rocky as the bed of a stream, zig-zagged higher and higher until the American fleet blockading Santiago was merely a collection of tiny, shapeless shadows on the steel bosom of an immense sea. The woods, the beautiful woods, were alive around us with the raucous voices of birds, black like crows.

[GOOD PLACE FOR A SANITARIUM.]

At the summit we looked upon a new series of ridges and peaks, near and far, all green. A strong breeze rustled the foliage. It was the kind of country in which commercial physicians love to establish

5. Sylvester Scovel of the New York *World*.

7. "The first breech-loading rifle manufactured at the Springfield Armory was . . . the Model 1866. This had the famous old 'Springfield' action with hinged breech-block. It used a .50 caliber, center-fire, brass cartridge, containing 70 grains of black powder and a 450-grain, grooved, lubricated, conical bullet. In 1873 this rifle was improved a little, and the caliber reduced to .45-70-405." It was used by the Army until the Krag-Jörgensen rifle was adopted. See Townsend Whelen, *The American Rifle* (1918), pp. 11–12.

The volunteer forces were armed with the Springfield.

8. Common name for *Panicum maximum*, a tall (three to eight feet) grass, native to Africa, used as a forage grass in the tropical Americas.

6. The *Triton* was a Navy tug used as a dispatch boat. Crane describes this incident in "War Memories" (*infra*, p. 274). "Hunger Has Made Cubans Fatalists" divides into two parts. It is possible that the second half, which begins here, belonged to a separate dispatch and was tacked on in the *World* editorial offices.

sanitariums. Then down we went, down and down, sitting on the pommels of our saddles, with our stirrups near the ears of the horses. Then came a brawling, noisy brook like an Adirondack trout stream. Then another ascension to another Cuban camp, where just at dusk the pickets in bunches of three were coming in to report to the captain, lazily aswing. One barefooted negro private paused in his report from time to time to pluck various thistle and cactus spurs from his soles. Scovel asked him in Spanish: "Where are your shoes?"

The tattered soldier coolly replied in English: "I lose dem in de woods."

We cheered.

"Why, hello there! Where did you come from?" To our questions he answered: "In New York. I leve dere Mulberry street. One — t'ree year. My name Joe Riley."

There he stood, bearded, black, a perfect type of West India negro, speaking the soft, broad dialect of these islands and — harp of Ireland — his name was Riley. I have heard of a tall Guatamalan savage who somehow accumulated the illustrious name of Duffy, but Riley ——

As we swung and smoked in our hammocks, the Cuban soldiers crooned marvellous songs in the darkness while the fire light covered with crimson glare some naked limb or made tragic some dark patient face. The hills were softly limned against a sky strewn with big stars.

We were up in the cold of the dark just before dawn. With fifteen men as escort, we moved again up the hills. In time, we arrived on a path that curved around the top of a ridge. Here we found Cuban posts. They having no tools with which to dig trenches, naturally turn to the machete. They can't dig down, so they build up.

These Cuban posts were each fronted with a curious structure, a mere rack made of saplings, tied fast with sinewy vines and then filled with stones. They were about six feet high, one foot thick and long enough to accomodate from five to eight riflemen. These structures paralleled the path at strategic points.

Soon we came to a point where upon looking across a narrow but very deep valley we could see in the blue dawn the shine of Spanish camp-fires. They were within rifle range, but we slunk along unseen. Our horses had now been left behind.

Then came a dive into the dark, deep valley — into Spain. The hillside was the steepest thing in hillsides which could well be imagined. We slid practically from tree to tree, our escort moving noiselessly below and above us. By the time we reached the bottom of this hill the day had broken wide and clear. A stream was forded and then a creep of five hundred yards through tall grass. There was a Spanish post upon either hand — 100 men in one, 50 men in the other. The Cubans had no tongues and their feet made no sound.

[LOOKED DOWN INTO SANTIAGO.]

To make a long story short, there were some nine miles of this sort of dodging and badgering and botheration — nine infernal miles, during which those Cubans did some of the best scouting and covering in the world. At last we were at the foot of a certain mountain. Olympus, what a mountain! Our weary minds argued that to this one the other hills were as the arched backs of kittens.

We ascended it — no matter how — it took us years. At the top we lay on the ground and breathed while the Cubans chopped a hole in the foliage with their machetes. Then we got up and peered through this hole and saw — what? Santiago de Cuba and the harbor, with Cervera's fleet in it and the whole show.

I had noticed that one of the men had carried with care something done up in a dirty towel and tied with creepers. When you see a man carrying with care something done up in a dirty towel and tied with creepers, what do you conclude he has? Why, a telescope, of course.

The hill was more difficult when going down than when coming up. We fell from tree to tree, from boulder to boulder.

The escort only behaved badly once. It seems they had had nothing to eat but mangoes for three weeks, barring a favorite mare which some stern patriot had sacrificed to the general appetite. We were within two miles of the insurgent lines and passing through a thick wood when the escort sighted a tree laden with mangoes and with luscious ripe ones crowding the ground. The captain raved in whispers and gestured sublimely, but it was of no benefit. That escort broke formation and scattered, flitting noiselessly and grabbing.

[MANGO-FED CUBANS REVOLT.]

There was a time when a Cuban nursed a cartridge and there are some disadvantages to his having a-plenty. When we reached the open ground we were a little reckless, being homeward bound, and the insurgents on the ridge, not valuing ammunition as they once did, began to pot genially away at us.

In one of the camps we stopped to lunch upon one can of beef. It was a mango camp. Our mango escort was still with us. That orange-colored fruit seemed to look reproachfully at us from the stomach of every man present. They gathered sadly around to see us eat the beef. It was too much for us. We divided one pound of beef among about thirty men, including ourselves.

We told our fifteen men, loyal save for the incident of the laden mango tree, that as they had only done twenty-five miles over impossible mountains since daylight they had better come six more miles over more impossible mountains to our rendezvous with the

Three Friends on the coast. Whereupon we would generously give them two good rations per man from the ship.

[WORLD'S BOAT DISAPPEARS.]

We mounted and rode away while they padded along behind us. As we breasted the last hillock near the coast we beheld the Three Friends standing out to sea, the black smoke rolling from her. We were about one half hour late. There is nothing in any agony of an ordinary host which could measure our suffering. A faithful escort — thirty-one miles — mangoes — three weeks — Three Friends — promises — pledges — oh, horrors.

Scovel rode like mad through the guinea grass to the beach to make desperate signals. The escort ran headlong after us. I could hear the captain screaming to his men "Run! Run! Run! Run!"

"I can't run any more! I am dying!" cried a hoarse and windless private.

"Run! Run! Run! Run!"

"If I take another step I will die of it," cried another hoarse and windless private.

"Ah," shrieked the captain wildly, "If you have to eat mangoes for another three weeks you'll wish you had run."

ARTILLERY DUEL WAS FIERCELY FOUGHT ON BOTH SIDES.

PLAYA DEL ESTE, July 1. — After seven hours of hard fighting our troops are now moving up the green hills toward the outer defenses of Santiago City.

The artillery duel this morning between Grimes's battery and the Spanish battery which he engaged was of the fiercest character. It was his second engagement of the kind.[1] His men threw their shrapnel directly into the Spanish trenches.

Reprinted here for the first time from New York World: *9 July 1898.*

1. At 8:20 A.M., July 1, Captain George S. Grimes, Battery "A," Second Artillery, opened the battle of San Juan. His position was on a hill to the left of the El Pozo-Santiago road, about 2,500 yeards from San Juan Hill. He engaged in an artillery duel with the Spaniards for forty-five minutes. Then at about 10:00 A.M., to protect the advance of Brigadier General Samuel S. Sumner's division, he opened fire again.

Grimes's career in the regular establishment is of interest to illustrate the slow promotion of the officer in the Army. Born in England, Grimes

Grimes was reinforced by a reserve battery late in the morning. Guns are being dragged up the hill through the dense chaparral and cactus.

Most of our troops are hidden in the thick woods, and so are not aware of the splendid advance of our advance guard. On the faraway hills large forces of Spaniards are being held in reserve. The Spaniards can be plainly seen in the trenches firing without exposing themselves in the slightest, simply thrusting their gun barrels over the breastworks.

CHASED BY A BIG "SPANISH MAN-O'-WAR."

The sea was like green satin, and at intervals the scud of the flying fish made bead-like traceries upon this oily, sheeny surface. Northward raised the tall blue mountains of eastern Cuba. The waters and the fair land composed one vast silence, and the seven correspondents under the awning at the stern of the newspaper despatch-boat[1] spoke of their tobacco famine as if it were the central fact in the universe. The tropic sun smote outlying parts of the ship until they scarred the careless hand. Thank heaven, there was still ice and apollinaris![2] The attire of the men was mainly pajamas, and sometimes it was less. Forward grimey and dripping stokers emerged frequently from a hatch and soused themselves with buckets of sea water. The bow of the boat steadily clove the flat sea and two curling waves wrinkled astern. It was about 1 o'clock in the afternoon.

The captain came aft and casually remarked, "Gentlemen, there is the smoke of a steamer close inshore." There was a general separation of correspondents from newspapers, novels and apollinaris bottles. "Eh, what? A steamer? Where? Let's have a look. Lend me your glasses, Jim." Sure enough there floated against the deep-toned hills a trail of tawney smoke. "Yes, there he is. That's one of them little Spanish gunboats. How is he heading, skipper?"

"He's heading straight for us," said the skipper at last. Well, what

---

served throughout the Civil War as an enlisted man; appointed a second lieutenant in 1867, he was promoted first lieutenant in 1868, and captain in 1887.

Reprinted here for the first time from New York World: *3 July 1898.*

1. The World dispatch boat, the Three Friends.
2. Properly Apollinaris water, an effervescent mineral water from the Apollinaris spring at Neuenahr, Germany; trademark, Apollinaris.

was to be done? There was a remote chance that it was an American cruiser prowling to and fro before Santiago de Cuba, but — at any rate, let's wait until we see it.

The captain climbed with his glasses to the top of the wheel-house. "He's heading straight for us and he's smoking up to beat hell." The jocular stage arrived.

"If he's a Spaniard, don't let a drop of whiskey fall into the enemy's hands."

"Wait until they get to stirring you up with a machete. Then you won't sleep so late in the mornings."

"Let's answer their hail in Chinese and say we are a junk loaded with tea."

Meanwhile the captain shinned down from the top of the pilot-house. "Two masts, two funnels and smoking up to beat hell."

A busy stage succeeded the jocular stage. "Now, what American cruiser could that be? It isn't the Marblehead nor the Montgomery,[3] because I know where they are."

"It isn't the Nashville,[4] because her stacks are almost as high as her masts."

"It isn't the Detroit either. I know about where she is."

"It's a Spaniard!"

"It's a Spaniard!"

The stranger had lifted rapidly from behind the shoulder of the sea and disclosed her two masts and her two funnels even to the people on the deck of the despatch-boat. "Better hook her up, chief," said the captain. The boat turned her head due south and the wake crumpled out into large and tumultuous waves.

A stern chase! Shades of Marryat and Cooper! And hail to the proverb asserting that the same is academically bound to endure a respectable prolongation.

"Got her hooked up, chief?"

"Hooked up! Well, I guess so! She's turning over about as fast as she ever did in her life."

Now, despite the fact that the despatch-boat was incapable under the circumstances of doing more than eleven knots, this chase was dramatic and fine. Over the great prairie of smooth water swept the little journalistic adventurer, and eight miles away sped her pursuer, with great clouds of dark smoke rolling from both funnels and tumbling in torn clouds close to the water and far astern. Spanish prisons

3. USS *Marblehead* (1892) and USS *Montgomery* (1891) were sister ships and designated as unprotected cruisers.

4. USS *Nashville* (1895) was a gunboat; tonnage (displacement): 1,371; length: 220 feet; speed: 16 knots; principal armament: eight 4-inch guns.

and practice of garotting! The absence of a British flag in the locker and the probability that the enemy would not believe it anyhow! A proclamation that newspaper men will be treated as spies and a boat going only eleven knots!

Seven idle men fixed their eyes astern and speculated rapidly, while in the stoke-room a devoted band, herculean for the time, at a bunker of coal — rampant, blind with the sweat that pours from the hair and the forehead into the eye cavities, cursing over a field that ranges from lichens to flying machines, bare to the belt, feet on hot iron plates, faces bloody with color from the glaring furnaces — they stoked, stoked themselves into the air, stoked themselves beneath the sea, stoked themselves into immortality, a fireless rest in a cool hereafter.

"Does she seem to be gaining?"

"Oh, yes, she's gaining."

"Can you hook her up any more, chief?"

"Hell! We are away over our limit now. We've got the safety valve weighted. If we do any more we'll blow up. We're carrying more pounds of steam than this packet ever saw before."

Well, give the boat a treat, man! Let her see more pounds of steam than she sees even now, when she sees more than she has ever seen before. Surprise and delight her with new wonders. Exhibit to her marvels. Blow her up, if need be, blow her up. Blow her into rat's-nest fragments. Blow her into a semblance of the outpost of a compound, eleven-story, triple-tooth coffee-grinder.

And Jamaica! Oh, happy isle, dream-haven, heart's ease, asylum, refuge, sanctuary, peace-place, resting spot, vast chamber of safety, paradise of the pursued, you are popular. Jamaica, however, was reported on the 29th of May to be 160 miles to the southward of a certain newspaper despatch-boat.

"He's smoking up to beat hell," said the captain.

"He's gaining," said one correspondent.

"No; he isn't," said another.

"He is," said another.

"I'll pass a cable under the ship and tie the valve with that," said the chief engineer.

"He's gaining," said everybody.

"——— ——— ** !!!" said the stoke-room.

The enemy was swelling out. He now exhibited a tremendous beam, and his spars could be counted without a glass. And still he grew. He was fairly flying. Billows of smoke were rolling out of his funnels, and a white shine at his forefoot told where his bow cut the sea.

Only four miles away! The game was up. He could fire and strike now whenever he liked. The despatch boat fled still, but hope was gone. The warship simply ate the distance between them. The correspondents began mournful preparations for capture. How many dagoes did they have up in Atlanta? Were there enough to go around in case an exchange was arranged? Well! well! this was a queer end to the cruise.

On swept the pursuing steamer — inexorable, certain as a natural law. She had fired no gun. She was a terrible water sphinx in her silence. Presently her wheel swung her to starboard, and to the eyes of the speechless and immovable crowd on the despatch-boat was presented the whole beautiful length of the American auxiliary cruiser St. Paul.[5]

NIGHT ATTACKS ON THE MARINES AND A BRAVE RESCUE.

GUANTANAMO, July 4. — Once upon a time there was a great deal of fighting between the marines and the guerillas here, and during that space things occurred.

The night attacks were heart-breaking affairs, from which the men emerged in the morning exhausted to a final degree, like people who had been swimming for miles. From colonel to smallest trumpeter went a great thrill when the dawn broke slowly in the eastern sky, and the weary band quite cheerfully ate breakfast, that scandalous military breakfast which is worst when men have done their best, advanced far or fought long. Afterward the men slept, sunk upon the ground in an abandon that was almost a stupor.

Lieut. Neville,[1] with his picket of about twenty men, was entirely

5. USS *St. Paul* (1895) was originally a liner owned by International Navigation Company, now converted into an auxiliary cruiser; tonnage (displacement): 14,910; length: 535 feet; speed: 22 knots; principal armament: six 5-inch guns. She had been commissioned April 20, 1898, and was commanded by Captain Charles D. Sigsbee, U.S.N., formerly of USS *Maine*.

Reprinted here for the first time from New York World: 16 July 1898.

1. Wendell Cushing Neville (1870–1930) was brevetted captain for this action. A graduate of the Naval Academy in 1890 and a first lieutenant since 1894, he was destined to become one of the legendary fighting men of the Marine Corps and its commandant, 1929–1930. In World War I he commanded as colonel the Fifth Marine Regiment and as brigadier general the Fourth Brigade. In 1914 he won the Congressional Medal of Honor.

cut off from camp one night, and another night Neville's picket and the picket of Lieut. Shaw[2] were cut off, fighting hard in the thickets for their lives. At the break of day the beleaguered camp could hear still the rifles of their lost pickets.

The problem of rescue added anxiety to the already tremendous anxiety of the fine old colonel,[3] a soldier every inch of him. The guerillas were still lurking in the near woods, and it was unsafe enough in camp without venturing into the bush.

Volunteers from Company C were called for, and these seventeen privates volunteered:

Boniface, Conway, Fitzgerald, Heilner, Harmson, Hemerle, Lewin, Mann, Mills, Monahan, Nolan, O'Donnell, Ryan, Riddle, Sinclair, Sullivan, W. A., and Smith, J. H.

They went out under Lieut. Lucas.[4] They arrived in Neville's vicinity just as he and his men, together with Shaw and his men, were being finally surrounded at close range. Lucas and his seventeen men broke through the guerillas and saved the pickets, and the whole body then fell back to Crest Hill. That is all there is to it.

STEPHEN CRANE'S VIVID STORY
OF THE BATTLE OF SAN JUAN

IN FRONT OF SANTIAGO, July 4, via Old Point Comfort, Va., July 13. — The action at San Juan on July 1 was, particularly speaking, a soldier's battle. It was like Inkerman,[1] where the English fought

2. Second Lieutenant Melville J. Shaw; a graduate of the Academy in 1894, he was appointed a second lieutenant in 1896. He and Neville were platoon leaders in Company "D" and both had been erroneously reported captured by the enemy.

3. Lieutenant Colonel Robert W. Huntington.

4. First Lieutenant Lewis C. Lucas was platoon leader, first platoon, Company "C." A graduate of the Academy in 1889, he was appointed second lieutenant in 1891 and promoted first lieutenant in 1892.

Reprinted from New York World: *14 July 1898. In* Harper's Weekly, *42 (23 July 1898) a short version appeared entitled: "In*

1. An intense and often savage battle in the Crimean War on 5 November 1854, between combined French and English forces against strong Russian columns. The English lost over twenty-seven per cent of their men and the Russians even more. The "fog" mentioned by Crane has also been called a mist or a rain.

half leaderless all day in a fog. Only the Cuban forest was worse than any fog.

No doubt when history begins to grind out her story we will find that many a thundering, fine, grand order was given for that day's work; but after all there will be no harm in contending that the fighting line, the men and their regimental officers, took the hill chiefly because they knew they could take it, some having no orders and others disobeying whatever orders they had.

In civil life the newspapers would have called it a grand, popular movement. It will never be forgotten as long as America has a military history.

A line of intrenched hills held by men armed with a weapon like a Mauser is not to be taken by a front attack of infantry unless the trenches have first been heavily shaken by artillery fire. Any theorist will say that it is impossible, and prove it to be impossible. But it was done, and we owe the success to the splendid gallantry of the American private soldier.

As near as one can learn, headquarters expected little or no fighting on the 1st. Lawton's division was to go by the Caney road, chase the Spaniards out of that interesting village, and then, wheeling half to the left, march down to join the other divisions in some kind of attack on San Juan at daybreak on the 2d.[2]

[MISINFORMED AS TO SPANISH STRENGTH]

But somebody had been entirely misinformed as to the strength and disposition of the Spanish forces at Caney, and instead of taking Lawton six minutes to capture the town it took him nearly all day, as well it might.

Front of Santiago." "Stephen Crane's Vivid Story of the Battle of San Juan" was reprinted in Stephen Crane: An Omnibus, *edited by R. W. Stallman (1952) and in* Stephen Crane: Stories and Tales, *edited by R. W. Stallman (1955). On the Three Friends Crane wrote this dispatch and also "Chased By a Big 'Spanish Man-O'-War' " (supra, p. 168). En route to Jamaica, Crane missed the destruction of Cervera's fleet on July 3. He filed his "Vivid Story of the Battle of San Juan" at Old Point Comfort on his arrival there aboard the* City of Washington *on July 13, having been ill a week with fever.*

The posthumous book, *Great Battles of the World* (1900), reflected Crane's seeming passion with military history, although Inkerman was not one of the battles described.

2. An error here; for Lawton, after securing El Caney, was to have proceeded to the San Juan area that same day, July 1.

The other divisions lying under fire, waiting for Lawton, grew annoyed at a delay which was, of course, not explained to them, and suddenly arose and took the formidable hills of San Juan. It was impatience suddenly exalted to one of the sublime passions.

Lawton was well out toward Caney soon after daybreak, and by 7 o'clock we could hear the boom of Capron's guns in support of the infantry.[3] The remaining divisions — Kent's and Wheeler's — were trudging slowly along the muddy trail through the forest.

When the first gun was fired a grim murmur passed along the lean column. "They're off!" somebody said.

The marching was of necessity very slow, and even then the narrow road was often blocked. The men, weighted with their packs, cartridge belts and rifles, forded many streams, climbed hills, slid down banks and forced their way through thickets.

Suddenly there was a roar of guns just ahead and a little to the left. This was Grimes's battery going into action on the hill which is called El Pasco.[4] Then, all in a moment, the quiet column moving forward was opposed by men carrying terrible burdens. Wounded Cubans were being carried to the rear. Most of them were horribly mangled.

The second brigade of dismounted American cavalry had been in support of the battery, its position being directly to the rear. Some Cubans had joined there. The Spanish shrapnel fired at the battery was often cut too long, and, passing over, burst amid the supports and the Cubans.

[SHORT LULL IN THE BATTLE.]

The loss of the battery, the cavalry and the Cubans from this fire was forty men killed and wounded, the First regular cavalry probably suffering most grievously. Presently there was a lull in the artillery fire, and down through spaces in the trees we could see the infantry still plodding with its packs steadily toward the front.

The artillerymen were greatly excited. Some showed with glee fragments of Spanish shells which had come dangerously near their heads. They had gone through their ordeal and were talking over it lightly.

In the mean time Lawton's division, some three miles away, was

3. At about 6:30 A.M., July 1, the battery under Captain Allyn Capron, U.S.A., opened the fight from a position about a mile south of El Caney. Capron's son, Captain Allyn K., had been killed at Las Guásimas. Capron, Sr., died of typhoid fever 18 September 1898, at Fort Meyer, Virginia. He was the son of Captain Allyn Capron, killed at Cherbusco in the Mexican War.

4. Properly El Paso; it is misspelled in various ways in the dispatches.

making plenty of noise. Caney is just at the base of a high willow-green, crinkled mountain, and Lawton was making his way over little knolls which might be termed foothills. We could see the great white clouds of smoke from Capron's guns and hear their roar punctuating the incessant drumming of the infantry. It was plain even then that Lawton was having considerably more of a fete than anybody had supposed previously.

At about 2,500 yards in front of Grimes's position on El Paso arose the gentle green hills of San Juan, dotted not too plentifully with trees — hills that resembled the sloping orchards of Orange County[5] in summer. Here and there were houses built evidently as summer villas, but now loopholed and barricaded. They had heavy roofs of red tiles and were shaped much like Japanese, or, better, Javanese houses. Here and there, too, along the crests of these curving hillocks were ashen streaks, the rifle-pits of the Spaniards.

At the principal position of the enemy were a flag, a redoubt, a block-house and some sort of pagoda, in the shade of which Spanish officers were wont to promenade during lulls and negligently gossip about the battle. There was one man in a summer-resort straw hat. He did a deal of sauntering in the coolest manner possible, walking out in the clear sunshine and gazing languidly in our direction. He seemed to be carrying a little cane.

[GRIMES SMASHED THEM.]

At 11.25 our artillery reopened on the central block-house and intrenchments. The Spanish fire had been remarkably fine, but it was our turn now. Grimes had his ranges to a nicety. After the great "shout of the gun" came the broad, windy, diminishing noise of the flung shell; then a fainter boom and a cloud of red debris out of the block-house or up from the ground near the trenches.

The Spanish infantry in the trenches fired a little volley imme-diately after every one of the American shells. It puzzled many to decide at what they could be firing, but it was finally resolved that they were firing just to show us that they were still there and were not afraid.

It must have been about 2 o'clock when the enemy's battery again retorted.

The cruel thing about this artillery duel was that our battery had nothing but old-fashioned powder, and its position was always as clearly defined as if it had been the Chicago fire. There is no secrecy about a battery that uses that kind of powder. The great billowy white smoke can be seen for miles. On the other hand, the Spaniards were

5. New Jersey.

using the best smokeless. There is no use groaning over what was to be, but! —

However, fate elected that the Spanish shooting should be very bad. Only two-thirds of their shells exploded in this second affair. They all whistled high, and those that exploded raked the ground long since evacuated by the supports and the timbers. No one was hurt.

[A MISPLACED BALLOON.]

From El Paso to San Juan there is a broad expanse of dense forest, spotted infrequently with vividly green fields. It is traversed by a single narrow road which leads straight between the two positions, fording two little streams. Along this road had gone our infantry and also the military balloon. Why it was ever taken to such a position nobody knows, but there it was — huge, fat, yellow, quivering — being dragged straight into a zone of fire that would surely ruin it.

There were two officers[6] in the car for the greater part of the way, and there surely were never two men who valued their lives less. But they both escaped unhurt, while the balloon sank down, torn to death by the bullets that were volleyed at it by the nervous Spaniards, who suspected dynamite. It was never brought out of the woods where it recklessly met its fate.[7]

In these woods, unknown to some, including the Spaniards, was fulminated the gorgeous plan of taking an impregnable position.

One saw a thin line of black figures moving across a field. They disappeared in the forest. The enemy was keeping up a terrific fire. Then suddenly somebody yelled, "By God, there go our boys up the hill!"

There is many a good American who would give an arm to get the thrill of patriotic insanity that coursed through us when we heard that yell.

Yes, they were going up the hill, up the hill. It was the best moment of anybody's life. An officer said to me afterward: "If we had been in that position and the Spaniards had come at us, we would

---

6. Lieutenant Colonel George McC. Derby, U.S.A., and Lieutenant Colonel Joseph E. Maxfield, U.S.A., Chief Signal Officer.

7. "The enemy opened fire. This fire appeared to be musketry alone. In a very few minutes it became apparent that the balloon had been struck, as there was a decided loss of gas, and . . . I gave the order that the balloon should be pulled down. . . . An examination of the balloon having shown several holes in the upper portion, and the loss of so much gas as to render the further use of it impossible, orders were given to secure it and to retreat along the river bottom." *Report of the Chief Signal Officer . . . for . . . 1898,* p. 91.

have piled them up so high the last man couldn't have climbed over."
But up went the regiments with no music save that ceaseless, fierce
crashing of rifles.

[FOREIGN ATTACHES SAID "IMPOSSIBLE"]

The foreign attaches were shocked. "It is very gallant, but very
foolish," said one sternly.

"Why, they can't take it, you know. Never in the world," cried
another, much agitated. "It is slaughter, absolute slaughter."

The little Japanese shrugged his shoulders. He was one who said
nothing.

The road from El Paso to San Juan was now a terrible road. It
should have a tragic fame like the sunken road at Waterloo. Why we
did not later hang some of the gentry who contributed from the trees
to the terror of this road is not known.

The wounded were stringing back from the front, hundreds of
them. Some walked unaided, an arm or a shoulder having been dressed
at a field station. They stopped often enough to answer the universal
hail "How is it going?" Others hobbled or clung to a friend's shoulders.
Their slit trousers exposed red bandages. A few were shot horribly in
the face and were led, bleeding and blind, by their mates.

And then there were the slow pacing stretcher-bearers with the
dying, or the insensible, the badly wounded, still figures with blood
often drying brick color on their hot bandages.

Prostrate at the roadside were many, others who had made their
way thus far and were waiting for strength. Everywhere moved the
sure-handed, invaluable Red Cross men.

Over this scene was a sort of haze of bullets. They were of two
kinds. First, the Spanish lines were firing just a trifle high. Their bullets
swept over our firing lines and poured into this devoted roadway, the
single exit, even as it had been the single approach. The second fire
was from guerillas concealed in the trees and in the thickets along the
trail. They had come in under the very wings of our strong advance,
taken good positions on either side of the road and were peppering our
line of communication whenever they got a good target, no matter,
apparently, what the target might be.

Red Cross men, wounded men, sick men, correspondents and
attaches were all one to the guerilla. The move of sending an irregular
force around the flanks of the enemy as he is making his front attack
is so legitimate that some of us could not believe at first that the men
hidden in the forest were really blazing away at the non-combatants
or the wounded. Viewed simply as a bit of tactics, the scheme was
admirable. But there is no doubt now that they intentionally fired at
anybody they thought they could kill.

You can't mistake an ambulance driver when he is driving his ambulance. You can't mistake a wounded man when he is lying down and being bandaged. And when you see a field hospital you don't mistake it for a squadron of cavalry or a brigade of infantry.

As we went along the road we suddenly heard a cry behind us. "Oh, come quick! Come quick!" We turned and saw a young soldier spinning around frantically and grabbing at his leg. Evidently he had been going to the stream to fill his canteen, but a guerilla had barred him from that drink. Two Red Cross men rushed for him.

At the last ford, in the shelter of the muddy bank, lay a dismal band, forty men on their backs with doctors working at them and bullets singing in flocks over their heads. They rolled their eyes quietly at us. There was no groaning. They exhibited that profound patience which has been the marvel of every one.

After the ford was passed the woods cleared. The road passed through lines of barbed wire. There were, in fact, barbed wire fences running in almost every direction.

The mule train, galloping like a troop of cavalry, dashed up with a reinforcement of ammunition, every mule on the jump, the cowboys swinging their whips. They were under a fairly strong fire, but up they went.

One does not expect gallantry in a pack train, but incidentally it may be said that this charge, led by the bell mare, was one of the sights of the day.

[BORROWE'S DYNAMITE GUN.]

At a place where the road cut through the crest of the ridge Burrowe and some of his men were working over his dynamite gun.[8] After the fifth discharge something had got jammed. There was never such devotion to an inanimate thing as these men give to their dynamite gun. They will quarrel for her, starve for her, lose sleep for her and fight for her to the last ditch.

In the army there have always been two opinions of the dynamite

8. The pneumatic "dynamite" gun was under the charge of Sergeant Hallett Alsop Borrowe. Actually, dynamite was not used but what was known as Nobel's gelatine. Invented by Dana Dudley, the gun consisted of two tubes, one placed over the other. The upper one, or projectile tube, was fourteen feet long; the under tube, some seven feet long, was the expansion or combustion chamber. The projectile contained a charge of four pounds of gelatine; the fuse could be set to explode on impact or to delay up to six to seven seconds. The range was said to be one to two miles and the rate of fire up to six times a minute. See the New York *Daily Tribune,* 10 July 1898, p. 2, and *The Literary Digest,* XVII (27 August 1898), 255. Both articles are illustrated.

gun. Some have said it was a most terrific engine of destruction, while others have called it a toy. With the bullets winging their long flights not very high overhead, Burrowe and his crowd, at sight of us, began their little hymn of praise, the chief note of which was one of almost pathetic insistence. If they ever get that gun into action again they will make her hum.

The discomfited Spaniards, recovering from their panic, opened from their second line a most furious fire. It was first directed against one part of our line and then against another, as if they were feeling for our weakest point, fumbling around after the throat of the army.

Somebody on the left caught it for a time, and then suddenly the enemy apparently devoted their entire attention to the position occupied by the Rough Riders. Some shrapnel, with fuses cut too long, passed over and burst from 100 to 200 yards to the rear. They acted precisely like things with strings to them. When the string was jerked, bang! went the hurtling explosive. But the infantry fire was very heavy, albeit high.

The American reply was in measured volleys. Part of a regiment would remain on the firing line while the other companies rested near by under the brow of the hill. Parties were sent after the packs. The commands knew with what other organizations they were in touch on the two flanks. Otherwise they knew nothing, save that they were going to hold their ground. They said so.

From our line could be seen a long, gray, Spanish intrenchment, from 400 to 1,000 yards away, according to what part of our line one measured from. From it floated no smoke and no men appeared there, but it was making a noise like a million champagne corks.

Back of their entrenchments, perhaps another thousand yards, was a long building of masonry tinted pink. It flew many Red Cross flags and near it were other smaller structures also flying Red Cross flags. In fact, the enemy's third line of defense seemed to be composed of hospitals.

The city itself slanted down toward the bay, just a glimpse of silver. In the clear, white sunshine the houses of the suburbs, the hospitals and the long gray trenches were so vivid that they seemed far closer than they were.

To the rear, over the ground that the army had taken, a breeze was gently stirring the long grass and ruffling the surface of a pool that lay in a sort of meadow. The army took its glory calmly. Having nothing else to do, the army sat down and looked tranquilly at the scenery. There was not that exuberance of enthusiasm which surrounds the vicinity of a candidate for the Assembly.

The army was dusty, dishevelled, its hair matted to its forehead with sweat, its shirts glued to its back with the same, and indescribably dirty, thirsty, hungry, and a-weary from its bundles and its marches and its fights. It sat down on the conquered crest and felt satisfied.

"Well, hell! here we are."

[LAWTON'S HEAVY LOSSES.]

News began to pass along the line. Lawton had taken Caney after a long fight and had lost heavily. The siege pieces were being unloaded at Siboney. Pando had succeeded in reinforcing Santiago that very morning with 8,400 men, 6,000 men, 4,500 men. Pando had not succeeded. And so on.

At dusk a comparative stillness settled upon the ridge. The shooting subsided to little nervous outbursts. In the trenches taken by our troops lay dead Spaniards.

The road to the rear increased its terrors in the darkness. The wounded men, stumbling along in the mud, a miasmic mist from the swampish ground filling their nostrils, heard often in the air the whip-lash sound of a bullet that was meant for them by the lurking guerillas. A mile, two miles, two miles and a half to the rear, great populous hospitals had been formed.

[CAMPING ON THE GROUND THEY WON.]

The long lines of the hill began to intrench under cover of night, each regiment for itself, still, however, keeping in touch on the flanks. Each regiment dug in the ground that it had taken by its own valor. Some commands had two or three shovels, an axe or two, maybe a pick. Other regiments dug with their bayonets and shovelled out the dirt with their meat ration cans.

Darkness swallowed Santiago and the new intrenchments. The large tropic stars illumined the sky. On the safe side of the ridge our men had built some little red fires, no larger than hats, at which they cooked what food they possessed. There was no sound save to the rear, where throughout the night our pickets could be faintly heard exchanging shots with the guerillas.

On the very moment, it seemed, of the break of day, bang! the fight was on again. The firing broke out from one end of the prodigious V-shaped formation to the other. Our artillery took new advanced positions, but they were driven away by the swirling Mauser fire.

When the day was in full bloom Lawton's division, having marched all night, appeared in the road. The long, long column wound around the base of the ridge and disappeared among the woods and knolls on the right of Wheeler's line. The army was now concentrated in a splendid position.

[CUBANS HELD IN CONTEMPT.]

It becomes necessary to speak of the men's opinion of the Cubans. To put it shortly, both officers and privates have the most lively contempt for the Cubans. They despise them. They came down here expecting to fight side by side with an ally, but this ally has done little but stay in the rear and eat army rations, manifesting an indifference to the cause of Cuban liberty which could not be exceeded by some one who had never heard of it.

In the great charge up the hills of San Juan the American soldiers who, for their part, sprinkled a thousand bodies in the grass, were not able to see a single Cuban assisting in what might easily turn out to be the decisive battle for Cuban freedom.

At Caney a company of Cubans came into action on the left flank of one of the American regiments just before the place was taken. Later they engaged a blockhouse at 2,000 yards and fired away all their ammunition. They sent back to the American commander for more, but they got only a snort of indignation.

As a matter of fact, the Cuban soldier, ignorant as only such isolation as has been his can make him, does not appreciate the ethics of the situation.

This great American army he views as he views the sky, the sea, the air; it is a natural and most happy phenomenon. He will go to sleep while this flood drowns the Spaniards.

The American soldier, however, thinks of himself often as a disinterested benefactor, and he would like the Cubans to play up to the ideal now and then. His attitude is mighty human. He does not really want to be thanked, and yet the total absence of anything like gratitude makes him furious. He is furious, too, because the Cubans apparently consider themselves under no obligation to take part in an engagement; because the Cubans will stay at the rear and collect haversacks, blankets, coats and shelter tents dropped by our troops.

The average Cuban here will not speak to an American unless to beg. He forgets his morning, afternoon or evening salutation unless he is reminded. If he takes a dislike to you he talks about you before your face, using a derisive undertone.

[DEMORALIZED BY AID.]

The truth probably is that the food, raiment and security furnished by the Americans have completely demoralized the insurgents. When the force under Gomez came to Guantanamo to assist the marines they were a most efficient body of men. They guided the marines to the enemy and fought with them shoulder to shoulder, not very skilfully in the matter of shooting, but still with courage and determination.

After this action there ensued at Guantanamo a long peace. The Cubans built themselves a permanent camp and they began to eat, eat much, and to sleep long, day and night, until now, behold, there is no more useless body of men anywhere! A trifle less than half of them are on Dr. Edgar's sick list, and the others are practically insubordinate. So much food seems to act upon them like a drug.

Here with the army the demoralization has occurred on a big scale. It is dangerous, too, for the Cuban. If he stupidly, drowsily remains out of these fights, what weight is his voice to have later in the final adjustments? The officers and men of the army, if their feeling remains the same, will not be happy to see him have any at all. The situation needs a Gomez. It is more serious than these bestarred machete bearers know how to appreciate, and it is the worst thing for the cause of an independent Cuba that could possibly exist.[9]

[THE BATTLE OF JULY 2.]

At San Juan the 2d of July was a smaller edition of the 1st. The men deepened their intrenchments, shot, slept and ate. On the 1st every man had been put into the fighting line. There was not a reserve as big as your hat. If the enemy broke through any part of the line there was nothing to stop them short of Siboney. On the 2d, however, some time after the arrival of Lawton, the Ninth Massachusetts and the Thirty-fourth Michigan[10] came up.

Along the road from El Paso they had to pass some pretty grim sights. And there were some pretty grim odors, but the men were steady enough. "How far are they off?" they asked of a passing regular. "Oh, not far; but it's all right. We think they may run out of ammunition in the course of a week or ten days."

The volunteers laughed. But the pitiful thing about this advance was to see in the hands of the boys these terrible old rifles that smoke like brush fires and give the regimental line away to the enemy as plainly as an illuminated sign.

I remember that on the first day men of the Seventy-first who had lost their command would try to join one of the regular regiments, but the regulars would have none of them. "Get out of here with that

9. Crane's opinions of the Cuban soldiers were echoed by other observers, commentators, and U.S. newspapers. H. H. Sargent was quite disapproving, for example: ". . . taken as a whole, they [the Cubans] had neither the discipline nor the courage to close with the enemy and fight . . . ," *The Campaign of Santiago de Cuba*, II (1907), 165–166.

10. The Thirty-fourth Michigan and Ninth Massachusetts arrived at the front on the morning of July 2, with the Michigan regiment taking position to the rear of Kent's division and the Massachusetts unit moving to the left of Brigadier General John C. Bates's brigade.

—— gun!" the regulars would say. During the battle just one shot from a Springfield would call a volley, for the Spaniards then knew just where to shoot. It was very hard on the Seventy-first New York and the Second Massachusetts.

At Caney about two hundred prisoners were taken. Two big squads of them were soldiers of the regular Spanish infantry in the usual blue-and-white pajamas. The others were the rummiest-looking set of men one could possibly imagine. They were native-born Cubans, reconcentrados,[11] traitors, guerillas of the kind that bushwacked us so unmercifully. Some were doddering old men, shaking with the palsy of their many years. Some were slim, dirty, bad-eyed boys. They were all of a lower class than one could find in any United States jail.

At first they had all expected to be butchered. In fact, to encourage them to fight, their officers had told them that if they gave in they need expect no mercy from the dreadful Americans.

Our great, good, motherly old country has nothing in her heart but mercy, and nothing in her pockets but beef, hard-tack and coffee for all of them — lemon-colored refugee from Santiago, wild-eyed prisoner from the trenches, Spanish guerilla from out the thickets, half-naked insurgent from the mountains — all of them.

SPANISH DESERTERS AMONG THE REFUGEES AT EL CANEY.

EL CANEY, July 5, via Port Antonio, Jamaica, July 7. — During to-day's lull in the hostilities a steady stream of refugees has poured into our lines from the beleaguered city of Santiago. Women, by far, have been in the majority. Men, strong and able-bodied, have been

11. So-called because of an order issued by Captain General Valeriano Weyler on 2 October 1896, the results of which brought untold horror and suffering upon the Cubans. Briefly the order required "all the inhabitants [noncombatants] of the country or outside of the line of fortifications of the towns" within a period of eight days to "reconcentrate themselves in the town occupied by the troops. Any individual who after the expiration of this period is found in the uninhabited parts will be considered a rebel and tried as such." See Elbert J. Benton, *International Law and Diplomacy of the Spanish-American War* (1908), p. 27.

Weyler issued other orders in similar terms for the several provinces.

Reprinted here for the first time from New York World: *8 July 1898. Juxtaposed with Crane's account of the refugees was Frank Norris' sketch entitled "Comida: An Experience in Famine."*

few indeed. Spain has urgent need of such, wherefore Santiago has given up few more than wrecked and helpless creatures, too far upon the road to death to aid in staying our advance.

Yet, as the truce advanced, it changed the number and the character of these refugees. More men flocked in, young men and strong men. Certainly among them were deserters. There was the air of the true Spaniard about them. They had cast aside their distinguishing uniforms, to be sure, but they could not so easily disguise the ways and bearing of the soldier. Undoubtedly they were renegades. But, then — what matter? They were permitted within the lines, the one place where they would find safety from the impending avalanche of death soon to roll down upon Santiago from the hillside.

One saw in this great, gaunt assemblage the true horror of war. The sick, the lame, the halt and the blind were there. Women and men, tottering upon the verge of death, plodded doggedly onward. Beyond were our lines and safety. But so long had this same horror of war been before them that no longer could they feel its horridness. Their air was stolid and indifferent. It was a forlorn hope at the best. If this was safety, well and good. If death, what difference how it came.

[WOMEN MEET INSURGENT KINDRED.]

In sharp contrast to this, one saw, now and again, women radiant with joy. These were the kindred of the insurgents. Some had been separated from those stout hearts in the field for many weary weeks — yes, months, and even years. At the crest of that weary slope they knew whom they should find. Toiling upward and onward they pressed, and finally, with glad cries, in the great gathering of troops they came upon the ones they sought. This, indeed, was another side of war.

Again, in the throng toiling on to safety were men and women carried in chairs and litters, some even in cot-beds. Our ambulances went forth to meet them. Then when these stolid, hopeless, unimpassioned ones found the dreaded enemy receiving and aiding them with kindness they showed, for the first time, some trace of feeling. What! Should these mad, despised Americanos spend time aiding the weak and aged! This was a wonder, indeed.[1]

1. The "emigration" to El Caney was the result of the intention of the American forces to bombard Santiago commencing at 12 noon, July 5. To avoid unnecessary slaughter, the governor of Santiago issued a decree permitting all noncombatants to leave the city between the hours of 5 A.M. and 9 A.M., July 5. The "emigration" began at daybreak.

Crane, who was at El Caney only for a short time, barely suggests the suffering of the "emigrants" there. Provisions were exhausted very shortly.

But, though the Americans' hands were turned to doing gentleness, it was otherwise with those Spanish miserables, Spain's ignoble pride, the guerillas.[2] They lurked along the roadsides, eager and ready for bloodshed, plunder and unnameable wickedness. To drive them back the American cavalry patrolled the road of the refugees, whereupon the guerillas withdrew.

At the church in Caney the American surgeons were laboring among the enemy's sorely wounded. Here fifty-two Spanish were under treatment. Their amazement was profound. In the centre of the church lies one of the Spanish commanders, sorely wounded. There never was a more astonished man than he. Like the others, he believed his position impregnable. How any mortal could cross the zone of fire and survive was a matter beyond his ken. By the saints, it was a miracle! Three thousand Mausers, he knew to his own knowledge, were trained down the one slope he guarded. Yet had the Americans plunged through the rain of death and driven all before them.

[AMAZED AT KIND TREATMENT.]

Almost as great was his amazement at our treatment of himself and his wounded men. Why should we waste time upon them, when so many of ours had been stricken? Why this kindness? They had expected to lie where they had fallen, waiting but to die. It was the fortune of war. Why should it not be?

Inside the limits of this town the foreign Consuls have made their headquarters. Here each one is ready to provide for the people of his flag. Also they are aiding in the care of the other refugees, so far as they are able. None of the refugees brought food — there was no food for them to bring. The Spaniards had planned to restock their commissary with the supplies they had arranged to capture from the Americans. It was a sad blow that the Americans declined to be captured.

Our course to all at Caney has been moderation. Sometimes we have been too kind. Everybody knows the story of the road from the battle-field — the guerillas hanging to the flanks of the long line of

---

"The bodies of those . . . killed on the 1st of July had only partly been buried. . . . Carcasses of horses and other animals, even corpses of persons, were thrown into the river. . . . Most of the people lived on mangoes and mamoncillos, and it is no wonder that malaria, fevers, and dysentery broke out. . . . Suffice it to say that El Caney, which was a town of 200 houses, was invaded by 20,000 people, who had counted on being there two days and who remained eleven . . . until the 16th." José Müller y Tejeiro, "Battles and Capitulation of Santiago de Cuba," *Notes on the Spanish-American War* (1900), p. 147.

2. Approximately one thousand guerrillas operated at Santiago during hostilities.

wounded going to the rear. Though these men of ours could fight no longer, though they were in sore distress, these fiends incarnate fired upon them. They picked off, where they were able, the ambulance men, the bearers of the Red Cross flag and the surgeons at their work. They bowled them over at every chance. Yet three of these miscreants, caught among the trees, wearing clothes stripped from our dead, have been set to work about headquarters.

CAPTURED MAUSERS FOR VOLUNTEERS.

GEN. SHAFTER'S HEADQUARTERS, July 7. — To men who have studied recent fighting in Cuba there is one point that occurs constantly and with increasing weight, and that point relates to the arms of the volunteers. The Springfield, 1873, was undoubtedly a good weapon in its time, and certainly it is even now a very strong shooting rifle, but if we are conducting a modern war on modern lines we may just as well understand once for all that black powder will not do.[1]

We cannot without cruel injustice send men using black powder into action against men who use a fair grade of smokeless. If any one wishes to learn more let him ask the Seventy-first New York or the Second Massachusetts or the Thirty-third Michigan.

The last-named regiment in particular has learned all the joys of being badly cut up by a force that they have never seen — whose positions they could not even suspect.

On July 1 the regiment was ordered to march on Aguadores and make an attack, which, it was hoped, would draw off a reinforcement from the Santiago trenches and make the work easier for Wheeler, Kent and Lawton.[2] The men were marched up the railroad track, which is the only practicable road between Siboney and Aguadores. Dense thickets were upon either side.

Reprinted here for the first time from New York World: 17 July 1898.

1. As has been stated, the volunteers, except for a small number, were armed with the Springfield, Model 1873. When war broke out, the War Department armed the expanded regular units and about 2,000 volunteers with Krag-Jörgensens. On hand were some 266,000 Springfields, but no smokeless powder cartridges for them and none obtainable. Black powder had to be used. From R. A. Alger, The Spanish-American War (1901), p. 13.

2. The Thirty-third Michigan, under General Duffield, and supported by the shellfire of two of Sampson's ships, attacked Aguadores while fighting was going on at El Caney and San Juan. The Aguadores operation was a feint to prevent the Spanish from sending reinforcements to Linares. In H. H. Sargent, The Campaign of Santiago de Cuba (1907), II, 122.

The action was opened by a Spanish battery, which had been placed so as to rake the railway track. This battery used smokeless powder. A moment later Spanish infantry opened a heavy fire. The infantry, too, used smokeless powder. The Thirty-third Michigan became then involved in one of those battles with spectres which is so hard on the nerves of the oldest soldiers. What force was hidden in the chaparral they could not estimate. They could tell nothing save that they were losing men.

On the other hand, their position and everything that they did were always perfectly clear to the Spaniards. If they deployed a line of skirmishers to the left and opened fire the Spaniards were able not only to locate this line exactly but to estimate from the puffs of smoke how many men were engaged. In a word, the proceedings of the enemy were all shrouded in mystery, while the movements of the Americans were always hopelessly palpable. So much for the Thirty-third Michigan and black powder.

It is plain reasoning that we have not armed the volunteers with Krag-Jorgensens, because we have not enough Krag-Jorgensens, and ordinarily there would be small use in scolding about it, but upon the fall of Santiago we should come into the possession of about ten maybe fifteen thousand Mauser rifles in good condition, and these should immediately go into the hands of our volunteers.

The Mauser is a more simple rifle than the Krag-Jorgensen, and in a good many respects it is a better arm. The volunteers could learn its use easily and quickly, and in a trice their effectiveness would be increased fourfold.

At the battle of San Juan it was not unusual to see, when a regular fell, some volunteers throw away an old Springfield and possess himself of the regular's Krag-Jorgensen and ammunition. The men find out what is good for them quickly enough. They would welcome the Mausers, and it is to be hoped they will get them. If there turns out to be not enough Mauser ammunition to last them any great length of time, let us set to work and make it. In war anything is justified save killing your own men through laziness or gross stupidity.

REGULARS GET NO GLORY.

SIBONEY, July 9. — Of course people all over the United States are dying to hear the names of the men who are conspicuous for bravery in Shafter's army. But as a matter of fact nobody with the

Reprinted here for the first time from New York World: *20 July 1898.*

army is particularly conspicuous for bravery. The bravery of an individual here is not a quality which causes him to be pointed out by his admiring fellows; he is, rather, submerged in the general mass. Now, cowardice — that would make a man conspicuous. He would then be pointed out often enough, but — mere bravery — that is no distinction in the Fifth Corps of the United States Army.

The main fact that has developed in this Santiago campaign is that the soldier of the regular army is the best man standing on two feet on God's green earth. This fact is put forth with no pretense whatever of interesting the American public in it. The public doesn't seem to care very much for the regular soldier.[1]

The public wants to learn of the gallantry of the Reginald Marmaduke Maurice Montmorenci Sturtevant, and for goodness sake how the poor old chappy endures that dreadful hard-tack and bacon. Whereas, the name of the regular soldier is probably Michael Nolan and his life-sized portrait was not in the papers in celebration of his enlistment.

Just plain Private Nolan, blast him — he is of no consequence. He will get his name in the paper — oh, yes, when he is "killed." Or when he is "wounded." Or when he is "missing." If some good Spaniard shoots him through he will achieve a temporary notoriety, figuring in the lists for one brief moment in which he will appear to the casual reader mainly as part of a total, a unit in the interesting sum of men slain.

In fact, the disposition to leave out entirely all lists of killed and wounded regulars is quite a rational one since nobody cares to read them, anyhow, and their omission would allow room for oil paintings of various really important persons, limned as they were in the very act of being at the front, proud young men riding upon horses, the horses being still in Tampa and the proud young men being at Santiago, but still proud young men riding upon horses.

The ungodly Nolan, the sweating, swearing, overloaded, hungry, thirsty, sleepless Nolan, tearing his breeches on the barbed wire en-

1. It so happened that the first American soldier killed in this war was a society soldier, Sergeant Hamilton Fish, killed when Roosevelt's Rough Riders were ambushed; and another society soldier was almost killed: Lieutenant Colonel Roosevelt. What irked Crane was that the newspapers were giving excessive adulation to the society soldier, dead or alive, while ignoring the common soldier — "Nolan." In counterattack Crane issued "Regulars Get No Glory," "Memoirs of a Private" (*infra*, p. 213), and "The Private's Story" (*infra*, p. 215).

"Just plain Private Nolan" reappears in Crane's short story "The Price of the Harness," which is the best thing in *Wounds in the Rain* (1900).

tanglements, wallowing through the muddy fords, pursuing his way through the stiletto-pointed thickets, climbing the fire-crowned hill — Nolan gets shot. One Nolan of this regiment or that regiment, a private, great chums in time of peace with a man by the name of Hennessy, him that had a fight with Snyder. Nearest relative is a sister, chambermaid in a hotel in Omaha. Hennessy, old fool, is going around looking glum, buried in taciturn silence, a silence that lasts two hours and eight minutes; touching tribute to Nolan.

There is a half-bred fox terrier in barracks at Reno.[2] Who the deuce gets the dog now? Must by rights go to Hennessy. Brief argument during which Corporal Jenkins interpolates the thoughtful remark that they haven't had anything to eat that day. End of Nolan.

The three shining points about the American regular are his illimitable patience under anything which he may be called upon to endure, his superlative marksmanship and his ability in action to go ahead and win without any example or leading or jawing or trumpeting whatsoever. He knows his business, he does.

He goes into battle as if he had been fighting every day for three hundred years. If there is heavy firing ahead he does not even ask a question about it. He doesn't even ask whether the Americans are winning or losing. He agitates himself over no extraneous points. He attends exclusively to himself. In the Turk or Cossack this is a combination of fatalism and wooden-headedness. It need not be said that these qualities are lacking in the regular.

After the battle, at leisure — if he gets any — the regular's talk is likely to be a complete essay on practical field operations. He will be full of views about the management of such and such a brigade, the practice of this or that battery, and be admiring or scornful in regard to the operations of the right flank. He will be a tireless critic, bolstering his opinions with technical information procured heaven only knows where. In fact, he will alarm you. You may say: "This man gabbles too much for to be a soldier."

Then suddenly the regular becomes impenetrable, enigmatic. It is a question of Orders. When he hears the appointed voice raised in giving an Order, he is a changed being. When an Order comes he has no more to say; he simply displays as fine a form of unquestioning obedience as there is to be seen anywhere. It is his sacred thing, his fetich, his religion. Nothing now can stop him but a bullet.

In speaking of Reginald Marmaduke Maurice Montmorenci Sturtevant and his life-sized portraits, it must not be supposed that the un-

2. Fort Reno, Oklahoma Territory, Department of Missouri. Prior to the war it was the headquarters of the Tenth Infantry and elements of the First Cavalry Regiments.

fortunate youth admires that sort of thing. He is a man and a soldier, although not so good either as man or soldier as Michael Nolan. But he is in this game honestly and sincerely; he is playing it gallantly; and, if from time to time he is made to look ridiculous, it is not his fault at all. It is the fault of the public.

We are as a people a great collection of the most arrant kids about anything that concerns war, and if we can get a chance to perform absurdly we usually seize it. It will probably take us three more months to learn that the society reporter, invaluable as he may be in times of peace, has no function during the blood and smoke of battle.

I know of one newspaper whose continual cabled instructions to its men in Cuba were composed of interrogations as to the doings and appearance of various unhappy society young men who were decently and quietly doing their duty along o' Nolan and the others. The correspondents of this paper, being already impregnated with soldierly feeling, finally arose and said they'd be blamed if they would stand it.

And shame, deep shame, on those who, because somebody once led a cotillion can seem to forget Nolan — Private Nolan of the regulars — shot through, his half-bred terrier masterless at Reno and his sister being chambermaid in a hotel in Omaha; Nolan, no longer sweating, swearing, overloaded, hungry, thirsty, sleepless, but merely a corpse, attired in about 40 cents' worth of clothes. Here's three volleys and taps to one Nolan, of this regiment or that regiment, and maybe some day, in a fairer, squarer land, he'll get his picture in the paper, too.[3]

A SOLDIER'S BURIAL THAT MADE A NATIVE HOLIDAY.

PONCE, Porto Rico, Aug. 5 (Special Correspondence of the *Journal* [1]). — A company of regular infantry marched into the plaza at Ponce, halted, stacked arms and broke ranks. In the cool shade of the trees the men loafed carelessly while the natives, always intensely interested

3. For information: a private's pay in the army was $13 a month; a sergeant's pay ranged from $18 to $23, a regimental sergeant major's from $36 to $41. Officers were fairly well paid, ranging from $1,400 a year for second lieutenants to $7,500 for major generals.

Reprinted here for the first time from New York Journal: *15 August 1898.*

1. At Siboney Crane boarded the transport *City of Washington* to return to the United States because he was ill with fever, and in order to obtain an advance from Pulitzer's *World*, which he didn't get. On board

in the soldiers, gathered near and began their comic, good-natured pantomime. The lazy, still, tropic afternoon drifted slowly, hour by hour, with only the rumble of passing carriages to interrupt its profound serenity.

The captain of the regulars went down the street to where, before the door of a house, waited a hearse. There was a carriage containing two American women, and on the pavement stood a little group of officers, with their battered old hats in their hands. The natives began to accumulate in a crowd, and from them arose a high-pitched babble of gossip concerning this funeral. They stretched their necks, pointed, dodged those who would interfere with their view. Amid the chatter the Americans displayed no signs of hearing it. They remained calm, stoical, superior, wearing the curious, grim dignity of people who are burying their dead.

The company of regulars swung down the street, drew up in front of the house, and presented arms with a clash. Six big, blue-shirted privates paced out with the coffin. The throng edged up suddenly, dodging and peering. The little band of Americans seemed like beings of another world, with their gently mournful, impassive faces, during this display of monkeyish interest.

[THE VOYAGE OF THE HEARSE.]

The cortege moved off, preceded, accompanied, followed by the crowd of natives. Ponce,² a large city, drowsed on peacefully in the

---

he had to isolate himself as a yellow-fever suspect. However, Crane's health had improved when the ship docked at Old Point Comfort, Virginia, on July 13. Here he bought new clothes, costing twenty-four dollars for the entire new outfit; but the New York *World* refused to reimburse him when he appeared in the *World* offices in late July.

The *World* had a grudge against Crane on two counts: one was that he had filed Edward Marshall's dispatch for the *Journal* when Marshall was severely wounded, and the other was that an unsigned dispatch in the *World* for July 16 accused the New York Seventy-first Regiment of cowardice. But Crane was back in the United States by the 13th, and this dispatch was filed from Port Antonio, Jamaica, and dated July 15. It was written not by Crane, but by Sylvester Scovel. (See Ames W. Williams: "Stephen Crane, War Correspondent," *New Colophon:* April 1948.)

Irked by his shabby treatment by the New York *World*, he covered the butt end of the war in Puerto Rico for the *Journal*. Peace was signed on 12 August 1898.

By the last week of August he was in Havana, and from Havana he sent the *Journal* more than two dozen sketches. It is reputed that he entered Havana as a tobacco buyer. So said Cora in her letter to the Secretary of War (*Letters*, p. 189).

2. At that time, Ponce was the first city in size, *ca.* 35,000, on the island, situated on the south-central coast on the Portugés River.

sun, and the passing of the small procession brought no particular emotion to its mind. In the suburbs women hurried out to the porches of the little wooden houses, and naked babies, swollen with fruit, strutted out to see, sucking their thumbs. A man walking directly behind the hearse was hailed interrogatively from a distance. He answered loudly, waving his arm toward the graveyard.

A girl called greetings to some friends in the crowd. Suddenly, close to the road, a woman broke out in a raucous tirade at some of her children. The crowd still babbled. All these sounds beat like waves upon the hearse; noisy, idle, senseless waves beating upon the hearse, the invulnerable ship of the indifferent dead man. And the Americans, moving along behind it, were still calm, stoical, superior. The spray of the chatter whirled against them and they were bronze, bronze men going to bury their dead, and the humming and swishing and swashing were only as important as the rattling of so many pebbles in a tin box.

The graveyard was circled by a high wall which was surmounted by broken bottles sunk into the mortar. The interior presented the appearance of a misused potato patch were it not for the gaunt wooden crosses which upreared here and there. The crowd of natives ploughed through each other in order to reach the gate.

The troops marched forward and faced up sharply before an open grave. A chaplain appeared. The Americans, barring the infantry, stood bareheaded. The natives, noting this, took off their hats. There was a moment of intense expectancy.

[THE HUMORS OF A FUNERAL.]

"I am the resurrection and the life" — The chaplain's words were quite smothered in the ejaculations, inquiries, comments which came over the wall where many people were pushing toward the gate. An enterprising lot had climbed a bit of old wall which overlooked the cemetery wall, and upon it they shrilled like parrots. The chaplain, beset, badgered, drowned out, went on imperturbably.

The first volley of the firing party created a great convulsion in the crowd outside, who could not see the proceedings and were taken by surprise. As the sound crashed toward the hills many jumped like frightened rabbits and then a moment later the whole mob, seeing the joke, burst into wild laughter.

A bugler stepped forward, into a medley of sounds such as would come from a combined baseball game and clambake, he sent the call of "taps," that extraordinary wail of mourning and song of rest and peace, the soldier's good-bye, his night, the fall of eternal darkness, the end.

The sad, sad, slow voice of the bugle called out over the grave, a soul appealing to the sky, a call of earthly anguish and heavenly tranquillity, a solemn heart-breaking song. But if this farewell of the soldier to the sky, the flowers, the bees and all life was heard by the natives their manner did not betray it.

THE PORTO RICAN "STRADDLE"

JUANA DIAZ, Porto Rico, Aug. 10.[1] (Special Correspondence of the Journal). — The American soldier alludes often to the natives here as handshakers. It is his way of expressing a cynical suspicion regarding all the "viva Americanos" business that he hears and sees in this city of Ponce. One cannot define a type at once when the type has just been captured, and knows that it must be very, very good, although the same may be foreign to its ordinary manners. It is correct enough that the American soldier should be suspicious; there is more or less in the handshaking idea.

Johnson,[2] one of the Journal's correspondents here, and myself had recently an opportunity to see the Porto Rican when he was right in the middle and couldn't tell which way to dodge. The incident was instructive.

Two companies of the Sixteenth Pennsylvania Infantry at that time formed the advance of the army along the main military road. They were encamped just beyond the town of Juana Diaz, which is nine miles from Ponce. We heard that General Ernst,[3] the brigade commander, was going to reinforce these pickets with five more companies and then extend the American advance five more miles into the hills. When we reached Juana Diaz we could see the men slinging

---

Reprinted here for the first time from New York Journal: *18 August 1898.*

1. How Crane "captured" Juana Diaz is told by Richard Harding Davis, *infra*, p. 196.

2. Unidentifiable.

3. Brigadier General Oswald Herbert Ernst (1842–1926), in command of the 1st Brigade, 1st Division, 1st Army Corps in Puerto Rico. Chiefly an engineering officer, Ernst had graduated from West Point in 1864 and served around the regular establishment, including such tours of duty as aide-de-camp to President Benjamin Harrison and superintendent of West Point (1893–1898). At the outbreak of war he was promoted brigadier general of volunteers and assigned to Chickamauga.

He was in direct command of troops at the skirmish at Coamo, August 9 (the day before Crane filed his dispatch), a battle which Crane seems to have ignored.

The Sixteenth Pennsylvania had taken part in the fighting.

their kits, preparatory to marching, and in the little hotel facing the plaza and the old church the General and his staff were just finishing their luncheon. We thought it was only a question of minutes, so we passed them and went on along the road which the troops were to take. We were under the impression that an advance party had gone on ahead. However, it was not long before a peasant's answers convinced us that Johnson, mounted on a bicycle, was the sure-enough vanguard of the American army. His immediate support bestrode a long, low, rakish plug, with a maximum speed of seven knots. We had no desire to win fame by any two-handed attack on the Spanish army, so, on receiving the peasant's information, we slowed down to a pace that was little more than a concession to one man's opinion of the other.

The road, beautifully hard, wound through two thick lines of trees. We circled spurs of the mountains, the grass upon them being yellowish green in the afternoon sunlight. We crossed tumbling brooks. With the palm trees out, it was a scene such as can be found in summer time in Southern New York. There was no man nor beast to be seen ahead on the road nor in the fields. We learned afterward that we were about two miles and a half ahead of the American scouts, the difficulties attending the work of the flanking parties causing the march to be extremely slow. Rounding a corner we came suddenly upon a country store. Chickens and pigs scouted in the road and in the yard of the house across the road. On the steps of the store, on a fence, on boxes and barrels, and leaning against trees were about thirty men dressed in civilian garb. As we appeared they turned their heads, and as we rode slowly up every eye swung to our pace. They preserved an absolute, stony silence. Now, here were men between the lines. The Americans were on one side and the Spaniards were on the other. They knew nothing of any American advance. They were, as far as they knew, on strictly independent ground, and could drop on either side of the fence. Americanism was here elective.

We drew up and looked at them. They looked at us. Not a word was said.

The native in the zone already ours is always quick to greet the American with a salute or with hat in hand. He cries out "Bueno!" at every opportunity, meaning, "I am glad you have come." When he is a crowd he is forever yelling "Viva Americanos!" When he is one he is forever nodding and smiling with absolute frankness and telling you that he prefers the Americans by all means. He is busy at it day and night.

But here was a contrast. This reception was new to our experience. These men were as tongue-tied and sullen as a lot of burglars met in the daytime. Not one of them could endure a straight glance, and if we turned suddenly we were likely to catch two of them whispering.

Time passed slowly, with no change in the situation. We remained in the road and grouped in front of the store was the crowd, with their strange foreign eyes moving in shifty glances. The situation got to be insupportable. It was no fun to stand there with an obligation of stoicism upon us and withstand this business of moving on a stage before an audience of thirty hostile dramatic critics. We finally developed a plan. We would concentrate our glance on one man and talk about him in English, ominously.

"Look at that brute on the barrel there. He certainly is glad to see us. Look at him, will you?"

"Ah, the whole crowd of 'em are Spanish — that's easy. Never mind. Let 'em wait. We'll know how it is later. Just size up the storekeeper. He'll be grinning, and charging the boys two prices to-morrow. But look at him, now. Never mind. We'll get even."

"Look at that Willie in the gray coat. See him stare back at us. Never mind. We'll fix him."

A half-hour passed as slowly as time in the sick room. Hardly a man in the crowd moved out of his place during this time. We called to the storekeeper for some cigarettes, and he came and handed them to us with a manner that was subtly offensive enough to be artistic. Some girls came out on the porch of the house and surveyed us impassively. A man talking with another glanced at us, and spat in a way that left a feeling in our minds that perhaps it was not altogether unlikely that he was referring insultingly to us.

We could not tell whether these people were all pro-Spanish Porto-Ricans or whether a part of them were really pro-American but afraid yet to give themselves away to the others or whether they were all simply timid people who wanted to play both ends against the middle until they were absolutely sure who were to be supreme. At any rate, they were a sulky, shifty, bad lot, with the odds strongly in favor of Spanish leanings. They had nothing but distrust in their eyes, and nothing but dislike in their ways.

Up the cool, shady country road toward Juana Diaz appeared a figure. It was a quarter of a mile away, but no one could mistake the slouched service hat, the blue shirt, the wide cartridge belt, the blue trousers, the brown leggings, the rifle held lightly in the hollow of the left arm. It was the first American scout.

He stood for almost two minutes, looking in our direction. Then he moved on toward us. When he had come ten paces four more men, identical in appearance, showed behind him. The crowd around the front of the store could not see them. Their first information was when a young American sergeant galloped up on a native pony. Then two of them mounted their horses quietly and started off in the direction of the Spanish lines. The young sergeant cried to us:

"Well, say, I guess I won't have that. Those Indians riding off to give us away!"

He galloped hastily down the road and we piled after him, but the two Porto Ricans came back docilely enough.

The five soldiers on foot arrived opposite the store. They did not stop, paying little heed to any one. With their passing the Porto Ricans began to brace up and smile. Then appeared the support of the scouts and flankers, forty men blocked in a solid wall of blue-black up the road. The Porto Ricans looked cheerful. After the support had gone on there was a considerable pause. Then six companies of Pennsylvania infantry marched past, with a rattling of canteens and shuffling of feet. The Porto Ricans looked happy. By the time the general clattered forward with his staff they were happy, excessively polite, overwhelming every one with attentions and shyly confessing their everlasting devotion to the United States. The proprietor of the store dug up a new English and Spanish lexicon and proudly semaphored his desire to learn the new language of Porto Rico. There was not a scowl anywhere; all were suffused with joy. We told them they were a lot of honest men. And, after all, who knows?

❋   ❋   ❋

HOW STEPHEN CRANE TOOK JUANA DIAS
By Richard Harding Davis

At the close of the Spanish-American campaign, the American forces that landed in Porto Rico were supposed to be invading a hostile territory. Politically, as a colony of the enemy, the inhabitants of the island should have been hostile, but they were not. They received our troops with one hand open and the other presenting either a bouquet, or a bottle. Our troops clasped both hands. There still remained in many of the towns a Spanish garrison, but from the greater number these garrisons had been withdrawn upon San Juana. As a result scouts and officers of our army on reconnaissance

---

Reprinted here for the first time from In Many Wars by Many War Correspondents, *edited by George Lynch and Frederick Palmer (Tokyo: Tokyo Printing Company, 1904).*

were constantly welcomed by the natives as conquering heroes, and at the approach of one of them entire villages would capitulate as readily as though the man had come leading an army corps. One town surrendered to an officer who had lost his way, and stumbled into it by mistake, another fell to the boss of a pack-train, whose only object in approaching it had been to steal some ponies.

In order to make quite sure, some towns surrendered several times. Ponce for instance surrendered four times to as many different American officers. It was not safe for an American wearing anything that resembled a uniform to approach a Porto Rican stronghold unless he was prepared to have it fall prostrate at his feet.

It struck me that in this surrendering habit of the Porto Ricans there lay a chance for great entertainment, and much personal glory, especially as one would write the story oneself. It would be a fine thing I thought to accept the surrender of a town. Few war correspondents had ever done so. It was an honor usually reserved for Major Generals in their extreme old age.

Halfway between Ponce and Coamo there is a town called Juana Dias which, at that time, seemed ripe for surrendering and I accordingly proposed to Stephen Crane, that at sunrise, before the army could advance to attack it we should dodge our own sentries, and take it ourselves. Crane was charmed with the idea, and it was arranged that on the morrow our combined forces should descend upon the unsuspecting village of Juana Dias. We tossed to see who should wake the other, and I won the toss. But I lost the town. For in an evil moment Crane confided the strategy of our campaign to the manager of his paper, the New York World,[1] Charlie Michaelson; and Michaelson saw no reason why in this effort to enlarge our country's boundaries, a man representing a rival newspaper, should take any part. So, no one woke me, and while I slumbered, Crane crept forward between our advance posts and fell upon the doomed garrison. He approached Juana Dias in a hollow square, smoking a cigarette. His khaki suit, slouched hat, and leggings were all that was needed to drive the first man he saw, or rather, the man who first saw him, back upon the town in disorderly retreat. The man aroused the village and ten minutes later the Alcalde, endeavoring to still maintain a certain pride of manner in the eyes of the towns-

1. Davis must be in error here, for Crane was filing a dispatch for the *Journal* on August 5 ("A Soldier's Burial"); he was no longer with the *World*. He describes the taking over of Juana Diaz (or Dias) in "The Porto Rican 'Straddle,'" in the *Journal* with file date of August 10, but characteristically he is silent about the part he played in the incident reported by Davis.

people, and yet one not so proud as to displease the American conqueror surrendered to him the keys of the cartel. Crane told me that no General in the moment of victory had ever acted in a more generous manner. He shot no one against a wall, looted no churches, levied no "forced loans." Instead, he lined up the male members of the community in the plaza, and organized a joint celebration of conquerors and conquered. He separated the men into two classes, roughly divided between "good fellows" and "suspects." Anyone of whose appearance Crane did not approve, anyone whose necktie even did not suit his fancy, was listed as a "suspect." The "good fellows" he graciously permitted to act as his hosts and bodyguard. The others he ordered to their homes. From the barred windows they looked out with envy upon the feast of brotherly love that overflowed from the plaza into the by streets, and lashed itself into a frenzied carnival of rejoicing. It was a long night, and it will be long remembered in Juana Dias. For from that night dates an aristocracy. It is founded on the fact that in the eyes of the conquering American while some were chosen, many were found wanting. To this day in Juana Dias, the hardest rock you can fling at a man is the word "suspect." But the "good fellows" are still the "first families."

In the cold grey dawn of the morning as Crane sat over his coffee in front of the solitary cafe, surrounded by as many of his bodyguard as were able to be about, he saw approaching along the military road from Ponce a solitary American soldier. The man balanced his rifle alertly at the "ready," and was dodging with the skill of an experienced scout from one side to the other of the long white highway. In a moment he was followed by a "point" of five men, who crept close to the bushes and concealed their advance by the aid of the sheltering palms. Behind them cautiously came the advance guard, and then boldly the Colonel himself on horseback and 800 men of his regiment. For six hours he had been creeping forward stealthily in order to take Juana Dias by surprise.

His astonishment at the sight of Crane was sincere. His pleasure was no less great. He knew that it did not fall to the lot of every Colonel to have his victories immortalized by the genius who wrote *The Red Badge of Courage*.

"I am glad to see you," he cried eagerly, "have you been marching with my men?"

Crane shook his head.

"I am sorry," said the Colonel, "I should like you to have seen us take this town."

"THIS town!" said Crane in polite embarrassment. "I'm really very sorry, Colonel, but I took this town myself before breakfast yesterday morning."

❖ ❖ ❖

HAVANA'S HATE DYING, SAYS STEPHEN CRANE.

HAVANA, Aug. 25, Special Correspondence of the Journal. — Conditions in this interesting city are much better than anybody on our side has supposed. The people await the coming of the Commission with a rather brave steadiness when you come to remember that they will not concede for a moment that Havana itself was ever in the remotest danger of being captured by the Americans.

The new condition of tranquillity has been established by the city's newspapers, which are printing Spanish news from Santiago, Porto Rico and Manila, descriptive of the temperance and justice of the Americans as well of their courage and prowess.

When I first landed here it was difficult to withstand the scowls that one met everywhere, particularly from Spanish officers, who at that time were all exaggerating their gaits and generally improving and rearranging their "fronts."

That has now changed for the better, and one can now inhabit the hotels, cafes and streets without meeting any particularly offensive looks.

Even some good manners have been publicly exploited by the police. What might be called a correspondent's corral was established out in the harbor, and nine birds fluttered therein. On a certain night one escaped and was trying his wings in Havana when the police swooped down on him. It is said that the air of distinguished consideration which surrounded the incident was beyond words. Spectators informed me the next morning that at a late hour they had left the correspondent and four police officials drinking cognac with almost supernatural courtesy in the Cafe Ingleterra.[1]

It becomes obvious that as time goes on many officials of many kinds here are arriving at the old Porto Rico proposition of playing

Reprinted here for the first time from New York Journal: 3 September 1898.

1. The Café Inglaterra, in the Hotel Inglaterra, was located on the west side of the Parque Central, more or less the center of Havana.

both ends against the middle. This is a tremendous change for the Spanish officials.

The Spanish merchant, however, has a supreme admiration for the American as a customer. He will wait for him and give him a welcome in which Peninsula patriotism plays no part.

There are four gunboats in the harbor besides the emaciated cruiser Alfonso XII[2] with no engines and no guns. The gunboats have been very useful in this war, but really they are boats which could have steamed out and destroyed the blockade at any time since our heavy ships have been away to Santiago. That is to say, they could have done so if their engines had been all right; but one can't tell whether it was a case of boilers or incompetence.

Their guns are all equivalent to six and twelve-pounders, and they could have wiped the ocean with ten or a dozen converted tow-boats if the Spaniard was only a sailor, and if the American was not such a fine sailor.

It is in the harbor where the war has marked Havana. The harbor is a soundless vacancy save for the gunboats. In the streets the change has not been so great. The cabmen charge fifty cents where once they charged thirty cents, and the commercial streets are dull, but it is on the water front where havoc has been wrought.

The prices for provisions have been about as known. The staples never went to really killing prices, if you limit the staples to rice, beans and meat. The proprietor of the Hotel Pasage[3] tells me, however, that at one time he had to pay fifty cents for a piece of bread as large as your hand in order to provide his customers at the hotel table. The luxuries simply passed out of sight, but then, to deprive people of luxuries is not necessarily to enforce a good blockade.

The spirit of the people here has not been broken, and as usual they regard the prospective ending of the war as some new betrayal of ignorance of the Government at Madrid. "Oh, yes, Santiago, I know. But, Havana? Never!" Still, their opinions of the Americans have entirely changed, and names like Sampson, Schley, Shafter and McKinley are spoken now with a change of voice.

Nobody — popularly speaking — has ever heard of Dewey, mainly because the existence of the Philippines is not a particularly well established fact.

2. Designated as a protected cruiser, Alfonso XII had a tonnage (displacement) of 3,090, a speed of 17 knots, and an armament of six guns of various caliber. She and the City of Washington (which carried Crane to Fortress Monroe) received casualties from USS Maine after the Maine blew up 15 February 1898 in Havana harbor.

3. Crane was living at the Pasaje.

The Spaniards may hate us, or, at least many of them hate us, but they will never again despise us.

The editors of the Havana papers have peculiarly difficult parts to play in this suspended crisis, and they are playing with splendid finesse and judgment.

Prominent citizens here do not see a convulsive future, the worst imagined being a time of festivities for the volunteers, when there is likely to be more or less ill-judged shooting. When that time comes certain prominent American journalists are likely to be seen writing their dispatches in the tops of tall trees.

STEPHEN CRANE SEES FREE CUBA.

HAVANA, Aug. 26, via Key West, Aug. 27. — Feeling here grows stronger for annexation. Every day the Spaniards fear anything like an onslaught from the Cuban troops, hungry for many things of which they have been long deprived.

Spaniards now respect the Americans, and probably will give hearty welcome to American troops. Reports from Santiago say the American soldiers have prevented any possible exuberance on the part of the insurgents, keeping them at the outskirts, and have made a great impression among the dominant mercantile classes. These regard the entrance of the Americans with tranquillity, and in many cases pleasure.[1]

Four Havana thieves talking yesterday said, "We must steal as much as possible before the Americans come, for then we will get into great difficulty if we steal." They had been used to paying $5 im-

---

Reprinted here for the first time from New York Journal: 28 August 1898.

1. By the terms of the Treaty of Paris, 10 December 1898, Spain relinquished her right and sovereignty over Cuba. The United States took temporary possession of the island and assumed its international obligations and, at the same time, through the War Department, administered the affairs of Cuba. In December 1901, after the people had adopted a constitution, they elected, almost unanimously, Tomás Estrada Palma (1835–1908), their first president. He was a veteran of the Ten Years War (1868–1878) and the revolution of 1895. On 20 May 1902 the United States formally withdrew from Cuba, and Palma replaced Governor General Wood.

munity for each case caught. Their sentiments give a line on the prevailing idea regarding Americans.

There will be no trouble from the volunteers provided the United States protect everybody. Even in the unconquered city of Havana the American is conqueror, if we may be allowed to speak in that way.

Steamships loading or unloading here are delayed owing to the physical weakness of the stevedores, but the higher classes in every case have had plenty of food, the difference being in quality, never quantity.

Advices from Matanzas[2] state that the condition of the poor people is simply horrible. Men, women and children lie in the street. The Consular authorities feel the Red Cross relief should come quickly. There is no such condition in Havana, where plenty of merchant ships are now coming.

The cane fields and sweet potato patches between here and Matanzas are well under way. The Spanish troops along the route look very hungry. No white flags are flying.

The better people of Matanzas also wish annexation. Along the route are temporary thatched villages for the reconcentrados. The armored cars still run on all trains, each car containing about thirty soldiers, their rifles in miserable condition, and the soldiers look as bad as reconcentrados. The garrison of Matanzas, amounting to 6,000, and a large force of insurgents under Betancourt,[3] are encamped within twelve miles.

STEPHEN CRANE FEARS NO BLANCO[1]

Havana, Aug. 28. — The change in the spirit of this city is something wonderful. It is signified by the increased use of a certain proverb. The proverb reads thus:

2. About 60 miles east of Havana, Matanzas was a city of some 35,000 population.

3. Miguel Betancourt Guerra (1835–1901), Cuban revolutionary, who participated actively in the 1868–1878 war and the uprising in 1895. In June 1896 he had successfully gotten a filibustering expedition through on S.S. *Commodore,* that ship's third venture (Crane's ill-fated journey was her fifth). He was one of the signers of the first Cuban constitution. In 1901 he was shot and rather than endure the pain he committed suicide.

Reprinted here for the first time from New York Journal: *31 August 1898.*

1. Ramon Blanco y Erenas, Marqués de Peña Plata (1833–1906), Spanish general and government official; he fought in Cuba during the

"It is better to be a lion's tail than a rat's head." If this doesn't edify any American who remembers the old rabid cries of the Havana populace, then all words have lost their significance.

Meantime everybody waits for the commission. Rumors both comic and serious fly in the streets. They do little more than indicate the desires of certain classes or parties. To-day it was said that the United States Government was going to buy for cash all the public buildings in Cuba, and that Spain was going to get the money to pay her troops.

An evening newspaper of yesterday printed an interview of over a column with Captain Stewart M. Brice, greatly to that young officer's astonishment. It seems that the interviewer breakfasted in Captain Brice's company, but as neither could speak the other's language none can tell why the interviewer thought he was interviewing anybody. Nevertheless, the article, apparently an outspoken statement by one of General Shafter's aids, set every tongue wagging.[2] It was distinctly hostile in its estimate of the Cuban character, and Spaniards were much tickled.

[AN IMAGINARY INTERVIEW.]

All the newspapers comment on it solemnly this morning. Four Americans who were also at the breakfast say that Brice and his supposed interviewer did not exchange five words. They couldn't.   .

Many of the Cubans think that as soon as the Americans come they are going to put the Spaniards out bag and baggage. They are happy over it. Columbus's bones are being dragged into the general misunderstanding to-day. Some high-priced dreamer got it into his head that the United States was going to seize the bones of the venerated discoverer. "These bones are ours, ours alone, and Spain cannot abandon them to the insults or indifference of an inimical race," he exclaims.[3]

Ten Years War and served in the Philippines as governor of Mindanao and in Cuba as governor general (captain general) twice: 1879–1881 and 1897–1898.

His last reign in Cuba was regarded as conciliatory and prudent, and he made some efforts to counteract the chaos left by Weyler, whom he replaced in October 1897. Specifically, Blanco revoked the concentration orders of Weyler.

2. Attempts to amplify this incident or to identify the officer involved have failed.

3. The bones mentioned here by Crane were alleged to be those of Columbus. On 26 September 1898 they were exhumed by the Spaniards from the cathedral of Havana and put aboard ship for transport to Spain. Prior to their being deposited in the cathedral at Seville, the coffin was

El Noticiero Universal this evening makes a laughable attempt to locate the future position of the Spaniards in Cuba. The article also indicates some of the popular misconceptions as to the intentions of the American Government. It begins with an expression of satisfaction that the American press has more or less changed its opinion of the Cubans, but sees very little on the horizon for the Spaniards, no matter which way the cat jumps.

"What are the Spaniards to do, facing this black future?" it asks. "Are we inclined to help the insurgents or are we inclined to favor the Yankees. The sentimentalism of blood and race alone calls us to the insurgents. If they rule we will have to leave this country in order not to become the victims of their hatred.

[LITTLE HOPE FOR SPANIARDS.]

"The instinct of preservation calls us to the Yankees, because we are at least bound to confess without hypocrisy that they are a people of order. But sooner or later we will be driven out of the island by them, and we will never be able to forget that they are the people who ruined us. What, then, have we to do? This is our opinion.

"We must be only Spaniards: amalgamate, form a powerful colony detailed in every way to help the prestige of the fatherland. Leave the insurgents and the Yankees to settle their own disputes, and when they have solved the problem we will decide as to our future course, after having studied the pros and cons of our own interests."

For a reason unannounced the authorities have raked up an old law which declares that no prisoner shall wear chains, although chains have been in vogue here for twenty-five years. The convicts who work on the streets are no longer to wear leg chains. People believe that the authorities are now willing to let prisoners escape in order to avoid the expense of them.

[WAITING FOR AMERICAN TROOPS.]

An American, who has been in Morro Castle,[4] who has been mobbed in the streets of Havana, who has been pelted and hooted throughout the Province of Havana because he was an American, said to me to-day:

---

opened on 4 January 1899 and found to contain about thirty bones and some ashes.

Actually, the remains of Columbus were in Santo Domingo, where they were transported in 1542, some thirty-six years after the admiral's death.

4. In addition to being used for defense of the harbor, Morro Castle also was used as a prison and place of execution.

"Oh, to see the regulars come up Obispo street.[5] We are all wait-ing for it." He had a memory for his wrongs, but we are all the same about one thing — we want to see the regulars march up Obispo street. There are few enough Americans here — maybe thirty, Red Cross members, tobacco buyers and correspondents.

"We are waiting to see our calm, steady, businesslike regulars swing up from the wharves to the Prado. It will be a great day in Havana."

To illustrate what I have previously said about the change of sentiment in Havana I must describe something which occurred this afternoon. With some friends I went to visit the graves of the dead sailors of the Maine. An old man conducted us to the pitifully bare little plot.[6] As we were going he came to the side of the carriage and said:

"There are a great many people sitting by the gate, and as you go out would you mind looking back and bowing to me? I want to show them what great and fine people are my friends."

We grinned at each other in abashed fashion at the idea of our being called great and fine, but at the gate we turned our heads and bowed fraternally to the old man, thus allowing him to work the cold bluff on the populace that he is on intimate terms with all the Ameri-cans.

In fact the position of an American changes from day to day. At first scowls, then toleration, then courtesy. For my part I came into Havana without permission from anybody. I simply came in. I did not even have a passport. I was at a hotel while the Government was firmly imprisoning nine correspondents on a steamer in the harbor. But no one molested me.

[HOW CRANE AVOIDS BLANCO.]

I don't doubt I could have been insulted if I chose. I often sus-pected Spanish officers of leaving a foot or an elbow too far in order that I might strike it and become involved in an altercation, but I dodged them all easily, without seeming to pay any heed. All I had to do was to keep from forcing any official recognition upon the Government, in which case they would have been obliged to deport me or to take some other means of disposing of me.

At present the position of an American in Havana is one that many

5. A principal east-west thoroughfare in Havana, stretching from Ca-valleria Wharf to Parque Central, along which were located the University of Havana and the governor general's palace.

6. The dead sailors from USS *Maine* were at first buried in Colon Cemetery, in the western outskirts of the city; later the remains were removed to Arlington National Cemetery.

another here envies. There is one thing which we have forgotten in our intercourse with the Spanish-Americans. People of this class not only admire splendor, they reverence it. They mistake it for excellence and power.

One remembers the visit of the British deputation to the court of King Menelek.[7] The men were decked out in all sorts of magnificence. They wore the shining uniforms of the Horse Guards, the Grenadier Guards and other lurid organizations. The sight smote the African soul of the monarch, and he promptly conceded more than he intended, even if that was not much.

The illustration is not perfect, but in dealing with a people of this kind we would find our path made much easier if we threw a few peacock feathers into our business.

I have said that the Spaniard here is going to make no trouble for the Americans. That is true; but there may be trouble. If so, it will be made by the man who is left behind — the Spaniard whose home and wealth is in Cuba and not in Spain. He is extremely likely to heave a few convenient rocks at the departing Spanish regiments.

STEPHEN CRANE'S VIEWS OF HAVANA.

Havana, Sept. 4, via Key West, Sept. 6. — Two years ago the Spanish merchants of Havana, filled with patriotic ardor, began a collection for the purchase of a war ship for the Spanish navy. A short time ago the money contributed had reached the comfortable sum of $800,000, which was given into the keeping of the Captain-General.[1]

But now ensues one of the strenuous and painful cases of bargain ruing the world has yet seen. The Spanish patriots want that money back, and they want it badly. They say with a deal of dry humor that they have discovered that a Spanish war ship is not a good investment.

7. King Menelek II (1844–1913) of Abyssinia ruled from 1889 to 1907. In May 1907, he received at Addis Ababa a British mission headed by James Rennell Rodd, 1st Baron (1858–1941), the British commissioner. Their discussions led to Menelek's agreement to settle Somali boundaries and to grant certain commercial rights for England.

The Royal Horse Guards, referred to as "The Blues," and the Grenadier Guards were very fashionable and old regiments of the British Army.

Reprinted here for the first time from New York Journal: 7 September 1898.

1. A captain general was the governor of a Spanish province or colony; the term is equivalent to governor general.

But does the Captain-General loosen his grip? Oh, no! He declares that
the money was donated to the Spanish navy, and it shall go to the
Spanish navy. The Havana merchants now see themselves in the position of people who got over-patriotic at the wrong time. Their only
solace now is to burst into tears.

An $800,000 joke is almost too expensive to incite laughter, es-
pecially in the man who pays, but the victims manage a feeble grin.
They tried to withdraw the money in order to build with it a great
Spanish clubhouse and in this way draw closer together Spaniards who
are to stay here and make them thus present a firmer front to the social
and commercial attacks of the Cubans and the coming American. Even
this fine idea did not catch the Captain-General.

About half a dozen unarmed men landed yesterday from the
relief ship in the uniform of the United States regular army. They
strolled around the streets, entered the cafes; did as they pleased. Of
course, they attracted a great deal of attention. They were very tall
men, giants to the people of Havana, and beside that they were American soldiers. I asked them how they had been treated and they
answered: "Oh, we've been used all right. We mind our own business
and nobody says anything to us." When all has been said and done,
the recent war was a most curious war.

The newsboys went screaming through the streets yesterday selling a translation of the Constitution of the United States. They flew
here and there with it excitedly, as if it were a war extra. So much so
that two or three Americans were misled into buying it, expecting to
read of the fall of New York.

The bones of Columbus still agitate a few minds. To-day the
papers announce joyfully that the Duke of Veragua,[2] lineal descendant
of the discoverer, has decided that he and he alone shall have the
bones.

The harbor is growing lively with shipping. The time to make
2,000 per cent on the sale of provisions in Havana has already past.
Merchants who think otherwise are likely to incur serious loss. In
three days the whole situation has changed. The wharves are now
piled high, and there is even more still in the bay. When Blanco decided to refuse Red Cross relief it was pretty certain that Havana had
plenty of food.

If the army is making any preparations for embarking for Spain
it is not apparent. Officially there is barely a mention of any such

2. The title of Duke of Veragua was bestowed on the grandson of
Christopher Columbus, Luís Colón (Columbus). In 1898, the holder was
Cristóbal Colón de la Cerda (1837–1910), who had been received in the
United States with great honors at the World's Columbian Exposition in
1893.

possibility. The great function of the soldier in Havana is to have nothing whatever to do. The Spanish officer has still less to do than the soldier. A brigade of volunteers is, however, aligned for inspection every morning in the Prado.[3] It is a weird scene. However, the hotel fronts the Prado and when the band plays it is worth even the endurance of an inspection of volunteers.

The authorities, by the way, have always spoken highly of these volunteers and valued them, but in action they certainly would make a sorry exhibition. Doubtless the standard of bravery would be creditable, but they don't know the business of soldiering at all. On drill they make a most unsoldierly appearance, and it is doubtful if one of them is sure whether he is carrying a gun or a handspike. But the Mauser is a fine weapon.

AMERICANS AND BEGGARS IN CUBA

The American commissions have had better care than any people who have yet invaded the island of Cuba. There has been more anxiety for their health and cuddling and precautions and general conference and discussions than is known in most sanitary philosophies. Five of them are dead.

In the meantime, there have been in Havana since about the 23d of August an unregenerate and abandoned collection of newspaper correspondents, cattle men, gamblers, speculators and drummers who have lived practically as they pleased, without care or restraint, going — most of them — wherever interest or whim led, with no regard for yellow fever or any other terror of the tropics. None of them are dead.

Probably it would be absurd to make any philosophic deductions from these certain facts but at least the facts remain interesting.

✱

There was at one time in Spain a regular commercial concern whose business it was to import into Cuba maimed and haggard beggars. The latter worked on a commission. The same company is said to be still doing business but that is quite impossible to learn. An

3. The main north-south thoroughfare of Havana, leading into the Parque Central, in which were the leading hotels and places of amusement.

Published here for the first time from an untitled holograph, three pages, in the Crane Collection at Columbia University Libraries, this unfinished article was written in pencil on the back of the Grand Hotel Pasaje (Havana) stationery probably in September 1898. It is an addition to the Crane canon.

organization of the kind does not advertise. At any rate, the streets of Havana are now infested with hideous spectacles. Creatures of disease squat on prominent corners and thrust their terrors pitifully out for the eyes of the passers-by and bands of shrill children haunt the cafes. It is like Italy.

The American is for a long time a quite reckless person with this kind of thing. He doesn't care for coppers anyhow and by profligate distribution he soon succeeds in calling all the beggars for miles down upon his own unhappy head. The beggars of Havana pay small heed to the rest of the world if they once sight an American. They at once head to cross his bows and if he escapes it is not because a wild clamor of begging has not whirled around him. One can note already that a little of the kindness of the average American's heart has already been fretted and pestered out of him.

It is also notable that the beggars rarely approach a Spanish officer. They will storm any American position and they will heroically besiege the Cubans but they habitually shy away from a Spanish officer. This is either because the Spanish officers are never known to give anything away or because they have frightened an immunity out of the beggars.[1] It is probably a combination of both.

An incident of another kind of begging occurred last Sunday at the camp of the Cuban general Cardenas.

STEPHEN CRANE MAKES OBSERVATIONS IN CUBA'S CAPITAL.

HAVANA, Sept. 20. — Well, it seems that the American regulars are not going to march up Obispo street for some time. War is long, and it makes no provision for impatient and exasperated patriots who refuse to attend strictly to their own affairs. Those of us who are waiting here to see the regulars march up Obispo street can wait and be damned. We thoroughly understand that part of it, and the present expression is intended more as a wail of anguish than as a plea to which anybody is likely to pay the slightest heed.

Still there are some things which might be said. In the first place, any intelligent person can see that the Spaniard is making a laudable effort to take every possible dollar out of Cuba before leaving it. His policy is necessarily a policy of delay. The longer he can stay the more

1. Crane first started to write *Cubans*.

Reprinted here for the first time from New York Journal: *2 October 1898.*

Cuban millions will he take back to Spain. He is in no hurry; he doesn't want to talk to a commission; he wants to collect duties and taxes.

Of course, we are a very generous people, and we so want to be kind to our fallen enemy that we hesitate to interrupt him in his occupation of robbing the populace of Cuba. That is all very charming as a sentiment, but it is doubtful if Bismarck's stern, quick terms to a conquered France were not more truly merciful than this buttermilk policy of ours. The intellectual result so far has been to reproduce here, at least, a state of absolute stupefaction. It is impossible to halt the economy of a country while a number of duly accredited gentlemen exchange notes. Yet that is what we are performing with great success. The next three months are likely to be more disastrous for Cuba than were the months of the war. The war was a tangible condition, plain as your nose. The present situation is a blank mystery. Merchants grope blindly, afraid to advance a step in any direction. Business pauses, waits. Business is the name of a process of exchange by which people are enabled to procure those things which support and protect life.

If a man lacks a spine it is not of a surety his privilege to enter heaven without challenge as a just and charitable spirit. The lack of a spine is not mentioned by any available authority as the supreme virtue of mankind. What we mistake for generous feeling for our late enemy is more than half the time merely a certain governmental childishness, and it benefits the Spaniard no more than it benefits us, and as for the inhabitant of this island, he finds a grim and inexplicable fate fall from a sky which he thought was the sky of promise.

In our next war our first bit of strategy should be to have the army and the navy combine in an assault on Washington. If we could once take and sack Washington the rest of the conflict would be simple.[1]

1. The barbs in this dispatch at the slowness of the peace negotiations are not too far out of line; nor indeed are the barbs at the peace terms, as the following recital of events will show.
July 26 (1898): At the request of the Spanish authorities, the French Ambassador at Washington, M. Jules Cambon, has an interview with McKinley; subjects: (1) a temporary halting of hostilities and (2) a discussion of terms of peace.
August 1: The U.S. State Department outlines acceptable peace terms: (1) Spain's relinquishment of all claims on Cuba, (2) cession of Puerto Rico and other West Indian islands, and (3) cession of Guam.
August 8: The reply of the Spanish Government, which practically accepts the terms, is forwarded to Washington.
August 10: Secretary of State William R. Day announces that a protocol has been agreed to which embodies the peace terms with Spain.
August 12: The protocol between the United States and Spain is signed at

THE GROCER BLOCKADE.

The Spaniard is evidently an epigrammatic person. He makes a
serious attempt to reduce everything to a basis of one line. Sometimes
he misses it, but more often he hits it. The people here are now saying,
"We were not blockaded by the war ships; we were blockaded by the
grocers." It is quite true. Immediately the blockade was declared the
grocers of Havana, stirred by a deep patriotism, arose to the occasion
and proceeded to soak the life out of the people. It was a wonder that
some sensible person did not go quietly about rearranging matters

Washington, M. Cambon acting as intermediary for Spain. Hostilities cease
as of that day.

September 5: The Spanish Cortes and the Ministry obtain leave to introduce a bill which would authorize renunciation by Spain of her colonies.

September 14: The Spanish Cortes passes such a bill, but only after a secret
and stormy session. The Cortes adjourns.

September 29: The Spanish and American Peace Commissioners meet in
Paris for the first time, guests of the French Minister of Foreign Affairs.

October 31: At a meeting of the Peace Commissioners in Paris, the United
States representatives submit a demand for complete cession of entire
Philippines.

November 4: Spanish Commissioners reject the U.S. demand, but admit
that they are powerless to oppose it.

November 21: The United States Commissioners offer, in exchange for cession of Philippines, an indemnity of $20,000,000 and the admission of
Spanish imports into the islands for five years on equal terms with American goods.

November 28: Spanish Commissioners declare they are constrained by force
to cede the Philippines and Sulu Archipelago in consideration of the indemnity.

December 8: The Commissioners of both nations complete the drafting of
the final treaty; six months to be allowed for its ratification.

December 10: Treaty of Paris signed, at 8:45 P.M. The final terms are:
(1) Spain's withdrawal from Cuba and her cession of Puerto Rico, Guam,
and the Philippines to the United States; (2) United States' agreement to
pay an indemnity of $20,000,000 and to grant Spain temporary commercial
rights in the Philippines; and (3) the inhabitants' political status in the
new possessions is to be determined by the new government.

*Reprinted here for the first time from New York Journal: 23
September 1898. The same ideas given in this article Crane recast
in "His Majestic Lie," published first in the New York Herald
(24 June 1900), and then in Wounds in the Rain (1900) and in
The Work of Stephen Crane, II (1925).*

with an axe, but no one did so, and the grocers throughout the war continued to gracefully pillage the public pockets.

Blanco's order establishing a standard of reasonable prices had no effect upon them. Before war was declared they put into hiding a large amount of stock. War came, and soon they declared that they had nothing to sell. Their stores were all empty. They had nothing; no, not so much as a pound of rice. The war had ruined them. Ah! those devils of Americans, thus to torment the honest grocers. In time, however, wealthy citizens might be seen wending their way with much gold to secret conferences with a grocer. Oh, no. Impossible! At no price! A pound of bread is worth more than a pound of gold. It is impossible. Well, if I sell some to you I would have to take it probably from the mouths of my own children, who are in danger of starving. A little, a very little; yes, perhaps.

Thereupon ensued the spectacle of a respectable citizen digging into his own bowels for gold to buy a little of the flour which the grocer had cleverly made to appear like pounded pumice stone.

Of course, in all wars there is invariably a class of patriots who seize their commercial opportunities to trade upon the preoccupation, the consequent vulnerability of the people who are deeply engaged with the palpable facts of the conflict. Doubtless during the civil war in America our particular breed of sutlers defended themselves in argument on the purest, most virtuous business lines. It was not until afterward that the people got their sense of proportion adjusted truly and saw that the system usually operated as a crime. And by that time the individual culprit was safely blurred in a sentimental resentment against a class. In the end, the affair was mainly a joke.

The grocers here were forced to play a bolder game. Upon the news of the raising of the blockade the market slumped from under them. The people simply refused to pay so much. They evidently felt capable of enduring until the supply ships came. The time of arrival of the supply ships was not known.

And now the grocers, as men with honest faces, were in a fair quandary. They would either have to give themselves away as cheats and lower prices and sell stocks as fast as possible, or — they would have to lose money.

What did they do? Did they lose money, like men who would care for an appearance of consistency, or did they give themselves away rather than lose a centavo?

In one day they lowered the price of rice 60 per cent. They lowered other staples proportionately. There had been no influx to the market. There had been simply a rumor that the blockade was about to be raised.

It was shameless. Our chill-blooded Northern race would have hung each grocer to his own signboard. These people, so fiery, so dangerous in temper, so volcanic, alive with p-p-passion, they did nothing. They perhaps expended themselves in talk — which is not impossible to their natures. They made an epigram: "We were not blockaded by the war ships; we were blockaded by the grocers." At any rate, one must admit that it is a good epigram.

MEMOIRS OF A PRIVATE.

As I understand it, the American public is now going about with a club crying: "Where is he? Where is he?" The American public is now about to chastise the one who can be proven responsible for the general incompetence and idiocy existing in several departments of the army during the last war.

I don't want to startle or anger the American public, but I feel impelled to point out to it that during the last few weeks it has caused a certain number of men in the regular army of the United States to laugh hoarsely and bitterly.

So you are looking for the responsible party, are you? You want to discover the culprit, do you? You want to visit dire punishment on him, do you?

Well, excuse the blunt language of a soldier, but you really strike me as being about the most comic spectacle that has yet crossed my thrilling journey toward a Soldiers' Home. Why, you are the culprit. You are responsible. Put up your search lights and your bludgeons and merely ruminate quietly and see if you can't get something into your peculiarly ingenuous head.

Here is the first test. Go out into the street and ask any person to name the secretaries of war of the last five administrations. The citizen will tell he doesn't know. Try another citizen; he won't know. There you are! Nobody knows; nobody cares. That is exactly the case. Nobody cares who is Secretary of War. It has been accounted — since Lincoln's time — a highly honorable post which is the proper loot of some faithful partisan. It goes to this man or it goes to that man, and in any case nobody makes any row or conceives the event to be of importance save those gentlemen who wished the post for themselves.

Then suddenly there comes on a war, and — behold — you find the chair occupied by a doddering fetless old man who can't even

Reprinted here for the first time from New York Journal: *25 September 1898. The subhead reads:* "Dictated to And Taken Down by Stephen Crane."

defend himself by remaining silent.[1] You talk about mismanagement! You talk about incompetence and gross criminality! Why, you are to blame! You are the criminals! You have for years persisted in raising monuments to your own incapacity for knowing anything about the army; for years you have conscientiously and steadfastly ignored every detail of it. What then, in the name of God, did you expect?

Every four years in our luxurious posts in Arizona or Wyoming we watched with feverish interest the appointment of the new Secretary of War. It was a solemn event always, for us. We cared who would be Secretary of War. But you never cared. You never gave three whoops in hades. In the first place you always proceeded on the stupid assumption that the country would never become involved in another conflict, and so you were constructively willing that any fool should be Secretary of War.

But the war came, my brothers, and found you dwelling in the midst of your blind idiocy. And now you are beating the tom-tom and screeching for somebody's blood. You know a real soldier always regards the civilian as an aimless, hapless, helpless blockhead, who tries to go three ways at once and say three things with one tongue, and

1. The secretaries of war in the last five administrations were for the most part faithful (but not always successful) party figures, most of them capitalists, many of them lawyers. The climax of such administrations was that of Russell Alger (1836–1907), ex-Civil War officer, Michigan lumber baron, ex-governor of Michigan (1885–1886), and ex-commander in chief of the G.A.R. (1889); he had the misfortune to be the Secretary during the Spanish-American War. According to *The New International Encyclopedia* (2nd ed., 1914), "His administration of the department during the . . . war met with the most vigorous criticism. He was charged with being directly or indirectly responsible for the unsanitary condition of camps, the overcrowding and unfitness of transports, the insufficiency of physicians and medicines, the bad quality of food, and the incompetence of subordinate officers."

General Nelson Miles, a powerful political figure, began the Alger affair after his arrival in Washington in September 1898. He laid a formal complaint against the War Department on September 9, charging it with being the cause of sickness and misery among the troops, and demanded an investigation. On September 24, President McKinley appointed a nine-member commission, with General Mellen Dodge (1831–1916), a railroad official and veteran of the Civil War, as its chairman, to investigate. Although the investigation exonerated Alger in the main, he resigned in August 1899. He was subsequently named to the Senate and in 1903 elected, the voters of Michigan apparently having forgotten or forgiven.

Alger defended himself vigorously and had defenders, T. R. Roosevelt among them, who regarded Alger as a victim of the system rather than a malefactor.

the idea never strikes me with such force as when I contemplate the frantic revolutions your belated conscience is now making.

Why, we knew all this long ago, and we cried out to you, we begged you to heed us, and you were deaf; you would not listen, and now you have paid for it — paid with the blood of your best beloved; paid with your dead. God pity you!

THE PRIVATE'S STORY

A hard campaign, full of wants and lacks and absences, brings a man speedily back to an appreciation of things long disregarded or forgotten.[1] In camp somewhere in the woods between Siboney and Santiago I happened to think of ice cream soda. I hadn't drunk anything but beer and whiskey for fifty moons, but I got to dreaming of ice cream soda and I came near dying of longing for it. I couldn't get it out of my mind, try as I would to concentrate my thoughts upon the land crabs and mud with which I was surrounded. All I could do was to swear to myself that if I reached the United States again I would immediately make the nearest soda water fountain look like Spanish fours.[2] I decided upon the flavor. In a loud, firm voice I would say: "Orange, please." What with the work and everything, I suppose some of us got to be a little childish.

But here is the funny part of it. In due time, I with many other heroes was loaded upon a Chinese junk.[3] We knew, however, that it was a United States transport because it was commanded by a fool who was all bluster and bad manners and fear of Spaniards. In rough weather we made a sort of a pool of all the sound legs and arms, and

---

Reprinted here for the first time from New York Journal: *26 September 1898. The subhead reads: "Stephen Crane Retells It for the Journal."*

The reader is invited to compare this account with that in "War Memories" (infra, p. 291).

1. Here follows the narrative of Crane's *own* homecoming to the United States after being shipped out of Cuba. He had the true marks of a hero, for it is typical of him that he should wryly describe such an event by completely ignoring himself.

2. As a colloquialism, "fours" means refection at four in the afternoon. The limiting adjective "Spanish" escapes us.

3. The "Chinese junk" was the *City of Washington*.

by dint of hanging hard to each other, we lived until the old trap reached Fortress Monroe.[4]

As we slowed down opposite the main battery — known to the department as Chamberlin's[5] — we witnessed something which informed us that with all our wounds and fevers and starvations we hadn't felt it all. We were flying the yellow flag,[6] but a launch came and circled swiftly about us. There was a little woman in the launch and she kept looking and looking and looking. Our ship was so high that she could see only those who hung at the rail, but she kept looking and looking and looking. Presently there was a commotion among some black dough-boys who had seen her, and two of them ran aft to their colonel. The old man got up quickly and appeared at the rail, his arm in a sling. He cried: "Alice."

The little woman saw him, and instantly she covered her face with her hands as if blinded with a flash of white fire. She made no outcry: it was all in this simple, swift gesture, but we — we knew then. It told us. It told us the other part. And in a vision we all saw our own harbor lights. That is to say, those of us who had harbor lights.

My difficulty being of a minor description, I was one of the first ashore. A company of volunteers dug a way for us through a great crowd. The verandas of the two big hotels were thronged with women and officers in new uniforms. Everybody beheld us. It was very hard to face it out. Some of the boys had something which might be called stage fright. I knew we looked tough, but I didn't know how tough we looked until I saw all this splendid five-dollar-a-day crowd.

Some of the boys could walk, but naturally there were many who couldn't, and these last they loaded upon a big flat car and towed it behind a trolley car. When that load passed the hotel, there was a noise made by a crowd which brought me up trembling. Perhaps it was a moan, perhaps it was a sob — but, no, it was something far beyond either a moan or a sob. Anyhow, the sound of women weeping was in it, for I saw many of those fine ladies with wet cheeks when that gang of bandaged, dirty, ragged, emaciated, half starved cripples went by in review.

And let me tell you, it brought something to my eyes which I was ashamed to have seen, and my sabre arm went stiff and strong as

4. Fortress Monroe, Virginia, located at Old Point Comfort, a resort center, lies opposite Norfolk at the mouth of the James River. In the peacetime Army it was an important artillery post, housing batteries of the First, Second, Third, Fourth, and Fifth regiments of artillery. It commands the entrance to Hampton Roads.

5. A misspelling for Chamberlain.

6. Signifying yellow fever aboard.

steel and I swore that, despite legislation and the appointment of incompetent quartermasters, I would live and die a good soldier, a true, straight, unkicking American regular soldier.

Now here is a funny thing. Avoiding the hospital people who were herding us, I entered a drug store and marched up to the soda water counter. The boy looked at me and I said: "Orange, please."

STEPHEN CRANE IN HAVANA.

HAVANA, Oct. 3. — The citizen of Havana has an extraordinary lack of what might be called the sense of public navigation. It is a common lack on all shores of the Mediterranean, and the dearth of it even extends to Paris, where it is always clear that a kind of special deity continually has to protect from the pain of collision all drivers of fiacres.[1]

But there is no special deity for the people here. They are children of pellucid chance, and if Havana was a tub and they were a lot of rubber balls prancing and bouncing within they could not be more joyously irresponsible and incompetent.

An opportunity to view this matter to good advantage is given every Thursday and Sunday evening, when a band plays in the square.[2] A great crowd attends, and with the lights and the music and all it is not unlike the board walk at Asbury Park,[3] without the boards and without the sea.

If two friends meet face to face on Broadway their greeting, if begun in the middle of the stream, is never finished there. They instantly move to the curb or in to the walls, to the slack water. They always do it, and there is nothing marvellous about it. But you should see two friends meet here when, for instance, the band is playing in the plaza and a great crowd is strolling.

Well, for their ceremony of greeting, they camp indefinitely right in the middle of everything. Of course, in Spanish countries it is customary to express joy and welcome by rushing forward and at once engaging the other in a catchweight wrestling contest.

Suppose that there are two hundred people coming along on the same route. They are stopped, bothered, compelled to change their

---

Reprinted here for the first time from New York Journal: 9 *October 1898.*

1. A *fiacre* was a small French hackney coach.
2. Actually the bandstand was in the Parque Central.
3. A seaside resort in New Jersey.

gait and their course. But they say not a word. They move around the impediment in silence and patience. It does not occur to them — they have no necessity for knowing — that traffic is blocked, as we say.

Nature is usually seeking to alleviate, to mend, but circumstance is always perverse, aggravating. The English are not a particularly amiable people; at least, they are not suave, and so circumstance provides them with a pattern of railway carriage which is the cruelest test of manners which life affords.

In Havana, where people do not comprehend public navigation, this perverse circumstance provides sidewalks from eighteen to forty inches wide, upon which only acrobats can make their way.

But, at any rate, a grand mystery of Spanish romance has been cleared for one mind, at any rate, by these Spanish sidewalks of Havana. In every one of those delightful tales there was a street scene in which a gallant cavalier going one way was met by a gallant cavalier going the other way. They stopped, then the first cavalier, twirling his mustache, said:

"Senor, I take the wall."

But the second cavalier, laying his hand upon his sword, invariably replied: "You are mistaken, senor. I take the wall."

Whereat they drew and fell upon each other like brave gentlemen, giving and receiving wounds in the groin, lungs, liver and heart, until one was down and after he had said, "Oh, I am dead," the other sheathed his sword and went home — taking the wall.

This fighting for the inside track, for the privilege of passing next to the wall, was a mystery and an annoyance to my boyish mind. I wanted my hero to fight over the lady behind the lattice. Anything connected with that intrigue was good cause for the gore of cavaliers.

But to go out and fight with comparative strangers over the privilege of passing next to the wall, giving and receiving wounds in the groin, lungs, liver and heart, seemed a very pointless proceeding. But it is all plain at present. It was because the Spaniard had as much sense of public navigation as he has now, and because the sidewalks of Seville were only from eighteen to forty inches wide.

HOW THEY LEAVE CUBA.

There is one thing relating to the Spanish evacuation of Havana of which, surely, the less said the better, and yet the exquisite mournfulness of it comes to one here at all times. For instance:

Reprinted here for the first time from New York Journal: 6 October 1898.

A friend and myself went on board the Alfonso XIII.[1] a few days ago as she was about to sail for Spain with an enormous passenger list of sick soldiers, officers, Spanish families, even some priests — all people who, by long odds, would never again set their eyes on the island of Cuba.

The steamer was ready to sail. We slid down the gangway and into our small boat. There were many small boats crowding about the big ship. Most contained people who waved handkerchiefs and shouted "Adios!" quite cheerfully in a way suggesting that they themselves were intending to take the next steamer, or the next again, for Spain. But from a boat near to ours we heard the sound of sobbing. Under the comic matting sun shelter was a woman, holding in her arms a boy about four years old. Her eyes were fastened upon the deck of the ship, where stood an officer in the uniform of a Spanish captain of infantry. He was making no sign. He simply stood immovable, staring at the boat. Sometimes men express great emotion by merely standing still for a long time. It seemed as if he was never again going to move a muscle.

The woman tried to get the child to look at its father, but the boy's eyes wandered over the bright bay with maddening serenity. He knew nothing; his mouth was open vacuously. The crisis in his life was lowering an eternal shadow upon him, and he only minded the scintillant water and the funny ships.

She was not a pretty woman and she was — old. If she had been beautiful, one could have developed the familiar and easy cynicism which, despite its barbarity, is some consolation at least. But this to her was the end, the end of a successful love. The heart of a man to whom she at any rate was always a reminiscence of her girlish graces was probably her only chance of happiness, and the man was on the Alfonso XIII., bound for Spain.

The woman's boatman had a face like a floor. Evidently he had thought of other fares. One couldn't spend the afternoon or three pesetas[2] just because a woman yowled. He began to propel the boat toward the far landing. As the distance from the steamer widened and widened, the wail of the woman rang out louder.

Our boatman spat disdainfully into the water. "Serves her right. Why didn't she take up with a man of her own people instead of with a Spaniard?" But that is of small consequence. The woman's heart was broken. That is the point.

1. Protected cruiser; tonnage (displacement): 5,000; speed: 20 knots; armament: 11 guns. During the fighting she had been stationed at San Juan, Puerto Rico.

2. The peseta had the same value as the franc — 19.3 cents. A one-peseta piece was a silver coin.

And that is not yet the worst of it. There is going to be a lot of it; such a hideous lot of it! The attitude of the Cubans will be the attitude of our old boatman: "Serves them right; why didn't they take up with men of their own people instead of with Spaniards?" But, after all — and after all — and again after all, it is human agony and human agony is not pleasant.

HOW THEY COURT IN CUBA

HAVANA, Oct. 17. — Cuban courting is on a plan that is strange and wonderful to us. It is full of circumlocution and bulwarks and clever football interference and trouble and delay and protracted agony and duennas. There is no holding hands in it at all, you bet. It is all barbed wire entanglements.

In the higher orders of society young men and young women have conventional opportunities of meeting each other and becoming acquainted, but that is not the situation among the masses. In the latter case a young man almost invariably falls in love with a fair face seen through a grated window. He could not tell if the lady was deaf and dumb. As for her disposition, she might, for all he knows, be accustomed to dragging her mother up and down stairs by the hair and beating her father daily with the cooking instruments. She might even have a wooden leg successfully concealed by her reposeful attitude. But, anyhow, he takes this wild whirl into romance, and only the gods know his end.

The first thing to be done is to attract the attention of the lady. This he usually accomplishes by a process of heroic patrolling to and fro in front of her house. She sits in the window and observes this scene. If she glances at him he smiles, looks foolish and adoring, acts like an ass.

This stage may be long or short; that depends upon the man and the maid. But sooner or later there comes a time when he shys up to the window and fillips a letter behind the bars, and the girl conceals it hastily in all likelihood, although the supposition is that she takes it immediately to her mother. And this letter! It breathes a passion which could only grow from the young man's lack of knowledge of the object of his devotion. It sings a perfect adoration, which could emanate only from a young man who is not thoroughly familiar with his subject. From it arises a perfume of love which could be created

Reprinted here for the first time from New York Journal: 25 *October 1898.*

only by a young man who had acted always as a spectator from without the bars.

Very well, then; this patrolling and grinning and this note have an effect, or else they don't have an effect. Let us suppose that the young man has not paced futilely to and fro, wearing out the pavements of a beneficent city government. In that case it is a race horse to a corn dodger[1] that she will not write an answer to his note without communicating news of the solemnity of the crisis to her anxious parent. It then becomes the duty of the anxious parent to collar the young man at some good time and ask him what the devil are his intentions, anyhow. He replies, of course, that his intentions are quite beyond reproach, and he hopes — he hopes — if he is not too unworthy — he — he will be allowed to pay his suit.

But, at any rate, the young man's position and prospects are weighed, and if they are satisfactory he is admitted to call upon the young woman. The young woman's opinion in the case is a blooming small matter. The young man is put on the scales, and if he don't tip them properly he goes, and if the girl wants to cry her eyes out she cries them out without moving the disposition of the ironclad parents.

The young man, being accepted, then begins the real courtship. A sort of schedule is established, and the young man runs on time. He turns up every evening — say — at 8 o'clock and goes away — say — at 10 o'clock.

It is not so much the uninterrupted punctuality. It is the length of the siege. It endures for ages. It is common for this sort of thing to last as long as eight years. Five years, or perhaps three years, is the habit.

What the young man does is to come into a drawing room, sit down in a chair near the young lady, and talk in a subdued and downtrodden voice, half to the young woman and half to the implacable mother, who holds her position with a courage born of the noble cause. She is always something like the Western man who chewed tobacco, and yet, in certain poker games, acknowledged that he dared not turn his head long enough to perform a certain obligation of men who chew tobacco.

Imagine this state of affairs enduring for eight years, or even for three years! It has all the fiery excitement of being cashier in a shoe store.

This call becomes a function of the daily life of the family, precisely like the morning coffee or dinner. If he failed to appear for one evening, there would be a panic in the household, and the young

1. Corn dodger: a bread made of cornmeal baked or fried hard in small pones.

woman would be heartbroken at this scandalous exhibition of infidelity. He would be obliged to make elaborate and fervid explanation.

Time moves at its allotted speed slowly over the years; nothing changes, routine is routine. And in the end, what? Who knows? Perhaps our fine young man sights a woman who rightly or wrongly blots out in four minutes the memory of the girl that he has arduously courted for three years. Then again, perhaps not.

After all, there is small use of discussing any such matters. Men seek the women they love, and find them, and women wait for the men they love, and the men come, and all the circumlocution and bulwarks and clever football interference and trouble and delay and protracted agony and duennas count for nothing, count for nothing against the tides of human life, which are in Cuba or Omaha controlled by the same moon.

STEPHEN CRANE ON HAVANA

HAVANA, Oct. 28. — When in other cities of the world the church bells peal out from their high towers, slowly and solemnly, with a dignity taken from the sky, from the grave, the hereafter, the Throne of Judgment — voices high in air calling, calling, calling, with the deliberation of fate, the sweetness of hope, the austerity of a profound mystic thing — they make the devout listen to each stroke, and they make the infidels feel all the height and width of a blue sky, a Sunday morning golden with sun drops. But — when at blear dawn you are sleeping a sleep of both the just and the unjust and a man climbs into an adjacent belfry and begins to hammer the everlasting, murdering Hades out of the bell with a club — your aroused mind seems to turn almost instinctively toward blasphemy. Religion commonly does not go off like an alarm clock,[1] and, as symbolized by the bells, it does not usually sound like a brickbat riot in a tin store. However, this is the

Reprinted here for the first time from New York Journal: 6 November 1898. Most of Crane's previous dispatches on the Spanish-American War bear the imprint of copyright by W. R. Hearst; but this dispatch, and most of the subsequent ones, bear the imprint "Copyright by Stephen Crane, 1898."

1. "Religion commonly does not go off like an alarm clock" connects curiously with Crane's striking image of his very religious-minded mother: "She spoke as slowly as a big clock ticks and her effects were impromptu." The syllogism seems to be: (a) Religion is not a clock; (b) my mother is a clock, etc.

Havana method. I fancy they use no such term here as "bell ringer;" they probably use "bell-fighter." But, such passion! Such fury! One can lie awake for hours and listen to the din of a conflict, which reminds one of nothing but a terrible combat between two hordes of gigantic blood-mad knights of the Middle Ages, whose armor had unfortunately been constructed from resonant metal. On feast days the clamor simply shakes out of one all faith in human intelligence. It is so endless, so inane, so like the din of monkeys with tin kettles. But the bells must be very good bells. Otherwise they could not stand these tremendous assaults. The bell fighters must be very good men. Otherwise they would soon succumb to the physical strain.

*

One apprehends that as soon as the tangled affairs of Cuba are arranged in some fashion there will be a considerable inflow of Americans looking for work. In a small way it has already begun. But there is no market for American labor in Cuba. Naturally, labor is one thing that the island contains in ever-increasing abundance. There is the remnant of reconcentrados; there are the refugees returning from foreign ports; there will soon be a great mass of disbanded insurgents, and, last, there are many Spanish soldiers who intend to stay here. Labor will be for a long time almost as cheap as it is in China.

Such a thing as a clerkship will be grabbed by competent, well-educated, but financially reduced, Cubans for a wage that would not support an American. The island is not at all a Klondike,[2] where a man might go with only his wits, a pick and a pan and yet win success.

The vanguard of a caravan of indigent Americans looking for fortune in this new country has already succumbed here, and one or two have even been shipped home by subscription of the newspaper men, cattlemen and others.

Cuba is the place for a wise investment of capital, but it offers no gold mine to the American who has none. Tobacco land, for instance, can be had very cheap, but before the appearance of the first crop a great deal of money — in proportion to acreage — has to be expended. Tobacco raising, indeed, is an expensive business, and, disclaiming all idea of speaking with authority, it is at least proper for me to warn all small capitalists to consider the question as something beyond small

2. The glorious gold rush into the Klondike was in full swing. Gold had been first discovered on 16 August 1896 on Bonanza Creek, but the outside world did not learn of it until the summer of 1897 when a cargo of gold came into Seattle from the Yukon Territory. By 1898 thousands were pushing through the Chilkoot and White passes down the Yukon River and into the Klondike district. Something like 28,000 people emigrated there.

farming in the United States and to thoroughly look into the matter before embarking for Cuba.

*

One newly arrived American announced that he had come to open a law practice. His equipments for this venture were youth, a very recent diploma, some few dollars and a perfectly ingenious ignorance of the Spanish tongue. The fortunes of men are in the wind, and the wind blows where it pleases. No one can say that this young man may not succeed, but at least it does seem that he is a little too soon.

However, his inexperience of American practice will not militate against him here. There is nothing in the American forms of procedure that resembles the Spanish forms of procedure. As near as one may learn, the function of a lawyer in Havana is mainly that of a go-between, who arranges a dicker between the honorable court and the client who has the most money. All that will be changed? Yes, but there are a great many things in Cuba which are not going to be changed in two minutes.

*

When the Earl of Malmesbury was Minister for Foreign Affairs,[3] he in 1852 wrote to the British Ambassador at Berlin about a certain political complication in the following terms: "You will, I hope, use all your influence at Berlin to show the King that the Duke of Augustenberg only delays his assent to the indemnity from a foolish hope that a row may take place somewhere and somehow among the five powers, and that in the scuffle he may get something more. It would be very desirable for the King of Prussia to make him understand that by further delays the only chance he runs is that of losing the terms now offered him."

If it would do any good the fine thing would be to have this straightforward parable printed on cardboard convenient for pasting in the hats of Spaniards here and elsewhere. They are figuring precisely on the lines of that illustrious Duke of Augustenberg. Some political miracle, some tremendous war that will force the United States to engage herself tooth and nail in the defence of her own soil, will enable Spain to sail in again and hold or regain her precious islands. It is stupid, but — what would you? The ordinary Spaniard has little knowledge of how the nations conduct their relations with each other. He interprets the mere land-hungry policy of Germany to mean a formidable enmity to the United States. He thinks the Parisian journals mean what they have said, and, meaning what they have said,

3. The third Earl of Malmesbury, James Howard Harris (1807–1889) was Secretary of State for Foreign Affairs in 1852 and in 1858–59.

that they voice a menace to the greater Republic. He thinks even that our Southern States are only waiting for a supreme crisis to again disengage themselves from the Union. In fact, he dreams still of a miraculous rescue of his country from her sorry plight.

Furthermore, he drinks in every sound of the tumult in the United States over the management of our army in the Santiago campaign and over the distress and illness in the American camps at Chickamauga[4] and other places. This uproar causes him to believe that if he had the whole thing to do over again he would have been victor. If he had known the plight of the American army at Santiago he would have done better: he would have held on: he would even have attacked. A thousand expedients occur to him now that he has all this information from inside the American lines, so to speak. And he gnashes his teeth over it.

✻   ✻   ✻

"YOU MUST!" — "WE CAN'T!"

HAVANA, Nov. 4. — The dull times in this city are in no way improved by the fact that an American commission and a Spanish commission are in a juxtaposition here which might be intended for the preservation of silence and inertia. For a long time everybody prayed for the coming of the American military commission.[1] All would be

4. Camp Thomas at Chickamauga Park in Georgia was one of the "notorious" camps during the Spanish-American War.

Reprinted here for the first time from New York Journal: 8 November 1898.

1. By Article IV of the Peace Protocol (signed by Spain and the United States on 12 August 1898) Spain would "immediately evacuate" Cuba, and to this end each government would appoint commissioners to meet in Havana — within thirty days after the signing of the protocol — and arrange and carry out "the details of the aforesaid evacuation of Cuba."
The two commissions from the start of their sessions engaged in arguments, mainly over "the meaning of 'evacuation,' whether in the sense of a 'military evacuation' or both 'military and civil evacuation,' over the property rights of Spain in Cuba, and over the legal status of Cuba if abandoned before the conclusion of a treaty of peace." (From E. J. Benton, *International Law and Diplomacy of the Spanish-American War* [1908], p. 233.)
The date for the evacuation was fixed for January 1, but the last of the Spanish troops did not leave Cuba until February 1899.

arranged and improved immediately after the arrival of that distinguished body. The Cubans rather expected them to come with trum-
peters and banners, escorted by both cavalry and infantry; field guns
and war ships would boom, and the Cuban populace and those Spaniards who have climbed hastily to the correct side of the fence were
prepared to line Obispo street and cheer themselves black in the face.
It was to be the grand emancipation, a magnificent ceremony of gold
lace and cocked hats. Even the little American colony often said to
itself: "Oh, just wait until the commission gets here."

The commission arrived ultimately, after we had been harrowed
in proper fashion by a series of rumors and false starts. For my part,
I was sitting in the Cafe Ingleterra one morning when some of the
waiters suddenly crowded toward the door and stared into the plaza.
Being interested in finding out what so attracted them, I looked also,
and saw a young man in a white duck uniform of the American navy
crossing the plaza. It was Lieutenant Marsh,[2] of Admiral Sampson's
staff.

This to the greater part of Havana was the arrival of the American
commission. It was an event, of course, but never a spectacle. Havana
opinion of the conquerors faded 50 per cent in a single day. The
reconcentrados found to their intense amazement that on that night
they were not merely as hungry as ever, but that they had now to
struggle with an appetite whetted out of all proportion by a false and
absurd anticipation. Really, in the strictest sense, nothing whatever
had happened.

At present the two commissions are engaged in a sort of a polite
and graceful deadlock. The Americans say: "You must!" The Spaniards
reply: "We can't." The Spaniards will soon have to make the best of
a bad business, but they hold on with the tenacity and hopeful inno-
cence of children.[3] It seems impossible to beat any truth into their
heads save with a hatchet. Something will turn up, they think. It is
impossible to many of these minds that such a calamity as this evacuation should come to pass. France, or Germany, or civil war in the
United States, or Divine Providence, will make interposition in time.

Meanwhile, although the reconcentrados are gradually getting
their voids partly occupied, the people who are the greatest sufferers
are the Cuban insurgents, who are still in the field. Their mental condition approximates stupefaction. They don't know whether they are
afoot or ahorseback. They ask the same questions of everybody who

2. Lieutenant Charles C. Marsh, U.S.N., a veteran of some twenty-three
years' service in the Navy.

3. Benton asserts that the Spanish Commissioners hoped, by their
quibbling, to gain "some advantages in the discussions in Paris." (*Op. cit.*,
p. 233.)

they think is entitled to know the slightest things. "Well, what is going to become of us, eh? Are we all Americans now? What are we, anyhow? [4] When are the Spaniards to be put out? When? When? When?"

There is a certain eloquence in the speech of a hungry, half-clad, homeless man who has lived three years in the manugue[5] and who is wondering if the sweetheart he left long ago in town could still distinguish between him and any other. They are marvellously patient about it — the men more than the officers. Just here it might be well to interpolate that the Havana province insurgents are very different from those patriots who so successfully did little or no fighting at Santiago. This province has been loaded, always, with Spanish troops, and the revolutionary bands have been kept on the keen jump, with perhaps a fight every day. They had none of those lovely mountain sanitariums which at critical times formed the safe abode of the Santiago warrior.

It is only fair to say that the present situation does not seem to be at all the fault of the American Military Commission. I have an idea that they are mad clear through to the bone, although they are as reticent as so many Russian diplomats. They have bucked squarely into the Spanish Commission, and have been met with the usual reply of "We can't," and also with "Wait until we hear from Madrid," and "Wait for the decision of the Paris Commissions." The first Spanish intrenchment is "We can't;" the second is "Wait." And they fight it out on those lines with heroism.

Some day we will get over considering these people clever in some ways. As a matter of truth, they are shockingly stupid. They are of the Mediterranean, that accursed sea which in modern times bathes only the feet of liars and of men of delay. Catch any Spaniard in a lie — it may be a Havana cabman or it may be the redoubtable Weyler[6] — and he fights you off with the unthinking desperation of a

4. The status of and use made of the insurgents by the United States in the war posed various diplomatic questions. "Most naturally," writes Benton, "the United States made use of the Cuban insurgents as allies, and particularly as scouts and guides." He points out that the American commanders claimed no control over the insurgent bands. "In neither Cuba nor the Philippines were the insurgents allowed to share the fruits of victory. . . . As long as Garcia's soldiers served under General Shafter they were furnished with rations and ammunition . . . but beyond informal relations with the Cuban . . . insurgents the Government of the United States steadfastly refused to go." (*Ibid.*, p. 144.)

5. Properly, *manigua* — meaning "jungle."

6. Valeriano Weyler y Nicolau, Marquess of Tenerife (1839–1930), a Spanish soldier of Prussian descent and formerly captain general in Cuba.

cat in a corner. He will never admit it — never — never. Confront him with proofs; show him a sworn statement signed by the flaming pen of the recording angel, but no — he looks at you with dull, senseless eyes and shakes his head eternally. "No, senor! No, senor! No, senor!" You can't move him. You can't even budge him an inch. There he sticks in his corner. You can only get a confession out of him by killing him and then journeying to hell to wrest it from his spirit.

This is about the measure of his intelligence. He has no knowledge of the tremendous and terrible art of half truth. He proceeds always on the basis of flat, wooden lying. A good many fine American tempers are doomed to be ruined in Cuba before the evacuation.

His other great principle of action is delay. Instead of opposing rational statement and argument, he will often meet the other side with seeming amiable acquiescence which is positively alluring and then he will proceed to organize a system for delaying the proceedings which can't be beaten anywhere in the world.

There are two elements at work in the Spanish mind at present. One is the dogged fatalism that Cuba will always belong to Spain. This arises simply from the fact that within everybody's recollection Cuba has always belonged to Spain. The other element arises from the opportunity, whatever betide, to pinch a few more millions out of Cuba. So naturally they have got their lies and their delays all up in harness, and are working them night and day. When our military commission returns to the United States, there wont be a sweet disposition left in it.

MR. CRANE, OF HAVANA.

HAVANA, Nov. 4. — One speaks of it with hesitation, but it is a fact sufficiently known among correspondents and other well-informed persons, that some of the regiments which have garrisoned the city of Santiago since the surrender have not behaved well or even decently towards the citizens of that town. They were not regiments which took part in the fights at El Caney or San Juan, but were commands that were sent in much later to relieve Shafter's troops. Particularly at fault were a certain regiment of immunes[1] and a certain volunteer colored

---

Reprinted here for the first time from New York Journal: 9 November 1898. The subhead reads: "We're First in War, But Not in Peace."

1. The act passed by Congress on 11 May 1898 authorized the organization of a volunteer force, not to exceed 10,000 enlisted men, who possessed immunity from tropical diseases. Thus the name "immunes."

regiment. In these two corps there were many cases of drunken sentries, and the promiscuous shooting at night by these men in the streets made it unwise to be too confident about one's safety if one had to travel after dark. On a certain evening a shot from one of these enthusiastically intoxicated gentlemen entered a window of the Santiago Club, breaking up a most virtuous poker game which was in progress there, and all Western gentlemen will agree with me that such conduct on the part of the sentry was unworthy an American soldier and a gentleman.

The occupation of surrendered cities is the most delicate business of war. It is plain that this applies threefold to towns in which the populace is favorably disposed to the victors. Soldiering at its best is cruel, hard work, and when the enwearied but triumphant soldier gets at last among the houses, where the people and their wine shops and other luxuries are practically at his mercy, he should not relax and go to pieces like a child, but, on the other hand, he should consider that he owes a double duty to his flag.

Indisputably the less said about these Santiago affairs the better, since every one has confidence in the admirable, soldierly and just administration of General Wood[2] and his ability to straighten out any of his force who get bumptious, but we must not forget that, in one sense, our men are now on exhibition alike before Spaniards and Cubans, and when two regiments who were not in the taking of Santiago at all, but are there now simply as military police — when these two regiments endanger by their behavior the prestige which the Fifth Army Corps so gallantly won and preserved as long as it remained in Cuba, it is time for us to blush a little and wonder if we can't improve matters.

No doubt the men in these regiments are good fellows enough, generous, kind, brave, devoted to their country, but they have not played the part of thorough soldiers, and the only man who has any business to engage in war is the soldier. The irresponsible whooper should remain at home.

The war is over, but — mark you this — that does not mean that we have no enemies. In the first place, the Cubans of Santiago province will never forgive us the fact that they took no part in the battle of San Juan and a distinctly secondary, even inconsequent, part in the

2. After the surrender of Santiago, General Leonard Wood was appointed military governor of the city. His administration was a particularly successful one. He brought the city "food, order, justice, sanitation, and public works." In October 1898, he was placed in command of the entire province of Santiago and in December 1899, he was appointed military governor of the island of Cuba. (Thomas J. Betts, "Wood," *Dictionary of American Biography* [1943], p. 467.)

fight at El Caney. They know perfectly well that they had nothing practical to do with either of these victories. It was the Americans alone who stormed these positions, and it was American blood that was poured out in the green fields. That is the truth, and none know it so well as the Cubans of Santiago province. If they could not know it with their own senses our men certainly told them it with great force both during the battle and after it.

But far more seriously distressing is the fact that tales of the adventures of our soldiers in the streets of Santiago have gone broadcast through the island. Here in Havana, for instance, La Lucha[3] — a newspaper which is against us as much as it dares — prints almost every day an account of the behavior of our troops in the city of the other end of the island. Of course, they are grossly and viciously exaggerated, according to the policy of a large body of Spaniards here; the articles are meant to establish a fear of American rapacity in the minds of the people of Cuba; their intention is thoroughly vindictive. But, nevertheless, there is not an American steamship agent, cattle man, provision speculator or correspondent who was in Santiago for any length of time after its fall who will not frankly tell you that such and such things happened there. The lamentable breaking up of the poker game heretofore described is merely used as an illustration of the quaint spirit of gayety which at times animates some of our men.

Now, Havana expects soon to be occupied with American troops. Havana listens with all her ears to these stretched-out yarns which La Lucha prints with such glee. To the citizen here they sound like truth. He wonders whether he will be let in for some game of the kind when the American troops occupy this city. His doubts are cheerfully encouraged by Spaniards of the La Lucha stamp. They laugh and say: "Oh, you will see! Your Americans so kind, so gentle, so just!" And yet anything in the way of ill-feeling or suspicion would never have occurred if a certain number of our soldiers could completely understand that whenever they wear the uniform of a United States soldier they carry upon their shoulders the weight of the honor and dignity of their country, and that their responsibility has increased a million fold.

For example, when four joyous privates enter a cafe in Santiago, order several drinks and then hilariously refuse to pay for them, they don't know that the story of it, enlarged and improved into a gigantic generalization, will go broadcast over Cuba, and that in countless minds they will have created a wrong opinion of every man who wears the

3. "This paper is in some respects the most important one in Cuba. . . . It is an evening journal. Two pages of each issue are printed in the English language" (A. J. Norton, *Complete Hand-Book of Havana and Cuba* [1900], p. 142).

blue, has worn it or ever will wear it. Tell one of these boys that to a million people he has dishonored the name of the United States army and he would probably drop dead. Tell him that he has insulted the flag and he would probably kill you. It all lies in the fact that he does not comprehend his new importance. He is not now just come to the tavern from a hard day in the fields, free of everything but a certain personal responsibility, free to be a regular wild ass of the desert if he so elects. He is part of the dignity, the justice, the even temper of the American Government.

It seems senseless that these silly little yarns from Santiago should stir so much apprehension, but it is no more senseless than any other natural law. It is what occurs in the lives of individuals, crowds, nations. A man spills some claret down his cuff and the report goes abroad that he has been drowned in a wine vat.

SPANIARDS TWO.

Havana, Nov. 5. — Then there is General Pando.[1] He claims to have found out by personal inspection absolutely everything concerning the army at Tampa. He ridicules it; calls it, in fact, an army of duffers; says our officers were so many wooden men. That is all very fine, but what did Pando do with all this wonderful information of his? Apparently what he did with it was to wait until the war was over and then use it as material for boisterous and insulting talk in the American and English newspapers. It is plain that he did not use one of the invaluable facts to benefit his country during the war. He did not say to Toral:[2] "Don't surrender; you are faced by a mere lot of incapable and illy provided people who will compass their own destruction if you give them a little time." In fact, what use did he

---

Reprinted here for the first time from New York Journal: 11 November 1898.

1. Luis Manuel de Pando y Sanchez (1844–1927) was one of Captain General Blanco's chief lieutenants in Cuba and closely identified with his chief's policies and actions. Just what Crane is stabbing at here is not clear — possibly a newspaper interview or story published in Havana or in a New York paper. On October 22 (1898) Pando presented a memoir to the Spanish senate which dealt with the Cuban situation prior to hostilities and which tried to justify Blanco's regime. It was attacked by General Weyler in his *Mi Mando en Cuba* (*My Command in Cuba*, 1910).

2. Brigadier General José Toral Vazques (1832–1904) was in command of the Spanish garrison at Santiago which surrendered to General Shafter.

make of his information, anyhow? None save in these uproarious and insolent interviews.

One does not expect a military spy to hold his own counsel until the war is over. Perhaps Pando did not do so. Perhaps he imparted his golden treasures to his comrades in arms. And what did they do with it? Where was this mine of information lost?

There is something wrong in this Pando game. Pando was undoubtedly a very genius of discovery and investigation, but he wandered into the woods somewhere and came out too late. In truth, Pando is but a soldier embittered because his side has been soundly whipped. After Waterloo, some of Napolean's superb gray veterans wrote pamphlets proving that the English knew nothing of the art of war.

But Havana hears Pando. Pando was always known as the active fighting commander. Havana listens to his howl and grows more chagrined, more anxious to contend that Spain lost by a fluke, more angry.

The frenzy for not losing any single chance at a dollar displays itself in more wonderful ways than in a tax upon American ships bringing relief for the people of Cuba. Montoro,[3] the chief of the treasury, has lately distinguished himself. Some Havana people projected a fair to be held at the Theatre Orajoa for the benefit of the hospitals which the Americans will establish for the sick among our troops. Although these hospitals are as remote and vague in point of time as the landing of a United States force here, yet these good people thought they would seize time by the hair and have a little fund all in readiness for the ailing boys in blue.

The response from the Cubans, from the Americans and from one or two straddling Spaniards was very hearty. Everything bloomed; it only remained for a committee to wait upon Montoro and gain his consent. But the gay Montoro at once announced to the committee when he saw it that they could hold the affair on condition that twenty-five per cent of the profits should go to the Government. Having recovered its composure with some difficulty the committee left him.

As far as goes the mere accident of birth Montoro is a Cuban, but even as the Tories of our Revolutionary War were usually too brutal for the stomachs of regular English troops, so this man is Cuba's most implacable and deadly foe. He and Fernando de Castro,[4] the Civil

3. Rafael Montoro (b. 1852 in Havana) was treasury secretary (*la secretaria de Hacienda*) during this time and was a member of the Evacuation Commission.

4. Fernando de Castro must remain merely a name; attempts at further identification have failed. Crane was partially correct: Montoro did leave Cuba but as Minister to Great Britain under Palma.

Governor, another Cuban, will have to go to Spain when the change comes. They can't stay here. The Cubans are going to be very law-abiding, but it would be too bad to stuff these two rascals down their throats.

OUR SAD NEED OF DIPLOMATS.

HAVANA, Nov. 9. — One of the foreign consuls, a man who has been for many years and in many lands in the diplomatic service of his country, when asked his opinion of the American commissions here, answered at once that they are too big, too unwieldy: there are too many men. He gave it as his idea that the European governments found it far more satisfactory and expeditious to leave the most important negotiations in the hands of three or four men trained to the game, who would have only such subordinates as were needed for bare clerkly duties, and practically carry everything in their own heads. He confessed that in a considerable experience at the London, Berlin and Vienna embassies of his country he had never succeeded in espying any such noble diplomatic caravans.

This seems partly true. For instance, the Evacuation Commission, or, rather, the Commission-Appointed-to-Negotiate-and-Superintend-an-Evacuation-Which-At-Some-Future-Date-is-More-or-Less-Likely-to-Take-Place,-Although-It-Must-Be-Said-There-Is-No-Direct-Evidence-at-Present-to-Prove-That-Said-Gentlemen-Might-Not-with-More-Com-fort-Have-Remained-at-Home-and-There-Drawn-the-Salaries-Duly-Provided — this commission lives in a hotel, an entire hotel, the best hotel. Of course, the private citizen is naturally aggrieved at having the best hotel and restaurant wrested from him, even by a commission. This is especially true in a town like Havana, where the best is not startling. But, after all, when the Standard Oil Company comes to town, it consists of a man with a valise. People like Senator Hanna[1] walk about with an entire State in a waistcoat pocket, and plenty of men jingle counties and cities carelessly, like so many coins. Alone, Napoleon once settled a treaty by hurling a porcelain vase to the floor in

---

Reprinted here for the first time from New York Journal: 17 November 1898.

Crane's dispatch, filed on November 9, has its companion piece in " 'You Must' — 'We Can't' " (supra, p. 225). The American military commissioners had arrived in Havana on September 10.

1. Marcus Alonzo Hanna (1837–1904) was an Ohio-born Republican politician and United States Senator, 1897–1904.

fragments and declaring to the Austrian Ambassador that his country would look that way if he did not instantly submit to the imperial terms. The great things of the world are invariably done by machines which do not require as housing an entire hotel.

One harrowing local phase of it is the absolute impossibility of getting familiar with all the faces of the commissioners and their suites. One will become quite convinced that one is well versed in the official countenances, when suddenly into some public place will come a bewildering string of colonels, majors and captains, all utterly new, and yet all obviously as important as the very devil. It makes one's head ache.

＊

If I may be allowed to say so, I have already pointed out in the Journal that one of the principal Spanish ideas of cleverness and craft is a policy of stone-faced delay. Heaven knows what they suppose it accomplishes, but at any rate they adopt it.

An American business man, many years the agent here of an important New York firm, remarked to me to-day: "When I came here first I tried to hurry these people. If I called on some firm and they kept me waiting an hour, I used to kick like blazes. I'd say: 'Look here, I'm in a hurry! My time is valuable! I can't wait here all day!' Then they would merely raise their shoulders in maddening indifference and say: 'Well, we are very sorry.'

It took me a long time to find out that it was merely a ruse, a trick, because the fools worked it often enough when it was greatly to their advantage to bring off a deal with me."

For my part, I believe all this is a direct inheritance from ancient Moorish vendors of fruit, tobacco, rugs, water jars, brass trinkets. We are, in fact, dealing with a lot of pedlers.

Colonel Hecker's[2] career here is highly amusing and instructive. "I want so-and-so. Have you got it? Yes? How much do you want for it? No — won't give it. Bang! — negotiations off!" While the pedler is just getting into shape to wheedle and dicker and snivel and bluff, Hecker is a mile away, dealing with another man. Hecker has greatly rumpled them up here. He charges them like a wild bull and wont stand for a minute their little Mediterranean tricks. For his dock and other works he has got nearly everything he wants in a short time, and

2. Frank Joseph Hecker (1846–1927), a Civil War veteran, railroad executive, and former police commissioner of Detroit, 1880–1890, who, as a colonel of volunteers in the quartermaster department, served as chief of the division of transportation of the Army (from 8 July 1898 to 1 May 1899). He was in Cuba with a board of officers appointed by the War Department (October 1) to select camp sites for the occupation troops.

— so business men tell me — he paid only the just price. The Spaniards think he is a marvel. They expected to have a pie.

*

Before the war, when the American colony was leaving Havana in haste, the Spanish pilot who was taking a steamer out of the harbor addressed one of the American passengers. "Well, good-by. I'll see you again soon."

"See me again soon?" said the American in surprise. "How will you see me again?"

"Oh, I'll soon be over there," answered the pilot grimly, pointing into the north. "I'm going on board one of our war ships."

The American laughed then. "Why, your war ships can't move. They haven't any coal."

"Yes; but," answered the Spaniard, "there is plenty of coal at Key West."

"How are you going to get it?"

"We will go and take it," said the pilot, with a shine in his eye and disclosing his teeth.

Well, the amount of coal captured by the Spaniards at Key West turned out to be not enough to carry them far, and at the end of the war the American returned to Havana. Luck had it that he was spoken of a great deal about the harbor as the probable American appointee as captain of the port. This turned the pilot quite woolly with fright, and his teeth have been chattering ever since in the expectation that when the Americans come his head will be among the first to fall.

There are plenty of people here who are sorry that they were so mighty cocksure in the early days. The roots of their existence are fastened in Cuba even as that pilot's sole hold on the world is his knowledge of the waters of Havana. Many of them who gratuitously insulted Americans before the war and in the early stages of the conflict now sometimes find that these individual Americans are likely to be their governmental masters.

A good many are trying to get in out of the wet, and although revenge is usually foreign to an American character, the reversal of form is so pitifully bald and shameless that it goes against the northern stomach.

*

An extraordinary number of people are inquiring the whereabouts of Joseph A. Springer.[3] He was consular agent here for over thirty-

3. Presumably Crane is referring to James H. Springer, consular agent at San Juan de los Remedios, province of Santa Clara, Cuba (an important

five years. He was the wheel horse of American diplomacy. In short, he was the consulate. He departed with Lee[4] just previous to the war.

We, as a people, know as much about diplomacy as we do about hatching fighting cocks by holding eggs over a gas jet, but unconsciously and without any virtue of our own, we have reared in certain places men who perfectly understand the business which, by mandate of Government, they are required to manipulate. These are invariably subordinate officers. The great men, the high-steppers, they come for a time, lean heavily upon the shoulders of the wheel horses and then retire to oblivion or Congress. The wheel horse puts some liniment upon his shoulder and stands then ready to pull the next high-stepper out of a mudhole.

Meanwhile, he never, by any chance, gets the slightest credit for anything. The great man, the Ambassador, or the Minister, may go home with his very boots full of laurels, but the wheel horse in all probability gets flung into some adjacent abyss without any one taking trouble to listen whether or no he hits a projecting ledge.

One familiar with our European affairs could cite unnumbered cases of the kind, but the case of Springer is point enough. On these commissions here is about everybody who ever officially sighted Cuba through a telescope. The young men who were under Springer's consular tutelage before the war are here, officially. Everybody is here but Springer. Springer has no influence. Heaven help Springer.

I often think of the fate of White,[5] the first secretary of our Embassy in London. He has pulled Ambassadors through knot holes and up through cracks in the floor until he is prematurely gray, and at last he will be flung out somewhere to die — all same Springer.

---

commercial town). The agent was paid no salary but rather was reimbursed by fees (e.g., $822.00 for the year 1893).

4. Fitzhugh Lee (1835–1905) of Confederate cavalry fame in the Civil War. He served as United States Consul to Havana, 1896–1898. In May 1898 he was put in command of the 7th Army Corps; later he was named military governor of Havana (1899), and subsequently he was appointed to command the Department of Missouri.

5. Henry White, Secretary of the Legation under Robert Todd Lincoln, Envoy Extraordinary and Minister Plenipotentiary to Great Britain, 1889–1893.

IN HAVANA AS IT IS TO-DAY.

THE insurgent posts are not far from Havana on all sides, and such is the present condition here that the main trouble of visiting any of them exists in the fabulous sums charged by the livery people for any kind of transportation. However, three of us yesterday combined to expend our hopes of a pensioned old age and hired a trap to take us to the camp of General Rodriguez,[1] insurgent commander-in-chief in Havana Province. The distance from Guanabacoa[2] is twenty-six kilometres over one of the few good military roads in Cuba.

The ground in front of the Spanish lines is favorable to the deploying of large bodies of troops, and the cavalry would have had considerable work cut out for it. The dense thickets of the ground before Santiago here do not exist. The high main position is led up to by a series of rolling, grassy mounds probably four miles in extent. Primarily there would have been some handy picket fighting and skirmishing around and over these mounds.

One must not leave discussion of these Havana defences without mentioning the barbed wire entanglements. They exist in profusion. They are not mere fences. Fences of barbed wire are the easiest of such entanglements. But these are laid in horizontal webs and meshes about nine inches from the turf, and so form a most formidable china shop for any living bull. The men who cut them would be within forty yards of the intrenchments, and men in these times do not cut barbed wire entanglements that are within forty yards' range of a rifle pit.

We had not gone three hundred yards from a pair of indolent cavalry pickets when we came upon five men in linen, yellow from dirt, who grinned at us in a most friendly fashion and arrived in some curious way at the position of order arms. As soldiers they were laughable. Yes, laughable, for those who do not know. Their pretence of coming to attention and doing us honor thereby was purely comic, but the first man in the file happened to resemble an insurgent whom I had seen killed at Cusco — really the tightest, best fight of the war — and thus I was enabled to know in some way that all was not to be judged by appearances.

They were armed with Remington rifles,[3] every one of which was

Reprinted here for the first time from New York Journal: 12 November 1898.

1. Beyond what Crane has to say about General Rodriguez, the insurgent chief remains obscure.
2. A suburb east of Havana.
3. Probably the Remington, Model 1873.

in more or less bad condition. However, in the Spanish army one never sees a rifle in good condition. In fact, the rifles of the insurgents are usually in better shape. They came to this grotesque attention and surveyed us with wide smiles — smiles of ivory purity on their black faces.

We supposed that, having passed this rebel outpost, we had entered the zone of the insurgents. But it was not so. To our military astonishment we found that the outposts interlaced. First you came upon the Spanish sentries; then an insurgent outpost; then a block house occupied by the Spaniards; then more insurgents; then another block house. During the war this road had been vigorously defended, and about all the Cubans could do was to cross it whenever they liked, but now, under the flag of truce, or peace, or whatever it is, the road seems to have come upon a manner of joint ownership, in which both sides exist on it without friction.

One incident will display the situation. A man in the coach, a Cuban, had come out heavily loaded with cigarettes for the patriots. Once he sighted an outpost and asked of a soldier: "How many are you here?"

The soldier answered: "Twelve men and a corporal, sir."

Whereupon our friend dished out a commensurate number of cigarettes. The soldiers were very grateful, very grateful indeed. They were Spanish soldiers. Our patriot kicked himself for some miles, but to no purpose. The cigarettes were gone, and they were gone firmly into the mouths of sundry hated Spanish infantrymen.

This happened to be the last Spanish post. Thirty yards from it were three serene insurgent pickets. They were apparently keeping out of sight of the enemy because of a sense of the decencies of the situation, but plainly theirs was a lazy job. They smiled at us, too — the same cavernous, ivory smile.

The carriage rocked tremblingly over a mile of wood road. We came upon other sentries more formal and then at last we arrived at that most interesting thing called an insurgent camp.

Evidently that wide avenue of palms led to the relics of a plantation, but now this palm-lined avenue was only the main street of an insurgent camp.

Primarily, we had come to see an American, Lieutenant-Colonel Jones,[4] on General Menocal's staff. Jones had been for three years on campaign. He had raised himself on his ability as an artilleryman. Artillerymen were almost as few as guns in the Cuban army, and every one was valuable. Jones, by his correct and intrepid handling of whatever guns went into action, was promoted steadily by Gomez un-

4. Another unknown figure of the time.

til he has now reached a position second to no artillery officer in the Cuban service.

We had some money for Jones; we had some tobacco for Jones; we had some sandwiches and some rum for Jones. We expected a welcome. Did we get it? We did. We got one of those open-armed, splendid welcomes which are written for the coming of dukes. After all, we were of his kind. He had been three years in the woods and with others, but when he saw us he was almost childishly delighted. It mattered nothing who we were or what we were: it was only that we were of his kind, and the hours we sat with him were glad ones, because he was glad, glad to be chock-a-block once more with his own. We could see him breathe in the outright Americanism as if it were some perfume wafted from the folds of the flag and we were not too noble representatives, either.

When we first sighted him he was lying in his hammock. It is impossible to state how universal is this condition of lying in a hammock — especially at this time when there is no occasion for activity, no fighting. Once the insurgents in Havana Province had more high stepping and tall jumping to do than has come to the lot of any military force in the world, barring the Apaches for some occasions. The present complacence of nature startles them into a curious state of fretful rest which they account almost as a disease after their three years of jumping, flying, aerial life.

The furniture of Jones's hut consisted mainly of a hammock and a soap box. In the soap box were some newspapers — now become universal in every jungle — a tin cup, a bottle of ink, some writing paper. On a rafter of his rude dwelling hung his belt, with his machete and his revolver. Beside him lay his saddle, which looked as if dogs had chewed it. This was apparently and truly all he possessed. The house was wide to the air; there were no sides. Outside crouched two of those quick-eyed military servants which one can find in any Cuban camp. To their services they imparted a good-natured or, rather, a friendly quality, which was infinitely grateful to the senses. They dodged, swung, lifted, carried in a certain indescribable way which impressed one that the will was good, all true, all amiable, all kind.

Presently we went to visit General Menocal.[5] General Rodriguez

5. Mario García Menocal (1866–1941) was, as Crane says, a graduate in civil engineering from Cornell, Class of 1888. His subsequent career is worth noting: President of Cuba, 1913–1921, succeeding General José Miguel Gómez and succeeded by Alfredo Zayas, an old political opponent. Menocal's administration has been called "businesslike and friendly" to the United States but only partly successful so far as reforms were concerned. In 1924, Menocal was defeated for the presidency by Gerardo Machado y Morales, but he was quite active in Cuban politics, 1931–1936.

was commander of the forces in the province, but he had gone away somewhere on horseback, riding a good white horse, and, for a wonder, riding it well.

We found Menocal to be a young man — not more than thirty-five years. His coat was much in the manner of a duck coat of an American naval officer. It had the same wide, white braid, but on the collar shone two gold stars, the sign of a general of division.

He is a Cornell graduate of the class of '88. He talks English consequently, clean out of all courier and hotel runner latitudes. He is soon to be a major-general, and it is a promotion that strikes every one with its extraordinary correctness. Menocal is one of the men in the game. When Garcia[6] was ploughing around the eastern end of Cuba Menocal was his chief of staff. Menocal had more to do with Garcia's success than we can talk about, and that is enough said. He will be one of the men who will comprehend the American point of view. He will know how honestly we mean in this affair.

The horseflesh to be seen was in bad condition, but no worse than the Spanish mounts. They were all odd, unmatched little beasts, with an infinite variety of accoutrement ranging from ragged and war-worn saddles with the padding leaking out to dazzling tan equipments

6. Crane is referring here to the Cuban patriot Calixto García y Iñigues (1836–1898), one of the great leaders against Spanish rule in the island. During the Spanish-American War he was in command of all Cuban forces in the eastern end of Cuba and he distinguished himself particularly in the fighting at El Caney. Elbert Hubbard's "A Message to García," a short editorial in *The Philistine* (1899), immortalized García and Lt. Andrew Summers Rowan, who told his own story in "How I Carried the Message to García," a pamphlet issued in 1923. Before the declaration of war, Rowan was sent in April 1898, not with a message to García (he carried no papers), but to "bring the military data up to date." Dressed as an English hunter, Rowan secured a small boat and, making the Cuban shore from Jamaica on April 23, he reached the general's headquarters at Bayamo on May 1 and obtained the information from him in the form of three staff officers to accompany Rowan back to the United States.

Crane objected strongly to Hubbard's piece about Rowan. "He didn't do anything worthy at all. He received the praise of the general of the army and got to be made a lieutenant col. for a feat which about forty news-paper correspondents had already performed at the usual price of fifty dollars a week and expenses. Besides he is personally a chump and in Porto Rico where I met him he wore a yachting cap as part of his uniform which was damnable. When you want to monkey with some of our national heroes you had better ask me, because I know and your perspective is almost out of sight." (Crane to Hubbard, 1 May 1899, in *Stephen Crane: Letters* [1960], p. 220.)

Nevertheless, Rowan was awarded by Congress in 1922 the Distinguished Service Cross.

from the best Havana saddlers, the latter being gifts of joyful friends since the pause in the conflict. In fact, the donations of Havana were everywhere plain. The officer of the day, for instance, wore a gorgeous crimson sash embroidered in white. The beloved, the sweetheart, has again entered the life of the lonely insurgent.

Food, if not exactly plentiful, was had in at least sufficient quantities for the troops. The pitiful sight was to see the last of the reconcentrados hanging about the camp, miserable women and babes, ragged, dirty, diseased, more than half famished. They are in desperate straits. Such, indeed, is the condition that a gift of a little bread sometimes brings the virtue of women to the feet of the philanthropist.

❉   ❉   ❉

MR. STEPHEN CRANE ON THE NEW AMERICA

Few men know as much of Cuba and the Cubans as Mr. Stephen Crane, who for the past three years has been in close touch with the people and leaders there. His late story, "The Open Boat," is a true account of an unenviable experience of his when on a filibustering expedition. His ship, the *Commodore*, was wrecked, and he himself with others given up as lost. He has a very interesting book made up of his own obituary notices which he greatly treasures. Mr. Crane's marked success as correspondent during the late war is well known, and, as far as United States battles on land are concerned, it can be truthfully said that he was the only man actually present at every engagement.[1] He has, however, had to suffer for these experiences, and is only just recovering from a sharp attack of yellow fever contracted during his services with the United States army and the insurgents. A mutual friend, calling upon him at his English home,[2] found Mr. Crane particularly communicative.

"That is a large question to ask a small man," he replied, in answer to this friend's inquiry as to the Future of Cuba. "The island has passed through practically thirteen years of continuous war.

An interview with Crane reprinted here for the first time from the London Outlook: *4 February 1899.*

1. That is, every major land engagement in Cuba and Puerto Rico. Sea engagements were something else again, Crane having missed the destruction of Cervera's fleet.

2. Ravensbrook. Crane sailed from New York on the *Manitou* and reached England in January 1899. He and Cora then moved into Brede Place, Sussex.

A very small war can destroy a very enormous commerce. Outside the American garrison the island now contains about one-fifth of a normal population. But its industries of tobacco, sugar, and ore are vast in possibility, and must exert an influence upon the shifting masses who are always searching for work.

"Under the evil Spanish Government, Cuba might as well have been a desert. No matter the wealth in the soil or in the rocks, it was kept there by thieving Spanish officials, unless it came forth with oppressive and almost murderous levy. I know this to be true. Everybody who knows the old life of Cuba knows that it was a life of officialdom, of corruption, ranging from petty bribes to grand gifts. This was true up to the very moment of the raising of the American flag on Morro Castle. I was present to see the wild fleeing of a multitude of little sharks. Parenthetically it might be said that Spain has been ruined mainly by men who in Cuba were engaged in babbling the loudest of their love for the Peninsula. It is easily then, my belief, that the new Government will be in the way of developing a Cuba of which the oldest Cubans could not dream. No one wants to speak of the Americans as an immaculate race; but I feel sure that my own people stand well in honesty with the rest of the world — else they would not accuse themselves so violently and continually.

"The Cubans will be given their independence — despite all cavilling and arguing — but they will be given it not until they have grown to manhood, so to speak."

Of influences to come Mr. Crane ventured to prophesy: "I think it can fairly be said that nations move without regard for either pledges or men; but the word that 'Cuba shall be free' has so freely been given through every city and village of the United States that I am confident it will be kept. I am sure that it has become almost a national creed that we shall do as we declared in the beginning. Governments break their word for the glory of nations, but people do so at their peril."

"And now comes the sore part," resumed Mr. Crane. "The Cubans have not behaved well in the most prominent cases. And this makes the common American soldier very angry. And the common soldier is the common American man. The Cuban says, 'We took San Juan Hill.' Any of us who were there know that there were no Cubans present within any other range than spent-shell range. The common American soldier, having died to some extent in Cuba, does not like these statements. Moreover, when he was in a hurry, the Cubans back of the firing line stole his blanket-roll and his coat, and maybe his hat. Sixteen thousand United States soldiers returning home, wofully ill of their Cuban ally, and being themselves brought from every corner of the United States, impress the entire people. And the entire people immediately say, 'Well, if this is the real Cuban, we know much more than we did previously.' And consequently I can assure you that they are perfectly willing to deal with the Cuban on a new basis, if the Cuban thinks he cares to have it done."

"As for annexation and its results," continued Mr. Crane, "Cuba is too small to affect the United States to an appreciable extent. Its financial question will grow easier and easier. As for the other questions, it seems to me to be a matter of the effect of the United States upon Cuba — that is the main consideration. The United States preponderates, and weighs down upon Cuba. With all mankind's sluice gates opened — I mean, at least, some of the sluice gates — I am, of course, a Free-trader — it is certain that the warmth from this natural mother-country will heat the little Cuba to its proper temperature. When you come to think of it, the island is only ninety miles distant from the United States."

And then they fell to talking of "American Imperialism." Here also Mr. Crane was enlightening.

"The people of the United States," he said, "consider themselves as a future Imperial Power only vaguely and with much wonder. The idea would probably never have occurred to them had it not been for foreign statements and definitions. The taking of Cuba was what they intended, and the taking of Porto Rico and the Philippines was a military necessity incumbent upon one country when it is engaged in war with another. The Philippines — speaking of them as the only international intrusion — were taken quite in the way of the most ordinary naval attack, the usual supports came for the attacking party, and after a time the United States finds itself confronted with some people — liberators, patriots, and others — who believed themselves valuable enough to appear as nuggets for which the entire world is going to scramble. That is as far as the United States went in Imperialism. The forces of the nation are now engaged in trying to comfort these people and tell them that they are not going to suffer oppression. If these people don't happen to believe it, there will be fighting on some Eastern islands. As far as I see, there is no direct American sense of Imperialism. America stands on her land and she meets what she meets; she challenges whomsoever she challenges, and whomsoever comes may find her weak, but will never find her unwilling. I say this because I believe it."

When the talk passed on to the Tsar's peace Rescript,[3] Mr.

3. On 24 August 1898, Count Michael Nikolaievich Muraviev (1845–1900), Minister of Foreign Affairs to Czar Nicholas II, and by his order, proposed to the several foreign ambassadors at St. Petersburg an inter-

Crane would formulate no personal opinion, but as to the opinion of the people in the United States he was more communicative. "I may say," he observed, "that in America I thought they took it in a fashion quite between the indifferent and the humorous. Outside of saying the ordinary thing, that nobody in America cares for what the Tsar of Russia says, it seems to me that they thought it quite unreal, the Tsar of Russia being notable to them as a man who obeyed his councillors, and otherwise being a man from whom nobody expected any heaven-sent statements. In reality, the United States has seldom been armed. An appeal of the sort from a completely military Power may properly strike them with a certain humour. The Powers of Europe have often plainly laughed at them as a great fat, unfortified mass. We can be military if we choose. The art of war is applied mechanics. It only needs one goading, two asides, and three insults. Thereupon we become a military people. If an apostle of peace does appear with true spirit and with true eloquence, he will not be the Tsar of Russia, nor will he be of the Russian General Staff. He will be some poor devil, and will probably be stoned to death for talking beyond his audience. And days will come and days will go before there appears a man who will stop the human race from 'Fighting like Hell for conciliation.' " [4]

---

national conference "on the preservation of peace and the reduction of armaments" (*Annual Register*, 1898, p. 50).

Regarded as "an extraordinary document" which produced "a great sensation in Germany and Austria" (*ibid.*, p. 282), it was also "generally regarded as impracticable, although all the powers sent a sympathetic reply" and agreed to be "represented at a conference to consider it."

On 11 January 1899 (30 December 1898, O.S.), Count Muraviev addressed a second circular to the Powers, outlining the proposals to be submitted for discussion. On January 19 (Vol. 68, 41), *The Nation* commented that it "restricts itself . . . to various proposals for making war less savage and for keeping down the future growth of armaments, and the burdensome taxes to pay for them. . . ." Invitations were also issued to send delegates. The eventual results were the first Hague Conference of 1899, and the second, of 1907, also called by the Czar.

It is not altogether clear which of the Czar's rescripts is being referred to in the article.

In March 1899, it was announced that the conference would meet at the Hague on May 18. Twenty-five nations were represented by 100 delegates. The U.S. contingent included Andrew D. White, Ambassador to Germany; Stanford Newel, Minister to the Netherlands; Seth Low, President of Columbia University; and Captain Alfred T. Mahan, U.S.N., Ret.

4. Crane's editorializing on the U.S. position *vis-à-vis* the rescripts may be compared with that of *The Nation*. On September 1 and 15 (1898) the magazine displayed a well-mannered skepticism toward the first letter. On

THE PRICE OF THE HARNESS

i

Twenty-five men were making a road out of a path up the hillside. The light batteries in the rear were impatient to advance, but first must be done all that digging and smoothing which gains no encrusted medals from war. The men worked like gardeners, and a road was growing from the old pack-animal trail.

Trees arched from a field of guinea-grass which resembled young wild corn. The day was still and dry. The men working were dressed in the consistent blue of United States regulars. They looked indifferent, almost stolid, despite the heat and the labour. There was little talking. From time to time a Government pack-train, led by a sleek-sided tender bell-mare, came from one way or the other way, and the

---

January 19 (Vol. 68, 41), Rollo Ogden said about Muraviev's second letter: "We are glad to see that the programme put forth is modest. Small beginnings are desirable in so great a movement. . . . His new circular letter brings the world distinctly nearer a practical agreement to make war a less constant preoccupation of civilized men. . . ."

Ogden was again skeptical on April 13, this time about the position of the United States: ". . . Indirectly the influence of the United States in the Czar's Congress will be great, and we regret to say that we cannot think it will be on the side of peace. This results not from what we say, but from what we do" (Vol. 68, 270). Of course, reference here is to the Spanish-American War and the campaigns in the Philippine Islands.

First published under the title "The Woof of Thin Red Threads" in Cosmopolitan: December 1898; also same month in Blackwood's Edinburgh Magazine.

Crane wrote it while in Havana, and in his October 1898 letter to Paul Reynolds, his agent, he calls it "The Price of the Harness." The "Woof of Thin Red Threads" title derives from the phrase Crane wrote in Part V of the story.

Writing Reynolds from Havana on November 3, Crane explained: "The name of the story is 'The Price of the Harness' because it is the price of the harness, the price the men paid for wearing the military harness, Uncle Sam's military harness; and they paid blood, hunger and fever." In Stephen Crane: Letters (1960), pp. 188, 193.

men stood aside as the strong, hard black-and-tan animals crowded eagerly after their curious little feminine leader.

A volunteer staff officer appeared and, sitting on his horse in the middle of the work, asked the sergeant in command some questions which were apparently not relevant to any military business. Men straggling along on various duties almost invariably spun some kind of joke as they passed.

A corporal and four men were guarding boxes of spare ammunition at the top of the hill, and one of the number often went to the foot of the hill swinging canteens.

The day wore down to the Cuban dusk, in which the shadows are all grim and of ghostly shape. The men began to lift their eyes from the shovels and picks, and glance in the direction of their camp. The sun threw his last lance through the foliage. The steep mountain range on the right turned blue and as without detail as a curtain. The tiny ruby of light ahead meant that the ammunition-guard were cooking their supper. From somewhere in the world came a single rifle-shot.

Figures appeared, dim in the shadow of the trees. A murmur, a sigh of quiet relief, arose from the working party. Later, they swung up the hill in an unformed formation, being always like soldiers, and unable even to carry a spade save like United States regular soldiers. As they passed through some fields, the bland white light of the end of the day feebly touched each hard bronze profile.

"Wonder if we'll git anythin' to eat," said Watkins, in a low voice.

"Should think so," said Nolan, in the same tone. They betrayed no impatience; they seemed to feel a kind of awe of the situation.

The sergeant turned. One could see the cool grey eye flashing under the brim of the campaign hat. "What in hell you fellers kickin' about?" he asked. They made no reply, understanding that they were being suppressed.

As they moved on, a murmur arose from the tall grass on either hand. It was the noise from the bivouac of ten thousand men, although one saw practically nothing from the low-cart roadway. The sergeant led his party up a wet clay bank and into a trampled field. Here were scattered tiny white shelter tents, and in the darkness they were luminous like the rearing stones in a graveyard. A few fires burned blood-red, and the shadowy figures of men moved with no more expression of detail than there is in the swaying of foliage on a windy night.

The working party felt their way to where their tents were pitched. A man suddenly cursed; he had mislaid something, and he knew he was not going to find it that night. Watkins spoke again with the monotony of a clock: "Wonder if we'll git anythin' to eat."

Martin, with eyes turned pensively to the stars, began a treatise. "Them Spaniards ——"

"Oh, quit it," cried Nolan. "What th' piper do you know about th' Spaniards, you fat-headed Dutchman? Better think of your belly, you blunderin' swine, an' what you're goin' to put in it, grass or dirt."

A laugh, a sort of deep growl, arose from the prostrate men. In the meantime the sergeant had reappeared and was standing over them. "No rations to-night," he said gruffly, and, turning on his heel, walked away.

This announcement was received in silence. But Watkins had flung himself face downward, and putting his lips close to a tuft of grass, he formulated oaths. Martin arose and, going to his shelter, crawled in sulkily. After a long interval Nolan said aloud, "Hell!" Grierson, enlisted for the war, raised a querulous voice. "Well, I wonder when we *will* git fed?"

From the ground about him came a low chuckle, full of ironical comment upon Grierson's lack of certain qualities which the other men felt themselves to possess.

ii

In the cold light of dawn the men were on their knees, packing, strapping, and buckling. The comic toy hamlet of shelter tents had been wiped out as if by a cyclone. Through the trees could be seen the crimson of a light battery's blankets, and the wheels creaked like the sound of a musketry fight. Nolan, well gripped by his shelter tent, his blanket, and his cartridge-belt, and bearing his rifle, advanced upon a small group of men who were hastily finishing a can of coffee.

"Say, give us a drink, will yeh?" he asked, wistfully. He was as sad-eyed as an orphan beggar.

Every man in the group turned to look him straight in the face. He had asked for the principal ruby out of each one's crown. There was a grim silence. Then one said, "What fer?" Nolan cast his glance to the ground, and went away abashed.

But he espied Watkins and Martin surrounding Grierson, who had gained three pieces of hard-tack by mere force of his audacious inexperience. Grierson was fending his comrades off tearfully.

"Now, don't be damn pigs," he cried. "Hold on a minute." Here Nolan asserted a claim. Grierson groaned. Kneeling piously, he divided the hard-tack with minute care into four portions. The men, who had had their heads together like players watching a wheel of fortune, arose suddenly, each chewing. Nolan interpolated a drink of water, and sighed contentedly.

The whole forest seemed to be moving. From the field on the other side of the road a column of men in blue was slowly pouring; the battery had creaked on ahead; from the rear came a hum of advancing regiments. Then from a mile away rang the noise of a shot;

then another shot; in a moment the rifles there were drumming, drumming, drumming. The artillery boomed out suddenly. A day of battle was begun.[1]

The men made no exclamations. They rolled their eyes in the direction of the sound, and then swept with a calm glance the forests and the hills which surrounded them, implacably mysterious forests and hills which lent to every rifle-shot the ominous quality which belongs to secret assassination. The whole scene would have spoken to the private soldiers of ambushes, sudden flank attacks, terrible disasters, if it were not for those cool gentlemen with shoulder-straps and swords who, the private soldiers knew, were of another world and omnipotent for the business.

The battalions moved out into the mud and began a leisurely march in the damp shade of the trees. The advance of two batteries had churned the black soil into a formidable paste. The brown leggings of the men, stained with the mud of other days, took on a deeper colour. Perspiration broke gently out on the reddish faces. With his heavy roll of blanket and the half of a shelter tent crossing his right shoulder and under his left arm, each man presented the appearance of being clasped from behind, wrestler-fashion, by a pair of thick white arms.

There was something distinctive in the way they carried their rifles. There was the grace of an old hunter somewhere in it, the grace of a man whose rifle has become absolutely a part of himself. Furthermore, almost every blue shirt-sleeve was rolled to the elbow, disclosing forearms of almost incredible brawn. The rifles seemed light, almost fragile, in the hands that were at the end of these arms, never fat but always with rolling muscles and veins that seemed on the point of bursting. And another thing was the silence and the marvellous impassivity of the faces as the column made its slow way toward where the whole forest spluttered and fluttered with battle.

Opportunely, the battalion was halted a-straddle of a stream, and before it again moved, most of the men had filled their canteens. The firing increased. Ahead and to the left a battery was booming at methodical intervals, while the infantry racket was that continual drumming which, after all, often sounds like rain on a roof. Directly ahead one could hear the deep voices of field-pieces.

Some wounded Cubans were carried by in litters improvised from hammocks swung on poles. One had a ghastly cut in the throat, probably from a fragment of shell, and his head was turned as if Providence particularly wished to display this wide and lapping gash to the long

1. Crane's story depicts the army moving up into the attack on Kettle Hill on July 1 (1898). Sumner's Brigade performed at Kettle Hill.

column that was winding toward the front. And another Cuban, shot through the groin, kept up a continual wail as he swung from the tread of his bearers. "Ay — ee! Ay — ee! Madre mia! Madre mia!" He sang this bitter ballad into the ears of at least three thousand men as they slowly made way for his bearers on the narrow wood-path. These wounded insurgents were, then, to a large part of the advancing army, the visible messengers of bloodshed and death, and the men regarded them with thoughtful awe. This doleful sobbing cry — "Madre mia" — was a tangible consequent misery of all that firing on in front into which the men knew they were soon to be plunged. Some of them wished to inquire of the bearers the details of what had happened; but they could not speak Spanish, and so it was as if fate had intentionally sealed the lips of all in order that even meagre information might not leak out concerning this mystery — battle. On the other hand, many unversed private soldiers looked upon the unfortunate as men who had seen thousands maimed and bleeding, and absolutely could not conjure any further interest in such scenes.

A young staff officer passed on horseback. The vocal Cuban was always wailing, but the officer wheeled past the bearers without heeding anything. And yet he never before had seen such a sight. His case was different from that of the private soldiers. He heeded nothing because he was busy — immensely busy and hurried with a multitude of reasons and desires for doing his duty perfectly. His whole life had been a mere period of preliminary reflection for this situation, and he had no clear idea of anything save his obligation as an officer. A man of this kind might be stupid; it is conceivable that in remote cases certain bumps on his head might be composed entirely of wood; but those traditions of fidelity and courage which have been handed to him from generation to generation, and which he has tenaciously preserved despite the persecution of legislators and the indifference of his country, make it incredible that in battle he should ever fail to give his best blood and his best thought for his general, for his men, and for himself. And so this young officer in the shapeless hat and the torn and dirty shirt failed to heed the wails of the wounded man, even as the pilgrim fails to heed the world as he raises his illumined face toward his purpose — rightly or wrongly, his purpose — his sky of the ideal of duty; and the wonderful part of it is, that he is guided by an ideal which he has himself created, and has alone protected from attack. The young man was merely an officer in the United States regular army.

The column swung across a shallow ford and took a road which passed the right flank of one of the American batteries. On a hill it was booming and belching great clouds of white smoke. The infantry looked up with interest. Arrayed below the hill and behind the battery were the horses and limbers, the riders checking their pawing mounts, and behind each rider a red blanket flamed against the fervent green of the bushes. As the infantry moved along the road, some of the battery horses turned at the noise of the trampling feet and surveyed the men with eyes as deep as wells, serene, mournful, generous eyes, lit heart-breakingly with something that was akin to a philosophy, a religion of self-sacrifice — oh, gallant, gallant horses!

"I know a feller in that battery," said Nolan, musingly. "A driver."

"Damn sight rather be a gunner," said Martin.

"Why would ye?" said Nolan, opposingly.

"Well, I'd take my chances as a gunner b'fore I'd sit way up in th' air on a raw-boned plug an' git shot at."

"Aw —— " began Nolan.

"They've had some losses t'-day all right," interrupted Grierson.

"Horses?" asked Watkins.

"Horses and men too," said Grierson.

"How d'yeh know?"

"A feller told me there by the ford."

They kept only a part of their minds bearing on this discussion because they could already hear high in the air the wire-string note of the enemy's bullets.

iii

The road taken by this battalion as it followed other battalions is something less than a mile long in its journey across a heavily wooded plain. It is greatly changed now — in fact it was metamorphosed in two days; but at that time it was a mere track through dense shrubbery, from which rose great dignified arching trees. It was, in fact, a path through a jungle.

The battalion had no sooner left the battery in the rear than bullets began to drive overhead. They made several different sounds, but as these were mainly high shots it was usual for them to make the faint note of a vibrant string, touched elusively, half-dreamily.

The military balloon,[2] a fat, wavering, yellow thing, was leading the advance like some new conception of war-god. Its bloated mass shone above the trees, and served incidentally to indicate to the men at the rear that comrades were in advance. The track itself exhibited for all its visible length a closely knit procession of soldiers in blue with breasts crossed with white shelter tents. The first ominous order of battle came down the line. "Use the cut-off. Don't use the magazine until you're ordered." Non-commissioned officers repeated the com-

2. The incident of the Army Signal Corps balloon, which puts the setting close by the trail leading up to the front, is retold in Crane's dispatch: "Vivid Story of the Battle of San Juan" (*supra*, p. 172).

mand gruffly. A sound of clicking locks rattled along the columns. All men knew that the time had come.

The front had burst out with a roar like a brush-fire. The balloon was dying, dying a gigantic and public death before the eyes of two armies. It quivered, sank, faded into the trees amid the flurry of a battle that was suddenly and tremendously like a storm.

The American battery thundered behind the men with a shock that seemed likely to tear the backs of their heads off. The Spanish shrapnel fled on a line to their left, swirling and swishing in supernatural velocity. The noise of the rifle-bullets broke in their faces like the noise of so many lamp-chimneys or sped overhead in swift cruel spitting. And at the front the battle sound, as if it were simply music, was beginning to swell and swell until the volleys rolled like a surf.

The officers shouted hoarsely, "Come on, men! Hurry up, boys! Come on now! Hurry up!" The soldiers, running heavily in their accoutrements, dashed forward. A baggage guard was swiftly detailed; the men tore their rolls from their shoulders as if the things were afire. The battalion, stripped for action, again dashed forward.

"Come on, men! Come on!" To them the battle was as yet merely a road through the woods, crowded with troops who lowered their heads anxiously as the bullets fled high. But a moment later the column wheeled abruptly to the left and entered a field of tall green grass. The line scattered to a skirmish formation. In front was a series of knolls treed sparsely like orchards; and although no enemy was visible, these knolls were all popping and spitting with rifle fire. In some places there were to be seen long grey lines of dirt, entrenchments. The American shells were kicking up reddish clouds of dust from the brow of one of the knolls, where stood a pagoda-like house. It was not much like a battle with men; it was a battle with a bit of charming scenery, enigmatically potent for death.

Nolan knew that Martin had suddenly fallen. "What —" he began.

"They've hit me," said Martin.

"Jesus!" said Nolan.

Martin lay on the ground, clutching his left forearm just below the elbow with all the strength of his right hand. His lips were pursed ruefully. He did not seem to know what to do. He continued to stare at his arm.

Then suddenly the bullets drove at them low and hard. The men flung themselves face downward in the grass. Nolan lost all thought of his friend. Oddly enough, he felt somewhat like a man hiding under a bed, and he was just as sure that he could not raise his head high without being shot as a man hiding under a bed is sure that he cannot raise his head without bumping it.

A lieutenant was seated in the grass just behind him. He was in the careless and yet rigid pose of a man balancing a loaded plate on his knee at a picnic. He was talking in soothing paternal tones.

"Now, don't get rattled. We're all right here. Just as safe as being in church. . . . They're all going high. Don't mind them. . . . Don't mind them. . . . They're all going high. We've got them rattled and they can't shoot straight. Don't mind them."

The sun burned down steadily from a pale blue sky upon the crackling woods and knolls and fields. From the roar of musketry it might have been that the celestial heat was frying this part of the world.

Nolan snuggled close to the grass. He watched a grey line of entrenchments, above which floated the veriest gossamer of smoke. A flag lolled on a staff behind it. The men in the trench volleyed whenever an American shell exploded near them. It was some kind of infantile defiance. Frequently a bullet came from the woods directly behind Nolan and his comrades. They thought at the time that these bullets were from the rifle of some incompetent soldier of their own side.

There was no cheering. The men would have looked about them, wondering where was the army, if it were not that the crash of the fighting for the distance of a mile denoted plainly enough where was the army.

Officially, the battalion had not yet fired a shot; there had been merely some irresponsible popping by men on the extreme left flank. But it was known that the lieutenant-colonel who had been in command was dead — shot through the heart — and that the captains were thinned down to two. At the rear went on a long tragedy, in which men, bent and hasty, hurried to shelter with other men, helpless, dazed, and bloody. Nolan knew of it all from the hoarse and affrighted voices which he heard as he lay flattened in the grass. There came to him a sense of exultation. Here, then, was one of those dread and lurid situations which, in a nation's history, stand out in crimson letters, becoming a tale of blood to stir generation after generation. And he was in it, and unharmed. If he lived through the battle, he would be a hero of the desperate fight at — and here he wondered for a second what fate would be pleased to bestow as a name for this battle.

But it is quite sure that hardly another man in the battalion was engaged in any thoughts concerning the historic. On the contrary, they deemed it ill that they were being badly cut up on a most unimportant occasion. It would have benefited the conduct of whoever were weak if they had known that they were engaged in a battle that would be famous for ever.

iv

Martin had picked himself up from where the bullet had knocked him and addressed the lieutenant. "I'm hit, sir," he said.

The lieutenant was very busy. "All right, all right," he said, just heeding the man enough to learn where he was wounded. "Go over that way. You ought to see a dressing-station under those trees."

Martin found himself dizzy and sick. The sensation in his arm was distinctly galvanic. The feeling was so strange that he could wonder at times if a wound was really what ailed him. Once, in this dazed way, he examined his arm; he saw the hole. Yes, he was shot; that was it. And more than in any other way it affected him with a profound sadness.

As directed by the lieutenant, he went to the clump of trees, but he found no dressing-station there. He found only a dead soldier lying with his face buried in his arms and with his shoulders humped high as if he were convulsively sobbing. Martin decided to make his way to the road, deeming that he thus would better his chances of getting to a surgeon. But he suddenly found his way blocked by a fence of barbed wire. Such was his mental condition that he brought up at a rigid halt before this fence, and stared stupidly at it. It did not seem to him possible that this obstacle could be defeated by any means. The fence was there, and it stopped his progress. He could not go in that direction.

But as he turned he espied that procession of wounded men, strange pilgrims, that had already worn a path in the tall grass. They were passing through a gap in the fence. Martin joined them. The bullets were flying over them in sheets, but many of them bore themselves as men who had now exacted from fate a singular immunity. Generally there were no outcries, no kicking, no talk at all. They too, like Martin, seemed buried in a vague but profound melancholy.

But there was one who cried out loudly. A man shot in the head was being carried arduously by four comrades, and he continually yelled one word that was terrible in its primitive strength — "Bread! Bread! Bread!" Following him and his bearers were a limping crowd of men less cruelly wounded, who kept their eyes always fixed on him, as if they gained from his extreme agony some balm for their own sufferings.

"Bread! Give me bread!"

Martin plucked a man by the sleeve. The man had been shot in the foot, and was making his way with the help of a curved, incompetent stick. It is an axiom of war that wounded men can never find straight sticks.

"What's the matter with that feller?" asked Martin.

"Nutty," said the man.

"Why is he?"

"Shot in th' head," answered the other, impatiently.

The wail of the sufferer arose in the field amid the swift rasp of bullets and the boom and shatter of shrapnel. "Bread! Bread! Oh, God, can't you give me bread? Bread!" The bearers of him were suffering exquisite agony, and often they exchanged glances which exhibited their despair of ever getting free of this tragedy. It seemed endless.

"Bread! Bread! Bread!"

But despite the fact that there was always in the way of this crowd a wistful melancholy, one must know that there were plenty of men who laughed, laughed at their wounds whimsically, quaintly inventing odd humours concerning bicycles and cabs, extracting from this shedding of their blood a wonderful amount of material for cheerful badinage, and, with their faces twisted from pain as they stepped, they often joked like music-hall stars. And perhaps this was the most tearful part of all.

They trudged along a road until they reached a ford.[3] Here under the eave of the bank lay a dismal company. In the mud and in the damp shade of some bushes were a half-hundred pale-faced men prostrate. Two or three surgeons were working there. Also, there was a chaplain, grim-mouthed, resolute, his surtout discarded. Overhead always was that incessant maddening wail of bullets.

Martin was standing gazing drowsily at the scene when a surgeon grabbed him. "Here, what's the matter with you?" Martin was daunted. He wondered what he had done that the surgeon should be so angry with him.

"In the arm," he muttered, half shamefacedly.

After the surgeon had hastily and irritably bandaged the injured member he glared at Martin and said, "You can walk all right, can't you?"

"Yes, sir," said Martin.

"Well, now, you just make tracks down that road."

"Yes, sir." Martin went meekly off. The doctor had seemed exasperated almost to the point of madness.

The road was at this time swept with the fire of a body of Spanish sharpshooters who had come cunningly around the flanks of the American army, and were now hidden in the dense foliage that lined both sides of the road. They were shooting at everything. The road was as

3. The ford Crane mentions is "Bloody Bend" on the San Juan River. It was here Crane encountered his Claverack school chum Reuben McNab, an encounter Crane describes in "War Memories" (*infra*, p. 000).

crowded as a street in a city, and at an absurdly short range they
emptied their rifles at the passing people. They were aided always by
the over-sweep from the regular Spanish line of battle.

Martin was sleepy from his wound. He saw tragedy follow tragedy, but they created in him no feeling of horror.

A man with a red cross on his arm was leaning against a great
tree. Suddenly he tumbled to the ground, and writhed for a moment
in the way of a child oppressed with colic. A comrade immediately
began to bustle importantly. "Here," he called to Martin, "help me
carry this man, will you?"

Martin looked at him with dull scorn. "I'll be damned if I do,"
he said. "Can't carry myself, let alone somebody else."

This answer, which rings now so inhuman, pitiless, did not affect
the other man. "Well, all right," he said. "Here comes some other
fellers." The wounded man had now turned blue-grey; his eyes were
closed; his body shook in a gentle, persistent chill.

Occasionally Martin came upon dead horses, their limbs sticking
out and up like stakes. One beast, mortally shot, was besieged by three
or four men who were trying to push it into the bushes, where it
could live its brief time of anguish without thrashing to death any
of the wounded men in the gloomy procession.

The mule train, with extra ammunition, charged toward the front,
still led by the tinkling bell-mare.

An ambulance was stuck momentarily in the mud, and above
the crack of battle one could hear the familiar objurgations of the
driver as he whirled his lash.

Two privates were having a hard time with a wounded captain,
whom they were supporting to the rear. He was half cursing, half
wailing out the information that he not only would not go another
step toward the rear, but that he was certainly going to return at once
to the front. They begged, pleaded at great length as they continually
headed him off. They were not unlike two nurses with an exceptionally
bad and headstrong little duke.

The wounded soldiers paused to look impassively upon this struggle. They were always like men who could not be aroused by anything
further.

The visible hospital was mainly straggling thickets intersected
with narrow paths, the ground being covered with men. Martin saw a
busy person with a book and a pencil, but he did not approach him to
become officially a member of the hospital. All he desired was rest
and immunity from nagging. He took seat painfully under a bush and
leaned his back upon the trunk. There he remained thinking, his face
wooden.

v

"My Gawd," said Nolan, squirming on his belly in the grass, "I can't stand this much longer."

Then suddenly every rifle in the firing line seemed to go off of its own accord. It was the result of an order, but few men heard the order; in the main they had fired because they heard others fire, and their sense was so quick that the volley did not sound too ragged. These marksmen had been lying for nearly an hour in stony silence, their sights adjusted, their fingers fondling their rifles, their eyes staring at the entrenchments of the enemy. The battalion had suffered heavy losses, and these losses had been hard to bear, for a soldier always reasons that men lost during a period of inaction are men badly lost.

The line now sounded like a great machine set to running frantically in the open air, the bright sunshine of a green field. To the *prut* of the magazine rifles was added the under-chorus of the clicking mechanism, steady and swift, as if the hand of one operator was controlling it all. It reminds one always of a loom, a great grand steel loom, clinking, clanking, plunking, plinking, to weave a woof of thin red threads, the cloth of death. By the men's shoulders under their eager hands dropped continually the yellow empty shells, spinning into the crushed grass-blades to remain there and mark for the belated eye the line of a battalion's fight.

All impatience, all rebellious feeling, had passed out of the men as soon as they had been allowed to use their weapons against the enemy. They now were absorbed in this business of hitting something, and all the long training at the rifle-ranges, all the pride of the marksman which had been so long alive in them, made them forget for the time everything but shooting. They were as deliberate and exact as so many watchmakers.

A new sense of safety was rightfully upon them. They knew that those mysterious men in the high far trenches in front were having the bullets sping in their faces with relentless and remarkable precision; they knew, in fact, that they were now doing the thing which they had been trained endlessly to do, and they knew they were doing it well. Nolan, for instance, was overjoyed. "Plug 'em," he said. "Plug 'em." He laid his face to his rifle as if it were his mistress. He was aiming under the shadow of a certain portico of a fortified house: there he could faintly see a long black line which he knew to be a loophole cut for riflemen, and he knew that every shot of his was going there under the portico, mayhap through the loophole to the brain of another man like himself. He loaded the awkward magazine of his rifle again and again. He was so intent that he did not know of new orders until he saw the men about him scrambling to their feet and running forward, crouching low as they ran.

He heard a shout. "Come on, boys! We can't be last! We're going up! We're going up." He sprang to his feet and, stooping, ran with the others. Something fine, soft, gentle, touched his heart as he ran. He had loved the regiment, the army, because the regiment, the army, was his life — he had no other outlook; and now these men, his comrades, were performing his dream-scenes for him; they were doing as he had ordained in his visions. It is curious that in this charge he considered himself as rather unworthy. Although he himself was in the assault with the rest of them, it seemed to him that his comrades were dazzlingly courageous. His part, to his mind, was merely that of a man who was going along with the crowd.

He saw Grierson biting madly with his pincers at a barbed-wire fence. They were half-way up the beautiful sylvan slope; there was no enemy to be seen, and yet the landscape rained bullets. Somebody punched him violently in the stomach. He thought dully to lie down and rest, but instead he fell with a crash.

The sparse line of men in blue shirts and dirty slouch hats swept up on the hill. He decided to shut his eyes for a moment because he felt very dreamy and peaceful. It seemed only a minute before he heard a voice say, "There he is." Grierson and Watkins had come to look for him. He searched their faces at once and keenly, for he had a thought that the line might be driven down the hill and leave him in Spanish hands. But he saw that everything was secure, and he prepared no questions.

"Nolan," said Grierson clumsily, "do you know me?"

The man on the ground smiled softly. "Of course I know you, you chowder-faced monkey. Why wouldn't I know you?"

Watkins knelt beside him. "Where did they plug you, old boy?"

Nolan was somewhat dubious. "It ain't much, I don't think, but it's somewheres there." He laid a finger on the pit of his stomach. They lifted his shirt, and then privately they exchanged a glance of horror.

"Does it hurt, Jimmie?" said Grierson, hoarsely.

"No," said Nolan, 'it don't hurt any, but I feel sort of dead-to-the-world and numb all over. I don't think it's very bad."

"Oh, it's all right," said Watkins.

"What I need is a drink," said Nolan, grinning at them. "I'm chilly — lying on this damp ground."

"It ain't very damp, Jimmie," said Grierson.

"Well, it is damp," said Nolan, with sudden irritability. "I can feel it. I'm wet, I tell you — wet through — just from lying here."

They answered hastily. "Yes, that's so, Jimmie. It *is* damp. That's so."

"Just put your hand under my back and see how wet the ground is," he said.

"No," they answered. "That's all right, Jimmie. We know it's wet."

"Well, put your hand under and see," he cried, stubbornly.

"Oh, never mind, Jimmie."

"No," he said, in a temper. "See for yourself." Grierson seemed to be afraid of Nolan's agitation, and so he slipped a hand under the prostrate man, and presently withdrew it covered with blood. "Yes," he said, hiding his hand carefully from Nolan's eyes, "you were right, Jimmie."

"Of course I was," said Nolan, contentedly closing his eyes. "This hillside holds water like a swamp." After a moment he said, "Guess I ought to know. I'm flat here on it, and you fellers are standing up."

He did not know he was dying. He thought he was holding an argument on the condition of the turf.

vi

"Cover his face," said Grierson, in a low and husky voice afterwards.

"What'll I cover it with?" said Watkins.

They looked at themselves. They stood in their shirts, trousers, leggings, shoes; they had nothing.

"Oh," said Grierson, "here's his hat." He brought it and laid it on the face of the dead man. They stood for a time. It was apparent that they thought it essential and decent to say or do something. Finally Watkins said in a broken voice, "Aw, it's a damn shame." They moved slowly off toward the firing line.

In the blue gloom of evening, in one of the fever tents, the two rows of still figures became hideous, charnel. The languid movement of a hand was surrounded with spectral mystery, and the occasional painful twisting of a body under a blanket was terrifying, as if dead men were moving in their graves under the sod. A heavy odour of sickness and medicine hung in the air.

"What regiment are you in?" said a feeble voice.

"Twenty-ninth Infantry," answered another voice.[4]

"Twenty-ninth! Why, the man on the other side of me is in the Twenty-ninth."

"He is? — Hey, there, partner, are you in the Twenty-ninth?"

A third voice merely answered wearily. "Martin of C Company."

4. The regiment is fictitious; there were but twenty-five regiments of infantry in the regular army.

"What? Jack, is that you?"

"It's part of me. — Who are you?"

"Grierson, you fat-head. I thought you were wounded."

There was the noise of a man gulping a great drink of water, and at its conclusion Martin said, "I am."

"Well, what you doin' in the fever place, then?"

Martin replied with drowsy impatience. "Got the fever too."

"Gee!" said Grierson.

Thereafter there was silence in the fever tent, save for the noise made by a man over in a corner — a kind of man always found in an American crowd — a heroic, implacable comedian and patriot, of a humour that has bitterness and ferocity and love in it, and he was wringing from the situation a grim meaning by singing "The Star-Spangled Banner" with all the ardour which could be procured from his fever-stricken body.

"Billie," called Martin in a low voice, "where's Jimmy Nolan?"

"He's dead," said Grierson.

A triangle of raw gold light shone on a side of the tent. Somewhere in the valley an engine's bell was ringing, and it sounded of peace and home as if it hung on a cow's neck.

"And where's Ike Watkins?"

"Well, he ain't dead, but he got shot through the lungs. They say he ain't got much show."

Through the clouded odours of sickness and medicine rang the dauntless voice of the man in the corner.

THE SERGEANT'S PRIVATE MADHOUSE

The moonlight was almost steady blue flame, and all this radiance was lavished out upon a still, lifeless wilderness of stunted trees and cactus-plants. The shadows lay upon the ground, pools of black and sharply outlined, resembling substances, fabrics, and not shadows at

First published in Saturday Evening Post: *30 September 1899, from which it is here reprinted in the original clusters of paragraphs separated by ornaments. It appeared also in* Wounds in the Rain (1900) *and in* The Work of Stephen Crane, IX (1926). *Major variants between the latter (referred to as Follett) and the present text are indicated in the footnotes.*

The action of this sketch occurs during the several days' fighting at Guantanamo, perhaps the night of June 12–13. The names of the characters are fictitious; and there was no "G" Company with the First Marine Battalion.

all. From afar came the sound of the sea coughing among the hollows in the coral rocks.

The land was very empty; one could easily imagine that Cuba was a simple vast solitude; one could wonder at the moon taking all the trouble of this splendid illumination. There was no wind; nothing seemed to live.

But in a particular, large group of shadows lay an outpost of some forty United States marines. If it had been possible to approach them from any direction without encountering one of their sentries, one could have gone stumbling among sleeping men and men who sat waiting, their blankets tented over their heads; one would have been in among them before one's mind could have decided whether they were men or devils. If a marine moved, he took the care and the time of one who walks across a death-chamber. The Lieutenant in command reached for his watch, and the nickel chain gave forth the slightest[1] tinkling sound. He could see the glisten in[2] five or six pairs of eyes that turned to regard him. His Sergeant lay near him, and he bent his face down to whisper: "Who's on post behind the big cactus bush?"[3]

"Dryden," rejoined the Sergeant just over his breath.

✿

After a pause the Lieutenant murmured: "He's got too many nerves. I shouldn't have put him there." The Sergeant asked if he should crawl down and look into affairs at Dryden's post. The young officer nodded assent, and the Sergeant, softly cocking his rifle, went away on his hands and knees. The Lieutenant, with his back to a dwarf tree, sat watching the Sergeant's progress for the few moments that he could see him moving from one shadow to another. Afterward, the officer waited to hear Dryden's quick but low-voiced challenge; but time passed, and no sound came from the direction of the post behind the cactus bush.

The Sergeant, as he came nearer and nearer to this cactus-bush — a number of peculiarly dignified columns throwing shadows of inky darkness — had slowed his pace, for he did not wish to trifle with the feelings of the sentry. He was expecting the stern hail, and was ready with the immediate answer which turns away wrath. He was not made anxious by the fact that he could not yet see Dryden, for he knew that the man would be hidden in a way practiced by sentry marines since the time when two men had been killed by a disease of excessive confidence on picket. Indeed, as the Sergeant went still nearer he

1. Follett has *faintest*.
2. Follett has *glistening*.
3. Follett has *plant*.

became more and more angry. Dryden was evidently a most proper sentry.

Finally he arrived at a point where he could see him[4] seated in the shadow, staring into the bushes ahead of him, his rifle ready on his knee. The Sergeant in his rage longed for the peaceful precincts of the Washington Marine Barracks, where there would have been no situation to prevent the most complete non-commissioned oratory. He felt indecent in his capacity of a man able to creep up to the back of a G Company member on guard duty. Never mind; in the morning back at camp —

But suddenly he felt afraid. There was something wrong with Dryden. He remembered old tales of comrades creeping out to find a picket seated against a tree, perhaps upright enough, but stone dead. The Sergeant paused and gave the inscrutable back of the sentry a long stare. Dubious, he again moved forward. At three paces he hissed like a little snake. Dryden did not show a sign of hearing. At last the Sergeant was in a position from which he was able to reach out and touch Dryden on the arm. Whereupon was turned to him the face of a man livid with mad fright. The Sergeant grabbed him by the wrist and with discreet fury shook him. "Here! Pull yourself together!"

*

Dryden paid no heed, but turned his wild face from the newcomer to the ground in front. "Don't you see'em, Sergeant? Don't you see'em?"

"Where?" whispered the sergeant.

"Ahead and a little on the right flank. A reg'lar skirmish line. Don't you see'em?"

"Naw," whispered the Sergeant.

Dryden began to shake. He began moving one hand from his head to his knee, and from his knee to his head rapidly, in a way that is without explanation. "I don't dare fire," he wept. "If I do they'll see me, and oh, how they'll pepper me!"

The Sergeant, lying on his belly, understood one thing. Dryden had gone mad. Dryden was the March Hare. The old man gulped down his uproarious emotions as well as he was able, and used the most simple device. "Go," he said, "and tell the Lieutenant, while I cover your post for you."

"No! They'd see me! And they'd pepper me! Oh, how they'd pepper me!"

The Sergeant was face to face with the biggest situation of his life. In the first place, he knew that at night a large or a small force of Spanish guerrillas was never more than easy rifle-range from any ma-

4. Follett has *Dryden*.

rine outpost, both sides maintaining a secrecy as absolute as possible in regard to their real position and strength. Everything was on a watch-spring foundation. A loud word might be paid for by a night attack which would involve five hundred men who needed their sleep, not to speak of some of them who would need their lives. The slip of a foot and the rolling of a pint of gravel might go from consequence to consequence until various crews went to general quarters on their ships in the harbor, their batteries booming as the swift searchlight flashed through the foliage. Men would get killed — notably the Sergeant and Dryden — and the outposts would be cut off, and the whole night would be one pitiless turmoil. And so Sergeant George H. Peasley began to run his private madhouse behind the cactus bush.

*

"Dryden," said the Sergeant, "you do as I tell you, and go tell the Lieutenant."

"I don't dare move," shivered the man. "They'll see me if I move; they'll see me. They're almost up now. Let's hide — "

"Well, then, you stay here a moment, and I'll go and — "

Dryden turned upon him a look so tigerish that the old man felt his hair move. "Don't you stir!" he hissed. "You want to give me away? You want them to see me? Don't you stir!" The Sergeant decided not to stir.

He became aware of the slow wheeling of eternity, its majestic incomprehensibility of movement. Seconds, moments,[5] were quaint little things, tangible as toys, and there were billions of them, all alike.

"Dryden," he whispered at the end of a century, in which, curiously, he had never joined the marine corps at all, but had taken to another walk of life and prospered greatly in it — "Dryden, this is all foolishness!"

He thought of the expedient of smashing the man over the head with his rifle, but Dryden was so supernaturally alert that there surely would issue some small scuffle, and there could be not even the fraction of a scuffle. The Sergeant relapsed into the contemplation of another century. His patient had one fine virtue. He was in such terror of the phantom skirmish line that his voice never went above a whisper, whereas his delusion might have expressed itself in coyote yells and shots from his rifle. The Sergeant, shuddering, had visions of how it might have been — the mad private leaping into the air and howling and shooting at his friends, and making them the centre of the enemy's eager attention. This, to his mind, would have been conventional conduct for a maniac. The trembling victim of an idea was somewhat puzzling. The Sergeant decided that from time to time he would reason

5. Follett has *minutes.*

with his patient. "Look here, Dryden, you don't see any real Spaniards. You've been drinking or — something. Now — "

But Dryden only glared him into silence. Dryden was inspired with such a profound contempt of him that it had[6] become hatred. "Don't you stir!" And it was clear that if the Sergeant did stir the mad private would introduce calamity. "Now," said Peasley to himself, "if those guerrillas *should* take a crack at us to-night, they'd find a lunatic asylum right in the front, and it would be astonishing."

The silence of the night was broken by the quick, low voice of a sentry to the left some distance. The breathless stillness brought an effect to the words as if they had been spoken in one's ear.

"Halt! Who's there? Halt, or I'll fire!" Bang!

At the moment of sudden attack, particularly at night, it is improbable that a man registers much detail of either thought or action. He may afterward say: "I was here." He may say: "I was there." "I did this"; "I did that." But there remains a great incoherency because of the tumultuous thought which seethes through the head.

"Is this defeat?" At night in a wilderness, and against skillful foes half seen, one does not trouble to ask if it is also death. Defeat is death, then, save for the miraculous ones. But the exaggerating, magnifying first thought subsides in the ordered mind of the soldier, and he knows, soon, what he is doing and how much of it. The Sergeant's immediate impulse had been to squeeze close to the ground and listen — listen; above all else, listen. But the next moment he grabbed his private asylum by the scruff of its neck, jerked it to its feet, and started to retreat upon the main outpost.

To the left, rifle-flashes were bursting from the shadows. To the rear, the Lieutenant was giving some hoarse order or admonition. Through the air swept some Spanish bullets, very high, as if they had been fired at a man in a tree. The private asylum came on so hastily that the Sergeant found he could remove his grip, and soon they were in the midst of the men of the outpost. Here there was no occasion for enlightening the Lieutenant. In the first place, such surprises required statement, question and answer. It is impossible to get a grossly original and fantastic idea through a man's head in less than one minute of rapid talk, and the Sergeant knew that the Lieutenant could not spare the minute. He himself had no minute to devote to anything but the business of the outpost. And the madman disappeared from his ken, and he forgot about him.

It was a long night, and the little fight was as long as the night. It was a heartbreaking work. The forty marines lay in an irregular oval. From all sides the Mauser bullets sang low and swift.[7] The

6. Follett has *was*.
7. Follett has *hard*.

occupation of the Americans was to prevent a rush, and to this end they potted carefully at the flash of a Mauser — save when they got excited for a moment, in which case their magazines rattled like a great Waterbury watch. Then they settled again to a systematic potting.

*

The enemy were not of the regular Spanish forces, but were of a corps of guerrillas, native-born Cubans, who preferred the flag of Spain. They were all men who knew the craft of the woods and were all recruited from the district. They fought more like red Indians than any people but the red Indians themselves. Each seemed to possess an individuality, a fighting individuality, which is only found in the highest order of irregular soldier. Personally, they were as distinct as possible, but through equality of knowledge and experience they arrived at concert of action. So long as they operated in the wilderness they were formidable troops. It mattered little whether it was daylight or dark, they were mainly invisible. They had schooled from the Cubans insurgent to Spain. As the Cubans fought the Spanish troops, so would these particular Spanish troops fight the Americans. It was wisdom.

The marines thoroughly understood the game. They must lie close and fight until daylight, when the guerrillas would promptly go away. They had withstood other nights of this kind, and now their principal emotion was probably a sort of frantic annoyance.

Back at the main camp, whenever the roaring volleys lulled, the men in the trenches could hear their comrades of the outpost, and the guerrillas pattering away interminably. The moonlight faded and left an equal darkness upon the wilderness. A man could barely see the comrade at his side. Sometimes guerrillas crept so close that the flame from their rifles seemed to scorch the faces of the marines, and the reports sounded as if from within two or three inches of their very noses. If a pause came, one could hear the guerrillas gabbling to each other in a kind of[8] delirium. The Lieutenant was praying that the ammunition would last. Everybody was praying for daylight.[9]

A black hour came finally when the men were not fit to have their troubles increase. The enemy made a wild attack on one portion of the oval which was held by about fifteen men. The remainder of the force was busy enough, and the fifteen were naturally left to their devices. Amid the whirl of it, a loud voice suddenly broke out in song:

8. Follett has *drunken*.
9. Follett has *daybreak*.

"While shepherds watched their flocks by night,
  All seated on the ground,
The[10] angel of the Lord came down,
  And glory shone around."

"Who the deuce[11] is that?" demanded the Lieutenant from a throat full of smoke. There was almost a full stop of the firing. The Americans were[12] puzzled. Practical ones muttered that the fool should have a bayonet-hilt shoved down his throat. Others felt a thrill at the strangeness of the thing. Perhaps it was a sign!

"The minstrel boy to the war has gone,
  In the ranks of death you'll find him,
His father's sword he has girded on
  And his wild harp slung behind him."

This croak was as lugubrious as a coffin. "Who is it? Who is it?" snapped the Lieutenant. "Stop him, somebody."

"It's Dryden, sir," said old Sergeant Peasley as he felt around in the darkness for his madhouse. "I can't find him — yet."

"Please, oh, please, — oh, do not let me fall!
  You're — gurgh-ugh —

The Sergeant had pounced upon him.

The singing had had an effect upon the Spaniards. At first they had fired frenziedly at the voice, but they soon ceased, perhaps from sheer amazement. Both sides took a spell of meditation.

The Sergeant was having some difficulty with his charge. "Here, you, grab 'im! Take 'im by the throat! Be quiet, you idiot." [13]

One of the fifteen men who had been hard pressed, called out, "We've only got about one clip apiece, Lieutenant. If they come again — "

The Lieutenant crawled to and fro among his men, taking clips of cartridges from those who had many. He came upon the Sergeant and his madhouse. He felt Dryden's belt and found it simply stuffed with ammunition. He examined Dryden's rifle and found in it a full clip. The madhouse had not fired a shot. The Lieutenant distributed these valuable prizes among the fifteen men. As they[14] gratefully took them, one said: "If they had come again hard enough, they would have had us, sir — maybe."

❀

10. Follett has *an*. 11. Follett has *hell*. 12. Follett has *somewhat*.
13. Follett has *devil*. 14. Follett has *the men*.

But the Spaniards did not come again. At the first indication of daybreak, they fired their customary good-by volley. The marines lay tight while the slow dawn crept over the land. Finally the Lieutenant arose among them, and he was a bewildered man, but very angry. "Now where is that idiot, Sergeant?"

"Here he is, sir," said the old man cheerfully. He was seated on the ground beside the recumbent Dryden, who, with an innocent smile on his face, was sound asleep.

"Wake him up," said the Lieutenant briefly.

The Sergeant shook the sleeper. "Here, Minstrel Boy, turn out. The Lieutenant wants you."

Dryden climbed to his feet and saluted the officer with a dazed and childish air. "Yes, sir."

The Lieutenant was obviously having difficulty in governing his feelings, but he managed to say with calmness, "You seem to be fond of singing, Dryden? Sergeant, see if he has any whiskey on him."

"Sir?" said the madhouse, stupefied. "Singing — fond of singing?"

❋

Here the Sergeant interposed gently, and he and the Lieutenant held palaver apart from the others. The marines, hitching more comfortably their almost empty belts, spoke with grins of the madhouse. "Well, the Minstrel Boy made 'em clear out. They couldn't stand it. But — I wouldn't want to be in his boots. He'll see fireworks when the old man interviews him on the uses of grand opera in modern warfare. How do you think he managed to smuggle a bottle along without us finding it out?"

When the weary outpost was relieved and marched back to camp, the men could not rest until they had told a tale of the voice in the wilderness. In the meantime the Sergeant took Dryden aboard a ship, and to those who took charge of the man, he defined him as "the most useful crazy man[15] in the service of the United States."

15. *Wounds in the Rain* has *useful* —— *crazy man*. Follett has *useful goddam crazy man*.

From "War Memories"

[I. GUANTANAMO]

"But to get at the real thing!" cried Vernall, the war-correspondent. "It seems impossible! It is because war is neither magnificent nor squalid; it is simply life, and an expression of life can always evade us. We can never tell life, one to another, although sometimes we think we can."

*   *   *

One day, our dispatch-boat[1] found the shores of Guantanamo Bay flowing past on either side. It was at nightfall, and on the eastward point a small village was burning, and it happened that a fiery light was thrown upon some palm-trees so that it made them into enormous crimson feathers. The water was the colour of blue steel; the Cuban woods were sombre; high shivered the gory feathers. The last boat-loads of the marine battalion were pulling for the beach. The marine officers gave me generous hospitality to the camp on the hill. That night[2] there was an alarm, and amid a stern calling of orders and a rushing of men, I wandered in search of some other man who had no

---

"War Memories" was published in The Anglo-Saxon Review: *December 1899. From it we have selected excerpts that show Crane reworking his journalism into his own method and style.*

1. The *Three Friends,* which we have encountered in previous newspaper dispatches, had four war correspondents aboard: Vernall, McCurdy, Brownlow, and Kary (all cognomens). McCurdy is Ernest W. McCready, who met Crane in Jacksonville, Florida, in 1896. Kary is Ralph D. Paine, who dedicated his *Roads of Adventure* (1922) to McCready: "My old comrade afloat and ashore." Brownlow is Harry Brown, dean of the New York *Herald* war correspondents. Vernall is Stephen Crane.

In the opening passage — here deleted — Crane describes how the *Three Friends* was tracked down and almost rammed by the USS *Machias.* (*cf., supra,* p. 134).

2. June 10–11.

occupation. It turned out to be the young assistant surgeon, Gibbs.[3] We foregathered in the centre of a square of six companies of marines. There was no firing. We thought it rather comic. The next night there was an alarm; there was some firing; we lay on our bellies; it was no longer comic. On the third night[4] the alarm came early; I went in search of Gibbs, but I soon gave over an active search for the more congenial occupation of lying flat and feeling the hot hiss of the bullets trying to cut my hair. For the moment I was no longer a cynic. I was a child who, in a fit of ignorance, had jumped into a vat of war. I heard somebody dying near me. He was dying hard. Hard. It took him a long time to die. He breathed as all noble machinery breathes when it is making its gallant strife against breaking, breaking. But he was going to break. He was going to break. It seemed to me, this breathing, the noise of a heroic pump which strives to subdue a mud which comes upon it in tons. The darkness was impenetrable. The man was lying in some depression within seven feet of me. Every wave, vibration, of his anguish beat upon my senses. He was long past groaning. There was only the bitter strife for air which pulsed out into the night in a clear penetrating whistle with intervals of terrible silence in which I held my own breath in the common unconscious aspiration to help. I thought this man would never die. I wanted him to die. Ultimately he died. At the moment the adjutant came bustling along erect amid the spitting bullets. I knew him by his voice. "Where's the doctor? There's some wounded men over there. Where's the doctor?" A man answered briskly: "Just died this minute, sir." It was as if he had said: "Just gone around the corner this minute, sir." Despite the horror of this night's business, the man's mind was somehow influenced by the coincidence of the adjutant's calling aloud for the doctor within a few seconds of the doctor's death. It — what shall I say? It interested him, this coincidence.

The day broke by inches, with an obvious and maddening reluctance. From some unfathomable source I procured an opinion that my friend was not dead at all — the wild and quivering darkness had

3. Acting Assistant Surgeon John Blair Gibbs, with rank of ensign, was thirty-nine years old at the time, a graduate of Rutgers, University of Virginia Medical School, and a well-known and respected surgeon in New York City. Unmarried, Gibbs had volunteered early in the war. He was to have been assigned to USS *Miantonomoh*, but upon reporting to Key West he was detailed to USS *Panther*. His father, a major, had been killed with Custer at Little Big Horn. John Gibbs was killed on the night of June 11–12. See "The Red Badge of Courage Was His Wig-Wag Flag" (*supra*, p. 140).

4. Not on the third night; Crane is confused. It was the second night — June 11–12. Gibbs died about 1:00 A.M. on June 12.

caused me to misinterpret a few shouted words. At length the land brightened in a violent atmosphere, the perfect dawning of a tropic day, and in this light I saw a clump of men near me. At first I thought they were all dead. Then I thought they were all asleep. The truth was that a group of wan-faced, exhausted men had gone to sleep about Gibbs's body so closely and in such abandoned attitudes that one's eye could not pick the living from the dead until one saw that a certain head had beneath it a great dark pool.

In the afternoon a lot of men went bathing, and in the midst of this festivity firing was resumed. It was funny to see the men come scampering out of the water, grab at their rifles, and go into action attired in nought but their cartridge-belts. The attack of the Spaniards had interrupted in some degree the services over the graves of Gibbs and some others.[5] I remember Paine came ashore with a bottle of whisky, which I took from him violently.[6] My faithful shooting-boots began to hurt me, and I went to the beach and poulticed my feet in wet clay, sitting on the little rickety pier near where the corrugated iron cable-station showed how the shells slivered through it. Some marines, desirous of mementoes, were poking with sticks in the smoking ruins of the hamlet. Down in the shallow water crabs were meandering among the weeds, and little fishes moved slowly in schools.

The next day we went shooting.[7] It was exactly like quail-shooting. I'll tell you. These guerillas who so cursed our lives had a well some five miles away, and it was the only water-supply within about twelve miles of the marine camp. It was decided that it would be correct to go forth and destroy the well. Captain Elliott,[8] of C company, was to take his men with Captain Spicer's company, D, out to the well, beat the enemy away, and destroy everything. He was to start at the next daybreak. He asked me if I cared to go, and of course I accepted with glee; but all that night I was afraid.[9] Bitterly afraid. The moon was very bright, shedding a magnificent radiance upon the trenches. I

5. "The attack of the Spaniards had interrupted in some degree the services over the graves of Gibbs and some others." That strikes off the germinal situation for Crane's remarkable short story "The Upturned Face," which Crane wrote at Brede Place in the fall of 1899; it was published March 1900 in *Ainslee's Magazine*.

6. The incident of Ralph D. Paine coming ashore with a bottle of whiskey is retold by Paine in his *Roads of Adventure* (1922).

7. That is, June 14.

8. Captain Elliott was engaged in the first serious encounter of our troops on Cuban soil. He figures in Crane's "Marines Signalling Under Fire at Guantanamo" (p. 148) and with Captain Spicer again in "The Red Badge of Courage Was His Wig-Wag Flag" (p. 140).

9. The night of June 13–14.

watched the men of C and D companies lying so tranquilly — some snoring, confound them — whereas I was certain that I could never sleep with the weight of a coming battle upon my mind, a battle in which the poor life of a war-correspondent might easily be taken by a careless enemy. But if I was frightened I was also very cold. It was a chill night, and I wanted a heavy top-coat almost as much as I wanted a certificate of immunity from rifle-bullets. These two feelings were of equal importance to my mind. They were twins. Elliott came and flung a tent-fly over Lieutenant Bannon and me as we lay on the ground in back of the men. Then I was no longer cold, but I was still afraid, for tent-flies cannot mend a fear. In the morning I wished for some mild attack of disease, something that would incapacitate me for the business of going out gratuitously to be bombarded. But I was in an awkwardly healthy state, and so I must needs smile and look pleased with my prospects. We were to be guided by fifty Cubans, and I gave up all dreams of a postponement when I saw them shambling off in single file through the cactus. We followed presently. "Where you people goin' to?" "Don't know, Jim." "Well, good luck to you, boys." This was the world's lazy inquiry and conventional Godspeed. Then the mysterious wilderness swallowed us.

The men were silent because they were ordered to be silent, but whatever faces I could observe were marked with a look of serious meditation. As they trudged slowly in single file they were reflecting upon — what? I don't know. But at length we came to ground more open. The sea appeared on our right, and we saw the gunboat *Dolphin* steaming along in a line parallel to ours. I was as glad to see her as if she had called out my name. The trail wound about the bases of some high bare spurs. If the Spaniards had occupied them I don't see how we could have gone farther. But upon them were only the dove-voiced guerilla scouts calling back into the hills the news of our approach. The effect of sound is of course relative. I am sure I have never heard such a horrible sound as the beautiful cooing of the wood-dove when I was certain that it came from the yellow throat of a guerilla. Elliott sent Lieutenant Lucas[10] with his platoon to ascend the hills and cover our advance by the trail. We halted and watched them climb, a long black streak of men in the vivid sunshine of the hill-side. We did not know how tall were these hills until we saw Lucas and his men on top, and they were no larger than specks. We marched on until, at last, we heard — it seemed in the sky — the sputter of firing. This devil's dance was begun. The proper strategic movement to cover the crisis seemed to me to be to run away home and swear I had

10. First Lieutenant Lewis C. Lucas, platoon leader in Company "C." He figures in Crane's dispatch "Night Attacks on the Marines" (*supra*, p. 171).

never started on this expedition. But Elliott yelled: "Now, men; straight up this hill." The men charged up against the cactus, and, because I cared for the opinion of others, I found myself tagging along close at Elliott's heels. I don't know how I got up that hill, but I think it was because I was afraid to be left behind. The immediate rear did not look safe. The crowd of strong young marines afforded the only spectacle of provisional security. So I tagged along at Elliott's heels. The hill was as steep as a Swiss roof. From it sprang out great pillars of cactus, and the human instinct was to assist oneself in the ascent by grasping cactus with one's hands. I remember the watch I had to keep upon this human instinct, even when the sound of the bullets was attracting my nervous attention. However, the attractive thing to my sense at the time was the fact that every man of the marines was also climbing away like mad. It was one thing for Elliott, Spicer, Neville, Shaw, and Bannon; it was another thing for me; but — what in the devil was it to the men? Not the same thing surely. It was perfectly easy for any marine to get overcome by the burning heat and, lying down, bequeath the work and the danger to his comrades. The fine thing about "the men" is that you can't explain them. I mean when you take them collectively. They do a thing, and afterward you find that they have done it because they have done it. However, when Elliott arrived at the top of the ridge, myself and many other men were with him. But there was no battle scene. Off on another ridge we could see Lucas's men and the Cubans peppering away into a valley. The bullets about our ears were really intended to lodge in them. We went over there.

I walked along the firing line and looked at the men. I kept somewhat on what I shall call the *lee* side of the ridge. Why? Because I was afraid of being shot. No other reason. Most of the men as they lay flat, shooting, looked contented, almost happy. They were pleased, these men, at the situation. I don't know. I cannot imagine. But they were pleased, at any rate. I wasn't pleased. I was picturing defeat. I was saying to myself: "Now if the enemy should suddenly do so-and-so, or so-and-so, why — what would become of me?" During these first few moments I did not see the Spanish position, because — I was afraid to look at it. Bullets were hissing and spitting over the crest of the ridge in such showers as to make observation to be a task for a brave man. No, now, look here, why the deuce should I have stuck my head up, eh? Why? Well, at any rate, I didn't until it seemed to be a far less thing than most of the men were doing as if they liked it. Then I saw nothing. At least it was only the bottom of a small valley. In this valley there was a thicket — a big thicket — and this thicket seemed to be crowded with a mysterious class of persons who were evidently trying to kill us. Our enemies? Yes — perhaps — I suppose so. Leave that to the people in the streets at home. They know and cry against the public enemy, but when men go into actual battle not one in a thousand concerns himself with an animus against the men who face him. The great desire is to beat them — beat them, whoever they are, as a matter, first, of personal safety; second, of personal glory. It is always safest to make the other chap quickly run away. And as he runs away, one feels, as one tries to hit him in the back and knock him sprawling, that he must be a very good and sensible fellow. But these people apparently did not mean to run away. They clung to their thicket, and amid the roar of the firing one could sometimes hear their wild yells of insult and defiance. They were actually the most obstinate, headstrong, mulish people that you could ever imagine. The *Dolphin* was throwing shells into their immediate vicinity, and the fire from the marines and Cubans was very rapid and heavy, but still those incomprehensible mortals remained in their thicket. The scene on the top of the ridge was very wild, but there was only one truly romantic figure. This was a Cuban officer who held in one hand a great glittering machete and in the other a cocked revolver. He posed like a statue of victory. Afterwards he confessed to me that he alone had been responsible for the winning of the fight. But outside of this splendid person it was simply a picture of men at work, men terribly hard at work, red-faced, sweating, gasping toilers. A Cuban negro soldier was shot through the heart, and one man took the body on his back and another took it by its feet and trundled away toward the rear looking precisely like a wheelbarrow. A man in C Company was shot through the ankle, and he sat behind the line nursing his wound. Apparently he was pleased with it. It seemed to suit him. I don't know why. But beside him sat a comrade with a face drawn, solemn, and responsible like that of a New England spinster at the bedside of a sick child.

The fight banged away with a roar like a forest fire. Suddenly a marine wriggled out of the firing-line and came frantically to me. "Say, young feller, I'll give you five dollars for a drink of whisky." He tried to force into my hand a goldpiece. "Go to the devil," said I, deeply scandalized. "Besides, I haven't got any whisky." "No, but look here," he beseeched me. "If I don't get a drink I'll die. And I'll give you five dollars for it. Honest, I will." I finally tried to escape from him by walking away, but he followed at my heels, importuning me with all the exasperating persistence of a professional beggar and trying to force this ghastly goldpiece into my hand. I could not shake him off, and amid that clatter of furious fighting I found myself intensely embarrassed, and glancing fearfully this way and that way to make sure that people did not see me, the villain, and his gold. In vain I assured him that if I had any whisky I should place it at his disposal. He could not be turned away. I thought of the European expedient in such

a crisis — to jump into a cab. But unfortunately — In the meantime I
had given up my occupation of tagging at Captain Elliott's heels, because his business required that he should go into places of great
danger. But from time to time I was under his attention. Once he
turned to me and said: "Mr. Vernall, will you go and satisfy yourself
who those people are?" Some men had appeared on a hill about six
hundred yards from our left flank. "Yes, sir," cried I with, I assure
you, the finest alacrity and cheerfulness, and my tone proved to me
that I had inherited histrionic abilities. This tone was of course a black
lie, but I went out briskly and was as jaunty as a real soldier, while
all the time my heart was in my boots and I was cursing the day that
saw me landed on the shores of this tragic isle. If the men on the distant
hill had been guerillas, my future might have been seriously jeopar-
dized, but I had not gone far toward them when I was able to recognize the uniforms of the marine corps. Whereupon I scampered back
to the firing-line and with the same alacrity and cheerfulness reported
my information. I mention to you that I was afraid, because there were
about me that day many men who did not seem to be afraid at all,
men with quiet, composed faces who went about this business as if
they proceeded from a sense of habit. They were not old soldiers; they
were mainly recruits, but many of them betrayed all the emotion and
merely the emotion that one sees in the face of a man earnestly at work.

I don't know how long the action lasted. I remember deciding
in my own mind that the Spaniards stood forty minutes. This was a
mere arbitrary decision based on nothing. But at any rate we finally
arived at the satisfactory moment when the enemy began to run away.
I shall never forget how my courage increased. And then began the
great bird-shooting. From the far side of the thicket arose an easy slope
covered with plum-coloured bush. The Spaniards broke in coveys of
from six to fifteen men — or birds — and swarmed up this slope. The
marines on our ridge then had some fine open-field shooting. No charge
could be made because the shells from the *Dolphin* were helping the
Spaniards to evacuate the thicket, so the marines had to be content
with this extraordinary paraphrase of a kind of sport. It was strangely
like the original. The shells from the *Dolphin* were the dogs; dogs
who went in and stirred out the game. The marines were suddenly
gentlemen in leggings, alive with the sharp instinct which marks the
hunter. The Spaniards were the birds. Yes, they were the birds, but I
doubt if they would sympathize with my metaphors.

We destroyed their camp, and when the tiled roof of a burning
house fell with a crash it was so like the crash of a strong volley of
musketry that we all turned with a start, fearing that we would have to
fight again on that same day. And this struck me at least as being an
impossible thing. They gave us water from the *Dolphin,* and we filled

our canteens. None of the men were particularly jubilant. They did not altogether appreciate their victory. They were occupied in being glad that the fight was over. I discovered to my amazement that we were on the summit of a hill so high that our released eyes seemed to sweep over half the world. The vast stretch of sea, shimmering like fragile blue silk in the breeze, lost itself ultimately in an indefinite pink haze, while in the other direction ridge after ridge, ridge after ridge, rolled brown and arid into the north. The battle had been fought high in the air — where the rain-clouds might have been. That is why everybody's face was the colour of beetroot and men lay on the ground and only swore feebly when the cactus spurs sank into them.

Finally we started for camp, leaving our wounded, our cactus pincushions, and our heat-prostrated men on board the *Dolphin*. I did not see that the men were elate or even grinning with satisfaction. They seemed only anxious to get to food and rest. And yet it was plain that Elliott and his men had performed a service that would prove invaluable to the security and comfort of the entire battalion. They had driven the guerillas to take a road along which they would have to proceed for fifteen miles before they could get as much water as would wet the point of a pin. And by the destruction of a well at the scene of the fight, Elliott made an arid zone almost twenty miles wide between the enemy and the base camp. In Cuba this is the best of protections. However, a cup of coffee! Time enough to think of a brilliant success after one had had a cup of coffee. The long line plodded wearily through the dusky jungle which was never again to be alive with ambushes.

[II. FORAY IN THE JUNGLE]

Later, I fell into the hands of one of my closest friends,[11] and he mercilessly outlined a scheme for landing to the west of Santiago and getting through the Spanish lines to some place from which we could view the Spanish squadron lying in the harbour. There was rumour that the *Vizcaya*[12] had escaped, he said, and it would be very nice to make sure of the truth. So we steamed to a point opposite a Cuban camp which my friend knew, and flung two crop-tailed Jamaica polo ponies into the sea. We followed in a small boat and were met on the beach by a small Cuban detachment who immediately caught our

11. Sylvester Scovel of the New York *World*. They landed June 17. See *supra*, p. 164.
    12. See note 14.

ponies and saddled them for us. I suppose we felt rather godlike. We were almost the first Americans they had seen, and they looked at us with eyes of grateful affection. I don't suppose many men have the experience of being looked at with eyes of grateful affection. They guided us to a Cuban camp where, in a little palm-bark hut, a black-faced lieutenant-colonel was lolling in a hammock. I couldn't understand what was said, but at any rate he must have ordered his half-naked orderly to make coffee, for it was done. It was a dark syrup in smoky tin cups, but it was better than the cold bottle of beer which I did not drink in Jamaica.

The Cuban camp was an expeditious affair of saplings and palm-bark tied with creepers. It could be burned to the ground in fifteen minutes and in ten reduplicated. The soldiers were in appearance an absolutely good-natured set of half-starved ragamuffins. Their breeches hung in threads about their black legs, and their shirts were as nothing. They looked like a collection of real tropic savages at whom some philanthropist had flung a bundle of rags and some of the rags had stuck here and there. But their condition was now a habit. I doubt if they knew they were half-naked. Anyhow they didn't care. No more they should; the weather was warm. This lieutenant-colonel gave us an escort of five or six men, and we went up into the mountains, lying flat on our Jamaica ponies while they went like rats up and down extraordinary trails. In the evening we reached the camp of a major who commanded the outposts. It was high, high in the hills. The stars were as big as coco-nuts. We lay in borrowed hammocks and watched the firelight gleam blood-red on the trees. I remember an utterly naked negro squatting, crimson, by the fire and cleaning an iron pot. Some voices were singing an Afric wail of forsaken love and death. And at dawn we were to try to steal through the Spanish lines. I was very, very sorry.

In the cold dawn[13] the situation was the same, but somehow courage seemed to be in the breaking day. I went off with the others quite cheerfully. We came to where the pickets stood behind bulwarks of stone in frameworks of saplings. They were peering across a narrow cloud-steeped gulch at a dull fire marking a Spanish post. There was some palaver, and then, with fifteen men, we descended the side of this mountain, going down into the chill blue-and-grey clouds. We had left our horses with the Cuban pickets. We proceeded stealthily, for we were already within range of the Spanish pickets. At the bottom of the canyon it was still night. A brook, a regular salmon stream, brawled over the rocks. There were grassy banks and most delightful trees. The whole valley was a sylvan fragrance. But — the guide waved his arm

13. June 18.

and scowled warningly, and in a moment we were off, threading thickets, climbing hills, crawling through fields on our hands and knees, sometimes sweeping like seventeen phantoms across a Spanish road. I was in a dream, but I kept my eye on the guide and halted to listen when he halted to listen and ambled onward when he ambled onward. Sometimes he turned and pantomimed as ably and fiercely as a man being stung by a thousand hornets. Then we knew that the situation was extremely delicate. We were now of course well inside the Spanish lines, and we ascended a great hill which overlooked the harbour of Santiago. There, tranquilly at anchor, lay the *Oquendo*, the *Maria Theresa*, the *Cristobal Colon*, the *Vizcaya*, the *Pluton*, the *Furor*.[14] The bay was white in the sun, and the great black-hulled armoured cruisers were impressive in a dignity massive yet graceful. We did not know that they were all doomed ships, soon to go out to a swift death. My friend drew maps and things while I devoted myself to complete rest, blinking lazily at the Spanish squadron. We did not know that we were the last Americans to view them alive and unhurt and at peace. Then we retraced our way, at the same noiseless canter. I did not understand my condition until I considered that we were well through the Spanish lines and practically out of danger. Then I discovered that I was a dead man. The nervous force having evaporated, I was a mere corpse. My limbs were of dough, and my spinal cord burned within me as if it were red-hot wire. But just at this time we were discovered by a Spanish patrol, and I ascertained that I was not dead at all. We ultimately reached the foot of the other mountain on whose shoulders were the Cuban pickets, and here I was so sure of safety that I could not resist the temptation to die again. I think I passed into eleven distinct stupors during the ascent of that mountain while the escort stood leaning on their Remingtons. We had done twenty-five miles at a sort of man-gallop, never once using a beaten track, but always going promiscuously through the jungle and over the rocks. And many of the mules stood straight on end, so that it was as hard to come down as it was to go up. But during my stupors, the escort *stood*, mind you, and chatted in low voices. For all the signs

14. Dispatched from Spain on April 9 (1898) under the command of Rear Admiral Pascual Cervera y Topete (1833–1909), the squadron had slipped into Santiago on May 19 and was then bottled up by Sampson's blockade. Spain's naval strength was inferior, although Cervera would have had some good modern ships had they been in first-class fighting trim. *Almirante Oquendo, Infanta María Teresa* (Cervera's flagship), *Cristóbal Colón,* and *Vizcaya* were sister ships and armored cruisers; tonnage (displacement): 7,000; length: 364 feet; speed: 20 knots; principal armament: two 11-inch and five 5-inch guns. *Plutón* and *Furor* were torpedo-boat destroyers.

they showed, we might have been starting. And they had had nothing to eat but mangoes for over eight days. Previous to the eight days they had been living on mangoes and the carcass of a small lean pony. They were, in fact, of the stuff of Fenimore Cooper's Indians, only they made no preposterous orations. At the major's camp, my friend and I agreed that if our worthy escort would send down a representative with us to the coast, we would send back to them whatever we could spare from the stores of our dispatch-boat. With one voice the escort answered that they themselves would go the additional four leagues, as in these starving times they did not care to trust a representative, thank you. "They can't do it; they'll peg out; there must be a limit," I said. "No," answered my friend. "They're all right; they'd run three times around the whole island for a mouthful of beer." So we saddled up and put off with our fifteen Cuban infantrymen wagging along tirelessly behind us. Sometimes, at the foot of a precipitous hill, a man asked permission to cling to my horse's tail, and then the Jamaica pony would snake him to the summit so swiftly that only his toes seemed to touch the rocks. And for this assistance the man was grateful. When we crowned the last great ridge we saw our squadron to the eastward, spread in its patient semicircle about the mouth of the harbour. But as we wound toward the beach we saw a more dramatic thing — our own dispatch-boat leaving the rendezvous and putting off to sea. Evidently we were late. Behind me were fifteen stomachs, empty. It was a frightful situation. My friend and I charged for the beach, and those fifteen fools began to *run*.

It was no use. The dispatch-boat went gaily away, trailing black smoke behind her. We turned in distress, wondering what we could say to that abused escort.[15]

[III. ADMIRAL SAMPSON]

Admiral Sampson[16] is to me the most interesting personality of the war. I would not know how to sketch him for you even if I could pretend to sufficient material. Anyhow, imagine, first of all, a marble

15. The story of this foray is told again in Crane's dispatch entitled "Hunger Has Made Cubans Fatalists" (*supra,* p. 161).

16. William T. Sampson (1840–1902) was at this time Acting Rear Admiral, commanding the North Atlantic Squadron. He had been graduated from the Naval Academy in 1861 and was promoted captain in 1889; in 1890 he took command of USS *San Francisco*, the first modern steel cruiser in the Navy. The ships under his command destroyed Cervera's fleet on July 3 (1898), but Sampson himself was not actually present throughout

block of impassivity out of which is carved the figure of an old man.
Endow this with life, and you've just begun. Then you must discard
all your pictures of bluff, red-faced old gentlemen who roar against
the gale, and understand that the quiet old man is a sailor and an
admiral. This will be difficult; if I told you he was anything else it
would be easy. He resembles other types; it is his distinction not to
resemble the preconceived type of his standing. When first I met him
I was impressed that he was immensely bored by the war and with
the command of the North Atlantic Squadron. I perceived a manner
where I thought I perceived a mood, a point of view. Later, he seemed
so indifferent to small things which bore upon large things that I
bowed to his apathy as a thing unprecedented, marvellous. Still I mis-
took a manner for a mood. Still I could not understand that this was
the way of the man. I am not to blame, for my communication was
slight and depended upon sufferance — upon, in fact, the traditional
courtesy of the navy. But finally I saw that it was all manner, that
hidden in his indifferent, even apathetic, manner there was the alert,
sure, fine mind of the best sea-captain that America has produced
since — since Farragut? I don't know. I think — since Hull.

Men follow heartily when they are well led. They balk at trifles
when a blockhead cries "Go on." For my part, an impressive thing of
the war is the absolute devotion to Admiral Sampson's person — no, to
his judgment and wisdom — which was paid by his ship-commanders
— Evans of the *Iowa*, Taylor of the *Oregon*, Higginson of the *Massachusetts*, Philip[17] of the *Texas*, and all the other captains — barring one.
Once, afterward, they called upon him to avenge himself upon a rival
— they were there, and they would have to say — but he said no-o-o,
he guessed it — wouldn't do — any — g-o-oo-d — to the — service.

Men feared him, but he never made threats; men tumbled heels
over head to obey him, but he never gave a sharp order; men loved
him, but he said no word, kindly or unkindly; men cheered for him
and he said: "Who are they yelling for?" Men behaved badly to him,
and he said nothing. Men thought of glory, and he considered the
management of ships. All without a sound. A noiseless campaign — on

the battle, Commodore Schley having taken command. This provoked an
argument between the supporters of each officer as to the credit for the
victory, an argument which darkened Sampson's last years. He retired from
the Navy in February 1902 and died that year.

17. Captain Robley D. Evans, commanding the *Iowa*, Sampson's former
command; Captain Henry C. Taylor (who, however, commanded the
Indiana, not the *Oregon*); Captain Francis J. Higginson, one of the senior
captains; and Captain John W. Philip, whose admonition to his men at
Santiago — "Don't cheer, the poor devils are dying" — was to become im-
memorial.

his part. No bunting, no arches, no fireworks; nothing but the perfect
management of a big fleet. That is a record for you. No trumpets, no
cheers of the populace. Just plain, pure, unsauced accomplishment. But
ultimately he will reap his reward in — in what? In text-books on sea
campaigns. No more. The people choose their own and they choose
the kind they like. Who has a better right? Anyhow he is a great man.
And when you are once started you can continue to be a great man
without the help of bouquets and banquets. You don't need them —
bless your heart.

[IV. THE DISEMBARKMENT]

. . . upon the morning of our return to the Cuban coast[18] we
found the sea alive with transports — United States transports from
Tampa, containing the Fifth Army Corps under Major-General
Shafter.[19] The rigging and the decks of these ships were black with
men, and everybody wanted to land first. I landed, ultimately, and immediately began to look for an acquaintance. The boats were banged
by the waves against a little flimsy dock. I fell ashore somehow, but I
did not at once find an acquaintance. I talked to a private in the Second Massachusetts Volunteers who told me that he was going to write
war-correspondence for a Boston newspaper. This statement did not
surprise me.

There was a straggly village, but I followed the troops, who at
this time seemed to be moving out by companies. I found three other
correspondents, and it was luncheon time. Somebody had two bottles
of Bass, but it was so warm that it squirted out in foam. There was
no firing; no noise of any kind. An old shed was full of soldiers loafing
pleasantly in the shade. It was a hot, dusty, sleepy afternoon; bees
hummed. We saw Major-General Lawton[20] standing with his staff

18. Crane had been in Jamaica briefly after his jungle foray with
Scovel.

19. See *supra*, p. 137.

20. Henry Ware Lawton (1843–1899) was yet another fine soldier
and commander. His service in the Civil War had gained him a brevet
colonelcy. He entered regular service in 1867, advanced steadily, and served
brilliantly throughout the Indian wars, capping his career with the capture
of Geronimo after a 1300 mile chase through Arizona and Mexico. He was
killed — 19 December 1899 — at the battle at San Mateo on Luzon in the
campaign against Aguinaldo. Crane describes him well: he stood six feet
four inches tall and was an erect and well-built man.

Most of his 2d Division had gotten ashore at Daiquiri the first day.

under a tree. He was smiling as if he would say: "Well, this will be better than chasing Apaches." His division had the advance, and so he had the right to be happy. A tall man with a grey moustache, light but very strong, an ideal cavalryman. He appealed to one all the more because of the vague rumours that his superiors — some of them — were going to take mighty good care that he shouldn't get much to do. It was rather sickening to hear such talk, but later we knew that most of it must have been mere lies.

Down by the landing-place a band of correspondents were making a sort of permanent camp. They worked like Trojans, carrying wall-tents, cots, and boxes of provisions. They asked me to join them, but I looked shrewdly at the sweat on their faces and backed away. The next day the army left this permanent camp eight miles to the rear. The day became tedious. I was glad when evening came. I sat by a camp-fire and listened to a soldier of the Eighth Infantry[21] who told me that he was the first enlisted man to land. I lay pretending to appreciate him, but in fact I considered him a great shameless liar. Less than a month ago, I learned that every word he said was gospel truth. I was much surprised.

[V. EDWARD MARSHALL]

The first of July? All right. My Jamaica polo pony was not present. He was still in the hills to the westward of Santiago, but the Cubans had promised to fetch him to me. But my kit was easy to carry. It had nothing superfluous in it but a pair of spurs which made me indignant every time I looked at them. Oh, but I must tell you about a man I met directly after the Las Guasimas fight. Edward Marshall, a correspondent whom I had known with a degree of intimacy for seven years, was terribly hit in that fight and asked me if I would not go to Siboney — the base — and convey the news to his colleagues of the New York *Journal* and round up some assistance. I went to Siboney, and there was not a *Journal* man to be seen, although usually you judged from appearances that the *Journal* staff was about as large as the army. Presently I met two correspondents, strangers to me, but I questioned them, saying that Marshall was badly shot and wished for such succour as *Journal* men could bring from their dispatch-boat. And one of these correspondents replied. He is the man I wanted to describe. I love him as a brother. He said: "Marshall? Marshall? Why,

21. The Eighth Infantry, a regular Army unit, was a part of the 1st Brigade, 2d Division.

Marshall isn't in Cuba at all. He left for New York just before the expedition sailed from Tampa." I said: "Beg pardon, but I remarked that Marshall was shot in the fight this morning, and have you seen any *Journal* people?" After a pause, he said: "I am sure Marshall is not down here at all. He's in New York." I said: "Pardon me, but I remarked that Marshall was shot in the fight this morning, and have you seen any *Journal* people?" He said: "No; now look here, you must have gotten two chaps mixed somehow. Marshall isn't in Cuba at all. How could he be shot?" I said: "Pardon me, but I remarked that Marshall was shot in the fight this morning, and have you seen any *Journal* people?" He said: "But it can't really be Marshall, you know, for the simple reason that he's not down here." I clasped my hands to my temples, gave one piercing cry to heaven, and fled from his presence.[22] I couldn't go on with him. He excelled me at all points. I have faced death by bullets, fire, water, and disease, but to die thus — to wilfully batter myself against the ironclad opinion of this mummy — no, no, not that.

[VI. ON THE ROAD TO SANTIAGO]

We will proceed to July 1st. On that morning I marched with my kit — having everything essential save a toothbrush — the entire army put me to shame, since there must have been at least fifteen thousand toothbrushes in the invading force — I marched with my kit on the road to Santiago. It was a fine morning, and everybody — the doomed and the immunes — how could we tell one from the other? — everybody was in the highest spirits. We were enveloped in forest, but we could hear, from ahead, everybody peppering away at everybody. It was like the roll of many drums. This was Lawton over at El Caney. I reflected with complacency that Lawton's division did not concern me in a professional way. That was the affair of another man. My business was with Kent's[23] division and Wheeler's[24] division. We came to El Poso —

22. This story of Marshall was told in the New York *World* for July 7, in Crane's dispatch: "Stephen Crane at the Front for the *World*" (*supra*, p. 154).

23. Jacob Ford Kent (1835–1918), graduate of West Point (1861), veteran of four years' service in the Civil War, went up the ranks with relative speed, being promoted colonel in 1895. His rank of general in the volunteers in the war led to a permanent brigadier generalship 4 October 1898. He retired eleven days later.

24. Joseph "Fighting Joe" Wheeler (1836–1906) was one of the Confederacy's bright and daring cavalry generals during the Civil War. He

a hill at nice artillery range from the Spanish defences. Here Grimes's battery was shooting a duel with one of the enemy's batteries. Scovel had established a little camp in the rear of the guns, and a servant had made coffee. I invited Whigham[25] to have coffee, and the servant added some hard biscuit and tinned tongue. I noted that Whigham was staring fixedly over my shoulder, and that he waved away the tinned tongue with some bitterness. It was a horse, a dead horse. Then a mule which had been shot through the nose wandered up and looked at Whigham. We ran away.

* * *

On top of the hill one had a fine view of the Spanish lines. We stared across almost a mile of jungle to ash-coloured trenches on the military crest of the ridge. A goodly distance in back of this position were white buildings, all flying great Red Cross flags. The jungle beneath us rattled with firing, and the Spanish trenches crackled out regular volleys, but all this time there was nothing to indicate a tangible enemy. In truth, there was a man in a Panama hat strolling to and fro behind one of the Spanish trenches, gesticulating at times with a walking-stick. A man in a Panama hat, walking with a stick! That was the strangest sight of my life — that symbol, that quaint figure of Mars. The battle, the thunderous row, was his possession. He was the master. He mystified us all with his infernal Panama hat and his wretched walking-stick. From near his feet came volleys and from near his side came roaring shells, but he stood there alone, visible, the one tangible thing. He was a Colossus, and he was half as high as a pin, this being. Always somebody would be saying: "Who *can* that fellow be?"

Later, the American guns shelled the trenches and a blockhouse near them, and Mars had vanished. It could not have been death. One cannot kill Mars. But there was one other figure which arose to symbolic dignity. The balloon of our signal corps had swung over the tops

---

served in the House of Representatives (with some breaks) from 1880 to 1900. In 1898, McKinley appointed him a major-general of volunteers, and a brigadier general in the regular Army, in 1900. He was buried in Arlington National Cemetery.

25. War correspondent for the Chicago *Tribune* and the London *Standard* in Cuba, Henry James Whigham (1869–1954) was a colorful and unique man. A native of Scotland and a graduate of Queen's College, Oxford (1893), Whigham had been drama critic for the *Tribune*, U.S. amateur golf champion, and a prisoner of the Spanish. In later years he edited *Town and Country* (1909–1935) and *Metropolitan Magazine* (1912–1922). Crane seems to have met Whigham at Guantanamo for the first time.

of the jungle trees toward the Spanish trenches.[26] Whereat the balloon and the man in the Panama hat and with a walking-stick — whereat these two waged tremendous battle.

* * *

Suddenly the conflict became a human thing. A little group of blue figures appeared on the green of the terrible hillside. It was some of our infantry. The attaché of a great empire was at my shoulder, and he turned to me and spoke with incredulity and scorn. "Why, they're trying to take the position," he cried, and I admitted meekly that I thought they were. "But they can't do it, you know," he protested vehemently. "It's impossible." And — good fellow that he was — he began to grieve and wail over a useless sacrifice of gallant men. "It's plucky, you know! By Gawd, it's plucky! But *they can't do it!*" He was profoundly moved; his voice was quite broken. "It will simply be a hell of a slaughter with no good coming out of it."

* * *

The trail was already crowded with stretcher-bearers and with wounded men who could walk. One had to stem a tide of mute agony. But I don't know that it was mute agony. I only know that it was mute. It was something in which the silence or, more likely, the reticence was an appalling and inexplicable fact. One's senses seemed to demand that these men should cry out. But you could really find wounded men who exhibited all the signs of a pleased and contented mood. When thinking of it now it seems strange beyond words. But at the time — I don't know — it did not attract one's wonder. A man with a hole in his arm or his shoulder, or even in the leg below the knee, was often whimsical, comic. "Well, this ain't exactly what I enlisted for, boys. If I'd been told about this in Tampa, I'd have resigned from th' army. Oh, yes, you can get the same thing if you keep on going. But I think the Spaniards may run out of ammunition in the course of a week or ten days." Then suddenly one would be confronted by the awful majesty of a man shot in the face. Particularly I remember one. He had a great dragoon moustache, and the blood streamed down his face to meet this moustache, even as a torrent goes to meet the jammed log, and then swarmed out to the tips and fell in big slow drops. He looked steadily into my eyes; I was ashamed to return his glance. You understand? It is very curious — all that.

26. The balloon had been sent up at dawn to find another path to San Juan. It discovered a second route, but the enemy knew about it too. The balloon fell, "dying a gigantic and public death before the eyes of two armies," as Crane reported it. It had of course drawn enemy fire!

✻   ✻   ✻

The two lines of battle were royally whacking away at each other, and there was no rest or peace in all that region. The modern bullet is a fairy-flying bird. It rakes the air with its hot spitting song at distances which, as a usual thing, places the whole landscape in the danger-zone. There was no direction from which they did not come. A chart of their courses over one's head would have resembled a spider's web. My friend Jimmie,[27] the photographer, mounted to the firing-line with me, and we gallivanted as much as we dared. The "sense of the meeting" was curious. Most of the men seemed to have no ideas of a grand historic performance, but they were grimly satisfied with themselves. "Well, be-gawd, we done it." Then they wanted to know about other parts of the line. "How are things looking, old man? Everything all right?" "Yes, everything is all right if you can hold this ridge." "Aw, hell," said the men, "We'll hold the ridge. Don't you worry about that, son."

It was Jimmie's first action, and, as we cautiously were making our way to the right of our lines, the crash of the Spanish fire became uproarious, and the air simply whistled. I heard a quavering voice near my shoulder, and, turning, I beheld Jimmie — Jimmie — with a face bloodless, white as paper. He looked at me with eyes opened extremely wide. "Say," he said, "this is pretty hot, ain't it?" I was delighted. I knew exactly what he meant. He wanted to have the situation defined. If I had told him that this was the occasion of some mere idle desultory firing and recommended that he wait until the real battle began, I think he would have gone in a be-line for the rear. But I told him the truth. "Yes, Jimmie," I replied earnestly, "you can take it from me that this is patent, double-extra what-for." And immediately he nodded. "All right." If this was a big action, then he was willing to pay in his fright as a rational price for the privilege of being present. But if this was only a penny affray, he considered the price exorbitant, and he would go away. He accepted my assurance with simple faith, and deported himself with kindly dignity as one moving amid great things. His face was still as pale as paper, but that counted for nothing. The main point was his perfect willingness to be frightened for reasons. I wonder where is Jimmie? I lent him the Jamaica polo pony one day, and it ran away with him and flung him off in the middle of a ford. He appeared to me afterward and made

27. Crane's friend, Jimmie, was James Henry Hare (1856–1946), one of the great war photographers of his day and a pioneer in aerial photography. He had been born in London, attended St. John College, and came to the United States in 1889. His war correspondence and photography carried him to South America, Mexico, the Balkans, and World War I.

bitter speech concerning this horse which I had assured him was a gentle and pious animal. Then I never saw Jimmie again.

*   *   *

Then came the night of the first of July. A group of correspondents limped back to El Poso. It had been a day so long that the morning seemed as remote as a morning in the previous year. But I have forgotten to tell you about Reuben McNab. Many years ago, I went to school at a place called Claverack, in New York State, where there was a semi-military institution.[28] Contemporaneous with me, as a student, was Reuben McNab, a long, lank boy, freckled, sandy-haired — an extraordinary boy in no way, and yet, I wager, a boy clearly marked in every recollection. Perhaps there is a good deal in that name, Reuben McNab. You can't fling that name carelessly over your shoulder and lose it. It follows you like the haunting memory of a sin. At any rate, Reuben McNab was identified intimately in my thought with the sunny irresponsible days at Claverack, when all the earth was a green field and all the sky was a rainless blue.[29] Then I looked down into a miserable huddle at Bloody Bend, a huddle of hurt men, dying men, dead men. And there I saw Reuben McNab, a corporal in the Seventy-first New York Volunteers, and with a hole through his lung. Also, several holes through his clothing. "Well, they got me," he said in greeting. Usually they said that. There were no long speeches. "Well, they got me." That was sufficient. The duty of the upright, unhurt man is then difficult. I doubt if many of us learned how to speak to our own wounded. In the first place, one had to play that the wound was nothing; oh, a mere nothing; a casual interference with movement, perhaps, but nothing more; oh, really nothing more. In the second place, one had to show a comrade's appreciation of this sad plight. As a result I think most of us bungled and stammered in the presence of our wounded friends. That's curious, eh? "Well, they got me," said Reuben McNab. I had looked upon five hundred wounded men with stolidity, or with a conscious indifference which filled me with amazement. But the apparition of Reuben McNab, the schoolmate, lying there in the mud, with a hole through his lung, awed me into stutterings, set me trembling with a sense of terrible intimacy with this war which theretofore I could have believed was a dream — almost. Twenty shot men rolled their eyes and looked at me. Only one man paid no heed. He was dying; he had no time. The bullets hummed low over them all. Death, having already struck, still insisted upon raising a

28. Crane attended Claverack (Hudson River Institute), 1889–1890.
29. Thomas Beer used as title for Chapter I in his biography of Crane: "Sunny Blue."

venomous crest. "If you're goin' by the hospital, step in and see me," said Reuben McNab. That was all.

* * *

At the correspondents' camp, at El Poso, there was hot coffee. It was very good. I have a vague sense of being very selfish over my blanket and rubber coat. I have a vague sense of spasmodic firing during my sleep; it rained, and then I awoke to hear that steady drumming of an infantry fire — something which was never to cease, it seemed. They were at it again. The trail from El Poso to the position along San Juan ridge had become an exciting thoroughfare. Shots from large-bore rifles dropped in from almost every side. At this time the safest place was the extreme front. I remember in particular the one outcry I heard. A private in the Seventy-first, without his rifle, had gone to a stream for some water, and was returning, being but a little in rear of me. Suddenly I heard this cry: "Oh, my God, come quick" — and I was conscious then of having heard the hateful zip of a close shot. He lay on the ground, wriggling. He was hit in the hip. Two men came quickly. Presently everybody seemed to be getting knocked down. They went over like men of wet felt, quietly, calmly, with no more complaint than so many automatons. It was only that lad — "Oh, my God, come quick." Otherwise, men seemed to consider that their hurts were not worthy of particular attention. A number of people got killed very courteously, tacitly absolving the rest of us from any care in the matter. A man fell; he turned blue; his face took on an expression of deep sorrow; and then his immediate friends worried about him, if he had friends. This was July 1.

[VII. REFUGEES]

Out on the slopes of San Juan the dog-tents shone white. Some kind of negotiations were going forward, and men sat on their trousers and waited. It was all rather a blur of talks with officers, and a craving for good food and good water. Once Leighton[30] and I decided to ride over to El Caney, into which town the civilian refugees from Santiago were pouring. The road from the beleaguered city to the outlying village was a spectacle to make one moan. There were delicate gentle families on foot, the silly French boots of the girls twisting and turning in a sort of absolute paper futility; there were sons and grandsons carrying the venerable patriarch in his own arm-chair; there were exhausted mothers with babes who wailed; there were young dandies

30. Possibly "Leighton" is Richard Harding Davis, war correspondent for the New York *Herald*, London *Times,* and *Scribner's Magazine.*

with their toilettes in decay; there were puzzled, guideless women who didn't know what had happened. The first sentence one heard was the murmurous "What a damn shame." We saw a godless young trooper of the Second Cavalry sharply halt a wagon. "Hold on a minute. You must carry this woman. She's fainted twice already." The virtuous driver of the U.S. Army wagon mildly answered: "But I'm full-up now." "You can make room for her," said the private of the Second Cavalry. A young, young man with a straight mouth. It was merely a plain bit of nothing — at — all, but, thank God, thank God, he seemed to have not the slightest sense of excellence. He said: "If you've got any man in there who can walk at all, you put him out and let this woman get in." "But," answered the teamster, "I'm filled up with a lot of cripples and grandmothers." Thereupon they discussed the point fairly, and ultimately the woman was lifted into the wagon.

The vivid thing was the fact that these people did not visibly suffer. Somehow they were numb. There was not a tear. There was rarely a countenance which was not wondrously casual. There was no sign of fatalistic theory. It was simply that what was happening to-day had happened yesterday, as near as one could judge. I could fancy that these people had been thrown out of their homes every day. It was utterly, utterly casual. And they accepted the ministration of our men in the same fashion. Everything was a matter of course.

❋   ❋   ❋

The fight at El Caney had been furious. General Vera del Rey with somewhat less than 1000 men — the Spanish accounts say 520 — had there made such a stand that only about eighty battered soldiers ever emerged from it. The attack cost Lawton about four hundred men. The magazine rifle! But the town was now a vast parrot-cage of chattering refugees. If, on the road, they were silent, stolid, and serene, in the town they found their tongues and set up such a cackle as one may seldom hear. Notably the women; it is they who invariably confuse the definition of situations, and one could wonder in amaze if this crowd of irresponsible, gabbling hens had already forgotten that this town was the death-bed, so to speak, of scores of gallant men whose blood was not yet dry; whose hands, of the hue of pale amber, stuck from the soil of the hasty burial. On the way to El Caney I had conjured a picture of the women of Santiago, proud in their pain, their despair, dealing glances of defiance, contempt, hatred at the invader; fiery ferocious ladies, so true to their vanquished and to their dead that they spurned the very existence of the low-bred churls who lacked both Velasquez and Cervantes.[31] And, instead, there was this mere

31. In a letter to an unknown recipient (Summer 1899) Crane wrote that the doughboys and the Jackies know nothing of Velázquez and

noise, which reminded one alternately of a tea-party in Ireland, a village fete in the south of France, and the vacuous morning screech of a swarm of sea-gulls.

❖   ❖   ❖

Pushing through the throng in the plaza, we came in sight of the door of the church, and here was a strange scene. The church had been turned into a hospital for Spanish wounded who had fallen into American hands. The interior of the church was too cave-like in its gloom for the eyes of the operating surgeons, so they had had the altar-table carried to the doorway, where there was a bright light. Framed then in the black archway was the altar-table with the figure of a man upon it. He was naked save for a breach-clout, and so close, so clear was the ecclesiastic suggestion that one's mind leaped to a fantasy that this thin, pale figure had just been torn down from a cross. The flash of the impression was like light, and for this instant it illumined all the dark recesses of one's remotest idea of sacrilege, ghastly and wanton. I bring this to you merely as an effect, an effect of mental light and shade, if you like; something done in thought similar to that which the French impressionists do in colour; something meaningless and at the same time overwhelming, crushing, monstrous. "Poor devil; I wonder if he'll pull through," said Leighton. An American surgeon and his assistants were intent over the prone figure. They wore white aprons. Something small and silvery flashed in the surgeon's hand. An assistant held the merciful sponge close to the man's nostril, but he was writhing and moaning in some horrible dream of this artificial sleep. As the surgeon's instrument played, I fancied that the man dreamed that he was being gored by a bull. In his pleading, delirious babble occurred constantly the name of the Virgin, the Holy Mother. "Good morning," said the surgeon. He changed his knife to his left hand and gave me a wet palm. The tips of his fingers were wrinkled, shrunken, like those of a boy who has been in swimming too long. Now, in front

---

Cervantes. "But there is an excellence of human conduct independent of Cervantes and Velasquez. The Spaniards who lay dead in El Caney knew something of it. Our men knew something of it. Mob-courage? — mob-courage. The mob has no courage. That is the chatter of clubs and writers. Pray go stand with your back to deadly fire from a painted drop for a pantomime and wave signals for half an hour without wincing and then talk of mob-courage." (In *Letters*, 1960, pp. 222–223.) Crane witnessed and reported this bravery in "Marines Signalling Under Fire at Guantanamo" (*supra*, p. 148).

Crane's own exploit of acting as signalman between outpost units of the Marine Corps during the naval engagement in Guantanamo Bay earned him a citation for bravery from the Department of the Navy.

of the door there were three American sentries, and it was their business to — to do what? To keep this Spanish crowd from swarming over the operating-table! It was perforce a public clinic. They would not be denied. The weaker women and the children jostled according to their might in the rear, while the stronger people, gaping in the front rank, cried out impatiently when the pushing disturbed their long stares. One burned with a sudden gift of public oratory. One wanted to say: "Oh, go away, go away, go away. Leave the man decently alone with his pain, you gogglers. This is not the national sport."

But within the church there was an audience of another kind. This was of the other wounded men awaiting their turn. They lay on their brown blankets in rows along the stone floor. Their eyes, too, were fastened upon the operating-table, but — that was different. Meek-eyed little yellow men lying on the floor awaiting their turns.

[VIII. HOBSON'S EXCHANGE]

I was on San Juan Hill when Lieutenant Hobson[32] and the men of the *Merrimac*[33] were exchanged and brought into the American lines. Many of us knew that the exchange was about to be made, and

32. Hobson's famous exploit — it captured the imagination of Americans — was his chillingly brave maneuvering and sinking, under heavy fire, of the collier *Merrimac* in the entrance of Santiago harbor on June 3 (1898). His attempt to plug the channel and block Cervera's fleet failed. He was captured. His exchange took place on July 6.

Richmond Pearson Hobson (1870–1937) was born in Alabama and graduated from the Naval Academy in 1889, after which he did post-graduate work in naval construction in Europe. Appointed assistant naval constructor (with rank of lieutenant junior grade) in July 1891, Hobson served in various capacities in the Navy. When war commenced he was number one on the list of assistant naval constructors.

"On March 1, 1899, President McKinley nominated him to be advanced ten numbers . . . for extraordinary heroism. This action placed him above all the lieutenant-commanders and nearly at the top of the commanders' list, so far as relative rank is concerned, and was said to constitute the greatest material promotion as a recognition of gallantry in the history of the naval service" (*National Cyclopedia of American Biography* [1899], X, 11).

In 1903, Hobson resigned from the service. He served in the House of Representatives, 1907–1915. In 1933, Congress got around to awarding him the Medal of Honor for his feat of thirty-five years before.

33. USS *Merrimac*, commissioned in April 1898, had arrived off Santiago on May 28. Hobson wrote of his experiences in *The Sinking of the "Merrimac"* (1899).

gathered to see the famous party. Some of our staff officers rode out
with three Spanish officers — prisoners — these latter being blindfolded
before they were taken through the American position. The army was
majestically minding its business in the long line of trenches when its
eye caught sight of this little procession. "What's that? What they goin'
to do?" "They're goin' to exchange Hobson." Wherefore every man
who was foot-free staked out a claim where he could get a good view
of the liberated heroes, and two bands prepared to collaborate on
"The Star-spangled Banner." There was a very long wait through the
sunshiny afternoon. In our impatience, we imagined them — the Americans and Spaniards — dickering away out there under the big tree
like so many pedlars. Once the massed bands, misled by a rumour,
stiffened themselves into that dramatic and breathless moment when
each man is ready to blow. But the rumour was exploded in the nick
of time. We made ill jokes, saying one to another that the negotiators
had found diplomacy to be a failure, and were playing freeze-out
poker for the whole batch of prisoners.

But suddenly the moment came. Along the cut roadway, toward
the crowded soldiers, rode three men, and it could be seen that the
central one wore the undress uniform of an officer of the United
States navy. Most of the soldiers were sprawled out on the grass,
bored and wearied in the sunshine. However, they aroused at the old
circus-parade, torchlight-procession cry, "Here they come." Then the
men of the regular army did a thing. They arose *en masse* and came
to attention. Then the men of the regular army did another thing.
They slowly lifted every weather-beaten hat and drooped it until it
touched the knee. Then there was a magnificent silence, broken only
by the measured hoof-beats of the little company's horses as they rode
through the gap. It was solemn, funereal, this splendid silent welcome
of a brave man by men who stood on a hill which they had earned
out of blood and death — simply, honestly, with no sense of excellence,
earned out of blood and death.

Then suddenly the whole scene went to rubbish. Before he
reached the bottom of the hill, Hobson was bowing to right and left
like another Boulanger,[34] and, above the thunder of the massed bands,
one could hear the venerable outbreak, "Mr. Hobson, I'd like to shake
the hand of the man who — " But the real welcome was that welcome
of silence. However, one could thrill again when the tail of the procession appeared — an army wagon containing the blue-jackets of the

34. This is a rather curious analogy on Crane's part between Hobson
and Georges Ernest Jean Marie Boulanger (1837–1891), French military
officer, whose stormy military-political career was the center of controversy
and support (e.g., the Boulangist movement) in France during the 1880's.
He committed suicide in Brussels.

Merrimac adventure. I remember grinning heads stuck out from under the canvas cover of the wagon. And the army spoke to the navy. "Well, Jackie, how does it feel?" And the navy up and answered: "Great! Much obliged to you fellers for comin' here." "Say, Jackie, what did they arrest ye for anyhow? Stealin' a dawg?" The navy still grinned. Here was no rubbish. Here was the mere exchange of language between men.

Some of us fell in behind this small but royal procession and followed it to General Shafter's headquarters, some miles on the road to Siboney. I have a vague impression that I watched the meeting between Shafter and Hobson, but the impression ends there. However, I remember hearing a talk between them as to Hobson's men, and then the blue-jackets were called up to hear the congratulatory remarks of the general in command of the Fifth Army Corps. It was a scene in the fine shade of thickly leaved trees. The general sat in his chair, his belly sticking ridiculously out before him as if he had adopted some form of artificial inflation. He looked like a joss. If the seamen had suddenly begun to burn a few sticks, most of the spectators would have exhibited no surprise. But the words he spoke were proper, clear, quiet, soldierly, the words of one man to others. The Jackies were comic. At the bidding of their officer they aligned themselves before the general, grinned with embarrassment one to the other, made funny attempts to correct the alignment, and — looked sheepish. They looked sheepish. They looked like bad little boys flagrantly caught. They had no sense of excellence. Here was no rubbish.

[IX. YELLOW FEVER?]

Very soon after this the end of the campaign came for me. I caught a fever. I am not sure to this day what kind of fever it was. It was defined variously. I know, at any rate, that I first developed a languorous indifference to everything in the world. Then I developed a tendency to ride a horse even as a man lies on a cot. Then I — I am not sure — I think I grovelled and groaned about Siboney for several days. My colleagues, Scovel and George Rhea,[35] found me and gave me of their best, but I didn't know whether London Bridge was falling down or whether there was a war with Spain. It was all the same. What of it? Nothing of it. Everything had happened, perhaps. But I cared not a jot. Life, death, dishonour — all were nothing to me. All I cared for was pickles. Pickles at any price! Pickles!!

35. George Rea was a reporter for the *World*, as were Scovel and Crane.

If I had been the father of a hundred suffering daughters, I should have waved them all aside and remarked that they could be damned for all I cared. It was not a mood. One can defeat a mood. It was a physical situation. Sometimes one cannot defeat a physical situation. I heard the talk of Siboney and sometimes I answered, but I was as indifferent as the star-fish flung to die on the sands. The only fact in the universe was that my veins burned and boiled. Rhea finally staggered me down to the army surgeon who had charge of the proceedings, and the army surgeon looked me over with a healthy eye. Then he gave a permit that I should be sent home. The manipulation from the shore to the transport was something which was Rhea's affair. I am not sure whether we went in a boat or a balloon. I think it was a boat. Rhea pushed me on board, and I swayed meekly and unsteadily toward the captain of the ship, a corpulent, well-conditioned, impickled person pacing noisily on the spar-deck. "Ahem, yes; well; all right. Have you got your own food? I hope, for Christ's sake, you don't expect us to feed you, do you?" Whereupon I went to the rail and weakly yelled at Rhea, but he was already afar. The captain was, meantime, remarking in bellows that, for Christ's sake, I didn't expect him to feed me. I didn't expect to be fed. I didn't care to be fed. I wished for nothing on earth but some form of painless pause, oblivion. The insults of this old pie-stuffed scoundrel did not affect me then; they affect me now. I would like to tell him that, although I like collies, fox-terriers, and even screw-curled poodles, I do not like him. He was free to call me superfluous and throw me overboard, but he was not free to coarsely speak to a somewhat sick man. I — in fact I hate him — it is all wrong — I lose whatever ethics I possessed — but — I hate him, and I demand that you should imagine a milch cow endowed with a knowledge of navigation and in command of a ship — and perfectly capable of commanding a ship — Oh, well, never mind.

I was crawling along the deck when somebody pounded violently upon me and thundered: "Who in hell are you, sir?" I said I was a correspondent. He asked me did I know that I had yellow fever. I said No. He yelled, "Well, by Gawd, you isolate yourself, sir." I said: "Where?" At this question he almost frothed at the mouth. I thought he was going to strike me. "Where?" he roared. "How in hell do I know, sir? I know as much about this ship as you do, sir. But you isolate yourself, sir." My clouded brain tried to comprehend these orders. This man was a doctor in the regular army, and it was necessary to obey him, so I bestirred myself to learn what he meant by these gorilla outcries. "All right, doctor; I'll isolate myself, but I wish you'd tell me where to go." And then he passed into such volcanic humour that I clung to the rail and gasped. "Isolate yourself, sir.

Isolate yourself. That's all I've got to say, sir. I don't give a goddamn where you go, but when you get there, stay there, sir." So I wandered away and ended up on the deck aft, with my head against the flagstaff and my limp body stretched on a little rug. I was not at all sorry for myself. I didn't care a tent-peg. And yet, as I look back upon it now, the situation was fairly exciting — a voyage of four or five days before me — no food — no friends — above all else, no friends — isolated on deck, and rather ill.

When I returned to the United States, I was able to move my feminine friends to tears by an account of this voyage, but, after all, it wasn't so bad. They kept me on my small reservation aft, but plenty of kindness loomed soon enough. At mess-time, they slid me a tin plate of something, usually stewed tomatoes and bread. Men are always good men. And at any rate, most of the people were in worse condition than I — poor bandaged chaps looking sadly down at the waves. In a way, I knew the kind. First lieutenants at forty years of age, captains at fifty, majors at 102, lieutenant-colonels at 620, full colonels at 1000, and brigadiers at 9,768,295 plus.[36] A man had to live two billion years to gain eminent rank in the regular army at that time. And, of course, they all had trembling wives at remote western posts waiting to hear the worst, the best, or the middle.

In rough weather, the officers made a sort of common pool of all the sound legs and arms, and by dint of hanging hard to each other they managed to move from their deckchairs to their cabins and from their cabins again to their deckchairs. Thus they lived until the ship reached Hampton Roads. We slowed down opposite the curiously mingled hotels and batteries at Old Point Comfort, and at our mast-head we flew the yellow flag, the grim ensign of the plague. Then we witnessed something which informed us that with all this ship-load of wounds and fevers and starvations we had forgotten the fourth element of war. We were flying the yellow flag, but a launch came and circled swiftly about us. There was a little woman in the launch, and she kept looking and looking and looking. Our ship was so high that she could see only those who hung at the rail, but she kept looking and looking and looking. It was plain enough — it was plain all plain enough — but my heart sank with the fear that she was not going to find him. But presently there was a commotion among some black dough-boys of the Twenty-fourth Infantry, and two of them ran aft to Colonel Liscum, its gallant commander.[37] Their faces were wreathed

36. As we have indicated by the careers of various officers, Crane is not far wrong.

37. The Twenty-fourth Infantry was a Negro regiment which, before the war, was commanded by General (then Colonel) Jacob F. Kent. Colonel Emerson H. Liscum had served as lieutenant colonel under Kent;

in darkey grins of delight. "Kunnel, ain't dat Mis'Liscum, Kunnel?"
"What?" said the old man. He got up quickly and appeared at the
rail, his arm in a sling. He cried, "Alice!" The little woman saw him,
and instantly she covered up her face with her hands as if blinded
with a flash of white fire. She made no outcry; it was all in this simply
swift gesture, but we — we knew them. It told us. It told us the other
part. And in a vision we all saw our own harbour lights. That is to
say, those of us who had harbour lights.

I was almost well, and had defeated the yellow fever charge
which had been brought against me, and so I was allowed ashore
among the first. And now happened a strange thing. A hard campaign,
full of wants and lacks and absences, brings a man speedily back to
an appreciation of things long disregarded or forgotten. In camp, somewhere in the woods between Siboney and Santiago, I happened to
think of ice-cream soda, and I came near dying of longing for it. I
couldn't get it out of my mind, try as I would to concentrate my
thoughts upon the land-crabs and mud with which I was surrounded.
It certainly had been an institution of my childhood, but to have a
ravenous longing for it in the year 1898 was about as illogical as to
have a ravenous longing for kerosene. All I could do was to swear
to myself that if I reached the United States again, I would immediately go to the nearest soda-water fountain and make it look like
Spanish fours. In a loud, firm voice I would say, "Orange, please."
And here is the strange thing: as soon as I was ashore I went to the
nearest soda-water fountain, and in a loud, firm voice I said, "Orange,
please." I remember one man who went mad that way over tinned
peaches, and who wandered over the face of the earth saying plain-
tively, "Have you any peaches?"

Most of the wounded and sick had to be tabulated and marshalled
in sections and thoroughly officialized, so that I was in time to take
a position on the veranda of Chamberlain's Hotel and see my late
shipmates taken to the hospital. The veranda was crowded with
women in light, charming summer dresses, and with spruce officers
from the Fortress. It was like a bank of flowers. It filled me with awe.
All this luxury and refinement and gentle care and fragrance and
colour seemed absolutely new. Then across the narrow street on the
veranda of the hotel there was a similar bank of flowers. Two companies of volunteers dug a lane through the great crowd in the street
and kept the way, and then through this lane there passed a curious
procession. I had never known that they looked like that. Such a gang
of dirty, ragged, emaciated, half-starved, bandaged cripples I had

---

he had been appointed second lieutenant in 1863 and promoted to the rank
of lieutenant colonel in 1896.

The Twenty-fourth Infantry had fought at San Juan.

never seen. Naturally there were many men who couldn't walk, and some of these were loaded upon a big flat-car which was in tow of a trolley-car. Then there were many stretchers, slow-moving. When that crowd began to pass the hotel the banks of flowers made a noise which could make one tremble. Perhaps it was a moan, perhaps it was a sob — but no, it was something beyond either a moan or a sob. Anyhow, the sound of women weeping was in it. — The sound of women weeping.

And how did these men of famous deeds appear when received thus by the people? Did they smirk and look as if they were bursting with the desire to tell everything which had happened? No, they hung their heads like so many jailbirds. Most of them seemed to be suffering from something which was like stage-fright during the ordeal of this chance but supremely eloquent reception. No sense of excellence — that was it. Evidently they were willing to leave the clacking to all those natural-born major-generals who after the war talked enough to make a great fall in the price of that commodity all over the world.

The episode was closed. And you can depend upon it that I have told you nothing at all, nothing at all, nothing at all.

3 SOUTH AFRICA AND THE BOER WARS

Introduction

IF STEPHEN CRANE had tried to visit South Africa to report on the
"Boer War" that broke out in 1899, he certainly would not have been
able to function as a war correspondent and he might never have got
there, for he was dying of pulmonary tuberculosis. However, war still
interested him. He was singularly adept at describing battles he could
only imagine, and in Greece and Cuba had had plenty of direct personal experience as a correspondent in the field. The New York *Journal's* readers still wanted to know what Mr. Stephen Crane might
have to say about the latest war.

The situation in the Transvaal provoked Crane's thoughts about
newspaper censorship in "Some Curious Lessons From the Transvaal,"
and stirred him to study the early history of the Boers in South Africa.
"The Great Boer Trek," in *Cosmopolitan* for June 1900, is as interesting
today as it was to that magazine's readers some sixty years ago. Here
once more Crane expresses his bias against missionaries and his con-
demnation of social injustices.

Not included are such dated articles as "Stephen Crane Says:
Watson's Criticisms of England's War Are Not Unpatriotic" (New
York *Journal*: 25 January 1900) and "Stephen Crane Says: The British
Soldiers Are Not Familiar With the 'Business End' of Modern Rifles,"
(New York *Journal*: 14 February 1900).

❁ ❁ ❁

SOME CURIOUS LESSONS FROM THE TRANSVAAL

The war in the Transvaal[1] is developing curious facts in regard to the reporting of battle news, and in some quarters it is even said that this generation will see the last of the war correspondent. The generals don't want him at all, and the public, even with its keen interest, does not want him if a dreadful censor is to sit perpetually on his chest. It all arrives at the question whether if an army loses an engagement the country and the world should know it. Military men seem to think that it is nobody's business whether or no an army has been whipped.

But when all is said and done, a strict censorship is an absolutely essential military thing, and it can also be said with confidence that the Spartan or the Stoic censor will not do in these days. He must be strict, but he must also have a feeling for the people at home, who for some centuries have understood that they pay for wars. They will not sew their sons up in black bags and hand them over to a government for a mysterious period of indefinite length. The military authorities of the more educated nations must learn that they must study the popular opinion at home as carefully as they study the enemy's ammunition supply.

The censorship at the Cape is apparently working to perfection. All the papers in London have been printing accounts of victories thus: "A strong column under General Blank advanced at daybreak this morning and gallantly drove the enemy for miles, inflicting enormous losses. At nightfall the column safely returned to its original position." It sounds like Mr. Dooley, but it is just as true in fact as the sage is true in point of view. Even a stupid public, a public so stupid that they can chuckle over the advantage gained, will not endure such conditions for long. It will come to them in time that there is something wrong. Then the censor must go. But he won't. Because of the swiftness of modern means of communication a modern war may not be conducted without the employment of a censor of news.

Then the war correspondent must go.

He must.

He must go because ocean beds are laid with cables, because range and plain are strung with telegraph, because fast trains and fast steamers are plentiful. His spark of information flies too quickly

Reprinted here for the first time from New York Journal: *7 January 1900.*

1. The South African War began with the Boer invasion of Natal in 1899, the first phase ending with the relief of Ladysmith on February 28 (1900).

around the world and into the enemy's camp. This is why London has been reading news carefully selected for Boer appetites.

There are now many people in England who would like to find the man who before the war constantly named the Boer reputation for valor and military ability as "the biggest unpricked bubble in the world." It had been for some years a favorite phrase to the minds of leader writers. I may say that it is now what might be termed a disengaged simile. No one is using it at present.

Also, several famous poets must be rather nervously considering the advisability of making a general overhaul of some of their proudest verse.

Nevertheless, the country remains very steady in its determination to fight everything out to a finish. Within a few days the Englishman has had to read of Gatacre's incomprehensible defeat, of Methuen's desperate attack and withdrawal and of Buller's reverse.[2] It would be idle to say that British pride has not sunk down into the tips of the national toes. But it would be just as idle to withhold admiration for the quick general decision, made on all sides and by all parties, that the painful business must be grimly and silently endured and the struggle in South Africa carried to a successful British conclusion. Writing under this date, the direct future is mysterious and filled full of shadows, but I conclude that one tangible thing is the resolution of the British people.

The bewildering thing to the British mind has been the mauling received at the hands of bewhiskered farmers by many regiments which were such favorites, whose records so blazed with glory that they were very popularly accounted invincible. For instance, "The Black Watch" (Royal Highlanders), a regiment composed of the old Forty-second Foot and the old Seventy-third Foot, has traditions which are superior to that of any regiment in the world, perhaps. Very well — an unimposing body of men who don't wash very often batter this regiment out of shape.

However, it might be said that of late years the "Gordon Highlanders," a regiment composed of the old Ninety-second and the old

2. On December 10 Sir William Forbes Gatacre in attempting a surprise attack upon the enemy was himself surprised near Stormberg and forced to retreat with the loss of 719 men. On the following day Lord Methuen delivered an attack, and that night the Highland Brigade lost 750 men and its general, and the next day 950 men. Methuen in previous attempts to relieve Kimberley, where Cecil Rhodes was, had suffered serious setbacks and was himself wounded. On December 15 General Redvers Buller made his effort and failed. He was replaced by Field Marshal Lord Roberts at supreme command, with Major General Lord Kitchener as his chief of staff.

Seventy-fifth, have had more campaigns and have achieved a name second to none. In the last campaign against frontier tribes of North-west India the Seventy-fifth made the famous charge at Darghal. Very well — the Ninety-second is with Sir George White and the Seventy-fifth is with Lord Methuen. Both battalions are at this writing mere skeletons, having been so hammered and pounded by the "unpricked bubbles" that they would do well in a representation of the famous picture "Roll Call After Quatre Bras."

It is not necessary to say much of the hammering received by the brigade of Foot Guards. The Foot Guards are a beautiful body of troops, but it has always been understood — notably by the line regiments, who envy them their swagger — that when the guards should meet hard-muscled, hard-shooting, tenacious foes there might be a great surprise. At this writing the brigade of Foot Guards is cut off with Lord Methuen, having already suffered severely.

In every report of an action in South Africa there has appeared a statement of the terrible execution done by the British guns. This may be accounted for by the fact that the observer posted near the position of the gun is not at all able to tell the amount of execution done by that gun's fire. These artillery duels have been fought at ranges which sometimes are as long as 7,000 yards. At a much lesser range than that the spectator is almost certain to conclude that every shell is bursting in the enemy's position.

However, there is one thing which guns may always do. If they are directed against the enemy's guns and handled in a superior fashion they are fairly sure to so involve him with flying showers of dirt and stones from his own earthworks that he is glad to run away for a time. It happened at Matanzas, when the New York, the Puritan and the Cincinnati made beautiful practice, and yet the Spanish loss was prob-ably the famous mule. It happened often enough before Santiago harbor, and it is happening every day in South Africa.

THE GREAT BOER TREK.

When, in 1806, Cape Colony finally passed into the hands of the British government, it might well have seemed possible for the white inhabitants to dwell harmoniously together. The Dutch burghers were in race much the same men who had peopled England and Scotland.

Reprinted here for the first time from Cosmopolitan: June 1900. Crane died at Badenweiler, Germany, in the Black Forest on June 5.

There was none of that strong racial and religious antipathy which seem to make forever impossible any lasting understanding between Ireland and her dominating partner.

The Boers were more devoid of Celtic fervors and fluctuations of temperament than the English themselves; in religion Protestant, by nature hard-working, thrifty, independent, they would naturally, it seems, have called for the good will and respect of their conquerors. But the two peoples seemed to have been keenly aware of each other's failings from the first. To the Boers, the English seemed prejudiced and arrogant beyond mortal privilege; the English told countless tales of the Boers' trickery, their dullness, their boasting, their indolence, their bigotry. The burghers had transplanted the careful habits of their home in the Netherlands to a different climate and new conditions. In South Africa they were still industrious and thrifty, and their somewhat gloomy religion was more strongly rooted than ever. Although they lived nomadic lives on the frontier, yet they had made themselves substantial dwellings within the towns; the streets were blossoming bowers of trees and shrubs; their flocks and herds increased, their fields produced mightily. In the courts of law they had shown conspicuous ability whilst acting as heemraden; they had made good elders and deacons in their churches, and good commandants and fields cornets in war — the ever-recurring conflicts with the Kaffirs.[1]

Many observers have noted the strong similarity of thought and character between the Dutchmen and the Scotchmen. There is the same thrift which is often extreme parsimony, combined with great hospitality, the same dogged obstinacy, and the same delight in overreaching in all matters of business and bargain-driving. Moreover, their religious ideals bear the strongest resemblance one to the other. In his character as a colonist the Boer certainly showed magnificent qualities; he could work and endure and fight. But in spite of his dour sanctimoniousness, he was not a perfect person, any more than his brother Briton. The English missionaries objected to his treatment of the natives, but there was never any of the terrible cruelty practised that the Spaniards used toward the natives during their colonization of Mexico — nor that of various French, English and Portuguese adventurers in Africa during the seventeenth century. But the fact remains that the entire race of Hottentots has been modified through the Dutch occupation; it is said that no pure-blooded Hottentot remains. This amalgamation was treated by the Boers as a commonplace thing. That habit of theirs of producing scriptural authority for all their acts must have begun with their settlement in Cape Colony.

1. Kaffirs belonged to the Bantu races of South Africa, of which the most advanced guard were the Xosas.

The "bastards," as they were openly called, were well treated, brought up as Christians and to lead a tolerably civilized life. The English missionaries were filled with disgust at this state of things, and the Boers were denounced from missionary platforms throughout England. Undoubtedly the missionaries were right, but the Boers, alas, are not the only white race who have taken this patriarchal attitude toward the natives of the country they were engaged in colonizing. The missionaries in their other charges were fanatical and ridiculous; they described the Boers as cruel barbarians, because they would not allow the vermin-haunted Hottentots to join them at family prayers in their "best rooms." The Colonial Office acted on these representations, and refused to listen to any complaints of the Boers. As they numbered less than ten thousand, and English emigrants were constantly pouring into the colony, the Boers were considered of little importance to the government; it was not imagined that they could do anything effectual in the way of resistance. In short, they, who had been the ruling race in the colony for over a century, were now a subject race; they were hampered and restricted on every side.

The first grievance of the Boers was the attitude of the English missionaries. Some of these were men of really high religious ideals, but most of them were politicians.[2] Mr. Vanderkemp and Mr. Read, missionaries of the London society, who had taken black wives, and announced themselves champions of the black race against the white, had sent to England reports of a number of murders and outrages said to have been committed upon Hottentots by the Dutch colonists. By order of the British government fifty-eight white men and women were put upon their trial for these crimes in 1812, and over a thousand witnesses, black and white, were called to give evidence. Several cases of assault were proved, and punished, but none of the serious charges was substantiated. In 1814 a farmer, Frederick Bezuidenhout, quarreled with his native servant, and refused to appear at a court of justice to answer the charge of ill treatment. A company of Hottentots was sent to arrest him; he fired on them and they shot him dead. A company of about fifty men joined an insurrection under the leadership of Bezuidenhout's brother Jan, but a strong force of Boers aided the government in putting down this rebellion; all surrendered but Jan, who was shot and killed.

Lord Charles Somerset, who drew a salary of ten thousand pounds a year, with four residences, was Governor at the time. He was arbitrary as a prince, and afterward suppressed a liberal newspaper and

2. The most famous missionary was the Scotsman Philip, whose policy was to segregate the natives in reserves supervised by Europeans. The Boers objected to reserves as it made it more difficult to obtain servants or slaves to work for them.

forbade public meetings. The prisoners taken were tried — they were thirty-nine in number — and six were sentenced to death, while the others all received some form of punishment. Somerset was entreated to annul the death sentence, but would do so only in one instance. The remaining five were executed in the presence of their friends, and the scaffold broke with their weight; they were all unconscious and were resuscitated. When they had been brought to consciousness their friends vehemently besought Somerset to reprieve them, but he was firm in his refusal and they were hanged again.[3]

This event caused a lasting bitterness among the Boers; the place of execution is known as Slachter's Nek to this day. In 1823, the Dutch courts of justice were abolished with their landrosts and heemraden, and in the place of them English courts were established, with magistrates, civil commissioners and justices of the peace. The burgher senate was abolished, also, and notices were sent to the old colonists that all documents addressed to the government must be written in English. Soon after, a case was to be tried at the circuit court at Worcester, and one of the judges removed it to Cape Town because there was not a sufficient number of English-speaking men to form a jury, though the prisoner and the witnesses could speak Dutch only, and whatever they said had to be translated in court. The judges were divided in their opinion as to whether it were necessary for every juryman to speak English; in 1831 an ordinance was issued defining the qualifications of jurymen and a knowledge of English was not one of them. But in the mean time the Boers had been greatly embittered by their exclusion from the jury-bow. They would not write memorials about it to the government, because they refused to write English.

During the years of English occupation the frontier aggressions of the Kaffirs were of frequent occurence. The document called, "An Earnest Representation and Historical Reminder to H. M. Queen Victoria, in view of the Present Crisis, by P. J. Joubert," published a few months ago, contains this reference to the frontier wars: "Natives molested them [the Boers]; they were murdered, robbed of their cattle, their homes were laid waste. Unspeakable horrors were inflicted on their wives and daughters. The Boer was called out for commando service at his own expense, under command and control of the British, to fight the Kaffirs. While on commando, his cattle were stolen by Kaffirs. After, they were made to wait until troops retook the cattle, which were afterward publicly sold as lost in the presence of their owners, the Boers being informed that they should receive compensation — not in money or goods, neither in rest nor peace, but instead,

3. At Slachter's Nek in March 1816. Somerset was the first British governor of the Cape (1814–1826). There was no representative government during his reign; he was an autocrat, and he antagonized both races.

indignities and abuse were heaped on them. They were told that they should be satisfied at not being punished as the instigators of the disturbance."

As far back as 1809, Hottentots were prohibited from wandering about the country without passes, and from 1812, Hottentot children who had been maintained for eight years by the employers of their parents, were bound as apprenticed for ten years longer. The missionaries were dissatisfied with these restrictions; both of them were removed by an ordinance passed July, 1828, when vagrant Hottentots began to wander over the country at will. Farming became almost impossible; the farm-laborers became vagabonds and petty thefts took place constantly.

Early in 1834, Sir Benjamin D'Urban, called "the Good," was appointed Governor. A legislative council was then granted the colony, but its powers were not great.

The Boers had never been greatly in favor (many opposed it strongly) of slavery, but they had yielded to the general custom and over three million pounds was invested in slaves throughout the colony in 1834. Sir Benjamin D'Urban proclaimed the emancipation of the slaves, who had been set free throughout the British Empire, in August, 1833. This freeing was to take effect in Cape Colony on the 1st of December 1834.

The news of the emancipation was felt to be a relief, but the terms on which it was conducted were productive of unending trouble. The slave-owners of Cape Colony were awarded less than a million and a quarter for their slaves — and the imperial government refused to send the money to South Africa; each claim was to be proved before commissioners in London, when the amount would be paid in stock. To make a journey of one hundred days to London was, of course, impossible to the farmers; they were at the mercy of agents who made their way down to the colony and purchased the claims, so that the colonist received sometimes a fifth, sometimes a sixth, or less, of the value of his slaves. The colonists had hoped that a vagrant act would have been passed by the Council when the slaves were freed, to keep them from being still further overrun by this large released black population, but this was not done.

In 1834, the first band of emigrants left the colony — forty-five men under a leader named Louis Triechard, from the division of Albany. He was a violent-tempered man, and so loudly opposed to the government that Col. Harry Smith[4] offered a reward of five hundred cattle for his apprehension. He left then at once, being of the class of

4. The most energetic governor the Cape ever had, Sir H. G. W. Smith aimed to extend British territory in all directions. Some hundreds of Boers left the colony between 1835 and 1837 under various leaders, the

Boers on the frontier who lived in their wagons, as though they were ships at sea, and had no settled habitation. His party was joined, before it left the colonial border, by Johannes Rensburg. Together they had thirty wagons. They traveled northward. All but two of Rensburg's party were killed, and those of Triechard's party who escaped the savages reached Delagoa Bay in 1838, after terrible hardships, where they received great kindness from the Portuguese. But their sufferings had been so great that only twenty-six lived to be shipped to Natal. But before the emigration reached its height another Kaffir war came on. There was a tremendous invasion of savages, between twelve and twenty thousand warriors, who swept along the frontier, killing, plundering and burning. December, 1834, under Col. Harry Smith a large force was raised; they marched into Kaffirland, and defeated and dispersed the invaders, who were compelled to sue for peace. As a security for the future, Sir Benjamin D'Urban, who was also at the front, issued a proclamation, declaring British sovereignty to be extended over the territory of the defeated tribes as far as the Kei River. But while the people were still suffering from the effects of the invasion, an order came from Lord Glenelg — who became Secretary of State for the Colonies in April, 1835 — peremptorily ordering that the new territory must be immediately given up, on the ground that it had been unjustly acquired.

The Boers now felt that no security existed for life or property on the frontier; all the support of the British government was given — with a philanthropy stimulated by the missionaries — to the black races as against the Boer farmers. The feeling had now become general among them that they must escape British rule at any cost. They left their homes and cultivated fields and gardens — the homes of over a century's growth — and started into the wilds. Purchases of the vacated property were not frequent; a house sometimes was sold for an ox; many of them were simply left, with no sale having been made. All over the frontier districts the great wagons set out, loaded with household goods, provisions and ammunition, to seek new homes farther north. Each party had its commandant and was generally made up of families related to each other. When the pasturage was good, the caravans would sometimes rest for weeks together, while the cows and oxen, horses and sheep and goats, grazed. General Joubert declares that they were followed as far as the Orange River by British emissaries who wanted to be sure that they took no arms nor ammunition with them. However, he adds, the Boers were able to *conceal* their weapons — a fact that seems a very modern instance, indeed.

North of the Orange River the colonists regarded themselves as

---

most noted being Potgieter, Retief, Uys, and Triechard. The latter is usually spelled "Trichart" in English histories.

quite free, for Great Britain had declared officially that she would not enlarge her South African possessions.

The emigrants were ridiculed for leaving their homes for the wilderness — "for freedom and grass," and were called professional squatters. One English writer said: "The frontier Boer looks with pity on the busy hives of humanity in cities, or even in villages; and regarding with disdain the grand, but to him unintelligible, results of combined industry, the beauty and excellence of which he cannot know, because they are intellectually discerned, he tosses up his head like a wild horse, utters a neigh of exultation, and plunges into the wilderness."

The number of "trekkers" has been estimated at from five thousand to ten thousand. The tide of emigration (they went generally in small bands) flowed across the Orange River and then followed a course for some distance parallel with the Quathtamba Mountains. By this route the warlike Kaffirs were evaded, the only native tribes passed through being small disorganized bodies. Near the Vaal River, however, resided the powerful Matabele nation, under the famous Moselekatze, a warrior of Zulu birth, who had established himself there and brought into complete subjection all the neighboring tribes.

One band of emigrants under Commandant Hendrik Potgieter, a man of considerable ability, arrived at the banks of the Vet River, a tributary of the Vaal. Here he found a native chief who lived in constant dread of Moselekatze, who sold to Potgieter the land between the Vet and the Vaal Rivers, for a number of cattle, Potgieter guaranteeing him protection from Moselekatze. After a while, Commandant Potgieter, with a party, went to explore the country, and traveled north to the Zoutpansberg, where the fertility of the soil seemed encouraging. They also believed that communication with the outer world could be opened through Delagoa Bay, so that the country seemed to offer every advantage for settlement. In high spirits they came back to rejoin their families, but a hideous surprise awaited them; they found only mutilated corpses. Expecting an immediate return of the Matabele who had massacred his people, Potgieter made a strong laager on a hill, by lashing fifty wagons together in a circle, and filling all the open spaces, except a narrow entrance, with thorn-trees. Presently the Matabele returned, and with great shouts and yells stormed the camp, rushing up to the wagon-wheels and throwing assegais. But the Boers, with their powerful "roers," or elephant-guns, kept such a rapid and skilful fire, while the women kept the spare guns reloaded, that the Matabele were forced to retire, but they drove with them all the cattle of the party. They left one hundred and fifty-five dead, and one thousand one hundred of their spears were afterward picked up.

The emigrants in the laager were left without the means of transportation, and very little food, while they had lost forty-six of their people. But fortunately they were near the third band of emigrants under Commandant Gerrir Maritz, who encamped near the mission station at Thaba Ntshu, and now sent oxen to carry away Potgieter and the others. Also a native chief, Marroco, brought them milk and Kaffir corn, and pack-oxen to help them away. It was resolved to revenge the massacre, to follow up Moselekatze and punish him. One hundred and seven Boers mustered for this service, besides forty half-breeds, and a few blacks to take care of the horses. A deserter from the Matabele army acted as guide. The commando surprised Mosega, one of the principal military towns, and killed four hundred. Then setting fire to the kraal, they drove seven thousand head of cattle back to Thaba Ntshu. Potgieter's party then formed a camp on the Vet (they called it Winburg), which was joined by many families from the colony. Another band soon reached Thaba Ntshu, under Pieter Retief, a man of great intelligence. June 6th, 1837, a general assembly of Boers was held at Winburg, when a provisional constitution, consisting of nine articles, was adopted. The supreme legislative power was intrusted to a single elective chamber, termed the Volksraad, the fundamental law was declared to be the Dutch, a court of landrost and heemraden was created, and the chief executive authority was given to Retief, with the title of Commandant-General. One article provided that all who joined the community must have no connection with the London Missionary Society.

New bands of emigrants were constantly arriving, and some of them wished to go into Natal, although the condition of the camp at Winburg was very satisfactory. Pieter Uys, one of their leaders, had visited Natal before, and had been impressed with its beauty and fertility. Retief finally decided to go and see for himself if Dingaan, the Zulu chief, would dispose of some land below the mountain.

While he was gone, a second expedition against the Matabele set out, consisting of one hundred and thirty-five farmers, under Potgieter and Pieter Uys. They found Mosega with twelve thousand warriors, brave and finely trained, but at the end of nine days' warfare, Moselekatze fled to the north, after a loss of something like one thousand men. Commandant Potgieter now issued a proclamation declaring that the whole of the territory overrun by the Matabele, and now abandoned by them, was forfeited to the Boers. It included the greater part of the present South African Republic, fully half of the present Orange Free State, and the whole of Southern Bechuanaland to the Kalahari Desert, except that part occupied by the Batlapin. This immense tract of land was then almost uninhabited, and must have remained so if the Matabele had not been driven out.

Much has been written of the beauties of Natal, with its shores washed by the Indian Ocean, its rich soil, luxuriant vegetation and noble forests. When Pieter Retief first saw it from the Drakensberg Mountains, it was under the despotic rule of the Zulu chief Dingaan, who had succeeded Tshaka,[5] the "Napoleon of Africa," the slayer of a million human beings. A few Englishmen, who were allowed to live at the port, gladly welcomed the emigrants, and took them to Dingaan's capital, called Umkunguhloon, acting as guides and interpreters. There was an English missionary clergyman living there, called Owen. Dingaan received them graciously and supplied them with chunks of beef from his own eating-mat, and huge calabashes of millet beer. But when Retief spoke about Natal, the despot set him a task, such as one reads of in folk-lore legends. Retief might have Natal for his countrymen to live in, if he would recover a herd of seven hundred cattle that had been recently stolen from him by Sikouyela, a Mantater chief. Retief accepted the condition, and actually made Sikouyela restore the cattle, which he drove back to Dingaan. The Boers at Winburg felt distrustful of Dingaan, and dreaded to have Pieter Retief trust himself again in the tyrant's hands. But in February, 1838, Retief started with seventy persons, armed and mounted, with thirty attendants. Again Dingaan received them hospitably, and empowered the missionary Owen to draw up a document granting to Retief the country between the Tugela and the Umzimvooboo. But just as the emigrants were ready to leave, they were invited into a cattle-kraal to see a war-dance, and requested to leave their arms outside the door. While sitting down they were overpowered and massacred, the horror-stricken Owen being a witness of the sight.

Immediately after the massacre, Dingaan sent out his forces against all the emigrants on the eastern side of the Drakensberg. Before daylight they attacked the encampments at Blaanwkrauz River and the Bushman River — ten miles apart. It was a complete surprise and a terrible slaughter of the Boers, although a brave defense was made. The township which has since arisen near the scene of the conflict still bears the name of Weemen — the place of wailing.

As soon as the emigrants on the west of the Drakensberg heard of the disasters, they formed a band of about eight hundred men to punish Dingaan for his treachery. But they were led into ambush, and finally defeated by the Zulus, and forced to retreat after a tremendous loss of life. The condition of the emigrants was now one of terrible distress and privation. They had many widows and orphans to provide for. The Governor of Cape Colony sent word to them to return, and there were many who felt willing to go, but it was the women of the party who sternly refused to go back; they preferred liberty, al-

5. Or "Chaka."

though that liberty had cost them so dear. In November, 1838, Andries Pretorius arrived in Natal from Graaff Reinet and was at once elected Commandant-General. He organized a force of four hundred and sixty-four men and marched toward Umkungunhloon. He took with him a sufficient number of wagons to form a laager; wherever the camp was pitched it was surrounded by fifty-seven wagons; all the cattle were brought within the inclosure, the whole force joining in prayers and the singing of psalms. The army made a vow that if victorious they would build a church, and set apart a thanksgiving day each year to commemorate it. The church in Pietermaritzburg and the annual celebration of Dingaan's bear witness that they kept their pledge. They were not fighting for revenge. On three occasions the scouts brought in some captured Zulus, and Pretorius sent them back to Dingaan to say that if he would restore the land he had granted Retief he would enter into negotiations for peace.

Dingaan's reply came in the form of an army ten thousand or twelve thousand strong, which attacked the camp on December 16, 1838. For two hours the Zulus tried to force their way into the laager, while the Boer guns and the small artillery made dreadful havoc in their ranks. When at length they broke and fled, over three thousand Zulu corpses lay on the ground and a stream that flowed through the battle-field was crimson. It has been known ever since as the Blood River.

Pretorius marched on to Umkungunhloon as soon as possible, but Dingaan had set the place on fire and fled.

Dingaan, with the remainder of his forces, retired farther into Zululand. There, soon after, his brother, Pauda, revolted, and fled with a large following into Natal, where he sought the protection of the Boers. Another and final expedition was made against Dingaan in January, 1840, the farmers having Pauda with four thousand of his best warriors as an ally. By February 10th, Dingaan was a fugitive in the country of a hostile tribe, who soon killed him, and the emigrant farmers were the conquerors of Zululand. On that day Pauda was appointed and declared to be "King of the Zulus" in the name and behalf of the Volksraad at Pietermaritzburg, where the Boers established their seat of government as "The South African Society of Natal."

Four days afterward, a proclamation was issued at the same camp, signed by Pretorius and four commandants under him, declaring all the territory between the Black Imfolosi and the Umzimvooboo Rivers to belong to the emigrant farmers. "The national flag was hoisted," says a chronicler, "a salute of twenty-one guns fired, and a general hurrah given throughout the whole army, while all the men as with one voice called out: 'Thanks to the great God who by his grace has given us the victory!'"

Now that the "trekkers" had freed South Africa from the destructive Zulu power, and had driven the Matabele away, they wished to settle in Natal, and rest from the nomadic existence that had so long been theirs. But the British now came forward to hunt them on again. The Governor of Cape Colony, Sir George Napier, proclaimed that "the occupation of Natal by the emigrants was unwarrantable," and directed that "all arms and ammunition should be taken from them, and the port closed against trade."

What followed — the British bombardment of the port, the Dutch surrender — are well-known facts of history. May 12, 1843, Natal was proclaimed a British colony, and the emigrants again took to their wagons, crossing the Vaal.

APPENDIX

Crane as Dramatist

SUCCESSFUL as novelist and short-story writer and as journalist, Crane from the start hankered to achieve also a name for himself as dramatist; and from the start he cast some pieces in dramatic dialogue-form. One such attempt is "Greed Rampant," summarized and quoted from in "Stephen Crane: Some New Stories," which Stallman edited for the *Bulletin of The New York Public Library* (January 1957).

Another dramatic dialogue is "At Clancy's Wake," published in *Truth* for June 1893. Much of Crane's fiction — "The Open Boat," for example — is dialogue readily convertible to the stage. Crane hoped that a dramatization would be made of his short story "The Upturned Face," but the actor Sir Johnston Forbes-Robertson turned down his proposal. In *Truth* for November 1893 the unpublished, unperformed dramatist issued "Some Hints for Playmakers."

In early 1896 Crane toyed with the idea of a play to be written in collaboration with Clyde Fitch, and in January 1898 Conrad was begging off collaboration with his friend Crane on the latter's proposal for a drama about a man who impersonates the dead lover of a girl, hoping thereby to win her. Hence the title: "The Predecessor." Says Conrad to Crane: "I have no dramatic gift. You have the terseness, the clear eye, the easy imagination. You have all — and I have only the accursed faculty of dreaming. My ideas fade — yours come out sharp cut as cameos — they come all living out of your brain and bring images — and bring light. Mine bring only mist in which they are born, and die. I would be only a hindrance to you — I am afraid" (*Stephen Crane: Letters* [1960], p. 167). But Conrad with two one-act plays drawn from his short stories and *The Secret Agent: A Drama in Four Acts*

(1923), drawn from his 1907 novel of that title, had much more success than Crane in writing for the stage.

In October 1899 Cora Crane sent a literary agent two chapters of Crane's novel *The O'Ruddy* (completed by Robert Barr, 1903), remarking: "I think it will make a popular success & a *good* play" (*Letters*, p. 236). Nothing came of that, and nothing by Crane ever got onto the stage except "The Ghost," a play written by ten collaborators and presented on 28 December 1899, at the schoolhouse in Brede village. Legend credited Brede Place, where the Cranes lived, with being a haunted house, and "The Ghost" exploited that legend. Collaborators included Henry James, H. G. Wells, Joseph Conrad, and George Gissing. For an extended discussion of "The Ghost" see *Letters*, pp. 244–247, with reproduction therein of one page of Crane's holograph manuscript, and "The Ghost at Brede Place," by John D. Gordan, *Bulletin of The New York Public Library*, 56 (December 1952), 591–595.

In the early 1920's it was announced in the papers that Lillian Gish proposed to appear in a film version of *Maggie: A Girl of the Streets*. But Thomas Beer, writing Miss Edith Crane (Stephen's niece) on 2 January 1923, said that Alfred Knopf, who two years later bought all rights in Crane's works from the Crane family for $5,000, had "moved to prevent any such catastrophe without Mr. William Crane's consent and the necessary contracts. If Miss Gish would provide a suitable and honest version of the story, it might not be a bad thing but you doubtless have observed what happens to good literature when it falls among thieves and movies belong in the same category." (William was Judge Crane of Port Jervis, New York; Stephen's oldest brother.) In 1951 when Gottfried Reinhardt (Max Reinhardt's son) produced *The Red Badge of Courage*, directed by John Huston, Crane finally got onto the screen. And in November 1962 Crane's *Red Badge* was produced on TV in a reading by Ben Gazzara synchronized with Brady photographs of the Civil War.

The stage fascinated Crane, and Crane's Maggie was likewise fascinated by theatrical and barroom performances. "Manacled" — published posthumously in *Argot* (August 1900) — is the story of a man trapped in a burning theatre. "Matinee Girls" is a fragment Stallman reproduced in *Bulletin of The New York Public Library* (September 1956) from Crane's Pocket Notebook. "The Fire Tribe and the Pale-Face," an unpublished six-page manuscript, is cast in dramatic form; and "In Search of a Quarrel," an untitled eighteen-page holograph manuscript, is a one-act play set in "a little inn in Old France." Its conception is much better than its execution. It ends with the appearance of Death, and his appearance has been prepared for; but in the interim there is too much repetitious and irrelevant twaddle. Whether Crane knew it or not, his general situation or "conceit" had already been manipulated brilliantly by Poe in "The Masque of the Red Death."

David Belasco corresponded with Cora Crane after Stephen's death for the purpose of obtaining permission to dramatize *The Red Badge*, and, in "The Genius of Stephen Crane" (*Metropolitan Magazine*: 1900), he declared that Crane, "by his directness and wealth of imagination, possesses eminently the qualities of a dramatic writer. He reveals the great human drama, its struggles and tragic climaxes, in a flash of the pen. His creations seem to rise in the flesh, vibrating with life and pulsating with passion. This is dramatic instinct *par excellence*."

This is certainly true of Crane's fiction, but none of his plays achieved the stage or saw print. His best attempt is printed below. The influence of Howells is manifest in the social comedy but is with great skill combined with some very realistic incidents of war, a combination that might well appeal to present-day "dramatists of the absurd." The work appears to be incomplete, but in view of the extremely unusual nature of the action the possibility cannot be ignored that Crane meant the play to end where the typescript ends. He submitted it to Reynolds, the literary agent, in its present form.

DRAMA IN CUBA

CHARACTERS

MR. JOHN STILWELL: *an English sugar-planter in Cuba*

MARJORIE STILWELL: *his daughter.*

LUCY STILWELL: *his daughter.*

DON PATRICIO DE MAVIDA Y AGUILAR: *colonel of the Tequila Battalion No. 206, of the Spanish army.*

HENRY PATTEN: *a first lieutenant commanding D Troop, 20th. United States Cavalry.*

SYLVESTER THORPE: *for the* New York Eclipse.

SERJEANT BROWN: *of D Troop.*

[ACT I]

SCENE: *The dining-room of John Stilwell's house on his plantation in the province of Santiago de Cuba.*

TIME: *The evening of a day in late July, 1898.*

John Stilwell, his two daughters, and Colonel Mavida discovered at dinner.

[SCENE I]

MAVIDA: (*gesturing*) "Well, you see, if the Americans come here, they will have some troubles. I have my mens — over 300 — in the blockhouse and in the town. And if the Americans come here they will not find that I am like General Linares."

JOHN STILWELL: "Well, you know, I don't like it. Directly, you know we'll have you chaps potting at each other here under our very noses."

MARJORY: (*shuddering*) "It will be dreadful" —

LUCY: "And, O, perhaps somebody will be killed!"

MAVIDA: (*puzzled and gentle*) "Killed! I think many mens will be killed, senorita. (*He plumes himself a trifle.*) If they come here, you will see — you will see. I myself will kill the first American — (*impressively*) — the first one."

MARJORY: "Oh, Don Patracio, please don't say it. It is too horrible" —

MAVIDA: (*solemnly*) "The first one!"

MARJORY: "And you really mean that you are going to kill the first American who comes here without particular discrimination! Oh, Don Patracio! It might be an awfully nice chap, you know."

LUCY: "And he may have a wife and babies and all that kind of thing."

STILWELL: (*soothingly*) "O, don't mind him. He don't mean it."

LUCY: "But Papa, he says he means it."

MAVIDA: (*earnestly*) "My friends, I cannot help myself. I am a soldier of Spain. I must meet the enemies of my country."

LUCY: "But, Don Patracio, don't you think the matter would be made so much more simple and agreeable if you just sort of casually surrendered, you know."

STILWELL AND MARJORY: (*together, scandalised*) "Lucy!"

MAVIDA: (*with gloomy dignity*) "The senorita is so good as to have been misinformed as to the honor of Spanish soldiers."

LUCY: (*sorry that she has hurt him*) "Oh, well, I didn't really mean surrender, you know. I meant giving in really, and of course" —

MARJORY: (*hastily interrupting*) "Yes, Don Patricio, but your honor does not require you to kill the American, you see. He may have, as Lucy so well has said, a wife and a number of babies at home."

STILWELL: "That is his own affair — his own affair. Hang it all, you can't hold Don Patricio responsible for every wife and baby in the American army."

MARJORY: (*coldly*) "I did not understand there were wives and babies in the American army."

MAVIDA: "The senoritas do not understand too much of the character of our nation. We have an enemy and we kill him. We are insult and we kill him, when first we see him."

LUCY: "But don't you ever think, Don Patricio, of all the mothers sitting up at night and waiting for the return of their sons?"

MAVIDA: "If a man has a mother it is his own fault."

MARJORY: "How do you mean? I don't understand."

STILWELL: "He is quite right. He doesn't mean exactly, my dear, that if a man has a mother it is his own fault. He means that when a man goes gratuitously into danger, he's got to pay the piper."

MARJORY: "Oh — I thought he must mean something like that. Of course at first, Don Patricio's sentiments sounded rather revolutionary."

MAVIDA: (*growing excited*) "I am convince. I am firm. The senoritas should understand the character of my nation. Our enemies — we kills them."

LUCY: (*to Marjory, tearfully*) "Isn't it horrible to think of all the new widows and orphans that will be in the United States within the next few weeks."

MAVIDA: (*haughtily*) "The senoritas misunderstands. I intend to make no move against the widows and orphans of the Americans."

STILWELL: "No! no! You misunderstand, Don Patricio. My daughter means merely to pity the new American widows and orphans."

MAVIDA: (*shrugging his shoulders*) "Well if they insist upon fight with Spain."

STILWELL: "No! no! you misunderstand again. There are no widows and orphans in the American army. My daughter means" —

MAVIDA: (*interrupting Stilwell with an impressive outstretched hand*) "I am sorry. The time is much serious. I am a Spaniard. I have been insult and I will kill the first American which I see."

(*a knock on the door, the dinner party start.*)

(*business*)

STILWELL: (*arising and moving toward the door*) "Who's there?"

PATTEN: (*without*) "An officer of the United States Army. Open the door."

(*a scene of agitation and consternation. Mavida arises and draws his revolver. He fiercely indicates his resolution to kill Patten upon his entrance. While the two girls, terrified, pantomine wildly at him. Stilwell stands near the door facing Mavida and making comic signs. Mavida is partly led and partly thrust through the doorway L, meantime protesting in dumb show that he will kill Patten.*)

PATTEN: (*without, sternly*) "Open the door."

(*Lucy and Marjory resume their seats and hastily compose themselves. Stilwell opens the door. Enter Patten*)

PATTEN: "You may stay outside, Serjeant."

(*Serjeant Brown is seen in the darkness and directly back of threshold.*)

SERJT. B.: "Yes sir."

PATTEN: (*he swiftly takes in scene before him*). "Extremely sorry, I'm sure, to give you any trouble. Fact is we find so many of these sugar-plantations deserted that I didn't expect to find so much — (*hesitates*) — civilization."

STILWELL: "Oh, of course, it's all right you know but then you did give us a bit of a start. I've got nothing to do with this business at all, you know, I'm an Englishman, you see."

PATTEN: "Oh, an Englishman? Well — that's all right."

LUCY: (*advances timidly toward Patten*) "But you are not going to fight anywhere about here, are you?"

PATTEN: "Fight? no! Not the slightest intention. You see, I'm merely running around with stores for the reconcentrados and — (*looking at Marjory*) — I wouldn't fight for worlds. That is — if it would annoy you any way."

STILWELL: "Won't you sit down?"

PATTEN: "Oh, thank you." (*takes rocking-chair the back of which is within two feet of the door L which leads into the room where Mavida is. A period of silence during which the Stilwells become gradually more and more agitated, while Patten watches them blandly.*)

PATTEN: "Of course, — I — I — it is rude to break in upon you in this manner and of course — (*suddenly and covering them all with a cold and contemptuous glance*) — I'm sorry that I disturbed you in the matter that some stranger menaces me at my back."

(*business*)

PATTEN: "I don't know — whether I should interfere in a thing which seems so purely domestic, but if you will allow me — (*suddenly*) — Serjeant!"

(*enter Serjeant Brown.*)

SERJT. B.: "Sir."

PATTEN: (*waves a hand carelessly behind him indicating the door.*) "Go in and see what that is."

SERJT. B.: "Yes — sir." (*exit, Serjt. B. — door L.*)

(*Patten speaks icily during some muffled sounds of a disturbance, L.*)

PATTEN: "I see that you have some machinery here for assaulting people who turn their backs to strange doors." (*the sound of disturbance increases*) (*business*)

STILWELL: "Look here, this won't do at all. It is strictly his own affair."

PATTEN: (*inflexibly*) "Whose affair?"

STILWELL: "I mean — look here you know — I'm not going to have you hurt in my house, and I am not going to give him away."

PATTEN: "I rather imagine the Serjeant is giving him away all well enough."

STILWELL: "He was dining here — and he said that he was going to kill the first American who came and we didn't want to have it done that's all there is to it."

PATTEN: "Oh, I see. I don't think we — you note that I say we — I mean the race — I don't think we lend ourselves readily to theories of assassination."

STILWELL: (*stiffly*) "Thank you very much."

PATTEN: (*calmly*) "It would have surprised me greatly to have been murdered in the house of an English gentleman."

STILWELL: "Quite so." (*after a pause*) "I hope — you are not alone?"

PATTEN: "Oh, no, the troop is outside. — thank you. I came to enquire for good camping ground with water and forage close by.

(*Twisting his head with swift impatience toward the door, L*) Why don't you bring him out, Serjeant?"

SERJT. B.: (*from without in muffled voice*) "All right, sir, in a minute."

PATTEN: "I suppose you wouldn't mind if we took a little sugar-cane for the horses?"

STILWELL: "Not at all — if you can find any. What between the Insurgents and the Spanish troops, I'm in doubt whether this is a sugar plantation or a stone quarry."

(*Private soldier opens the door C and steps aside for the entrance of war-correspondent.*)

THORPE: (*over his shoulder to private*) "Thank you". (*looks about him in some bewilderment and bows hurriedly at sight of the girls.*) "I beg your pardon. I was told — oh, there you are, Patten."

PATTEN: (*immovable in chair*) "Hullo, Thorpe."

WAR CORRES.: (*staring at Patten*) "What is the matter?"

PATTEN: "Nothing."

WAR CORRES.: "What's the row in the next room?"

PATTEN: "That is my first Serjeant engaging the enemy."

WAR CORRES.: "Why don't you go and help him?"

PATTEN: "I don't think he needs it."

(*commotion inside door L.*)

MARJORY: (*unable to contain herself; moves toward Patten; her hands are clasped*) "Will you please move away from that door — or — or — or — turn about so that you will face it in some way."

PATTEN: (*with alacrity*) Why of course. (*he moves R down stage*) (*enter Serjt. B. and Mavida; Brown has Mavida by the scruff of the neck; Mavida is furious but disarmed*).

SERJT. B.: (*bursting out excitedly*) "I had an awful time with him, sir. He fought like a cat and he bit my finger — see. If it hadn't been that I was on duty, I would have taken and everlastingly broken — "

PATTEN: (*swiftly, in a hard voice*) "Be quiet, Serjeant." (*sudden rigidity of Serjt.; Patten looks at Mavida*) "Who is he, Serjeant?"

SERJT. B.: Well he's a Spanish officer, sir. That's all I know. And he bit me on the fing — "

PATTEN: "Be quiet, I tell you." (*he turns deferentially to Stilwell.*) "I'm sorry but I'm afraid that I will have to ask you who is this remarkable man?"

STILWELL: "Well, you know — your man here says he bit his finger — and of course when people begin to bite other people's fingers — by Gad you know! But — he was dining here you know and — of course — you — you will have to make your own investigations you know."

PATTEN: (*promptly*) "Of course; I see." (*he turns to the Serjt.*) "Does he speak English, Serjeant?"

SERJT. B.: "I don't know, sir. I've only heard him swear and it has been all in Spanish."

PATTEN: (*addressing Mavida*) "Do you speak English?"

MAVIDA: "None of your beesness."

PATTEN: "Thank you, I thought you did. Well then, I have a few serious words to speak to you. Your force has been surrendered by your superior in the city of Santiago who has surrendered the entire Spanish force in the Province of Santiago de Cuba. It is thus clear that he has surrendered you — . A colonel inclusive so to speak. Now I'm here with a force of American cavalry guarding and bringing some stores for the people in the town and — really you ought to behave yourself you know."

STILWELL: (*interpolating*) "I have always found Don Mavida a gentleman and I'm sure you can trust — but still if it's true that he bit the Serjeant's finger you know, by Gad" —

LUCY: "Oh, it can't be possible that Don Patricio really bit the poor man's finger.?"

MARJORY: "No! no! the idea is outrageous."

SERJT. B.: "But — he did!"

PATTEN: (*formally to Marjory*) "I am sorry but the Serjeant's communications are always reliable. I do not think he would have the genius to invent such a mishap for himself."

STILWELL: "Well, you know, it is incredible that I should have a guest who would bite another man's finger. — Now if he had punched him" —

SERJT. B.: (*heatedly*) "If he had — why — "

PATTEN: "Stop it, Serjeant."

WAR CORRES.: (*laughing*) "What a strange way to conduct military operations."

LUCY: (*to War Corres.*) "Oh, what are they going to do to him, please?"

WAR CORRES.: (*differentially*) "Why, I wouldn't worry if I were you. I suppose Patten will just take and sort of naturally run him off the face of the earth."

LUCY: "Oh, that's in the American language. I want to know whether it will hurt."

WAR CORRES.: (*gently*) "What to be run off the face of the earth? Why no, I don't suppose so. Don't you be worried. I'll keep an eye out."

PATTEN: (*addressing Mavida*) "I know perfectly well that it would be impossible for you to disobey the orders of your superiors."

MAVIDA: (*quietly*) "What are you going to do with me?"

PATTEN: (*slowly*) "Technically you are a prisoner of war and I expect that you will march your battalion into Santiago and take ship for Spain with the others."

MAVIDA: "Yes officially I am given to my enemies but actually I and my battalion can still fight for our honor."

PATTEN: "I thought that was what you were doing in the next room."

MAVIDA: "I will tell you with much clear, that I will not march my men to Santiago and deliver my honor into the hands of your accursed nation."

PATTEN: "You will sooner or later. We don't want your honor, particularly but we are somewhat serious about having you."

MAVIDA: "Sir, you talk as if you had many men at your command."

PATTEN: "Well, I've got thirty six. I'm not here to fight you. I'm here to distribute stores to reconcentrados. As I said, I tell you plainly I have thirty six men and — mark you — I'm going to let you run off home, but don't you come shooting in this particular locality because if you do — many things might happen and most irregular proceedings would occur."

MAVIDA: "Sir, I shall bring my battalion against you as soon as I can reach my subordinates."

SERJT. B.: (*suavely*) "Of course, sir, as far as reaching his subordinates is concerned" —

PATTEN: "Of course." (*he addresses Mavida*) "But to me you are simply a man who has been officially surrendered and you do not appeal to me as an addition to the baggage. So you trot along and behave yourself."

MAVIDA: (*furiously*) "I shall attack" —

PATTEN: (*interupting*) "Oh, no you won't. Run along."

(*exit Mavida.*)

MARJORY: "Oh, but he will."

PATTEN: "Well if he does, I suppose we will be able to manage it somehow."

(CURTAIN)

[ACT II]

SCENE: *same.*

TIME: *daybreak, next morning.*

> (*Patten discovered having breakfast alone. After an interval — enter Marjorie. Patten arises hurriedly with his napkin in his hand*)

PATTEN: "Oh, it seems I'm taking a tremendous advantage of you in accepting your invitation to breakfast at day-light. I didn't expect to see anybody down" —

MARJORIE: (*simply*) "I couldn't sleep."

PATTEN: "I'm very sorry. Was it the — was it the — the — possibility?"

MARJORIE: "Yes. I feel sure that he will fight with you. He is a very determined man."

PATTEN: "Is he?"

MARJORIE: "Yes. Of course a lot of these stories of cruelty are exaggerated, but then there is something in them, you know — more or less."

PATTEN: (*insidously*) "You mean that perhaps it is possible that you may have some small cursory interest in my welfare?"

MARJORY: (*hastily*) "Not at all."

PATTEN: "Oh, — (*impudently*) — I thought that I might have been honored by some part of your consideration."

MARJORIE: "You were entirely mistaken. You are impudent."

PATTEN: "You don't mean to say that you warned me about that Spanish colonel on — on simply human ground? I thought you did it because we were — cousins you know, or some-thing like that."

MARJORIE: (*she sees that he is teasing her; she speaks sharply*) "I'm very sorry to admit that I thought of you merely as a human being — I understand on good authority that there are many millions of human beings."

PATTEN: (*he makes a sudden submissive bow in which there is no derision*) "I am glad to be considered among those whom you recognise in existence."

MARJORY: "But I do not know — I do not know whether it is proper to admit you quite that far."

PATTEN: (*submissively*) "It would of course be a great concession on such short acquaintance." (*again insidious and impudent*) "Of course if you mean that it would please you that this Colonel Mavida should come to no harm through D troop of the 20th. Cavalry" —

MARJORIE: "I can't understand you."

PATTEN: "Well it would be hard to keep from shooting him if

he tries to rush the sugar mill. But then (*insinuatingly*) I might prevail on my men to miss him somehow. You don't want him killed, I judge?"

MARJORY: (*indignantly*) "It is nothing to me whether he is killed or no."

PATTEN: (*serenely*) "Oh, then we shall kill him."

MARJORY: (*aghast*) "Oh, no! no! no! I didn't mean that. You mustn't kill him."

PATTEN: "Well then I understand that you make a personal request for the life of this Spanish colonel."

MARJORY: (*ingenuously*) "Do I?"

PATTEN: "Why of course you did. You request that I should take particular pains to preserve Colonel Mavida. I look at the matter in a broad way and I say that if the preservation of this invaluable Colonel Mavida is of special importance to you, I shall try my best to do as you wish."

MARJORY: (*after deliberation; strainedly*) "Well — it is of importance."

PATTEN: (*after a pause*) "Of special importance?"

MARJORY: (*abruptly*) "Yes."

PATTEN: "Oh, I daresay I can manage it somehow."

MARJORY: "Of course you know this Colonel Mavida will do even as he announces."

PATTEN: (*suavely*) "I have no doubt but what he is the most excellent of men. For my part I shall not be surprised if he does about twice as much as he announces."

MARJORY: "He is extremely dangerous — really."

PATTEN: (*abruptly*) "I understant what you mean but if he gets within my line of fire at fair range, I don't see what I'm going to do about it."

MARJORY: "You don't understand at all. I mean — (*hesitates; and then rapidly*) I mean — here you are sitting down quietly at breakfast and at any moment he might be down upon you like rain."

PATTEN: "Well, previous to the rain there will be heard some picket-shooting from the north, east, south and west and from any other cardinal point of the compass which I may happen to have forgotten."

MARJORY: (*stiffly*) "I understand your type, now. You're one of those young officers who have just left school."

PATTEN: "Oh, no; I've just come apparently."

MARJORY: "Well, I hope the time is not approaching when I shall be compelled to be sorry for you."

PATTEN: "I don't think it is and then again it might be."

(*enter Sylvester Thorpe*)

THORPE: "Good morning, Miss Stillwell. Hullo Patten."

MARJORY: "Good morning, Mr Thorpe. Where's your note-book?"

THORPE: (*looks in a puzzled way about the room*) "Note book! Note book!"

MARJORY: "Yes. I always thought that war-correspondents appeared with note books and wrote in them at inconsequent times."

THORPE: "Oh, — yes, I guess they do — only, you see, I'm new to the business."

MARJORY: "But look here, seriously, Mr Thorpe — I do not at all know how to interfere in the affairs of men — but can not you explain to Mr Patten the great danger he is in?"

THORPE: (*in great amazement*) "Who! Patten?"

MARJORY: (*she begins as if it were her duty to explain all that she apprehends*) "Yes, I've been saying to him that he is in great danger and he insists that it is a foolish — foolish — foolish — "

THORPE: (*to Patten, agitatedly*) "Patten, have you no pickets out?"

PATTEN: (*angrily*) "Don't be a fool."

MARJORY: (*relieved*) "Oh, then you mean that you have everything arranged so nobody will be hurt at all?" (*small business by Patten and Thorpe*)

THORPE: "Well — no — not exactly that."

MARJORY: (*she turns in an appealing manner to Patten*) "But really Mr — Mr Patten, I beg you to understand that Colonel Mavida is a dangerous man."

(*noise without, enter Serjt. Brown*)

SERJT. B.: (*saluting*) "Sir, a man has come in from the out-post down the road with the report that the Spaniards are advancing."

PATTEN: "Were they able to make out the number of the enemy, Serjeant?"

SERJT. B.: He says, sir, that they thought it was the whole battallion of Spaniards advancing from the blockhouses and the town."

PATTEN: "Send word to the outpost to fall back on us, firing as they come. That is, if they need the word. The troop will occupy the sugar-mill." (*a few far-away shots are heard*) "Drive the wagons into the Sugar house. The door is wide enough."

(*In meantime Patten and Serjeant are headlong off stage simultaneous with entrance of John Stilwell; a small volley is heard which sounds nearer than previous fire.*)

STILWELL: "Oh, I say! What is this you know? Damn it, I'm not going to have a battle fought on my own place you know."

MARJORY: (*panic-stricken*) "Father, father you'll be killed! Don't you hear them, father! They're fighting!"

STILLWELL: "Fighting, are they? I thought I heard a funny sound."

MARJORY: "Oh, it's going to be dreadful, and perhaps somebody will be killed."

(enter Lucy — precipitately)

LUCY: "Oh! — Oh! — Oh! I was looking out of my window and I heard them fighting and then seven or eight Americans came running as fast as they could and — (ingenuously) — I was awfully frightened."

STILWELL: "I hope to Heaven I've not made a serious mistake in keeping you two little people here during this war."

(the door C flies open and Patten enters)

PATTEN: "I'm awfully sorry but I'm about to be attacked and I thought that I would rather invite you — inasmuch as your house is of thin wood and the sugar-mill is of stone — I rather thought I would invite you — oblige you — compel you to take refuge in the sugar-mill."

(the door flies open, a corporal appears)

CORPORAL MULLIGAN: "Lieutenant, they're on us."

(CLOSE OF SCENE)

[SCENE II]

SCENE: *Interior of sugar-mill. Open windows L and back stage. These windows are long and wide. Each window is occupied by four or five American soldiers. The floor is cluttered with haversacks. From time to time can be heard the sing of bullets entering the deep windows. A man is hit in the arm. He sits down quietly on the floor of the sugar-mill and binds up his arm as best he can. The Americans have not yet opened fire. Enter, R, Patten.*

PATTEN: (sternly) "Use the cut-off. Don't let me hear any magazines."

(enter John Stilwell)

STILWELL: "Well, look here, you know, this is a devil of a funny business. I don't quite understand. I've got a plantation here you know which is worth £23,000. Of course if you want to fight on it, I suppose you will but" —

PATTEN: "Where are your daughters?"

STILWELL: "They are right behind me."

(enter Marjory and Lucy.)

PATTEN: (advancing upon Marjory and Lucy) "Oh, please — will you lie down? I can't bear to see you stand up. One can't tell what might happen. Please lie down." (the last words were addressed particularly to Marjory)

MARJORY: "Lie down?"

PATTEN: "Oh, of course, I didn't mean exactly to lie down — but — if you could manage in some way to sort of — get your head below the line of fire — of course that's what I mean."

(*Marjory, Lucy and John Stilwell seat themselves upon the floor of the sugar-mill; the firing has continued steadily but in skirmishing shots; Patten walks along the line of his men; he exits R but returns immediately. — finally there is a lull in the firing; he returns to the group of three seated on the floor of the sugar-house.*)

PATTEN: "I am afraid that it is our friend of last evening who is making us this little trouble."

MARJORY: "Oh, but nobody is hurt?"

PATTEN: "I don't know whether they are hurt or not but two of my men have been hit. They failed to say whether or not they were hurt."

LUCY: "But don't you think we are all going to be killed?"

PATTEN: "Well, I don't know. Of course it's possible. — But I'm sure they wouldn't kill you anyhow. Of course they might kill me you know —"

MARJORY: "No, but why would they kill you?"

PATTEN: "Oh, I don't suppose there would be any particular reason — they might do it simply as a matter of course — but then you know when I have D Troop playing away in a sugar-mill, I don't anticipate death to any great extent."

MARJORY: "D Troop? What do you mean by D Troop? Do you mean those men there?"

PATTEN: "Yes, I mean those men there. They are all I've got in the world. I own them as you might own a diamond necklace. They may be no good but — I hope they may be able to protect you from any slight inconvenience."

STILWELL: "Look here, when's this thing going to stop, you know?"

PATTEN: "Well the firing up to the present has merely indicated that an attack is beginning. I apprehend that after the attack begins I may be able to get an idea of when it's going to stop."

STILWELL: "But I thought this was the attack."

PATTEN: "You have been misinformed. This is the introduction. Else, much as I would like it, I could not be here. The enemies' advance are firing from three hills which I have already noted and then of course as a detail your house is on fire."

STILWELL: (*uprising in great rage; thunderously*) "Sir, my house on fire?"

PATTEN: "Pardon me; your house is on fire through the inability of your friend to understand that he has been surrendered. I would order out my men to save what were possible if it were not for the fact that they would probably be killed in doing so."

STILWELL: "You are quite right. Really you know I — I — I wouldn't like to play the goat and if the house is burning down by Gad let it burn down."

PATTEN: "Thank you very much."

STILWELL: "I don't mean you know that I wont make a big claim against the American government — of course it is a very rich government — but by Gad when you come to think that he bit the Serjeant's finger — it's different all around you see."

PATTEN: "Well of course I would understand what you mean by that but I want you to understand a matter far more important than your attitude towards me or my attitude toward you. The simple strange fact is that I and my 36 men have to fight for our lives."

STILWELL: (*politely*) "And of course I and my daughters are unavoidably involved in this."

PATTEN: "I think I may say unavoidably. Colonel Mavida might prove unable to use the word."

STILWELL: "Well, we're in it. And we'll have to play the game. And — I don't know — but I suppose the best way to play a game is to play it the best way you can."

PATTEN: (*with feeling*) "Of course you understand that it is far from my wish that you are caused the slightest annoyance."

LUCY: "Not in the least, Mr Patten. I think Colonel Mavida is a regular wretch to come here and fight you without any warning."

PATTEN: "Oh, no, not at all."

LUCY: "And when he knows that he might hurt somebody."

PATTEN: "Oh, well, it's all right."

STILWELL: "But look here, he is shooting at you. Why don't you shoot at him?"

PATTEN: "Oh, this shooting is of no matter. I'd rather wait."

MARJORY: "It isn't? Why I thought this was a battle."

PATTEN: "Oh, no."

LUCY: "Mr Patten, when it is a really-truly battle, will you let me know? I don't want to be frightened over a little — er — popular amusement, you know, but of course if a really-truly battle comes, I'd like to be told about it."

PATTEN: (*bowing*) "I'll make a point of it."

(*enter Serjeant Brown*)

SERJT. B.: "Lieutenant, they're coming down through those trees at the other end." (*exit Patten and Brown R. Stilwell, Marjory and Lucy are seated on some low thing C.*)

LUCY: "I wish that nice Mr Thorpe would come and tell us when it is a really-truly battle."

(*a voice is heard without R*)

VOICE: "Eight hundred yards! use the cut-off! Fire at will — Fire!!"

(*a noise of shooting, agitation of the girls. Enter Serjt Brown. He prowls along the line of men. Some of the men have turned their heads to look back of them at that part of the sugar house that is now supposed to be more severly attacked.*)

SERJT. B.: "What are you looking at? You want to see it do you? Your own affairs are not enough for you, eh? — You've got to get busy with other people's? Don't let me catch a man of you turning his head again."

(*He scolds vigorously in pantomime. The pop of Mausers — the long mellow thudding of Craig-Jorgensens — business by the Stilwells. Enter Thorpe R*)

THORPE: "Oh, here you are. Patten told me to come and tell you that it was really nothing — so far."

LUCY: "Why! Isn't it a battle yet?"

THORPE: (*frankly*) "Well, I think it is, but Patten is a man of peculiar ideas."

MARJORY: "Have they hurt any of the Spaniards, Mr Thorpe?"

THORPE: (*gently*) "Er — I don't know, Miss Stilwell. Er — some of them acted as if they were rather hurt."

(*enter Patten hurriedly. He is dirty and a trifle disheveled. Pays no heed to Stilwells.*)

PATTEN: (*loudly, resolutely*) "Now men, here's where they are going to make their main attack. Sight for 300 yards. But don't use the magazine until I tell you. Now! — hold it on them — Fire!!"

(*The rattle of fire. The men buckle up to the six windows sills and fire carefully. Big business. Men shot here and there. The roar increases, indicating the close approach of the Spaniards.*)

PATTEN: (*yelling*) "Magazines. Point blank."

SERJT. B.: (*yelling*) "Magazines. Point blank."

THORPE: (*cooly drawing revolver and holding it on his knee*) "Well here they come."

(*The Stilwells look at him in horror. Fight continue; suddenly Patten jerks his whistle from his pocket and blows. The firing ceases entirely after a few scattered shots indicative of men who have been too excited to pay heed to the whistle.*)

PATTEN: (*calling out loudly*) "Steady now men. They are going to palaver." (*he mounts a window-sill and calls out L*) "Come on, you won't be hurt." (*a pause*) "What can I do for you?"

VOICE: (*from without*) "I have the honaire to present the compliments of Colonel Mavida of the 206 Battalion of the Spanish Army. He would like to know if you are ready to surrender."

PATTEN: "Why no! I hadn't thought of it."

VOICE: (*from without*) "Then Colonel Mavida of the 206 Battalion of the Spanish Army is very sorry, but he will have to continue the battle."

PATTEN: "Why of course."

VOICE: "Then you will not yet surrender? You will continue ze battle?"

PATTEN: "Yes, I — I think so. You tell the colonel I will let him know when I'm through."

VOICE: "Colonel Mavida wishes to say that because you have taken prisoner three of his English friends he will spare no American at the end of the battle."

STILWELL: (*Moves to window beside Patten*) "No! no! That is a mistake. We're all right here. We're not prisoners. You tell the Colonel not to worry."

PATTEN: "If Colonel Mavida guarantees the safe conduct of the three non-combatants, I will of course agree not to fire until they have passed his lines."

THORPE: (*hurriedly to Marjory and Lucy*) "Look here, you had much better be in here having the Spaniards shoot at you than to be out there having *these* men shooting at you."

LUCY: "And anyhow after all the trouble that dear Lieutenant has taken and all those men bleeding and — everything."

MARJORY: "Oh, I hope Father won't consent."

STILWELL: (*calling out the window*) "Thank you very much but we'll just stay here and sit tight." (*Patten bows to Stilwell*)

PATTEN: (*calling through the window*) "I shall withhold my fire until the flag of truce has disappeared, when I shall conclude that hostilities have been resumed."

LUCY: (*to Thorpe*) "Oh, now you are all going to be killed because we are here with you."

THORPE: "But it doesn't matter, really."

LUCY: "What, that you will all be killed?"

THORPE: "Oh, no. I mean — we would like to do anything you know to oblige you."

MARJORY: "Well I will tell you now. (*strenuously*) Beat them!"

THORPE: (*calling out to Patten who is busy looking from the window*) "Patten!"

PATTEN: (*impatiently*) "What?"

THORPE: "Miss Stilwell requests that you beat them."

PATTEN: "Oh, thank you. I daresay I will be able to manage it somehow. It is very kind of Miss Stilwell to trouble herself on our account."

STILWELL: (*Turning from window*) "Since I found out that he bit that soldier's finger, my opinions have been changing."

PATTEN: (*suddenly*) "Look out, now! Use the magazine! Fire at will — Fire!"

(*The fighting is resumed. From time to time men fall. Light smoke. Chatter of Krag-Jorgensens. Pop-pop-pop of Mausers. Song of bullets. Suddenly Patten winces. He looks at his left arm.*)

LUCY: "Oh, he's hit."

MARJORY: "Oh —" (*She advances upon Patten who continues to attend his business*)

PATTEN: (*to his men*) "Now take it cooly. They'll never get that charge home."

MARJORY: (*to Patten*) "Let me bind it, will you?"

PATTEN: (*waving her away without looking*) "Pardon me. You are in danger. Please get down. (*to his men*) Look at that squad sneaking in the tall grass there, Mulligan."

(*He walks along his men followed by Marjory with a handker-chief*)

MARJORY: (*finding a temporary pause*) "Please, let me tie it up."

PATTEN: (*seeing her*) "Oh, — pardon me. Yes — if you care to (*she begins*) You may find it amusing."

(*Brief exchange between Marjory and Patten. Enter Serjt. B. on a run R*)

SERJT. B.: (*breathless*) "Lieutenant, we can see four mounted men on a hill that way (*pointing R*) and they look" —

TROOPERS ON STAGE: (*yelling*) "Ammunition. Ammunition. Good God, can't you give us ammunition."

PATTEN: (*yelling toward R*) "Ammunition there."

SERJT. B.: (*yelling toward R*) "Ammunition. Ammunition."

(*Enter two men with regulation box 1000 cartridges. They drop box on stage and it breaks open. Men from firing line grab feverish handfuls. Close pop of Mausers*)

STILWELL: "God help us, this *is* a fight."

LUCY: (*wailing*) "I don't want to die. Oh, I don't want to die."

MARJORY: "Lucy — Lucy — poor little sister."

(*A distant bugle is heard calling the charge for United States cavalry*)

SERJT. B.: (*leaping in air*) "I can name the man that blew that bugle."

PATTEN: (*turning hastily to Marjory*) "It's all right now. Here come some friends of mine."

(*A crescendo roar and thud of many hoofs sweeping past the sugar mill. One or two hoarse orders. Shots. Grand excitement in sugar house.*)

PATTEN: (*shouting*) "All ready to double out now. Magazines full — Charge."

(*Troopers led by Patten leap through windows. Stilwell, Marjory and Lucy crowd up to a window-ledge*)

LUCY: "Oh — oh — look at those men on horses."

Reproduced here from the typescript in the Crane Collection at Columbia University Libraries, complete with misspellings and crazy punctuation. There are thirty-one typed sheets and one holograph. The holograph sheet is the original for the typed sheet listing "Characters." The manuscript is untitled, the present title having been added by the Editors. It was first published in Bulletin of the New York Public Library *(October 1963) and is an addition to the Crane canon.*

INDEX

INDEX